Environment, Power, and Injustice
A South African History

This book presents the socio-environmental history of black people in the area near Kuruman, on the edge of the Kalahari in South Africa. Considering successive periods – Tswana agropastoral chiefdoms before colonial contact, the Cape frontier, British colonial rule, Apartheid, and the homeland of Bophuthatswana in the 1980s – *Environment, Power, and Injustice* shows how the human relationship with the environment corresponded to differences of class, gender, and race. While exploring biological, geological, and climatological forces in history, this book argues that the challenges of existence in a semidesert arose more from human injustice than from deficiencies in the natural environment. In fact, powerful people drew strength from and exercised their power over others through the environment. At the same time, the natural world provided marginal peoples with some relief from human injustice.

Nancy J. Jacobs is Assistant Professor in the Department of Africana Studies and the Department of History at Brown University, Providence, Rhode Island, USA. She is a recipient of the Alice Hamilton article prize from the American Society for Environmental History.

STUDIES IN ENVIRONMENT AND HISTORY

Editors

Donald Worster, University of Kansas
J. R. McNeill, Georgetown University

Other books in the series

Environment, Power, and Injustice

A South African History

NANCY J. JACOBS

Brown University

CAMBRIDGE
UNIVERSITY PRESS

PUBLISHED BY THE PRESS SYNDICATE OF THE UNIVERSITY OF CAMBRIDGE
The Pitt Building, Trumpington Street, Cambridge, United Kingdom

CAMBRIDGE UNIVERSITY PRESS
The Edinburgh Building, Cambridge CB2 2RU, UK
40 West 20th Street, New York, NY 10011-4211, USA
477 Williamstown Road, Port Melbourne, VIC 3207, Australia
Ruiz de Alarcón 13, 28014 Madrid, Spain
Dock House, The Waterfront, Cape Town 8001, South Africa

http://www.cambridge.org

First published 2003

Printed in the United Kingdom at the University Press, Cambridge

Typeface Times New Roman 10/13 pt.   *System* LATEX   [TB]

A catalog record for this book is available from the British Library.

Library of Congress Cataloging in Publication Data
Jacobs, Nancy Joy.
  Environment, power, and injustice : A South African history / Nancy J. Jacobs.
   p. cm. – (Studies in environment and history)
  Includes bibliographical references (p.) and index.
  ISBN 0-521-81191-0 – ISBN 0-521-01070-5 (pbk.)
   1. Human ecology – South Africa – Kuruman – History. 2. Kuruman (South
Africa) – Social conditions. 3. Kuruman (South Africa) – Economic conditions.
I. Title. II. Series.
 GF758 .J33 2003
 306.3′49′0968 – dc21   2002025654

ISBN 0 521 81191 0 hardback
ISBN 0 521 01070 5 paperback
ISBN 0 521 53457 7 African edition

To my father, Fred Jacobs,
and the memory of my mother, Irene Jacobs

Contents

Contents

Contents

List of Illustrations

Cover illustration: Sophie Tshekoeng near Ncweng, 1998. (Photograph courtesy of Peter Heywood.)

List of Tables

Preface

The research that became this book was possible because of several generous grants. I have been a recipient of the following support: a Fulbright-Hays Grant in 1991; an Indiana University College of Arts and Sciences Second Semester Fellowship in 1994; an American Council of Learned Societies/Social Science Research Council International Postdoctoral Fellowship (made possible with funding from the National Endowment for the Humanities) in 1997–8; and a Bernadotte E. Schmitt Grant from the American Historical Association in 1998. I am also grateful to the Brown University Office of the Dean of the Faculty for a Junior Sabbatical in 1997 and for a subvention to underwrite the costs of producing this book. I would like to acknowledge the permission of the Chief Directorate of Surveys and Mapping in South Africa to use their copyrighted map material and aerial photographs to make the maps and reproductions of aerial photographs in this book. I also thank the MacGregor Museum in Kimberley for permission to use copyrighted historic photographs of the Kuruman area.

Of all the people I must thank for their assistance and support, I will begin with my teachers. First, I thank my professors at Calvin College, who taught me to consider justice and encouraged me to take up the academic life. I am especially grateful to Wallace Bratt and Barbara Carvill. Alan Boesak, who taught me at Calvin College for one semester, was a tremendous influence. At UCLA, where I did an MA in African Studies, I received generous guidance from Richard Sklar and Joseph Lauer. The best decision I made in my academic life may have been to enroll in a Ph.D. program in the History Department at Indiana University. There, I received stimulating instruction and unfailing support. I am extremely indebted to Phyllis Martin for serving as my doctoral advisor. She remained cheerful and encouraging, while reading critically and asking probing questions. She also gave me the freedom to pursue environmental history.

Also at Indiana University, I benefited greatly from working with many other members of the faculty, including Randall Baker, George Brooks, William Cohen, Paula Girshick, John Hanson, C. R. D. Halisi, and Patrick O'Meara.

My next acknowledgment must be to the collegiality of my peers. I am especially honored to have been a classmate of the late Christopher Gray at Indiana University. I have also enjoyed knowing and learning from Allison Shutt. In Bloomington, Moira Wedekind and Hank Huffman taught me that the environment was important in ways I had not recognized. As I formulated this book, conversations with many people instructed me about new ways to consider environmental and African studies. I would like to acknowledge my long-standing debts to the following: Kevin Shillington, Pieter Snyman, Neil Parsons, Charles van Onselen, Jan-Bart Gewald, John Wright, Robert Harms, Jim Giblin, Jim McCann, Jane Carruthers, the late Ruth Edgecombe, Greg Maddox, Teresa Barnes, Jamie Monson, Tom Johnson, Chris Conte, Immanuel Krieke, Ravi Ravjan, Laura Mitchell, Derick Fay, Joshua Forrest, Robert Gordon, Jock McCulloch, David Ward, Suzanne Vetter, Richard Madsen, Kim Euston-Brown, Kees Bootsman, Andy Manson, James Drummond, Lerato Thahome, and David Phalatse. These people helped me in many ways by asking me the right questions, by answering the questions I asked them, and by reading earlier versions of this manuscript. Of these colleagues, Ruth Edgecombe, Andy Manson, Neil Parsons, and James Drummond generously opened their homes to me.

As an American, conducting research in South Africa is a logistical challenge. Over the years, I have received the generous hospitality and assistance of people at the Moffat Mission, including Alan and Hilda Butler, the late Joseph and Marjory Wing, Steve De Gruchy and Marian Loveday, and Sophie Rieters. In addition to providing me with housing, Moffat Mission staff helped me create a research network. In Cape Town and Johannesburg, I thank Nick Binedell, Rob and Sue Stelzner, and Jeannine Jennings and Peter Ibbotson for giving me a place to live for extended periods.

Doing worthwhile interviews is a difficult project and other people helped me find success. I thank my old friend Steve Michmerhuizen for introducing me to Rapid Rural Appraisal (RRA). I have a tremendous debt to two former students who joined me in Kuruman to do RRA interviews. Working as volunteers, Megan Waples and Kristin Russell figured out the RRA technique, found their way around Kuruman villages, cooked, cleaned, and kept the car running and entertained everyone. Bhangi Mosala and Kgomotso Tshetlho joined us as interpreters but became RRA interviewers in their own right. Other interpreters worked with me for shorter periods: Richard Mogwera, Constance Paul, Rosey Molokoane, Poppy Afrikaner, Bhangi Mosala, Tsolo Steenkamp,

Victoria Tsatsimpe, and Kopano Chirwa. I hardly know how to thank Julius Mogodi, Benjamin Barnette, Gaogonelwe Motsamai, Peter Mokomele, and especially Stephen Kotoloane. At times they worked as interpreters, but their contribution was more fundamental. They all took interest in the project, introduced me to people and encouraged them to trust me, and advised me on my work. Clearly, the interviews for this book were a collaborative effort, and I am deeply indebted to all who helped with them.

I must also address my tremendous outstanding debt to the people who allowed me to interview them. My research brought no evident benefits to people in Kuruman, and I was touched that so many were willing to consider my questions. As John Molema told a neighbor, "Nancy is not here to help us, we must help her," and he and others taught me much. I would like to thank all individual informants cited by name in the references. Because many of my interviews were in groups, I will thank those people by recognizing the villages they lived in. My research assistants and I were hospitably received in the following villages: Bothetheletsa, Manyeding, Ncweng, Ga-Mopedi, Batlharos, Seodin, Kagung, Sedibeng, Ga-Sebolao, Ga-Lotlhare, Maipeneke, Ga-Diboe, Logobate, and Churchill and by many individuals in Mothibistad and the town of Kuruman.

Finding the right documents is another challenge, one that archivists and librarians helped me meet. I am particularly grateful to the staff at the National Archives in Pretoria and the Cape Archives in Cape Town. They were unfailingly helpful and patient. Furthermore, my research on removals has benefited considerably from the assistance of the staff at The Association for Community and Rural Advancement (AnCRA) in Kuruman and from researchers at the Department of Land Affairs in Pretoria. Both organizations unstintingly shared materials on removals of Kuruman reserves.

At Brown University, I thank members of the Departments of History and Africana Studies, especially those who considered my ideas: John Thomas, Jim Campbell, Rhett Jones, Maud Mandel, Michael Vorenberg, Kerry Smith, Karl Jacoby, and Amy Remensnyder. Conversations with Shepard Krech, Peter Uvin, and Blenda Femenias have also helped me refine my thoughts. I have also relied on the particular skills of Lynn Carlson, who made my maps, and Jess Lopez, who prepared illustrations. I must thank Nancy Soukup for support and proofreading. One joy of being at Brown University is working with the students. The following students have read and commented helpfully on parts of the manuscript: Matthew Lange, Katherine Bayerl, and Adam Schupack. I thank the Brown Undergraduate Teaching and Research Assistantship Program that enabled me to work with Elisa Margolis on the history of rinderpest and with Joe Winter on graphics.

I am also grateful to my collaborators in the 2001 asbestos research project that made Kuruman its case study. I thank my colleagues Sophia Kisting, Lundy Braun, John Trimbur, and Simphiwe Mbuli, as well as our students Scott Bulcao, Kristen Erickson, Alice Kidder, Theo Luebke, Marc Manseau, Mpho Matsipa, Almea Matanock, Kagisho Motseme, Fanomezantsoa Endor Rakoto, Casey Roberts, Kat Saxton, and Lucia Trimbur. We also owe a debt of gratitude to the new director of the Moffat Mission, Richard Aitken, who with Jane Argall, supported the project and became our valued collaborators. A Richard B. Salomon Faculty Research Award from Brown University and supplemental funding from the Dean of the Faculty allowed me to return to South Africa for the asbestos research. Returning to Kuruman with this group gave me new perspectives on its history and a much deeper understanding of contemporary environmental problems. I thank them for their dedication to the work and to the international collaboration.

Following convention, in this last paragraph of the acknowledgments I thank my family. My parents, Fred Jacobs and the late Irene Jacobs, of Holland, Michigan, always encouraged me to study and travel. Their support was crucial to my studies and research. Even after years of hearing about it, my siblings and in-laws usually took interest in my work and were always humorous when they did not. I am especially grateful to the other historians in the family, my sister Chris and brother-in-law Dirk Mouw, who read parts of the manuscript. Finally, my husband Peter Heywood, a biologist who committed to both me and Kuruman in a ceremony in the Moffat Church, astounds me with his generosity, insight, integrity, and talent. In countless ways he has supported my research and helped me turn it into this book. His most evident contributions are the photographs of contemporary Kuruman and my understanding of photosynthesis, but he has been involved in many less obvious ways as well. Not least, he has been a thoughtful companion in seeking equitable ways of using and preserving the environment, and of living in this world.

Nancy Jacobs
2002

Abbreviations

ANC   African National Congress
AnCRA   The Association for Community and Rural Advancement
ARD   Asbestos-Related Disease
BAD   Union and Republic of South Africa Bantu Administration
        and Development Department
BB   British Bechuanaland
BBLC   British Bechuanaland Land Commission
BIC   Bantu Investment Corporation
BP   Bechuanaland Protectorate
CC   Cape Colony
GLW   Griqualand West
LMS   London Missionary Society
LSU   Large Stock Unit
NAC   Native Affairs Commission
NAD   Native Affairs Department
OFS   Orange Free State
SANT   South African Native Trust
SAR   South African Republic
UCDP   United Christian Democratic Party

1

Approaching Kuruman

O NCE, outsiders considered Kuruman* in the Kalahari thornveld an interesting place, but today its popular allure is gone. In the early nineteenth
century, the area just north of the Orange River (Figure 1-1) was a remote and
exotic destination for visitors from the Cape, but its dusty and bleached-out
landscape could not long distract explorers from the lush allure of the interior.
Thus, it was "left to wither on the vine," on a "bygone road to Africa."[1] Once,
historians found that this southern Tswana region provided good evidence about
a process that interested them – imperial annexation in the nineteenth century –
and wrote about the area including Kuruman. Eventually, however, the interests
of Africanist historians changed from imperial annexation to colonial struggles
and negotiations. While twentieth-century South Africa was a dynamic scene
of political contest and cultural innovation, observers have perceived this region
as an underpopulated and quiescent backwater. In short, in earlier times some
visitors and historians found the place interesting, but few have found anything
in its more recent past worth dwelling upon.

This book returns to Kuruman to construct its socio-environmental history.
My project has been to comb rich sources about this place for evidence of people
interacting with the environment and, through their environmental relations,
with each other. By looking at different groups of people and their relations with
the nonhuman world around them, I have united the nineteenth and twentieth
centuries in one extended narrative and found a historical dynamic behind the
quiescence. This book is about power, social difference, and the biophysical
realm. It is about how people related to the environment as they interacted with
each other.

---

* Kuruman is both a town and an administrative district. By "Kuruman," I usually mean the district
  as defined before 1949, but sometimes I refer to the town. This study focuses on the black people
  in that district.

1

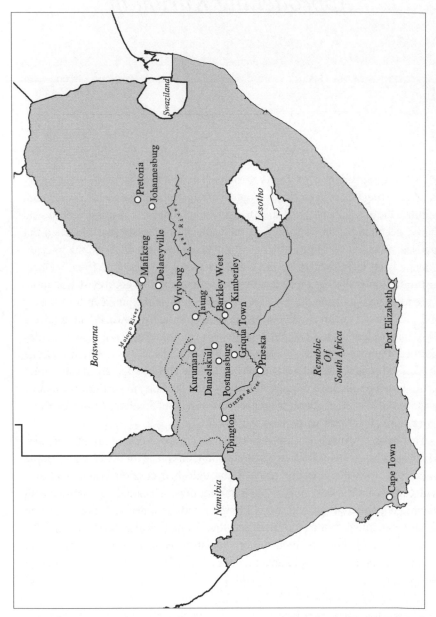

Figure 1-1 South Africa. Based on information in the public domain.

A recent episode illustrates these interactions dramatically. The donkey, often viewed as a comical beast of burden, articulated relations between poor people, the environment, and the colonial economy. Donkeys are not indigenous to South Africa, but after 1900 blacks in Kuruman acquired them. They were better adapted to the semi-arid and diseased environment than cattle were and became very useful to people without much cash. During the twentieth century, racial segregation excluded blacks from citizenship in the modern state, even as the state appropriated the right to intervene in their food production and settlement patterns. Donkeys became, in the official construction, an environmental menace, and by the mid-twentieth century state programs curtailed their numbers. Furthermore, unlike cattle, donkeys had no market value and therefore did not contribute to the "development" visions of economic planners. The policy of Separate Development, the infamous form of segregation in South Africa in the 1960s and 1970s, had a powerful impact on donkeys in Kuruman. Separate Development dictated the establishment of an "independent" Tswana state called Bophuthatswana. In Bophuthatswana, the concerns of the well-connected dominated rural governance, and elite cattle ranchers benefited from state assistance. A crisis came with the terrible drought of 1983. Cattle died at higher rates than donkeys, and the Bophuthatswana government blamed the donkeys for wasting grazing resources that would be better reserved for cattle. The police and army descended on villages, and in a chaotic and brutal operation, they shot over 10,000 donkeys, approximately half of those living in this area. Donkey owners were not consulted and were threatened when they protested. For many people, the gunfire, suffering, and intimidation made this the most traumatic experience of Apartheid, and today many still resent the oppressive state and rich people who obstructed their humble ways of subsisting in this environment.

The donkey massacre is the most dramatic episode in this book, and fresh memories make it a powerful story. The environmental character of power is also evident before Separate Development. In earlier periods, too, those with more power arrogated the most advantageous relations to themselves. Very often, power was divided along racial lines. Under segregation in the mid twentieth century, many black people had been forced from long-occupied river valleys into the southern Kalahari. Whites took over more of the river valleys, and blacks on the dry veld found it impossible to farm as they had. Working backwards from that point, we see that in the early part of that century, Kuruman, the new white town upstream from black villages, drew precious water from the small Kuruman River, parching the black community downstream. The loss of water echoed land alienation during colonial annexation in the late nineteenth century, when Tswana people lost much of their land and the ability to own it as whites did, thus becoming impoverished. Yet the precedent for environmental oppression even predated segregation and colonial rule. At the turn of the nine-teenth century, Tswana chiefs arrogated to themselves rights over cattle. Cattle owners were secure, while common men served as their clients. Barred from cattle ownership, women cultivated and poor people foraged.

In each of these dispensations, people differentiated by race, class, and gender had different access to power and relations with the environment. The powerful always drew strength from relating to the environment in particular ways and retained their positions by manipulating against others' beneficial uses of it. However, throughout all these events, even as the powerful appropriated the best ways of using the environment to themselves, the disinherited found some way of mitigating their circumstances through their relations with it. Even when people seemed quiescent, they acted with creativity and deliberation in their relations with the environment.

The environment has been more than a backdrop in these power struggles. It has shaped outcomes, both as a prize and a player. People negotiated its characteristics by particular ways of living and farming, and new social re-lations resulted. Capitalism, Christianity, colonialism, and segregation mani-fested themselves at the level of hoeing, plowing, tending animals, and working local asbestos deposits. In fact, relations with the environment have filtered the impact of the major social forces in South African history. The semi-arid thorn-veld and its river valleys constituted the *immediate* environment of Kuruman people, and whatever their other concerns, rain, crops, stock, access to land the costs and yields of production, and rights to produce food ranked high among their preoccupations.

Thus, an environmental approach brings an added authenticity to our un-derstandings of the way people once lived and reveals unrecognized forces for change. The socio-environmental approach shows new aspects of power, its sources and motives for exercising it. Essentially, the issue is one of environ-mental justice, which is often viewed as the concern of contemporary activists in industrialized societies who seek cleaner, healthier environments for marginal-ized people. Yet environmental injustice – structured inequalities in the ways people related to the biophysical world – has existed in nonindustrial societies and in earlier times. Seen from this angle, Kuruman's past is eventful and its present is fraught.

THE KALAHARI THORNVELD TODAY: A TOUR

On the edge of the Kalahari is a dry savanna known as the thornveld, and from whatever direction you approach, to reach Kuruman you must cross much of it. The thornveld is named for the thorny acacias that dominate the landscape. In some places near Kuruman, a two-storied savanna of tall acacia and grass prevails, but the typical scene is scragglier than the ideal captured in African nature photography. The soil is stony, thin, and patchy, leaving exposed rock in places. There are not many large trees and not much tall grass. Rather, bushes of the intermediate story define the profile, and their small, hard leaves testify that rain is not abundant here. On the edge of the Kalahari you do not take rain for granted. The Tswana word for rain, "*pula*," is a salutation at public meetings, and Botswana has even given the name to its currency. However, pula, being so erratic, might not merit this esteem. Drought is so familiar here that H. C. Bosman chose Kuruman for a send-up of small town gossip in his short story, "The Homecoming." An abandoned wife weeps over news from her husband, but claims the letter was from "her sister in Kuruman, who wrote about the drought there . . . 'It seemed to be a pretty long drought,' " an observer comments, " 'judging from the number of pages.' "[2]

There were indeed long droughts and many of them. The thornveld is a sub-tropical region; hence, it receives rainfall mostly in the summer months of October to March through the seasonal movements of the inter-tropical convergence zone (ITCZ), the low-pressure tropical weather system (see Figure 1-2). However, because it is south of the Tropic of Capricorn and close to the high-pressure zone over the Namib and Kalahari, the ITCZ brings little rain to this area. The average annual rainfall measured between 1932 and 1992 at the meteorological station in Kuruman town was 416 millimeters. Such low precipitation has had great impact on land use. Even sorghum cultivation fails in dry years, although periodic years of good rains and good harvests tease farmers into believing the possibilities of maize cultivation. The question is: do good and bad years occur in cycles or has there been a long-term desiccation trend? This is a critical question for historians, because people suffer through and adapt to difficult years, but long-term desiccation can undermine a society, independent of any human factors. As discussed in Chapter 9, people who live in Kuruman hold the latter interpretation. The conventional wisdom is that there is less rainfall than there used to be. This theory dates back to the early nineteenth century – not just for Kuruman, but for the country as a whole. However, if rainfall has indeed been declining for nearly 200 years, it is a wonder that any at all falls today.

Since the early twentieth century, South Africa has kept regular records of rainfall at stations throughout the country. Climatologists have analyzed these data, and P. D. Tyson has delivered a decisive rebuttal to the conventional wisdom: "The earlier hypothesis that South Africa has undergone progressive

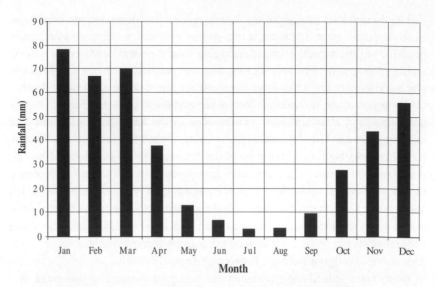

Figure 1-2 Kuruman District mean monthly rainfall, 1931–97.

desiccation consequently must be rejected as untenable." Instead, Tyson proposed a theory of cyclical variation, the strongest being a cycle of around eighteen to twenty-two years.[3] In Kuruman, the South African Weather Bureau has kept monthly statistics since 1932. I contracted a meteorologist, Mark Majodina, to analyze the data for rainfall variability, and he performed regression analyses on the data from the months of maximum rainfall (January, February, and March from 1932–92).[4] He found no trend in the data, although variability did increase in the second half of the study, with the largest fluctuations in the 1970s and 1980s. The data did reveal cycles, the dominant one being twenty years, which fall within Tyson's model. Also present were episodic events related to a global weather phenomenon – the El Niño/Southern Oscillation event affecting weather and precipitation over much of the tropics and subtropics.* If the recent intensification of El Niño is creating a global climate change, it will have repercussions on farming and herding in the future. For most of the recorded history of Kuruman, however, change in climate patterns is not a sufficient explanation for environmental and economic change. Therefore, the history that follows examines droughts as episodes and does not hypothesize a desiccation trend. Lack of rainfall is a serious difficulty, but long-term changes have been in the effects of drought, not the amount of rain.

---

* The Southern Oscillation involves pressure changes over the southeastern Pacific Ocean and Indonesia. El Niño involves a warming of the Pacific Ocean off the coast of Peru.

Figures 1-3 and 1-4* show annual rainfall broken down by season from 1932–97. The figures illustrate the unpredictability of rainfall by year and season and help us take the empathetic leap toward understanding what it was like to live in this environment in those years. Picture yourself as a farmer who wants to plant sorghum or maize. Every October you would begin to watch the sky and begin to calculate when enough rain had fallen to justify sowing. Imagine the anxiety of predicting whether this year would bring enough rain to sustain a crop. Imagine the disappointment of a year like 1943 with excellent spring rains, but marginal summer ones, or the surprise of a year like 1991 when summer rain far surpassed any expectations set by the poor spring performance. Consider your astonishment in 1974 when unprecedented flooding and several years of high rainfall followed the drought of 1973. Feel the helpless frustration during the prolonged dry spell in the 1980s as you watched your stock die from lack of grass.

In Kuruman, the most reliable source of water is not the heavens, but the earth. Today's travelers driving on the major highways from Upington, Kimberley, or Vryburg pass though huge expanses of bushy thornveld, but upon entering the town they suddenly encounter large green lawns informing them that they have arrived at an oasis (see Figure 1-5). The green grass, exotic palms, and cattle egrets inspecting the grass for insects contradict the lesson evident in history: there is not enough water for all who want it. The illusion of plentiful water is possible, because those who own the grass control the water supply. Underground water is a blessing of the Ghaap Plateau, the landform that stretches 150 kilometers from the Harts River valley in the east to the Kuruman hills in the west. Its surface is calcrete, a whitish chalky porous rock formed from alluvial deposits. Bedrock of dolomite, or calcium manganese carbonate, underlies it. Like other dolomite areas, this is "karst" topography, meaning the bedrock is riddled with caves, sinkholes, and underground waterways. At intervals dolerite dikes interrupt the caverns, and the dikes block the underground flow of water, forcing water to surface springs, known in South Africa as "fountains" or often as "eyes."† Unfortunately, there has never been a thorough survey of all springs in the area of study, and the Ghaap Plateau has scores of them, ranging from small trickles to the Eye of Kuruman, which yields approximately 20 million liters of water a day. Some springs are seasonal; larger ones have big catchment areas and are not affected by one year's rainfall; and some have dried up

---

* Figures 1-3 and 1-4 show rainfall by climatological rather than calendar year. Thus, the column for 1932 represents the season beginning in October 1931. The data were collected at weather stations near Kuruman town.
† The usage of "eye" originates in the Dutch Old Testament in, for example, Deuteronomy 33:28. Personal communication, Alan Butler, January 18, 1994.

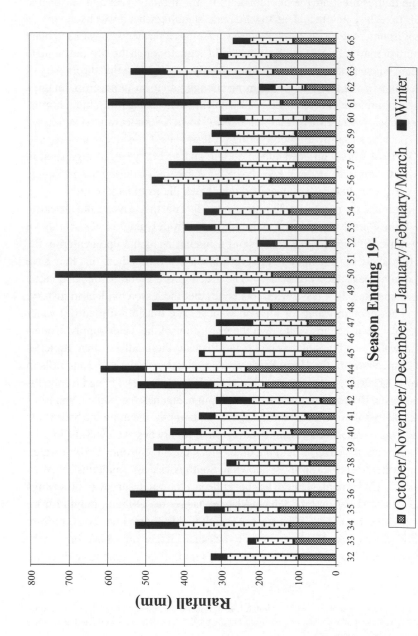

Figure 1-3 Kuruman rainfall, 1932–65.

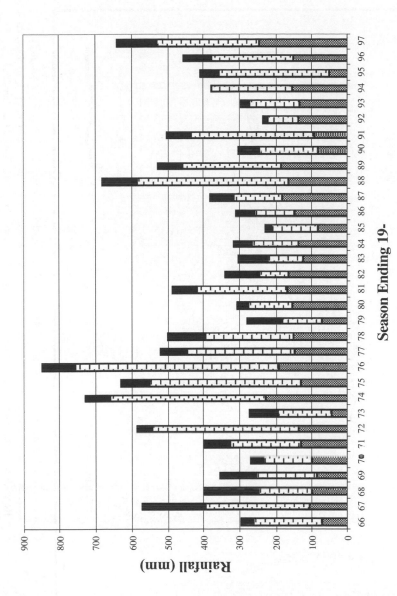

Figure 1-4 Kuruman rainfall, 1966–97.

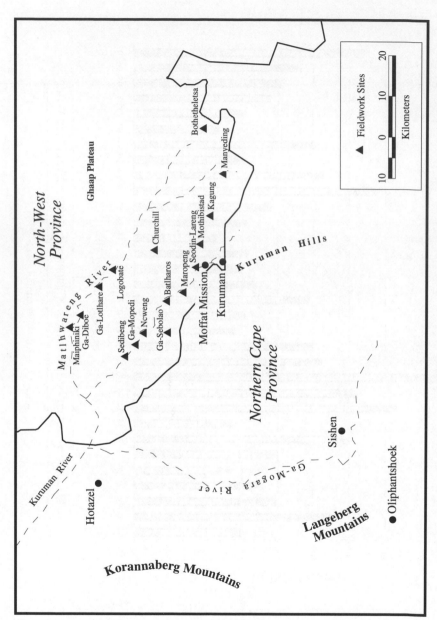

Figure 1-5 The Kuruman area today. Based on 1:250,000 topocadestral sheets 2622 Bray, 2722 Kuruman, 2724 Christiana, 2822 Postmasburg, 3634 Vryburg. From the Chief Directorate of Surveys and Mapping in South Africa. Reproduced under Government Printer's Copyright Authority No. 11012 dated 9 October 2001.

permanently.[5] While the springs are a great resource, the dry surroundings help them appear more prolific than they really are.*

The most famous spring in South Africa is the Eye of Kuruman, a major attraction in the town and often claimed to be the largest spring in the country. Its Tswana name is "Gasegonyane," "little calabash," after the cave that produced the flow. The charming name is no longer appropriate, because in the 1970s planners remodeled the Eye by closing the cave, allowing much of the water to be siphoned off to supply the town. Today, some water is pumped to the top of a rock ledge and allowed to fall into a pond below, a picturesque but manufactured display. Surrounding the Eye is a neatly kept park planted with palms to accentuate the oasis mystique, but the Eye is in contemporary South Africa, not an exotic desert of imagination. When the water flows beneath the high iron fence surrounding the park, it enters a racialized landscape. The Eye is the source for the Kuruman River, which runs northwest, first watering garden plots owned by white families. These plots and the water supplied to them were the object of the first major segregation effort in Kuruman. What little water is left in the stream below these gardens then makes its way into areas where blacks live.

The town of Kuruman grew up around the Eye. Today, it is an undistinguished South African *dorp*.† On the through highway and the town's main streets are branches of the same banks, retailers, and petrol stations present throughout South Africa.[6] The residential areas were restricted to whites by law until 1994, and today only a few black families own houses here. On the north side of town, however, travelers approach the section of town where black people receive services. There are shops with unique names: "No Jokes Fruit and Veg" and "Tlharo Tlhaping Butchery." Near the bus stop and taxi ranks are informal traders and many black pedestrians. Past this, on the northbound highway, the town rapidly gives way to a fringe of bungalows on both sides and another green lawn. The transition from garden back to thornveld is an abrupt one, but the course of the river and the location of the irrigated plots are marked on the east side of the highway with rows of trees, parallel to the road.

Five kilometers downstream is the Moffat Mission Trust, an ecumenical center on the historic grounds of the London Missionary Society station, tracing its roots to nonconformist evangelism among Tswana people in 1816. The mission made Kuruman the anchor on the Road to the North and gave British

---

* For comparison's sake, it is helpful to note that the Eye of Kuruman is surpassed in output by many springs in the karst regions of Florida, Missouri, and Indiana, which receive much higher rainfall. Richard L. Powell, "A Guide to the Selection of Limestone Caverns and Springs in the United States as National Landmarks," unpublished document, Indiana Geological Survey, 1970. I thank Hank Huffman for this reference.

† "Dorp" is Afrikaans and South African English for a small town.

authorities a reason to locate an administrative center here. Today, it gives tourists a reason to stop in Kuruman. The mission was placed here because the land could be irrigated. Old trees of the former orchard still yield tiny fruit, but the missionaries' garden and wheat field are now a pasture. The mission homes from the 1820s are well tended and the 1838 stone church, seating up to 800 people, is still impressive. It stands empty on Sundays, however. With the implementation of the Group Areas Act of 1950, black parishioners were no longer allowed to attend services at the mission, which was proclaimed to be in a white area. The rejuvenation of the site as a church retreat center and an excellently preserved historical artifact and national monument has occurred since the 1980s. Today, the church is the setting for weddings (local villagers and visiting academics alike exchange vows here) and occasionally for special worship services.

Just downstream from the mission, the river, by now just a ditch nearly narrow enough to jump across at the center of the shallow valley, crosses a border to the area where blacks live. Historically, the valley has been home to members of the Tlhaping and Tlharo chiefdoms. Under colonial rule, the lower valley became a black reserve, and under segregation, it was part of the homeland of Bophuthatswana. Since 1994, the same line divides the Northern Cape and North–West Provinces. Along the Kuruman River are more springs of different sizes and endurance. In Batlharos, the largest village in the lower river valley, there is a wide green vlei (marsh) where animals graze and people find shade on summer afternoons. Another spring in Ga-Mopedi creates a pond in winter (see Figure 1-6). The eyes along the river do not usually provide sustained flow of water for any distance; most times the riverbed is a series of ponds and marshes, which disappear a short distance downstream, varying by season. Summer is the time of rain, but lower evapotranspiration in winter keeps the rivers fuller when it is colder. These ponds and rivers sustain bird life – waterfowl as well as gorgeous lilac-breasted rollers, little bee-eaters, and crimson boubous, anomalous splashes of color in the faded landscape. Queleas, "feathered locusts," also gather in the river valley. Queleas are the cultivators' bane, but they do not find much grain here. Although the river valleys have the dampest soil in the area and are fenced into gardens, most are abandoned.

By the time the Kuruman River reaches the confluence with the Matlhwareng River, both rivers are dry, except under exceptional circumstances. As the riverbed trails off the Ghaap Plateau onto the sandy surface of the Kalahari, there are no springs to refresh it. If sufficient rain allows water to flow this far, it soon sinks into the sand or evaporates into the dry air. The Kuruman River has flowed into the Molopo River, the usually dry river valley on the South Africa/Botswana border, only four or five times in the past 100 years.[7]

Figure 1-6 The Eye at Ga-Mopedi, 2001. Although most of the Kuruman River Valley is dry, at intervals eyes replenish the flow. At the village of Ga-Mopedi, sheep, donkeys, and other creatures refresh themselves at the water. In the background, note the fences and boxy houses of a Betterment village. (Photograph courtesy of Peter Heywood.)

The Kuruman Hills to the west of the river are not high or steep, but the ridgeline is distinctive because of a conical hummock, Ga-Mogana, standing 1,614 meters tall. The chain forms the northern portion of the Asbestos Hills, beginning at Prieska on the Orange River to the south. The rock is banded ironstone, bearing blue asbestos or crocidolite, and is a major source of the semi-precious stone tiger eye, asbestos embedded in quartz. Since the 1970s, as the health risks of asbestos became known, usage of crocidolite has stopped worldwide. Until demand dropped, crocidolite was the most valuable type of asbestos in South Africa, with most of it coming from the Northern Cape and North–West Provinces. Crocidolite is also the deadliest type of asbestos. Thus, it brought relative prosperity, but also many deaths from lung diseases, not only in miners, but also in the general population, because merely living there entails high exposure to airborne fibers. The last mine in Kuruman closed in 1997, leaving the economy and the environment devastated. In spots in the Kuruman Hills above the villages, the earth is blue with asbestos fibers, open to disturbance by wind, rain, and animals, and the hillside placement of the mines spreads their dust over the plains and villages below. In 1997, a visiting American journalist ventured that they would qualify as Superfund sites in the United States.[8] The post-Apartheid government is committed to making this and other asbestos-producing areas safe for breathing, but resources are limited and many former mines on communal lands will remain unreclaimed in the near future. In spite of the health danger, people told me they wish the mines would reopen and provide them with jobs.

East of the hills and rivers is the Ghaap Plateau, with an elevation of 1,341 meters above sea level at the town of Kuruman. It slopes down to the north, causing the northward flow of the rivers. True to its name, it is flat and largely feature-less, a wide savanna of grass, trees, and bush, with an occasional farmhouse or village. The only evident geological features are the dolerite dikes, slight bush-covered protrusions on the surface that mark the best places to drill for water. In the 1950s and 1960s, the segregationist government positioned villages at intervals on the communal lands of the Ghaap Plateau. The new communities were organized on platted grids and placed at artificial water points. Apart from the largest settlement at Mothibistad, these villages are largely indistinguish-able from each other. Dusty places of close settlement, taxis and buses stop on the main roads; coming and going are disproportionate components of hu-man activity. The villages are platted on rutted dirt roads studded with natural rocks. Most homes are modest places of earthen bricks, but here and there is a luxurious one. There are many partially completed houses, brick walls and window frames awaiting a roof or panes that will arrive as funds become avail-able. Besides houses, there are schools, churches, small shops, liquor stores, and clinics, but only Batlharos has a hospital. There are no cultivated fields on the communal lands on the plateau, but goats and donkeys browse along the road (and have little fear of traffic). Lots are always fenced, and the wire, like the acacia shrubs, captures stray plastic bags that litter the streets. Inside the fences are shade trees, fruit trees, gardens, or raked earth. The villages follow regimented design and have little charm. The earth is dry and the people are poor. Yet when it rains in summer, the plateau can be beautiful. Once I saw a complete double rainbow, two perfect arcs bridging as wide a horizon as earth can offer. Shadows of retreating thunderheads fled across the greening veld.

More cattle and small stock are on the Ghaap Plateau than in the river val-leys, and they testify to the most significant human use of the environment. Because the area is too dry for regular high-yielding cultivation, pastoralism has been more important – originally subsistence herding and now commer-cial production. Herds and herders alike might be happier in greener pastures, but keeping few animals over a wide area allows them to survive on the thin grass. All the same, cattle tend to be bony in dry seasons and plumper when rain makes the grass thicker. Between villages is open veld, grassy on parts of the Ghaap Plateau but more often bushy. In his 1953 landmark *Veld Types of South Africa*, J. P. H. Acocks classified the region around Kuruman as the Kalahari Thornveld.[9] A 1996 survey of vegetation, *Vegetation of South Africa, Lesotho and Swaziland*, includes this area in the savanna biome. A savanna is an unstable and transitional environment between grassland and woodland. The 1996 study describes this savanna as an intermediate form, with three types of "bushveld" differentiated by different rainfall levels, soil types, and plant types.[10] The proper proportion of bush, trees, and grass is a matter of concern to herders and ecologists. After the 1880s, the wood trade to Kimberley claimed the big trees. Smaller acacia and other bushes have certainly increased during this period. A conventional explanation for the change is that bushes have increased because of intensive grazing; since grass is a better fodder, the increased bushes mean less sustainable herding. However, there are good reasons to question the received wisdom on the processes and effects of change. As discussed in Chapter 6, range ecologists have identified many factors besides grazing that contribute to bush growth.

Since 1994, the infrastructure in black areas has improved. The development most anticipated and celebrated is the parastatal corporation Eskom's extension of electricity service. Yet the grid grows only slowly, and some people awaited the new millennium to see the shiny new wires connected to their houses. Another parastatal, Telkom, is increasing telephone service in many villages, and a cellular provider has a public service in Seodin. Changes I saw around the region in 1997 and 1998 included an informal marketplace in Kagung constructed after a cheery rondavel-like design, which unfortunately went unused. At convenient intervals around the village of Ga-Mopedi were water supply points operated with prepaid cards. Large Reconstruction and Development Programme (RDP) signs announced projects at intervals along the roadside, but since the independent RDP ceased to exist in 1996, the government's continuing commitment to investment in rural areas is less clear.

Beyond the river valley, reserves and trust lands on the Ghaap Plateau are lands limited under colonial rule and Apartheid to white ownership. These lands include the southern Kalahari, the Ga-Mogara Valley, and the Langeberg Mountains. Today, blacks find work on mines and farms on the alienated lands. Although not as attractive for farming as the Ghaap Plateau, the Ga-Mogara Valley has yielded the greatest wealth in the Kuruman region: metals. In fact, the Ga-Mogara Valley is one of the richest manganese sites in the world. There, at the southern edge of the Kalahari, defined by the lack of water and a sandy surface, is the aptly named company town Hotazel, pronounced "hot-as-hell," although it can be almost as cold in winter. Rising on the quiet savanna, the iron and manganese mines are eerie outposts of heavy industry. East of the

Ga-Mogara valley are the quartzitic Langeberg Mountains that begin at the Orange River and stretch nearly 200 kilometers north, with the highest rising to a height of 1,836 meters. The Kalahari, an expanse of hardy grass and bushes on red sand, makes a semi-circle beginning west of the Langeberg Mountains and arcing north of the Ghaap Plateau. There are no permanent rivers in the Kalahari, the geology does not provide any springs, and the rainfall is less than 125 millimeters per year. Aridity keeps the population there very low, and the only farming is stock ranching. The Kalahari proper has always had a low population and thus is not central in this book.

I close this description of the landscape with a note about a distinctive characteristic of the Kuruman environment. The area is ideally suited to parasailing. From November through January, dedicated enthusiasts from around the world converge here to fly under unparalleled conditions; summer thermal currents have carried fliers to distances of over 300 kilometers and altitudes of over 4,000 meters. At those heights, they have a unique perspective on the landscape and the people living there. However, while the landscape can serve as an historical source, a casual outside viewing, even from high above, will not give answers about how people interacted with the environment. Answering these questions requires an understanding of the ecology and physical environment and a consultation of more traditional historical sources. The parasailer who wrote an article entitled "Kuruman: Bad for Farming, Good for Flying"[11] may have been right about flying, but as for farming, it is not so simple. Even in this challenging environment, the difficulties people have had supporting themselves have more to do with injustices among humans than with deficiencies in the nonhuman world.

TWO HISTORIES FROM BELOW: A SOCIO-ENVIRONMENTAL APPROACH

An historical narrative, as much as a tour, has an approach. Since practitioners of both social history and environmental history have claimed to write from "below,"[12] it is interesting that they have not encountered each other more often. Below, evidently, is not a fixed point. For social historians of South Africa, the lowest stratum is composed of black workers and peasants. For environmental historians, the land and its ecological communities form the fundamental layer. Both schools of historians have sought to show that the history of those at the bottom has been suppressed, their voices ignored and their agency unrecognized. Given the different starting points but similar treatments, both schools may be understood as parallel approaches to history. Certainly, most works in both schools have shown too little indication that the fields might intersect. However, they must be brought together for the benefit of both parties.

The integral role of the environment in South African rural history is not evident in most writing on the subject. To be sure, the historians C. W. De Kiewiet, William Beinart, Jane Carruthers, and Charles van Onselen have paid close attention to the importance of the biophysical world in human history.[13] Yet much work by South African radical historians brings to mind an environmentalist critique of Marx: that by ignoring the environment, he was not *enough* of a materialist.[14] During the 1970s and 1980s, South African social historians concentrated on issues of political economy, particularly the proletarianization of Africans. Without denying their contributions, their focus does not give sufficient attention to some very important issues in rural history, such as methods of production and environmental and technological factors.[15] Although structured inequalities are the major theme of South African history, environmental oppression has been too often absent from the master narrative. Environmental factors are central in a growing body of writing on the history of conservation. These works examine degradation and the attempts of the state to halt the destruction of soil and game, and while they do consider society and the environment, the environment appears as a protected object rather than a factor in production.[16]

The major agenda of environmental history is to analyze biophysical forces in historical processes. This means considering how people have operated in relation to biological entities and physical forces – plants, animals, pathogens, seas, lakes and rivers, fire, weather systems, the soil, and the bedrock. Introducing the nonhuman world has perhaps made some environmental historiography less sensitive about the human one. William Cronon has remarked that environmental history has failed "to probe below the level of the group to explore the implications of social division. . . . In the face of social history's classic categories of gender, race, class, and ethnicity, environmental history stands much more silent than it should."[17] Although underdeveloped, such analysis is not absent in environmental historiography, and this study continues the discussion with the conviction that the analysis will strengthen the field of environmental history for all regions. It is fundamentally necessary to understand that social difference shapes people's relations with the environment.

Understanding that different categories of people have different experiences can counteract a trend evident in much environmental history toward "declensionist" narratives, stories of degradation in ecology and the collapse of society. Works such as Richard White's *Roots of Dependency* make valuable contributions by revealing environmental components in the rise and fall of societies and economies.[18] Yet, in the words of White, historians mislead if they suggest that "only a miracle has preserved life on this planet." Similarly, John M. MacKenzie warns against a view of environmental history as "one long free fall, with imperialism as its global accelerator."[19] In Africa, narratives of degradation and decline support different political tendencies. Colonial officials decried African land use practices as destructive, while a later school of historians described imperial annexation as an apocalypse eradicating precolonial sustainable land use. The works of James Fairhead, Melissa Leach, and others, including James McCann, have exposed that colonial degradationist narratives about the African environment are often based on untested assumptions.[20] The imperial annexation-as-apocalypse view is also problematic and has been criticized for romanticizing precolonial relations with the environment.[21] Africans in the precolonial period neither lived in harmony with nor had control over their environment.[22] What they did was work it with particular methods that were affected by colonial annexation.

A further problem of the association of imperial annexation with the end of indigenous environmental management is that it underestimates the resilience of "processes that have maintained life and culture."[23] This tension between environmental histories of decline and continuation has points of intersection with the question in African historiography about the ways people existed within oppressive and exploitative structures. Changing interpretations of African agency in migrant labor to southern African mines provide a good example. Early structuralists emphasized the capacity of the state and capital to accumulate wealth and impose social control on exploited workers. Social historians challenged this view by giving agency a more central analytical position. They concluded that working-class Africans had played a role in the creation of migrant labor and had created their own culture in the workplace.[24] In both environmental and African social history, the point has been made that imperial annexation entailed trauma and loss. However, if resilience, environmental or otherwise, is evident, conditions after the loss of precolonial sovereignty cannot be interpreted primarily as a degraded state.

Avoiding declensionism and degradationist narratives does not mean shining a rosy light on change. It means recognizing that change happens with every generation, that it brings winners and losers, that societies can survive terrible developments, and that ecological change must be analyzed before being decried. My point is not to deny environmental trauma or to champion African agency as the moral of history. My point is the one Cronon has made about environmental history, that the emphasis on decline or continuing agency is a narrative issue.[25] The narrative of decline impoverishes our understandings. Portraying tightening structures and a general decline yields a "cut-away view" of peaks and troughs. Rather, I attempt to follow the road over the up-and-down terrain, to survey the circumstances at points of interest, and to identify the forces operating on people and the decisions they made. My goal is to assess the contingencies at different moments without aiming the story at a low point over the next horizon. Every generation inherited an understanding of how to live from its parents, and each faced new circumstances that forced it to innovate. Even those generations that were forced to innovate a lot for only a little return do not exist primarily as a degraded version of what went before. They exist as a testament to their own circumstances, values, and perseverance.

In contemporary thinking, it is not a given that "nature" is a force in human history. Let me state two countervailing positions starkly: modernists display confidence in humans' ability to control nature, while postmodernists are convinced that humans construct it. There is truth in both positions, but in their extreme forms, they can make it difficult to see that biophysical forces act on human history. Modernist influences appear only toward the end of this history in the form of the segregationist state. Although the segregationist state acted in the biophysical realm, it intervened more to control people than the environment. The history of Kuruman before this point shows, however, that the simplifications and impositions by the state came at the cost of indigenous adaptations to the environment.[26]

For this study, it has been more important to triangulate with the postmodernist positions. Nature, of course, is an entirely human construct and a culturally bound one at that. The first problem with the term is that it suggests that biophysical forces are somehow wild and separate from human influences. This does not hold for biophysical forces in the history of Kuruman, where the biology of the domesticated donkey is an important consideration and where humans have influenced the biology of the savanna. So, the term nature requires deconstruction; yet becoming preoccupied with the deconstruction of the term has its costs. We can forget that the biophysical world has an existence and influence independent of human conceptions. Therefore, rather than a reified and constructed nature, I prefer to approach biophysical entities as people's "environment." This terminology underscores that my subject is the interactions between people and the nonhuman realm surrounding them, and leaves us open to seeing that these biophysical entities and forces interact with each other as well as with people. This is not to say that a history can achieve a neutral representation of voiceless nonhumans, but that my point in peeling away layers of representation of nature will be primarily to gain some conception of an actually existing nonhuman biophysical world with its own integrity.

Readers will note less of an emphasis on culture or consciousness of the environment in this book than in some other recent environmental histories. There are several reasons for this. First, documentary sources for the nineteenth century give practically no indication about the ways that people thought about the biophysical world around them. The most insightful formulation of an early Tswana construction of the human and nonhuman worlds is by Jean and John

19

Comaroff, who postulate that Tswana people held a stark opposition between the domesticated space of their households and the wild bush, with a higher valuation on the domesticated. This analysis informs my discussion of production and power in Chapter 2. This partiality toward domesticated environments persisted throughout the period of study, but apart from the supplication at chiefs' graves during droughts and other well-covered rainmaking practices, I found no rituals or markers of domestication, although perhaps herding and growing crops served to claim the environment and were themselves processes of symbolic domestication. My interviews likewise yielded little evidence of a spiritual significance to the landscape. Apart from their respect for graves, people did not indicate that memory or spirit shaped their interactions with specific microenvironments. The less cultural concerns of this research – poverty, power, dispossession, and agency as they relate to the nonhuman environment – arise from the data I collected, including evidence from open-ended interviews. In general, my experience has been that while it is difficult to say how people thought about their environment, it is easier to surmise from social and biophysical evidence why they worked their environment as they did. Because social and biophysical evidence have a cultural context, in the final chapter I explore the human values – essentially indigenous ideas about environmental justice – conveyed in my interviews.

It is noteworthy that, compared with North American environmental historians or South African social historians, historians of tropical Africa have shown consistency in folding together the history of society, culture, and the environment. For example, Philip Curtin and Jan Vansina, senior historians who shaped the field from its beginnings, have paid close attention to environmental forces.[27] Other leading historians who have not taken an explicitly environmental approach, but who have brought environmental factors into their works on culture and production, are Steven Feierman and Elias Mandala.[28] Additionally, John Iliffe has written a textbook of African history that considers how people have adapted to the environment, albeit a relentlessly hostile one.[29] Regarding east and east–central Africa, especially, a school of writing has made the environment central to the analysis. As early as 1977, eastern African historians wrote about the relation of imperialism and environmental change.[30] A recent generation of historians of eastern, central, and west Africa has developed a more critical analysis of ecological management, production, conservation, and consciousness of the environment. These historians of Africa are among the first to have used categories of social history to look at human relations with the environment.[31] This nuanced Africanist environmental historiography, with its sensitivity to cultural and social issues, offers useful models to environmental historians of North America and other parts of the world. The invigorating work of the American environmental historians Alfred Crosby, Carolyn Merchant, Richard White, and Donald Worster;[32] the oversights in the existing historiography of southern Africa; Cronon's call to environmental historians to take social categories into account; and the example of historians of tropical Africa have inspired me to write a socio-environmental history of one South African region, the Kalahari Thornveld.

DOING SOCIO-ENVIRONMENTAL HISTORY IN KURUMAN

To construct the history of Kuruman, my primary questions have been those of environmental history. Environmental history requires considering human–environmental interactions at several different levels. According to Worster, reconstruction of past environmental conditions is the first level of enquiry; ecological implications of production, including technological and social considerations, are the second; and human perceptions of the environment are the third. Merchant's model varies only slightly from Worster's, adding a level for reproduction between production and consciousness.[33] Like these and other environmental historians, I begin my exploration in the biophysical world: what are the environmental characteristics, and how have they changed over time? Understanding environmental characteristics is essential to this method, but by no means does environmental history involve environmental determinism. It is obvious in Kuruman's history that the characteristics of the environment do not determine how people farm. For a landscape with a reputation for harshness, the thornveld scattered with springs has offered people a good number of options. People frequently changed their relations with the environment according to what was possible and what seemed auspicious.

Merchant and Worster agree that consideration of production follows environmental characteristics, and these questions dominate this book. Like Worster, who has sought to develop an "agro-ecological" historical perspective, I see the most fundamental interactions between people and the environment at the level of production, specifically food production.[34] Throughout this history, food production has been a major activity, and the historical forces that change human relations with the environment are explicitly evident at this level. I am not suggesting that production determines reproduction or environmental perceptions in any functionalist way; certainly, the relationship is reciprocal, but production is the more dynamic and influential sphere of analysis in rural environmental history. My conviction is that to understand rural history, to understand rural social relations, one must analyze the work that occupied much of people's lives. This involves scrutinizing techniques and methods of production in an environmental context.

The work of Elias Mandala demonstrates this point extremely well, but Mandala observes that, in general, Africanist historians have been more interested in relations than in methods of production.[35] Investigating production methods reveals their economic logic and gives specificity to relations of production. This is an effort, as John Sutton has put it, "towards a history of cultivating the fields."

> This should encompass more than the tools for cultivating and the techniques employed in the fields, more again than the annual and seasonal arrangements of crops, either interplanted or grown on separate plots, and the various ways by which livestock are combined. It needs to comprehend the whole organisation, social as well as physical, of the agricultural practices and strategies for succeeding year by year.[36]

My analysis of the social organization and strategies of production is centered on two issues: the choices people made about investing their labor and the ways they interacted with each other as they practiced specific production methods.

In understanding labor decisions, I have benefited from the work of Ester Boserup, who postulated that people intensified cultivation and moved from shifting to permanent cultivation, in response to population growth. Different periods of fallow and different levels of intervention into ecological processes marked steps on a continuum of intensification.[37] Shortening fallow and domesticating the landscape meant a larger population could be fed on the same area of land; however, this required investing more work. Intensification increased the total amount of food but also the relative amount of labor. She argued that, in the absence of population growth, people avoided intensification because of the greater work requirement. By no means does Boserup's theory provide a complete explanation for intensification in human history. For example, it deals only with cultivation and not with pastoralism or foraging, which are more extensive land uses than even shifting cultivation. Furthermore, population has not been the sole determinant of land use, and Boserup does not explain the ways environment, human culture, and historic circumstances influence people's practice of food production. Her argument that population is an independent variable is less critical to this study than its corollary that people defer intensification because of the greater work requirement. The 1920s Soviet economist Chayanov devised an evocative term for this preoccupation: "drudgery aversion."[38]

Boserup's observation about labor requirements and changing production practices provides insight into the advantages and disadvantages of pastoralism, foraging, shifting cultivation, and irrigation. Sutton and Thomas Spear have considered the history of intensive and extensive production in east African cases, but to my knowledge, southern Africa remains without this sort of study.[39]

Applying these insights to the history of Kuruman, I explain how the agro-pastoral and Cape frontiers, British colonialism, and segregation created forces that changed the way people used the environment and persevered in their lives. With its semi-arid thornveld and its flowing eyes, the Kuruman environment presented people with a variety of constraints and possibilities, thus giving good ground to explore the history of intensive and extensive land uses. There has not been a consistent effort to maximize agricultural use of the water. Understanding why intensification of land use has been maintained at certain levels requires historical consideration of human, biological, and physical factors. Classification of "extensive" and "intensive" land uses is difficult because the terms are relative. Despite what nineteenth-century missionaries and some modern commentators have said, extensive production is not an underdeveloped land use retarded by rudimentary technology. Rather, the rudimentary technology and reliance on ecological processes are its strengths, allowing people to get food with lower effort and risk. In Kuruman, the lower drudgery levels of extensive production provided good reason to hesitate about intensification, a consideration evident in the nineteenth century, until conditions in the twentieth century undercut extensive production and made it nearly impossible to intensify.

Although I begin my study of production with questions about how people interact with the biophysical environment, questions of social history, how people interact with each other, complete my analysis. Humans do not interact with the environment as an undifferentiated whole; in Kuruman, social divisions by race, class, and gender determined which uses prevailed and how the benefits were shared.* There are admirable precedents for this line of enquiry in the environmental history of tropical Africa. The works of James Giblin and Robert Harms show that patronage is an environmental issue, that powerful classes hindered others in developing independent productive activities, and that disadvantaged people chose particular forms of production to promote their interests. Giblin explores how class relations facilitated trypanosomiasis management and food security but with unequal benefits for patrons and clients.[40] Harms considers tactical decisions about different forms of production in different microenvironments as people strategized how to survive and succeed at social competition.[41] Henrietta Moore and Megan Vaughan reveal that gender is another salient category in African environmental history. Looking at agricultural history and nutrition, they analyze the history of *citemene*, the system of shifting agriculture in Zambia, and show that different opportunities and obligations among

---

* Ethnicity is certainly an important consideration in southern Africa and in environmental history; however, ethnicity in its modern form was not a factor on the Bantu-Khoisan frontier, and in twentieth-century Kuruman, the Tlhaping and Tlharo had not developed notably differentiated forms of ethnic consciousness.

women and men have led to different production and distribution strategies. Constraints on women's access to resources made it difficult for them to gain from farming as men did.[42] Racial and ethnic identity also has environmental aspects. In a West African case, James Webb argues that climate change created conflict on the desert frontier and contributed to the construction of the *Bidan* or "White" identity among pastoral people in the southwestern Sahara.[43] In this book, I will explore an underdeveloped aspect of socio-environmental history: the state. Because the state has exercised power on behalf of dominant social groups, its impact on people's relations with the environment requires sustained consideration. These questions of social history will show that although the environment of Kuruman is largely arid, relatively infertile, and prone to stock disease and overgrowth by bushes, it has been human society that has presented the greater hindrance to people using it to create adequate support for themselves. At the same time, some poor and disempowered people found independence and sustenance in this environment.

My methodology for constructing a social and environmental history has been to conduct fieldwork; to search documentary records; and to explore disciplines, including atmospherics, climatology, geology, geomorphology, and biology. Scientific evidence helped me identify qualities of the biophysical world that influenced human history. These included rainfall cycles, soil characteristics, underwater karst systems, vegetation change, stock disease, and diet. In developing an understanding of these issues, I consulted specialists.

As for my documentary sources, in this research, I have benefited greatly from three published studies: Kevin Shillington's history of the colonization of the southern Tswana, P. H. R. Snyman's local history of Kuruman, and the works of Jean and John Comaroff who include evidence from Kuruman in their study of Christianity among the southern Tswana.[44] With thorough and well-researched explanations of cultural, political, and economic processes, these books provided me with a framework for doing environmental history. It would be difficult to overestimate the importance of these books for my own research.

For primary sources, my research draws most heavily on documentary records, which varied greatly in quantity and quality over the time span of the study. Compared with much of Africa, documentary sources are particularly rich for this area in the nineteenth century. The early chapters are dependent on published travelers' accounts and missionary archival records. For the period after colonial annexation, published and archival governmental records are the chief sources. However, the quantity of descriptions is not usually matched by insight into African experiences. The problem remains that these biased outsider depictions represent the writer more than the observed environment and the people in it. Mary Louise Pratt has criticized the interpretive impositions of European travelers who provide source material for this book. Still, read critically, these sources reveal insight into the landscape and the people, plants, and animals in it.[45] In the early decades of British and Cape rule, bureaucrats left detailed descriptive records, but the quality of information drops off considerably by the 1950s as government officials increasingly turned their attention to their own projects and less to the circumstances of Africans. I found no Tswana-language documentary histories, and in documentary sources left by outsiders, testimony by Africans is frustratingly scarce. However, I have made it a priority to include as many writings by Kuruman people as possible. In reading these documentary sources, my goal has been to peer through the environments, cultures, and societies to view the people and the nonhuman world behind them. It is necessary to read outsider sources on two levels: for their context and prejudices and for evidence about people operating within their historic environments.[46] Although outsider observations run indigenous voices through a very fine filter, it is possible to hear farmers' testimony in others' descriptions of their work. As Moore and Vaughan say, "concrete practices are as much evidence of agency and self-presentation as are 'voices.' "[47] Farming practices, even those described prejudicially, can be read as a text on how people assess their options.

I have been cautious about projecting contemporary indigenous knowledge or information gained by observing practices backward into earlier times. Food production changed radically during the period of this study, and today people around Kuruman practice little cultivation at all. Therefore, enhancing colonial records with ethnographic evidence seemed untenable. This changes for the period within living memory. For much of the twentieth century, farmers' voices were accessible. To tap such memory and knowledge, I twice did fieldwork.[48] My fieldwork goals were to see the environment, production processes, and social interactions through the eyes of people who lived this history. In 1991, I did doctoral research on the replacement of subsistence production with wage labor in the period before 1935. At that time, I spent about two months in Kuruman getting to know the people and the place. I stayed at the Moffat Mission and drove across the border into Bophuthatswana for my interviews. Living in white South Africa was not ideal, but given my race and the political realities, it was unavoidable. The benefit of this removed base was that I developed a wide perspective, as I made contacts in many villages within a sixty-kilometer radius of Kuruman town doing twenty-nine interviews. My contacts began with Alan Butler, then director of the Moffat Mission Trust, who put me in touch with black church and community leaders, who in turn introduced me to the elderly men and women who remembered the period before 1935, who in turn introduced me to their relatives and neighbors. Anticipating that group interviews could stifle some voices, I mostly interviewed individuals.[49] Some interviews were in English and some were in Tswana. I had studied Tswana in graduate school, but needed assistance with translation and hired interpreters from the University of Bophuthatswana (now the University of the North–West). As the research progressed, they conducted their own interviews with a question-naire that I created. Peter Mokomele, who lived at the Moffat Mission, was extremely helpful with contacts in the community and checking the translation. Seeking corroboration or dissenting opinions, we asked the same questions of many people and found great conformity about farming and herding practices, about what they produced, and about how people cooperated in their work. The consistency gave me confidence in the results, but made me wonder if ques-tioning a succession of elderly people was the ideal procedure. There were a few exceptional informants and interviews. The headman in Ga-Mopedi, Isaac Seamecho, who was born in 1909, became my valued teacher on local history. He had a gift for dates, an excellent memory, and the ability to put events in Kuruman in a larger context. With him I had my best extended open-ended conversations. Also, I found that my group interviews were invigorating and productive exchanges.

I had made one lightning visit to Kuruman during the 1994 elections, but when I returned for more research in 1997, I found much had changed since 1991, par-ticularly in efforts toward development, restitution, and democracy. There were new networks, an increased openness, and a new hope for positive change. Because it was an ideal central location, I again made the Moffat Mission my base; Alan and Hilda Butler had moved to England, and their replacements at the mission, Steve De Gruchy and Marian Loveday, were equally helpful. Very importantly, researchers investigating claims for restitution for forcible removals under segregation were doing work that intersected with mine. Peter Mokomele had become a researcher for the Association for Community and Rural Advancement (AnCRA), a local nongovernmental organization that as-sisted removed communities in the area with land claims. I shared my archival research with Peter and his colleagues at AnCRA, and they allowed me to cite their interviews. Also, land claim committees in villages that were seeking restitution for their removals were good contacts. They supported my work and I shared information with them. Sadly, Mr. Seamecho and other elderly friends had passed away, but many other people were extremely receptive to us.

At this time, I took a different approach to fieldwork, using the research methodology of Rapid Rural Appraisal (RRA).[50] RRA uses exercises and open-ended questions to set up discussions and visual communication. It was devised by development specialists to replace time-consuming and costly quantitative surveys and superficial "development tourism" by experts visiting from urban areas. Its techniques proved well suited to historical research. The cardinal principles are to avoid leading questions, to be relaxed, to be less intrusive in discussions, to encourage informants to direct discussions, to triangulate information between interviews, and to question critically the process and one's role in it. The RRA philosophy is that local people have the knowledge outsiders seek and that outsiders can tap into it more easily, more deeply, and with less distortion than with previously used methods. My research assistants inestimably enhanced the use of RRA in this project. Two of my former students, Kristin Russell, a graduate of Carleton College, and Megan Waples, a graduate of Brown University, volunteered to help me from September through December 1997. In Kuruman, I hired Tswana-speaking research assistants, including Poppy Afrikaner, Bhangi Mosala, Tsolo Steenkamp, Kgomotso Tshetlho, and Victoria Tsatsimpe, who facilitated the interviews and translated for the Americans. In teams of two to four, we did fifty-two group interviews in the villages of Ncweng, Ga-Mopedi, Batlharos, Seodin, Kagung, Sedibeng, Ga-Sebolao, Ga-Lotlhare, Maiphinike, Ga-Diboe, Logobate, and Churchill. I returned in March and July of 1998 for more interviews, when I worked with the assistance of Peter Heywood and Stephen Kotoloane for twelve semistructured interviews. Over the course of this period, we supplemented the group interviews with twenty-four individual ones, when we took life histories and talked with those who could not come to our meetings. In individual interviews, people sometimes clarified sensitive information.

Our RRA interviews involved inviting a group to meet us at a venue suggested by community members, usually a church hall, a clinic, or a school. In our first RRA interviews, we asked people to use colored pens and large pieces of paper to draw maps that showed changes in land use since they were young. Another technique we used early in the research was to take transect walks through villages, pastures, and cultivated fields. As time progressed, we frequently used matrices. For example, in interviews on fodder vegetation, I first asked informants "What veld plants do animals eat?" They brainstormed a list of the most common fodder plants, which Bhangi wrote on a piece of paper. We did this exercise in two or three groups to check and expand the list. Later, in a tour of the veld, several men identified the most important plants for me, and together we used field guides to determine the scientific names. David Phalatse, a botanist at the University of the North–West, also helped me with identification. In the next round of interviews, people did rankings on the preference of cattle, sheep, and goats for different plants. They also modeled with dried beans the relative importance of different fodder plants – making bean piles sized in proportion to their perception of the importance of the plant. They also assessed the value of different fodder plants. Finally, people used bean quantification to show their memories of grass tree ratios over time. Without a doubt, dried beans became our most important research tool. Using up to four types of beans to signify different categories, people modeled change over time in many different subjects – social division, rainfall levels, herd composition, strategies to gain a livelihood, stock diseases, diet, and poverty levels. The visual representation in these exercises conveyed much information quickly, but the most valuable exchange of information came from listening to the discussion during the exercise and asking people about the resulting schematic. We usually taped the sessions and afterwards wrote notes on the discussions, either paraphrasing the discussion or recording quotations, depending on our assessment of the quality of the information. In these interviews people spoke English and Tswana. Quotations in the text are either in the original English or in translations by my research assistants.

These methods were particularly well suited for research in the recent environmental history of a rural, farming society. RRA tools reveal the logic and dynamic of mundane everyday existence and evoke a structured analysis of economic activities and commentary on environmental conditions. In contrast to my previous research, the middle-aged people who remembered this period were hale enough to come to group meetings at a central location. Topics such as ethnobiology, farming methods, household economies, and general historical overviews were not contentious issues in community politics and thus were less likely to be skewed by group interviews. We witnessed people working through the RRA exercises, discussing the topics, and adding to and disagreeing with each other's statements. We repeated important questions in several interviews to crosscheck information. The method was also valuable in allowing people to discuss sensitive subjects, such as wealth distribution within the community, by modeling them abstractly. Yet we did find that group interviews created disincentives for dissent on the sensitive subject of the donkey massacre. The advantage of the RRA technique is that it ensures that the interview is open to participation and direction by informants. The interaction is less directed by the intention and needs of the interviewer than a question-and-answer format.

AN OVERVIEW: THE FRONTIER, COLONIALISM, AND SEGREGATION

I have organized the chapters in this book around three successive and overlapping dispensations familiar in both African and environmental history: the frontier, the colonial, and the segregationist periods. I will draw on the understanding of these themes in both bodies of historiography as I explore how relations between people and the environment changed through political, cultural, and economic forces.

Frontiers are zones of contact between different societies, meeting places for people with different cultures, economies, and political systems. Frontiers are most interesting to historians when they are dynamic, when the line of contact encroaches onto one party's territory, and when people join through amalgamation or subjugation. The history of Kuruman is enlivened by two separate frontier encounters between 1700 and 1820. Both brought transformation in the ways people related to the environment and to each other. In South African history, the frontier often is associated with the Cape after the seventeenth century. However, the introduction of European influence followed an earlier internal African frontier that spread new cultures, languages, human physical types, and production methods.[51] This was the frontier between Bantu and Khoisan cultural groups that spread agro-pastoralism and Bantu languages, first through immigration by Bantu agro-pastoralists. Thereafter, their presence, along with other incentives, led many in the autochthonous Khoisan population to join them in creating Tswana chiefdoms – the Tlhaping and Tlharo. In my discussion of agro-pastoral production, I establish that this was a very extensive land use. In contrast to the usual depiction of Bantu-speaking chiefdoms, the Tlhaping and Tlharo had a foraging class. Full-time foraging was the practice of the destitute, but some people seemed to prefer it to working as clients of the rich. The most powerful people, chiefs, controlled cattle, and other men aspired to acquire herds. Women were excluded from stock ownership, so they cultivated, but I see agriculture as a sphere of female autonomy separate from the male world of stock, not as a case of male exploitation of female labor. Men and women practiced reciprocity in their production, although among men the benefits were greatly skewed. In this society and all those that followed, social divisions determined who had power to practice their preferred uses of the environment, although those with less power found respite from domination in their environmental niches.

The nineteenth century saw the opening of the second frontier between the Cape Colony and the societies in the interior. The frontier has been a useful concept among historians of white settlement in South Africa. Particularly valuable to this study is the work by Martin Legassick on the Griqua, Tlhaping, and Tlharo in the context of the Cape frontier.[52] Ironically, it was Legassick's refutation of the tradition that the frontier was the crucible of racial conflict that pushed southern African history away from frontier studies in the 1970s and 1980s.[53] Of course, even if it was not the origin of racial division in modern South Africa, the frontier is worthy of study and historians have returned to considering the Cape frontier for what it was, a zone of interchange and change.[54] On the Cape frontier new environmental relations emerged. More than cattle keeping had been, irrigation and commercial hunting were open to common men as well as the elite, and the fact that these practices dispersed power from the agro-pastoral hierarchy may have contributed to their popularity. Yet I argue that people adapted irrigation and commercial hunting into their extensive land use system. While the Cape frontier brought innovations to men, the environmental activities of women and the poorest people changed little.

The second dispensation in this book, discussed in Chapters 4, 5, and 6, is colonialism. Concepts of colonialism in southern African and environmental history have an awkward fit. Environmental histories of colonialism and imperialism focus on white settlement.[55] Of course, there were great numbers of white settlers in South Africa, but unlike other settler societies, there was no demographic decline among the indigenous people. My goal is to contribute to an understanding of colonial environmental history for areas where the indigenous population was stable. Of course, while Africans remained in the majority, they still experienced colonization. Therefore, African environmental history of the colonial period must explore how state administration shaped people's relations with the nonhuman world. While most comparisons involving the environmental history of South Africa have involved settler societies in temperate zones, focusing on the state will bring out the similarities between South African and continental African environmental history. The state was not a dispenser of justice, environmental or otherwise, in colonial Africa. Still, the earliest colonial state in Kuruman governed through Direct Rule by a paternalist administration, and thus, it was less interventionist than the late colonial state in South Africa or elsewhere.

The aspect of colonialism that has most interested South African historians is the capitalist transformation of society and economy. Among black South Africans this process occurred through the entrenchment of migrant wage labor. The history of Kuruman shows that biophysical forces contributed extensively to this process. When rural African societies lost their political and economic autonomy to colonial rulers and the cash economy, migrant wages were not sufficient to support households. An environmental approach to this history shows that people earning wages did not stop having deliberate and calculated interactions with the biophysical world. Therefore, I analyze the production methods of people who were dependent on wage labor and how they change over time. By the 1950s, people reduced their supplementary subsistence production and became more heavily dependent on cash. I also examine the social relations of this work and find that the desire to escape socially unequal reciprocal relations was one cause of the decline of cultivation.

The last section of the book, Chapters 6 and 7, considers a period when segregationist policy further changed people's relations with the nonhuman world. Race is not a prominent topic in environmental history.[56] One work

30

that does consider race is Andrew Hurley's book documenting unequal exposure to pollution in Gary, Indiana. Yet the similarities between Hurley's work on Gary and mine on Kuruman are limited. He finds class to be a more basic determinant than race, and his and other environmental histories of race in the United States are urban.[57] Unfortunately, environmental historiography offers no models for understanding racial segregation in an agrarian, colonial setting. Racial segregation was best developed in settler societies, but implementing it entailed state policies that were similar to those throughout colonial Africa. My understanding of segregation in South Africa is indebted to Mahmood Mamdani's work *Citizen and Subject: Contemporary Africa and the Legacy of Late Colonialism*. Mamdani's argument that in colonial Africa under Indirect Rule, including segregationist South Africa, the state "was organized not as a racial power denying rights to urbanized subjects, but as an ethnic power enforcing custom on tribespeople."[58] This subject status allowed Africans fewer rights and less ability to use their land. Exploiting these constricted rights, the state extended segregation into the environmental sphere by restricting where blacks could live and what they could do on their land. Through forced removals and coercive conservation, most notoriously the donkey killing, the state became an active and unwelcome partner in people's relations with the environment.

In fact, C. S. Lewis's declaration resonates in many events throughout this history: "What we call Man's power over Nature turns out to be a power exercised by some men over other men with Nature as its instrument."[59] In this book, I critique the ways the powerful have exerted themselves to extract the most wealth from the environment and have assailed weaker people's relations with the environment. I also show that weaker people have found their own ways of interacting with the environment to mitigate their circumstances. I hope this critique of power will contribute to efforts to reform and develop the black communal areas in this region. I also hope that those with expertise, resources, and commitment will work to encourage and improve the environmental innovations of poor people to avert the trend of displacing them with commercial production by a few. Finally, I hope my interpretation of this history will give new insights to people who live in communal areas about the many possible ways to live in this environment and will help them plan a more just dispensation. Relations with fellow humans shape the choices people make about how to use the environment, and everyone does not have the same freedom of choice. At least as much as any challenges posed by "nature," people have been challenged by the task of how to live with each other in this environment.

2

Goat People and Fish People on the Agro-Pastoral Frontier, c. 1750–1830

A Matchappee, being told that cows, oxen, sheep, and other animals
were made for certain purposes, such as to feed and clothe men, was
asked for what purpose he thought man was made. He answered, to
go on plundering expeditions against other people.[1]

W HEN groups meet in frontier zones, they have to negotiate many issues,
including the ways of using the environment. Because these encounters
introduce and establish new environmental relations, they are of particular interest to environmental historians. In early Kuruman, as in other places, frontier
encounters provided fuel for a dynamic of change. In fact, the two major considerations of this book – social difference in environmental relations and the
process of intensification – first appeared with the agro-pastoral frontier wash-
ing over Kuruman in the eighteenth century. Thus, our starting point for the
environmental history is the shift from foraging to herding and growing crops
and the associated political and social changes on the agro-pastoral frontier.

Broadly speaking, southern African frontiers involved contact between three
economic groups that largely correspond to linguistic groups. The first inhabitants were foraging "bushmen," or "San," who spoke the click languages of
the Khoisan family. Second were the Khoikhoi, also speaking a Khoisan language, who kept stock, although they did not cultivate. Third and last appearing
were the agro-pastoralists, whose men herded cattle, sheep, and goats, while the
women cultivated with iron tools. In the summer rainfall areas, agro-pastoralism
supported the densest populations in southern Africa, although the population
thinned toward more arid regions where people depended more on herding than
on cultivating. Agro-pastoralists spoke the Bantu languages that have developed
into Zulu, Xhosa, Sotho, Shona, Tswana, Herero, and others.[2]

Early in the second millennium of the Common Era (CE), the agro-pastoral
frontier moved from the forested Indian Ocean coast to the grassy interior

plateau.[3] Centuries later, Kuruman became one of the last areas to host its arrival. In fact, by 1800, when the frontier zone from Cape Colony entered this region, the transformation to agro-pastoralism was not as complete as in neighboring areas, and land use remained relatively extensive. So, visitors from the Cape Colony to Kuruman documented a society still in transition, and their records allow us to probe the shift to agro-pastoralism in exceptional depth. This chapter explores the establishment of agro-pastoralism in two newly formed Tswana chiefdoms near Kuruman, the Tlhaping and the Tlharo. It discusses the foundation of stock keeping and cultivation, even while foraging endured. It also assesses the social organization of extensive production. Food production activities corresponded to social power, which cleaved along lines of class and gender. Foraging had its advantages, because it involved less labor for the food acquired, but full-time foragers were vulnerable to exploitation by more powerful neighbors. Men with power monopolized pastoralism, the most propitious land use. Cultivation, the form of production that entailed the most drudgery, was relegated to women. Social divisions corresponding to forms of production were the result a combination of factors: the risks and benefits of production, a culture that esteemed men and cattle over women and the wild, and the concentration of power among some men.

GOAT PEOPLE AND FISH PEOPLE BECOME TLHAPING

The transition from foraging to agro-pastoralism accompanied cultural, linguistic, and political changes common to much of Africa, "the Bantu expansion."* [4] The spread of Bantu languages was once considered the result of population movement, but the population expansion model may not adequately explain the evidence. Jan Vansina has argued that rather than a relentless move through contiguous territory, a limited immigration would have been sufficient to introduce a new language to the existing population.[5] In this process of limited migration and language shift, "the largest numbers of agents were descendants of autochthons themselves."[6] Applied to southern Africa, this paradigm suggests that Bantu-speaking agro-pastoralists did not necessarily displace Khoisan foragers and herders, but that Bantu-speaking agro-pastoral societies emerged from the fluid, heterogeneous cultures of frontier zones. Archeological evidence about the Khoisan/Bantu frontier north of the Orange River supports this supposition.[7] The earliest identifiable inhabitants of the northern Cape were

---

* The Bantu language subfamily of the Niger-Congo group has 450 closely related languages. They are widely spoken in central, eastern, and southern Africa, but their origins were in Nigeria and Cameroon. It has been a major task of Africanist historians to explain the spread of these languages and their speakers over such a large area.

foragers. Archeologists have postulated that pastoralists, probably Khoikhoi, joined them in the thornveld around 800 CE. Agro-pastoralists, presumably Bantu speakers from the northeast, first appeared in the region around contemporary Kuruman and Vryburg by the seventeenth century or earlier, but did not immediately displace or dominate previous residents.[8]

Oral tradition about the foundation of the Tlhaping chiefdom also supports Vansina's model of cultural shift rather than population movement. Before the mid-eighteenth century, people in the Kuruman–Vryburg area had been foragers, small-stock pastoralists, and clients of agro-pastoralists. There was no local Tswana chiefdom, but the Rolong, an established Tswana chiefdom to the east, claimed some authority over the people who lived there. We do not know which language they spoke, but we know they had kinship and trading connections with both Khoikhoi and Tswana. In later years they were remembered as poor fish eaters and goat keepers. Toward the end of the eighteenth century, through trading and raiding, these people acquired wealth and formed chiefdoms along Tswana lines. The prevailing fluidity gave way to conformity, as many people made the transition from foraging and small-stock herding in bands to agro-pastoralism under newly formed local Tswana chiefdoms. In the process, Khoisan cultural tendencies yielded to Tswana ways, but Khoisan connections and markers remained. Several early historians of southern Africa – George Stow, George Theal, and Silas Molema – shared the belief that the Tlhaping were a vanguard of Sotho-Tswana migration whose Bantu authenticity had diminished through mixture with the Khoisan. These historians considered them to have become degraded because of Khoi influence in language, economy, and physique.[9] In contrast, I use the same evidence to argue that this was a young chiefdom still coming into conformity with Sotho-Tswana patterns.

Two separate published historical traditions exist for the origins of the Tlhaping chiefdom before the nineteenth century. These traditions are incomplete simplifications of the frontier zone dynamics, providing only limited historical evidence, but critical readings reveal the fundamental point that the Tlhaping did not migrate to Kuruman as Tswana agro-pastoralists, but arose from Khoisan and Bantu foragers, clients to Tswana agro-pastoralists. The first tradition, that of "Briqua" or "Goat People," is that the Tlhaping were mixed Tswana-Khoisan with roots among Sotho-Tswana and Khoikhoi west of the Langeberg Mountains. (See Figure 1-5.) The second tradition is of "Tlhaping," Tswana for "Fish People." (These Tlhaping are not necessarily the exclusive ancestors of the nineteenth-century chiefdom of the same name.) The Fish People tradition holds that they were originally Rolong, but settled near the Vaal-Harts confluence, near Taung (see Figure 1-1) where they intermarried with the Korana, a local Khoikhoi group. The fact that the early Tlhaping were known to one set of neighbors as goat herders and to the other set of neighbors as fish eaters is good evidence that they were not agro-pastoralists on the Sotho-Tswana model.

Colonists at the Cape first learned about the Goat People from Khoikhoi on their frontier.[10] Closer contact came in 1778 and 1779 when two separate travelers, H. J. Wikar and R. J. Gordon, traveled on the middle Orange River between present-day Upington and the Augrabies Falls (see Figure 1-1).[11] They recorded meeting the "Gyzikoa" (Wikar) or "Geissiqua" (Gordon), people who had close connections with the "Blicquoas" (Wikar) or Briqua (Gordon), a term that may have referred to the Sotho-Tswana in general or perhaps more particularly to the Tlhaping. Wikar recorded that Gyzikoa were a divided people, half living among the Blicquoa and half on the Orange River; therefore, he called them the "Twin Folk." He attributed several characteristics of the Gyzikoa to Blicquoa influences: their size, hair texture, language, karosses (leather blankets), and metal ornaments. From them he learned that the Blicquoa lived three days' journey north along a river; that they cultivated; that they kept cattle at posts in the mountains; and that they traded valuable handicrafts, the metal specularite (used as a sparkly cosmetic), tools, and weapons in exchange for heifers. The Gyzikoa offered to take the travelers to the Blicquoa, but the road and river were both without water, and Wikar's companions refused.[12] Gordon gave fewer indications that the Geissiqua exhibited Briqua culture and physiognomy, but he recorded a few Tswana words and noted that the Briqua had recently suffered smallpox and that their more proper name was "Bitjoana," the first recorded use of the name "Tswana." Like Wikar he noted the route to the "Moetjoanaas," but did not journey there.[13] * In a scholarly elaboration of the Goat People tradition, L. F. Maingard postulated that the mixed Gyzikoa/Geissiqua were the original Tlhaping. As evidence for a strong Korana heritage among the Tlhaping, he noted that the Tlhaping name for the Korana identified them as a kindred people.[14] He corroborated the Gyzikoa/Geissiqua testimony about being related

---

* In the Tswana language, prefixes designate singular and plural forms. Of the noun class pertaining to familiar and respectable humans, "mo" is the singular form and "ba" is the plural form. Tswana-speaking groups referred to themselves and each other with "ba," for example, *Batlhaping* or *Bakwena*. Maingard observes that the name for the Khoikhoi was "Bakxoto." The ba plural prefix signifies them as a known people. In contrast, unfamiliar people were given the "le" prefix, such as the Xhosa, *Lekhonkhobe*, and whites, *Lekhoa*. Maingard argued that the ba/le distinction was the best indication of identification. This presents an opportunity to explain my usage of Tswana names in this book. The Tswana language requires declensions of plural, singular, and adjectival forms. Because declensions of noun prefixes are unknown in English, and because the prefixes make English definite and indefinite articles redundant, I do not use noun prefixes in this book. I use only the familiar root of proper nouns – for example, Tswana – as the form for plural and singular nouns as well as adjectives. However, I use the Tswana plural term "balala," for the poor class, because it is used as a proper noun in documentary sources.

to the Blicquoa/Briqua with nineteenth-century testimony from Tlhaping and Korana that they had previously lived together at Nokaneng,* southwest of Kuruman.[15] He put this site about half way between modern Kuruman and Upington, west of the Langeberg Mountains, on a now dry tributary of the Orange River, the Nokanna. Although Maingard did not seem to realize it, the archeologist T. Maggs noted that his hypothesis placed the settlement very close to a present-day farm of the same name, thirty kilometers southwest of Olifantshoek.[16] (For these and other settlements mentioned in this chapter, see Figure 4-1.)

The second tradition of the Fish People has been more influential, perhaps because the Tlhaping themselves used the name. The first travelers from the Cape to reach the Tlhaping capital at Dithakong in 1801 pointed out that the Briqua referred to themselves by a form of the term Tswana.[17] Lichtenstein, who visited in 1805–1806, was the first to observe that there were several separate "Beetjuana" tribes, one of which was the "Maatjaping" [Motlhaping]. Because the Fish People ate little fish, he gave the name Tlhaping some consideration:

> No food is more horrible to them than fish, even if they are very hungry. Their rivers are full of fish. I have tried my utmost, but in vain, to find the reason for this superstition. The name Maatjaping [Motlhaping] points in that direction. According to the missionary (Jan Mathias) Kock [*sic*] a close relation of the name to this animal can be seen; tjapi [tlhapi] meaning fish.[18] †

In fact, fish are not a totem, forbidden to the Tlhaping diet. The name arose, as the traveler Andrew Smith later learned, because "the Baclapins [Batlhaping] used to catch fish and eat them when they were poor."[19]

In general, travelers could not learn much about Tlhaping history. John Campbell learned about five generations of chiefs and that the Tlhaping had resisted a Rolong attempt to collect tribute. The Tlhaping chief responded, "Am I then your servant?"; this caused a war which scattered the people.[20] One account, published in the twentieth century by the missionary J. Tom Brown, has been very influential. The story was that the Tlhaping broke away from the Rolong, "moved to the banks of the Vaal River and began to use fish as part of their diet, hence their name. At and near the river they came into contact with Korana and Bushmen and intermarried with them."[21] As a tribal history, the Fish People

---

* "Nokaneng," meaning "at the river," was a common name.
† Lichtenstein confuses the singular and plural prefixes, referring to the Tlhaping chiefdom as "Motlhaping." The name for tilapia, a fresh-water fish available in some North American grocery stores, has Bantu origins and is derived from "tlhapi."

tradition of migration and politics resembled those of scores of other groups; however, it had insufficient corroboration among the Tlhaping themselves. P.-L. Breutz, the government ethnologist who did fieldwork among the southern Tswana in the late 1950s, noted:

> The baRolong usually say that the baTlhaping were Rolong originally, and it is very likely that they were not. . . . It appears that certain Rolong chiefs . . . merely ruled foreign Tlhaping clans. Large Tswana tribes know all about their earliest migrations, the baTlhaping do not. They there-fore must have consisted of very early small isolated groups with no tradition . . . . All these early populations mixed more or less with the orig-inal populations in the country, mainly related to Korana Hottentots.[22]

Martin Legassick made an insightful interpretation for the origins of the name Tlhaping. Since fish was a distateful wild food among the Sotho-Tswana, the name Tlhaping probably connotes very poor foragers, and the term is "more likely to be applied to a *class* of people than a chiefdom."[23] He argued that "they were a cluster of dispersed Bantu-Khoisan clients" who formed a chiefdom between 1750 and 1800. Before this point, there were many different groups who only later consolidated as the Tlhaping.[24] By using evidence other than that collected in the tradition, Legassick gave clarity to the processes of political consolidation.

Traditions of origins among the second chiefdom in the area, the Tlharo, are not as well developed, so no similar treatment is possible. One memory maintains that they are an offshoot of the Hurutshe, an older Tswana group. Their more proper name is "*Batho baga Motlhware*," or "people of the wild olive," for the original sojourning group took shelter under a tree. Despite this tradition of pure Tswana origins, they also lived in communities with Korana.[25]

The traditions reveal cultural homogenization as well as political transforma-tion. Early nineteenth-century travelers do not record ethnic diversity among the Tlhaping. As we shall see, the foragers in this society were not typically identi-fied as Bushmen, and since these same travelers had encountered Bushmen in other areas, their absence is noteworthy. The Korana were nearby and remained throughout the century. However, relations between them and the Tlhaping had changed. In contrast to the diversity among the Twin Folk, people recognized as Korana and Tswana no longer lived together. Testimony from both groups taken in the nineteenth century indicates that the mixed community at Nokaneng broke apart before 1800 because the site was vulnerable to raiding.[26] After 1800, visiting Europeans recorded meeting "Beetjuanas" who understood the Korana language.[27] This suggests a process of cultural homogenization, of becoming Tswana. As these chiefdoms consolidated and conformed to Tswana culture, the dominant class became agro-pastoralist and its language and production meth-ods gained hegemonic value throughout the territory. In the early nineteenth century, there was still intermarriage between the Tlhaping and the Korana, the brides joining their husbands' people. Presumably, a Korana bride joining the Tlhaping at Dithakong had to assimilate to Tswana ways more than her grand-mother at Nokaneng would have. Consolidation around Kuruman and Vryburg could have weakened Sotho-Tswana presence to the west. In fact, a mirror im-age of Tswana cultural homogenization among the Tlhaping must have been taking place among the Korana on the Orange River who were incorporating Sotho-Tswana clients as Khoikhoi.[28]

As the Tlhaping and Tlharo were coming into being, other people throughout the region were experiencing transformations of their own. Recently, discus-sions have sought to link the causes of the conflict and political change in the region before 1820 with those of the spectacular conflict that climaxed through-out southern Africa after that date, usually known as the *mfecane* or *difiqane*. In fact, Parsons has described the period after 1750 as "the proto-*difiqane.*"[29] The endemic stock raiding of this period is the most obvious link between the establishment of independent agro-pastoralism among the Tlhaping and Tlharo and the bursts of violence everywhere.[30] Plundering herds was the "princi-pal object" of warfare.[31] Through raiding, stock-poor people could establish themselves as a chiefdom, as seen in the case of the Thamaga, a client group of the Tlhaping who became an independent chiefdom:

> They formed a considerable body in the days of Molehabangue . . . who, in his commandoes for the capture of cattle, was wont to take them with him. Taught this mode of warfare, and being of an intrepid character, they sallied forth and took cattle for themselves, which Molehabangue's generous dis-position allowed them to keep, and they became an independent tribe.[32] *

Campbell was disturbed to discover acceptance of the ubiquity of raiding vi-olence: "A Matchappee [Motlhaping], being told that cows, oxen, sheep, and other animals were made for certain purposes, such as to feed and clothe men, was asked for what purpose he thought man was made. He answered, to go on plundering expeditions against other people."[33] However, outside forces also fed this violence. By the 1790s, the Cape raiding frontier had reached the Tlhaping and began to funnel cattle and captive people to the Colony.[34] The Korana-Tlhaping community at Nokaneng dissolved under Korana attacks around that time, and the Tlhaping moved northeastward to the Kuruman and Matlhwareng River valleys (see Figure 4-1).[35]

---

* The reference is to Molehabangwe, chief of the Tlhaping at the turn of the nineteenth century.

Tlhaping territory is notorious as a major site of violence during the "mfecane/difiqane." The violence was prominent in 1823 at the famous conflict at Dithakong (by this time no longer the Tlhaping capital).* One factor identified as a cause for the constant raiding during the early nineteenth century is a food shortage. This has been attributed to population growth and drought after the 1790s. These were not necessarily local causes; land shortage due to Khoikhoi and Griqua migration away from the Cape may have been a factor.[36] Another development related to the violence and political consolidation is an increase in and the redirection of long distance trade with the Cape. The new trading opportunities increased the wealth of the chiefs, who then attracted more followers, contributing to the establishment of towns where people found some protection from raiding.[37] Because food production revolved around them, the growth of towns made a greater reliance on agro-pastoralism likely. The founding of the towns brought people who had previously not grown crops or spoken a Bantu dialect into the realm of the Sotho-Tswana, further entrenching food production and Tswana identification among a new population.

The transformation was significant. By 1778, when Wikar heard about them, Fish and Goat People had become cattle owners and cultivators.[38] In later years, the Tlhaping remembered that "they had never been so rich nor so numerous" as they were under Molehabangwe, the ruler at the turn of the nineteenth century.[39] However, the people who remembered being rich did not speak for everyone. Some people still foraged for wild food. Travelers and missionaries who visited this region after 1801 agreed that agro-pastoralism did not sustain everyone in the thornveld society.

THE ECOLOGICAL CYCLE IN AN AGRO-PASTORAL SOCIETY

That food production did not yield enough to support everyone is evident in the existence of a Tswana foraging class, *balala*. However, the existence of *balala* as a genuine and significant part of this society must be established. At times Tswana chiefdoms have been depicted as unstratified and secure food producers with a small chiefly class.[40] When the poor do attract historical attention, they are not considered integral.[41] There has been an assumption that the existence of lower, foraging classes resulted from outside factors. The most common explanation for lower classes is that they were ethnic outsiders, such as the San and the Kgalagadi, a subservient Tswana group among northern Tswana

---

* The engagement was between Griqua, missionaries, and Tlhaping on one side and "Mantatees" on the other side. See page 63.

chiefdoms.[42] However, among the Tlhaping and Tlharo, there is no correlation between poverty and ethnic difference. Another tendency has been to argue that stratification arose through foreign market forces: either that upper classes consolidated with increased wealth arising through trade or that lower classes plummeted because of the collapse of that trade.[43] Certainly, trade affected society in this period; it contributed to the founding of Tswana chiefdoms. However, stratification manifested itself around stock ownership, a form of food production, and must be studied in that context.[44]

John Iliffe argues that poor people were an integral part of Tswana societies: "The structural poor of nineteenth-century Tswana society were a complex stratum and perhaps an unusually large one by African standards" and "the whole process of Tswana history, with groups repeatedly incorporated in subordinate capacities, suggests recurrent disaster and destitution."[45] This observation about "recurrent disaster and destitution" is reminiscent of Richard Elphick's theory of the ecological cycle. Elphick devised this theory to describe a class-based dynamic between Khoisan herders and foragers in the western Cape. He argued that there was no great gulf between pastoralists and foragers. As the Khoikhoi people spread in search of new grazing, they incorporated San foragers as hunting clients, herders, and wives. However, not all Khoikhoi were equally successful as herders, and foraging continued among them as a low-prestige activity.[46] The upward phase of the ecological cycle involved San foragers acquiring stock through work as clients or raiding. Conversely, the cycle had a downward phase, for Khoikhoi who lost their herds through ostracism by their band, warfare, or disease could assume the life of foragers, becoming bushmen. Elphick hesitated to apply the ecological cycle to agro-pastoral societies. He cautioned:

> Here the Khoikhoi experience contrasted sharply with that of most eastern and southern African peoples, who combined a ritual and emotional attachment to pastoralism with an economic reliance on cultivation. In Southern Bantu society, for example, all persons have the right to use a section of tribal land, even though the actual distribution of the land rests in the hands of the chief. Thus, though individuals and lineages may be poor in stock, they rarely starve unless the whole community is starving with them. The Khoikhoi approach to wealth was by contrast individualistic; fortune was unstable, and the gap between rich and poor could be very pronounced.[47]

Other historians seem to have been convinced by this caveat; there has been no attempt to extend Elphick's analysis to agro-pastoral societies. This may be because of misconceptions about the efficacy of cultivation and the egalitarianism of agro-pastoral societies, apparent in Elphick's statement.[48] Despite Elphick's hesitation, the concept of the ecological cycle can provide a starting point for examining the relations between those who had enough food and those who did not, between foraging and food-producing people in the same Bantu-speaking, agro-pastoral society.

Identifying foraging as the defining characteristic of *balala* is problematic because people of all classes ate wild food. Wild plant food consisted of roots and fruits, especially *moretlhwa* from the raisin tree (*Grewia flava*). Roots of the *motlope* or shepherds' tree or witgatboom (*Boscia albitrunca*) yielded a sweet coffee-like beverage when boiled, and *tamma*, the boiled root of the gemsbuck beans (*Tylosema esculentum*), was a staple at certain times of the year. Also, swarms of grasshoppers, boiled and pounded into a powder, provided food.[49] This area is native to many wild plant foods not specifically mentioned in the earliest accounts: one contemporary study lists over fifty roots, tubers, seeds, flowers, fruits, berries, and leaves with many uses as staples, hunger foods, relishes, and beverages.[50] While the Tlhaping ate fish only during a crisis, game was relished and probably provided more meat than flocks and herds did. Game consisted of large and small antelope, Cape buffalo, wild birds, hares, giraffe, and zebra. There were grand hunts with hundreds of participants armed with knobkerries and assegais and employing pitfalls.[51]

Households with flocks and fields supplemented their diets with *veldkos* ("food from the veld" in Afrikaans and South African English) and game, but contemporary observers describe an underclass who were not able to produce enough for themselves, *balala*. The term most likely derives from the Tswana verb "to lie down" and means "low ones" or "those who have been laid low."[52] Our evidence on *balala* comes from outside observers, who probably exaggerated their hardships. Still, their writings consistently indicate that *balala* were ethnically Tswana full-time foragers, differentiated from others by lacking the ability to produce food.[53] Robert Moffat claimed *balala* "live a hungry life, being dependent on the chase, wild roots, berries, locusts, and indeed anything eatable that comes within their reach."[54] The process that reduced them to these circumstances is similar to the downward phase of Elphick's ecological cycle. We can cite individual examples of agro-pastoralists being reduced to hunting and gathering: one man was impoverished because of "measles," or smallpox. He lost "a great many cattle . . . and became a poor man, which obliged him for some time to live among the wild bushmen, in order to obtain subsistence."[55] In another case, a man suffered during Korana raids on Tlhaping herds. He recalled that the entire population had dispersed from towns and foraged to survive.[56] In the case of a girl "almost a skeleton," a breakdown of the producing household reduced her and her mother to poverty; her father had gone away with another woman, reducing the mother to foraging for survival.[57] A woman and her two children, similarly abandoned, subsisted by begging.[58] Losing ties to patrons further impoverished those who could not provide for themselves, as in the case of two poor and depressed men who lost positions as herdsmen for the chief. They were reduced to foraging "and in this employment, it was unnecessary for them to say, that they had not lately been very successful."[59] Missionaries recognized something akin to the ecological cycle, explaining that *balala* had once lived in towns but now lived "in the same relation to the Bechuanas in which the Bushmen formerly stood to the Hottentots"(Khoikhoi)[60] or using the telling term, "Bootchuana Bushmen."[61]

Balala were differentiated from the class of "vassals," the *batlhanka*, who were usually taken as prisoners in raids and lived as serfs. There was a fine and sometimes loose distinction between *balala* and *batlhanka*, but it was evident that the *batlhanka* were more like serfs or slaves than the destitute *balala*.[62] *Batlhanka* were not originally saleable property, but as the market for slaves developed on the Cape frontier, they were traded.[63]

Both of these lower classes were more vulnerable to starvation than was the community as a whole. The missionary Philip's depiction may be extreme, but his general point is that hunger existed:

> Such was the state of wretchedness to which many of Mateebe's people were reduced, that Mr. Gleig remarked, that although he had seen many famines in India, he had never seen the effect of famine in such a manner as he had witnessed at Lattakoo [Dithakong]. Many of the common people were literally walking skeletons; and those among them who were in possession of cattle, were really passing such of their neighbours as were perishing among the bushes, with the leaves in their mouths, with as much indifference as if they had been so many dogs.[64]

Begging was common, but often did not yield adequate results.[65] Some masters allowed "a scanty portion of food or milk and leave them to make up the deficiency by hunting or digging up wild roots."[66] Foraging did not provide abundance, but it was necessary for the poor's survival.

Foraging can be an ideal way to procure sustenance: converting wild plants and animals into food required less time spent in labor and less drudgery than managing domesticated plants and animals did. However, there was little surplus and there were risks of hungry periods. Furthermore, foraging was probably not sufficient to feed the entire population. Therefore, most households farmed and herded and then foraged as a supplement. The poorest only foraged. My emphasis on the foraging and the lower classes does not suggest that *balala* necessarily made up a large proportion of the population. The crucial issue is not their numbers, but that they were genuinely part of the thornveld society and that full-time foraging was the recourse of the poorest.

PASTORALISM: A PROPITIOUS FOOD SOURCE

Under such pressure, managing herds was the most auspicious way humans interacted with the thornveld. Herding was more intensive than foraging, but it was still a relatively extensive land use. Herding required less labor than cultivation, but provided for the same number of people on a smaller area than foraging could. Grazers and browsers consumed the grasses and bushes that grew naturally under the low rainfall and converted the vegetation into a relatively reliable source of food. Their value was enhanced because they were mobile during drought, disease, or raiding. They reproduced themselves without assistance and required only herding from humans. Furthermore, pastoralism was a level of intensification appropriate to the population size: the relatively few people could rely on wide expanses for herding. Herding was well suited to the thornveld, but it was not the only way that people obtained food. What proportion of calories pastoralism provided to the diet is difficult to state, and such a question can only be answered by asking who was doing the eating: rich men, members of their households, or *balala*. Domestic stock did not provide much meat; however, many travelers testified that the "principal food" was milk. People usually drank it curdled or cooked sorghum and beans in it to make porridge.[67]

The significance of pastoralism, however, went beyond dietary contribution. Cattle had the greatest cultural and political significance, although they were less productive than other domesticated animals. The Tlhaping (Goat People, after all) had many more goats and paid high prices for sheep.[68] Despite this, Tlhaping men who owned stock treasured cattle most of all. Records from the 1801 Truter–Somerville expedition stress this point strongly. One account described the scene of stock returning to the kraal at night, when "the cattle, in particular, are welcomed and caressed by their owners, and the favourites spoken to in terms of endearment or high eulogium." One man reportedly spoke for nearly an hour in praise of his cattle.[69] Another record of the trip states that in a song about cattle "the fortune of those who possessed such treasure was compared with the misery of those who were destitute."[70] The accumulation of cattle, more than the practice of cultivation, marked the transformation of Fish and Goat People into a Sotho-Tswana chiefdom and allowed individual men to develop power and influence. Cattle were at the center of Tswana society, having a symbolic and ideological value as the essence of socialized life.[71] Only men had rights over cattle.

Pastoralism was a propitious and preferred use of the environment, which made use of available land and had limited labor requirements. Stockowners scattered their animals across huge areas, keeping stock at many posts that sent leather bags filled with milk to people in town.[72] The posts could possibly be several days journey from town.[73] Stockowners' sons and client herders lived at the posts to care for the cattle.[74] A man received rights to springs and pastures by asking the chief for permission to use them; thereafter, he seemed to have a priority over them.[75] Watching herds is not arduous work, and one herder can take care of many animals successfully. If animals wandered, it was time consuming to search for them, but some were trained to return to a call.[76] Yet there were difficulties and risks in this system of herding. First, there were not great production surpluses. The Truter–Somerville expedition contacted the Tlhaping with hopes of trading for their cattle, but was disappointed. As Somerville reported,

> No endeavour has succeeded in procuring for purchase a single milk cow.... But the Chief declared that there were really not cows enough to give milk for the maintainance [*sic*] of his people, and that the few quarts he daily sent us was felt, which may be readily conceived when it is considered that between 7 and 8000 people are maintained principally upon milk.[77]

The tight supply may have resulted from low production per cow.[78] Alternately, it may have resulted from a shortage of animals, which was Somerville's understanding: "The number of cattle possessed by the inhabitants of Litakone [Dithakong] is very far from being great compared with that of their owners – and the fact I believe truly to be that they have sense enough to value their oxen more than beads, knives or any of the baubles offered in exchange for them."[79] Numbers grew slowly because cattle reproduce more slowly than small stock and suffer more from disease. In fact, anthrax and bovine botulism, the two endemic environmental stock diseases in the area, worsen as herd populations grow. One or both of these diseases posed challenges to Tlhaping herders in this period. Environmental conditions in the Tlhaping pastures at Nokaneng and at Tlharo areas in the Langeberg Mountains were not conducive to disease, but by 1801 the Tlhaping already experienced stock disease on the Ghaap Plateau, reporting that pastures at Kuruman were healthier than those at Dithakong. Kuruman did not remain disease free, however, for disease was a factor in the Tlhaping move to eastern areas in 1828.[80]

Extensive production created a system conducive to violence and theft, for the scattered pastures opened herds to attack from raiders. Chief Molehabangwe explained this to a visitor:

> We found the cattle all very lean: this the king said was owing to the treacherous conduct of Makkraki [a Rolong chief] which constrained him to keep them in the neighbourhood, lest they should all be stolen; the consequence was, that all the fields near were eaten quite bare, and scarcely any means of subsistence now remained for the cattle.[81]

Gathering animals to protect them put stress on the grass supply and also raised mortality and lowered milk production. Also, the grass supply and therefore stock keeping was affected by drought.[82] Consequently, there was competition between herders for grass and water. In short, flocks and herds had great practical and symbolic value; yet herders faced constraints in keeping them, and this strain sustained a competitive politics of stock keeping.[83]

SOCIAL POWER AND THE ECOLOGICAL CYCLE

Although the Tswana were reliant on extensive land uses, they lived in settlements where large populations were concentrated. These places could be very large: travelers in the early nineteenth century compared the size of the Tlhaping capital with Cape Town.[84] The Tswana town was, according to Jean and John Comaroff, "a centralized polity, one in which distinctly unequal classes enjoyed very different access to the means of production and redistribution."[85] The chief had particular rights over townspeople: the right to demand tributary labor; the right to organize cattle raids and grand hunts and claim most spoils; the right to claim a portion of ivory, hides, and feathers captured in other hunts; the right to the brisket of all meat, known as "sehuba" (Tswana for chest); and the right to levy fines. With his wealth in cattle, the chief could provide bridewealth for many wives who labored in fields and bore children, who provided more labor, and, if they were girls, who brought more cattle when they married. He could also attract clients and thus increase his prestige and wealth. Chiefship brought added wealth to men who were already rich. In fact, a chief who was not the richest man in the community was in a precarious position.[86]

The chief played a disproportionate role in rituals of food production, particularly of cultivation. Women waited for the chief to open the agricultural season.[87] They brought the first of the harvest to his court for the first fruits ceremony to open the harvest season. Also, he was responsible for providing rain for the crops. Not only the living chief, but chiefly ancestors protected rain, fertility, and reproduction of stock and the success of the hunt.[88] The richest man at the center of the society defined by its agro-pastoralism, the chief was most removed from the foraging past, and he and his ancestors embodied the ability to succeed as herders and cultivators.

Throughout Tswana areas, the chief was understood as *modisa*, literally "shepherd." Peters makes the point that "trustee" is not a sufficient translation for the term, that the chief had more privilege: "Inherent in the Tswana authority role of *modisa*, a label for a wide range of roles that incorporate responsibility for a group, is a notion of privileged appropriation of the corporate property."[89] Still, the *kgotla*, or community council of men, tempered the power of the chief.

> The mobilization of support behind the chief on a major issue was needed in a system of governance that was seen as consultative and was bound up with the disposition of cattle, servants, and other privileges by the chief. It was difficult for a Tswana ruler to be an autocrat, still less a despot, for long; but he was not the pawn of his people.[90]

Town households interacted at the level of the ward, an administrative, spatial, and social unit. The genesis of a ward may have started with a successful man consolidating his position. "Each chieftain or *kosi* [*kgosi* "chief"] pitches his house on a separate spot, while all his relations, friends or dependents build theirs around him."[91] These separate wards remained strong, and rich men could challenge the paramount chief by breaking away with their followers.[92] There were few people capable of attracting clients: "All independent persons, or such as have cattle sufficient to support their families, are captains, or rank as such, though only one in a district be really so."[93] The 1812 traveler William Burchell believed all dependents were "in fact, the unpaid servants of either the chief or of the various chieftains."[94] Estimates of ward size are impressionistic, but provide a rough indication of the size of a headman's retinue. There was great variation among wards, but these estimates allow a rough guess that the average size may have been around 150 people.[95] Not everyone below the headman was impoverished, but there was a great difference between rich and poor: "One man alone will sometimes be the owner of eight or ten considerable herds."[96]

An important interaction between chiefs, headmen, and their clients revolved around the care of cattle. Rich men needed assistance with herding, sometimes more than their sons could give. Also, it reduced risk and labor to scatter their animals among many herders across different pastures. On the other side, poor but ambitious men needed to build herds. These requirements encouraged men of different households to come together in *mafisa* relationships, involving the transfer of one or two young heifers from a rich man to a poorer one: "A poor Beetjuana with one wife and half a dozen head of cattle seeks the protection of a richer one. He adds his few oxen to the large herd of the rich one and for a share in the 'profit' he serves as a herdsman."[97] The receiver cared for a cow and kept it for several years, consuming all its milk. During that time, he had obligations to assist the cattle owner with labor, and although he had no rights over the cow or its offspring, the owner usually allowed the caretaker to add an animal to his own herd.[98] *Mafisa* brought men together in cooperative relationships with benefits to all sides, but their distribution was sometimes uneven.

Given the brake on milk production and stock reproduction, even rich owners were concerned with maintaining the viability of their herds. Also, they were concerned with keeping others from accumulating stock and a power base, so reciprocal herding did not always allow poorer herders to accumulate herds. This description of *mafisa* under Chief Mothibi, Molehabangwe's son, describes it as a very uneven reciprocity:

> Mattivi possesses numerous herds of cattle; these are pastured in various parts of the country, and furnish employment for a considerable number of the *poorer class* of his people. They receive for their service, nothing more than mere sustenance, and, as it would appear, barely that; being allowed only a certain portion of the milk, and left to supply themselves with meat by occasional hunting.[99]

The distinction between milk and stock as payment for herding is critical. Milk provided calories, but a heifer provided the means to build a herd and to achieve independence from patrons.

> This class of the inhabitants is greatly oppressed, not only by a *despotic*, but by an *aristocratic* power also: for, that authority which the chief exercises over the *kosies* or richer order, these exercise over their servants and immediate dependents, to so unjust a degree that they will not suffer them to acquire any property whatever; and should any of this illfated class become, by means however honest, possessed of a cow or a few goats, he would be a rare instance of good fortune or favor, if his master did not take them from him. This tyrannical conduct the *kosi* would justify by telling him that a *muchunka* or *mollala* (poor man or servant) had no need of cattle, as he had only to mind his duty in attending those of his superior, and he might always be certain of receiving as much milk and food as would be necessary for his support.[100]

There were benefits to both parties, but they were uneven. Burchell noted: "The chief will always be the richest man; for once arrived at supreme authority he holds within his own hands the power of obtaining property." "The poor," he continued "are always kept poor; and if I might judge by appearances, there are many of that description."[101]

In addition to the difficulties in accumulating stock, *balala* and *batlhanka* experienced other hardships. Members of poor classes could be victims of exceptional violence.[102] Dependents were permitted to leave the towns, but when they were in the bush, they might be required to yield some wild products, including berries, meat, and skins for karosses.[103] It was possible, however, at least when they acted as a group, for clients to challenge domination, as the cases of Fish People and the Thamaga show.

The power exerted by the chief and headmen to maintain their positions suggests that the theory of the ecological cycle as such is not adequate to describe relations between cattle owners and client herders and foragers. As identified by Elphick, hostile and benevolent forces acting on individual men powered the ecological cycle: competition and good fortune, victory or defeat, drought, disease, and the reproductive capacity of stock. The same processes of destitution and accumulation were evident among the Tlhaping and Tlharo. However, in their case, these processes were not a cycle and ecology was not the primary force behind them. Class difference resulted not only from a two-way interaction between people and nature; rather, successful men exerted their power to protect themselves from the vagaries of the ecological cycle, and this entailed keeping underlings at a disadvantage. The need to minimize risk and obtain labor and the desire for status and power through the accumulation of animals motivated the rich to perpetuate clientship. Expropriation of stock, under-remuneration in *mafisa* relations, tribute requirements, violence, and forced labor were protective measures erected by the rich and powerful. These interventions impeded their descent or others' ascent through a cycle fueled by individual effort, environmental possibility, and chance.

The denigration of the wild and those who lived on its foods and the exaltation of production and cattle are also evident in the cultural values and ritual activity. We have no direct evidence for indigenous attitudes toward nature in this period, and it would be untenable to project contemporary thinking backwards. However, Jean and John Comaroff have extrapolated attitudes from recorded behavior and spatial organization, describing a Tswana worldview that ranks categories of people and their associated spaces in a hierarchy. The wild bush and the unfortunate people who lived there were understood to be in opposition to the town, the seat of the chief, the most successful man. The Comaroffs find no esteem for "wilderness" among southern Tswana people. Despite human effort, the natural environment remained a challenging force, and the best antidote to its caprice was human achievement, best exemplified by the ruling cattle owners who were removed the furthest from the wild.[104] It became a truism among European observers that Tswana people lacked an appreciation for nature. As Campbell stated, "Nothing in creation attracts their attention, unless it can be converted into food or used as an ornament."[105] To state it positively and more neutrally, they appreciated their biophysical environment most when it was transformed into a space that produced for people.

Poverty, stratification, clientship, and dependence rather than reciprocal egalitarianism characterized male society in the early nineteenth century. Fortune or impoverishment hung on the successful management of cattle, the most efficacious use of the semi-arid thornveld. Accumulating herds brought wealth and power, while losing them reduced a man to the foraging *balala* class, to be a Tswana bushman. However, this particular interaction between people, animals, and the environment was limited to men. Women in southern African agro-pastoral societies were excluded from the opportunities of cattle herding and worked as cultivators instead. The place of women and the role of cultivation need to be considered, as the most intensive form of food production which was practiced in the thornveld society by people excluded both from stock ownership and political power.

SHIFTING CULTIVATION AS EXTENSIVE PRODUCTION

Women's lower position corresponded to the status of cultivation, which was less efficacious than stock keeping and did not provide wealth or influence. Of the ways of getting food, cultivation was the most intensive use of the land and the most consuming of human effort, but the amount of labor involved was lower than has been assumed. According to the argument that people intensify production when conditions force them to do so, the Tlhaping and Tlharo cultivated because the older forms of food production, pastoralism and foraging, did not provide sufficient food. Yet women's methods were not particularly arduous, and the practice increased available calories while giving women more control over food.

Shifting cultivation is sparing in the use of labor rather than land. Fields are partially cleared with fire and an ax, rather than painstakingly weeded. Undisturbed soil will have fewer weeds than regularly used plots, so only light hoeing is necessary. The natural vegetation provides fertility, and burning it releases minerals to enrich the soil. Therefore, the labor of applying fertilizer is avoided. Such farming requires little investment in making or purchasing tools. It does require large land areas, because when fertility drops and weeds increase, cultivators move to new plots and clear them along the same lines. According to Boserup, shifting cultivators might clear a new plot every year or every ten years. The fields can lie fallow for twenty-five years or more, regaining their fertility, before cultivators return to them and clear them as practically virgin land. Boserup maintains that most working days consist of a few hours of labor, and there are many days with no work in the fields at all.[106]

Cultivation among the Tlhaping certainly qualifies as extensive.[107] The settlement history of the eighteenth-century Tlhaping suggests cultivation was a recent development, for Nokaneng was extremely dry. From the 1790s to 1829, the Tlhaping capital moved around the upper valleys of the Kuruman and Moshaweng Rivers, where rainfall was still uncertain in some years, but cultivation was part of the complement of food production practices.[108] This was shifting cultivation with indefinite, even infinite, fallow periods, since the Tlhaping never returned to previously cultivated sites. The extensive nature of cultivation is also evident in tenure arrangements, in the open access to land. The chief was responsible for granting fields, but Burchell recorded that, in contrast to cattle, the chief did not exert his authority to confiscate land. The nature of land tenure, with secure usufruct rather than saleable title, was unfamiliar to Europeans, drawing comment from Burchell.

> [A]s long as the occupier chuses afterwards to remain there, he is never disturbed or interrupted in his right, nor does he pay any other acknowledgment for this privilege, than the first ceremony of asking leave. It must not, however, be concluded that this nation are acquainted with any of those distinctions of landed property, which would class such possessions either as *allodial* or *feodal* lands; or that the soil, as I have before stated, is ever regarded as the property, either of the Chief or his subjects.[109]

Burchell elaborated: "In fact, with respect to *territory*, they have none of those ideas which a European would attach to the word. The soil never appears to be considered as property, nor is it hardly ever thought worth claiming or disputing the possession of: the water and pasturage of it, is all that is rated of any value; and when these are exhausted the soil is abandoned as useless."[110] Burchell's assertion that water was more valuable than land held true for some later travelers who had difficulty gaining access to water sources.[111]

Another characteristic of a very extensive form of cultivation is that it did not produce great surplus, as Burchell explained:

> The pursuit of agriculture, though deemed by them of high importance, is not, however, carried so far as to push the nation in a state of plenty; . . . To fill up this deficiency, and escape starvation, or at least to mitigate their daily hunger, they are reduced to the necessity of searching the plains for those *wild roots* which nature offers.[112]

Actually, in extensive food production this relationship is reversed from what

Burchell described. Rather than foraging to make up for a shortfall in cultivation, people cultivated to make up the shortfall of wild foods. Many observers noted that the diet was usually not bountiful, but that the Tlhaping ate lots when food was available. Missionaries put this down to gluttony.[113] Yet enthusiastic eating made sense as long as it did not threaten the future food supply: "They have been accustomed to habits of industry and economy from their early years and would find means of living where others would starve, and I believe they would rather die of hunger than eat the seeds of grain intended for next year's sowing."[114]

Cultivated fields surrounded the towns. Somerville estimated fields were three to four miles across, but did not consider the plots given to each family very large. He explained that "the quantity of land cultivated is only great, when compared with the means by which labor is performed."* [115] The main tool for clearing and preparing the fields was a hoe: "A flat piece of iron fixed into the knob of the Kaffer *keerrie*. When its horizontal edge is so fitted that it stands at right angles with the handles, it serves as a hoe; when turned round so as to be parallel with the handle, it is then a hatchet."[116] The hoe sufficed because fire helped clear fields and not all of the natural vegetation was removed. Cultivators applied no manure, but burned fields, which provided some nutrients, before using them.[117] Brush and trees reduced the amount of grain produced on any plot, but leaving them standing reduced labor as well. Tree removal was for convenience of cultivation, for fencing and fuel, and to remove bird habitat. Since the veld type was an open savanna, clearing fields was not as large a task as in forested regions. Several observers commented on the scarcity of trees near the towns. In fact, Moffat gave the Tlhaping notoriety as "a nation of levellers."[118]

Short uses of each plot further reduced labor. Weeds and grasses increased in successive years of cultivation, and shifting cultivators avoided this problem by moving to new plots. Somerville suggested plots were used for only one year, but his visit was too short to ascertain this.[119] We do know that they prepared new fields at least as often as the Tlhaping capital moved, six times at an average of every four and one-half years between 1800 and 1827.[120] It is possible that soil exhaustion was a chief reason for the frequent movement of the town. In choosing fields, they avoided rocky places and may have preferred sowing in less dry spots.[121] To prepare the fields, women "scratched a few inches deep."[122] Sowing took place after the first rains, which could come as early as November or not at all. People broadcast their seed, sowing beans, pumpkins, squash, melons, sweet reed, and sorghum, in the same field. The next step was hoeing for weeds. The greatest labor of the season came just before harvest: protecting

---

* Somerville did not realize that a cultivation system with rudimentary technology required less labor than the plows he was more familiar with.

the crops, especially sorghum, from birds. Melons and beans came into harvest before sorghum. Threshing and winnowing were the last tasks, and then grains and beans were stored in clay granaries.[123] Cultivation was the most labor- and land-intensive activity within an extensive food procurement system.[124] Seeing it in the context of its particular methods, the practices of pastoralism and foraging, and the social relations connected to them will help us understand the gender differences and the position of women in the thornveld society.

CULTIVATION – A SPHERE OF FEMALE AUTONOMY

Thornveld society excluded the category of females from stock ownership and relegated grain ownership to them instead. In good years, at least, chiefs and wealthy men coerced poorer people to help in their fields.[125] Does it follow, as Jeff Guy suggests, that women were also, perhaps more subtly, impelled to work for male benefit?[126] Iris Berger cautions that rather than asking what role women played in a male-dominated society, we should consider the behavior of people with certain levels of power and the ways this corresponded to gender. In this light, I argue that the relationship between men and women in food production cannot be primarily understood in terms of exploitation and control for the sake of production. Rather, the division of responsibilities between men and women resulted from fundamental conceptions of gender. By no means am I implying that women and men had equal privileges; women were excluded from male power and pastoralism. However, once excluded from pastoralism, they cultivated not because male pastoralists demanded they do so, but because they needed food. More than a sphere of female exploitation, cultivation was a sphere of female autonomy. It was a hedge against male failure within the ecological cycle. Children and women were particularly vulnerable during hard times, and growing crops gave women their own source of food. Supplying the household provided a motivation for women's work that was independent of the dictates of men.[127]

The nature of the work and its product differentiated female production from male production. Unlike pastoralism, producers could not gain durable wealth through cultivation. The absence of opportunity for individual profit has been cited as a cause of female subordination.[128] However, cultivation was based on reciprocal exchange of labor rather than communal sharing of produce. One disincentive toward individualism among cultivators was that the accumulation of agricultural produce could not lead to real status. Grain was a less durable, higher risk commodity than stock, requiring more labor for these lesser rewards. Furthermore, households were drawn to share labor because it was more efficient than working alone. Because women had different strengths, being speedy weeders, hoers, or harvesters, working together on the many tasks evened out work time.[129] A woman could draw on the labor of her children and make arrangements with her mother and sisters, with her daughters as she aged, with her neighbors in the ward, or with poor retainers. Large groups of women departed for the fields together, but work parties could be small.[130] Work parties had the added benefit of teaching Khoikhoi women about cultivation. Women joined for all phases of the agricultural season, including clearing fields, hoeing, planting, weeding, and harvesting. Tellingly, the Tswana word for harvest, *letsema*, also means "working together."

Although women suffered structural inequalities that excluded them from the ecological cycle, their production methods and ownership patterns were not the opposite of the individual ambition motivating men. Since they responded to incentives and controlled their product, their work was not a form of gender exploitation. Although they bore the greater burden of sustaining life than men did, their work was not the resource that created male wealth.[131] This is evident in production methods and ownership. The two existing descriptions of work parties suggest that self-interest coexisted with reciprocal activity. Observers noted that women of the highest rank worked side by side with commoners.[132] Work was egalitarian, but it was not a communal arrangement requiring from each according to her ability. Contributions were measured: "They all sing while at work, and strike the ground with their axes according to time, so no one gives a stroke more than another; thus they make labour an amusement."[133] Also, there were motivations besides bringing in the harvest:

> The manner in which the females cultivate the soil is not unworthy of notice. They may be seen, perhaps fifty together, working in a line on the same spot, and holding their pioche or native spade in the hand ready to strike it into the ground when the signal for commencing is given. . . . While at work they repeat a kind of song as a means of animating them amidst their toils; repeating at the same time all the names of all the animals with which they are acquainted. The origin of this custom of repeating the names of animals is supposed to be found in the following practice: when a Bechuana has succeeded in obtaining game, his wife invites her neighbors to partake in the pleasures of the feast, on the condition that, when the period arrives for cultivating the ground, those who were guests, and had shared the spoil, should assist in working the soil.[134]

Such a work party offered reciprocal benefits, labor for food. These parties probably included a good number of those who, for physical and social reasons, could not produce for themselves. Although households shared their labor and a meal, they kept their own granaries from their own fields.[135]

Women have been called "beasts of burden,"[136] and this requires some consideration in the light of what they did. Men and women had different responsibilities: "It is the province of the women to build their houses, to dig the fields, to sow and reap; and that of the men to milk the cows, make the clothes and go to war."[137] This was not an equal division of duties: "Men are seen asleep in different parts of the town at all times of the day, but a woman asleep I have not yet seen."[138] Women's work was compared to the *batlhanka*: "Two thirds of the nation are women and even without any wars they would have to belong to the working class."[139] Of course, outsider evidence about male and female labor must be read with an awareness of the observer's thinking on the proper spheres of men and women, the fields, and the home. It should also be read with awareness about women's circumstances and motivations.[140] Now, all indications are that women worked harder than men. They worked harder because cultivation was harder than stock keeping. Although it demanded more time and effort than stock keeping, it was not as arduous as intensive cultivation. Shifting cultivators can provide for themselves with a few hours labor per day, and we know that available household labor was not always maximized. The lower classes were required in the fields only sporadically, and parents did not seem to demand much labor from children.[141] Seasonally high demands for labor could be met by working longer hours. The fact that cultivation was extensive does not mean that women had a lot of free time. They also had other tasks – cooking, childcare, and house building. However, by practicing extensive cultivation, women limited the proportion of their time that they spent on it.

Other evidence that men did not control female production is that the cultivators themselves chose extensive production that produced low yields. Because milk provided much of the diet of townsfolk, and because people also gained food through foraging, there was less pressure on cultivation to provide the food supply. This supports Berger's prediction that women's labor might be less strenuous in stock-based economies.[142] In fact, the political and cultural significance of cattle made female labor power *less* critical. Men gave stock much attention, increasing the number of cows and the amount of milk, which was gained with less human effort than sorghum was. The importance of stock motivated greater *male* effort in food production and lessened the amount of food women had to produce through their labor.

Women worked harder than men and were excluded from owning cattle, but male wealth was based on ownership of cattle rather than on female labor. The "acquisition, creation, control, and appropriation"[143] of labor power did not approach the competition for stock in importance for male success. Bridewealth exchanges provide evidence. An average of five to twelve head prevailed as bride payments among rich Tlhaping, and the lower classes might pay no stock at all.[144] Furthermore, bridewealth was not restricted to cultivating societies: there were also gifts of cattle to the bride's family among Khoisan herders, including the Korana,[145] and the Tlhaping and Tlharo would not have had a completely separate logic for bridewealth than their Korana ancestors and relatives did. At a fundamental level, bridewealth was something other than a transfer of cattle for labor power. Rather than being a means to control and exchange a highly valued resource, bridewealth was more of a symbolic and political exchange.[146]

Nothing about production methods required a class of women to be restricted to cultivation.[147] A more satisfying explanation for women's subordinate position lies in culture and cosmology. Tswana cultural values about the environment correspond to the distribution of political and economic power. According to Jean Comaroff, female reproductive capability was associated with wild food and cultivation and was feared to have the power to threaten production, particularly cattle and the social achievements of men. Rituals sustained this worldview and reproduced the social order resting on it.[148] This presentation of the symbolic ordering of the world of men, women, the nonhuman environment, and production corresponds to the way social difference determined who practiced which forms of food production. However, these beliefs about gender, power, and well-being are not unique to Tswana people, and the concerns about power and gender are very broad. Eugenia Herbert has examined the importance of gender in processes of transformation throughout sub-Saharan Africa. She has explored a wider belief that female reproductive abilities might endanger such varied actions as iron making, pottery, and hunting. Processes of transformation, she maintains, are characterized by three features: designation of work roles by gender, age, and social criteria, resulting in the exclusion of a significant number of people; anthropomorphism and genderization of paraphernalia; ritual and prescriptive behavior.[149] The first and last of these are obvious in the food production activities of the Sotho-Tswana agro-pastoralists, but the anthropomorphism and gendered paraphernalia are not obvious. Consideration of herding and cropping as processes of transformation could allow us to consider gender and food production among the Sotho-Tswana within the context of other practices across a broader region. If these observations about gender and power hold, they will give further weight to arguments that relations between men and women cannot be understood as the exploitation of female labor by men. There was a logic behind the division of labor arising from a worldview and not the immediate requirements of production.[150] Yet, as an explanation for agricultural practices, cultural values should not eclipse environmental characteristics or population and the concern about controlling labor inputs. All these functioned together, and each alone has a limited explanatory power; however, the environmental characteristics and the calculus about labor requirements are fundamental to any understanding of food production.

ENVIRONMENT, PRODUCTION, AND CLASS AND GENDER

The ways people produced, the efficacy of their production, and how these changed in the agro-pastoral frontier zone reveal that the early Tlhaping and Tlharo chiefdoms practiced extensive food production. The diversity reduced risk, yet the risk and the benefits of successful production were not divided evenly. Lower class people and women in towns did less efficacious work, not because their daily activities were dictated by politically powerful men, but because they were excluded from stock ownership, and foraging and cultivation were what they could do. Certain men controlled stock because they had the political power and cultural right to do so, and benefits from herding reinforced their position. People in the thornveld developed a way of providing food for themselves which was not bountiful, but was usually adequate for the population of the towns, the households of the fortunate and powerful. Work patterns arose because of environmental conditions, the subsistence requirements of the population, the machinations of the powerful, and the understanding of male and female potential. These were truly "games against nature," but the rules were different for rich and poor and for men and women.

3

Intensification and Social Innovation on the Cape Frontier, 1820s–1884

Till the present system shall undergo a complete revolution, such a population can never abound in grain.[1]

S OON after the agro-pastoral frontier engulfed the thornveld, the Cape frontier began to lap at its southern edge. As on other frontiers, the European-indigenous encounter in southern Africa involved renegotiating the ways people interacted with the environment.[2] It is widely understood that the Cape frontier introduced Christianity and cash-based commerce to the Kuruman thornveld, but it is less often recognized that these had a definite impact on people's relations with the environment. Christianity entailed irrigated cultivation, while commerce depended on exploiting wild fauna and flora as resources, and both were challenges to existing land uses. Irrigated cultivation is sedentary and more labor intensive than the shifting cultivation practiced by the Tlhaping and Tlharo. Commercial hunting and woodcutting brought a way to accumulate wealth without investing in cattle. Clearly, these new forms of production had the potential to revolutionize social relationships. However, by no means did Christianity, commerce, irrigation, commercial hunting, or woodcutting displace older ways of thinking about and producing from the biophysical world. Irrigation and trading were grafted onto older practices of agro-pastoralism, and their revolutionary impact was muted. The fundamentals of thornveld society and production methods endured, at least until colonial annexation.

IRRIGATION AS AN INNOVATION IN PRODUCTION AND SOCIETY

Channeling water from their springs to cultivated areas was a foreign notion to people in Kuruman. Rather, they devoted themselves to making rain. Probably because Tswana-speaking people lived primarily in semi-arid regions, they esteemed *pula*, or rain, with the word being used as a greeting or a blessing. In times of drought, the chief himself was responsible for rainmaking. However, despite the high regard for water, the response to the water shortage was to conserve rather than invest labor in enhancing the supply. In dry times communities guarded their water supply against outsiders, and the Tlhaping appear to have adapted to water scarcity; travelers remarked on how little water they drank, even during exertion.[3] In keeping with the logic of extensive food production, development of water resources was rudimentary; people cleared fields in wet spots, and in dry seasons they dug holes in riverbeds for humans and stock.[4] Access to water was not the chief consideration when the Tlhaping chose sites for settlements. Women at Maropeng walked about one mile for water, and Tlhaping men rejected a site on the Kuruman River because it lacked thorn trees for construction and fencing stock.[5] From 1802–6 the Tlhaping capital was at the Eye of Kuruman, but thereafter, that spot was merely a cattle post.[6] Irrigation began only after visitors from the Cape cast their eyes on the springs and river valleys.

The first contact with the Cape came by the 1770s through frontier renegades who raided the Tswana.[7] A more stable and mutually beneficial relationship developed after the establishment of the Griqua state north of the Orange River around 1800. The Griqua, Dutch-speaking Creoles escaping the racial order developing in the Cape, served as trading partners and powerful allies of the Tlhaping and Tlharo.[8] After the turn of the nineteenth century, visitors from Cape Town came as missionaries, explorers, and traders. The Tlhaping chiefdom, especially, drew many foreigners. The first visitors were emissaries from the colonial government who came to Dithakong in 1801 to trade for cattle. Since nothing was more valuable to the Tlhaping than their cattle, the expedition left with few beasts.[9] These literate observers left rich records about the young chiefdom migrating between Dithakong, northwest of modern Vryburg, and the upper Kuruman River Valley.

Two London Missionary Society (LMS) missionaries went to the Tlhaping territory with that expedition and stayed five years, finding more success procuring ivory than proselytizing the people.[10] Thereafter, the LMS sent no missionaries until 1816, when James Read, an experienced missionary among the Khoikhoi, took up residence.[11] Representatives of the LMS were explicit that their mission included altering relations with the environment. For John Campbell, an LMS scout who made two journeys to the area, intensification – greater labor inputs to support a larger population – was a stated goal:

> Till the present system shall undergo a complete revolution, such a population can never abound in grain, nor can it become an article of trade. The land that may fairly be claimed by each nation is capable of supporting

more than twenty times the population if the ground were to be cultivated, which would require comparatively little labour.[12]

Robert and Mary Moffat, who arrived in 1821, were particularly effective in this regard. Over the next fifty years they had tremendous impact on Tlhaping society, on religion and economy, and, most definitely, on relations with the environment. Unlike neighboring regions, the many springs produced by the karst geology advertised the possibility of making the thornveld bloom. In this environment Robert Moffat and his colleagues could challenge the Tswana appreciation of cattle (and social structure!) by raising tilling of the soil to the pinnacle of their environment management. Previous historians have analyzed the ways that missionaries' moral, political, and religious reactions to the semi-arid environment promoted irrigation. Environmental historian Richard Grove proposed that Moffat's theory of environmental change motivated him to irrigate. Reading the landscape as an exposition on Genesis, he believed long-term desiccation and drought resulted from the Fall from Eden and from unsustainable wood cutting. Therefore, the introduction of irrigation was an attempt to redeem the landscape itself.[13] Anthropologists Jean and John Comaroff emphasized the metaphysical vision – agriculture was a metaphor for civilization and Christianity and missionaries believed that irrigation, like their preaching, brought the water of life to a wasteland.[14] In addition to these were immediate and personal motivations: Moffat's position as a father with a hungry family in an unfamiliar environment as well as his training as a gardener in England predisposed him toward exploiting the river valleys.[15] Irrigation was an attempt to reverse desiccation and was a metaphor for mission work, but in a very real sense its fruits made missionary existence possible.

The multiple motivations for irrigation sustained the missionaries through early difficulties. The first attempts by missionary Read to irrigate at the Tlhaping settlement at Maropeng, approximately sixteen kilometers downstream from the Kuruman Eye, were hampered by the lack of water and by the missionaries' lack of rights to land and water. Their irrigation ditch ran several miles from the river past rain-fed gardens to the mission plots. In 1821, women, led by Mothibi's chief wife Mahutu, diverted water from the missionaries' ditch to their own fields. Read's successors, Robert Moffat and his colleague Robert Hamilton, protested, arguing that their labor gave them rights to the water. Among the Tswana, however, water and land rights derived from residence and community membership. Angry with Moffat and unwilling to accommodate this system of intensive agriculture and private tenure, the women destroyed the dam with their picks.[16] The water rights struggle and other challenges of living and evangelizing within the Tlhaping capital led the missionaries to seek

Figure 3-1 The pond at the Eye of Kuruman in the 1880s. (Photograph courtesy of MacGregor Museum in Kimberley.)

an independent site for a mission, ten kilometers upstream from the Tswana town. They petitioned Mothibi and received permission to use the land, which they received on Tswana terms, but reciprocated according to European custom by paying £5 worth of beads for rights over land later surveyed at approximately 223 hectares.[17] The agreement between Mothibi and Moffat had very different meanings for both men. For Mothibi, the transaction amounted to granting use rights to a subordinate, and Moffat's gift served as tribute rather than payment. Moffat, however, understood that the agreement transferred permanent ownership, a proposition that made no sense to shifting cultivators. In 1824 Moffat and Hamilton built a dam five kilometers below the Kuruman Eye and irrigated the valley downstream. (See Figure 3-1.) This section of the river became known as "Seodin," the Tswana word for "elbow," named for a bend in the river.

Even before the mission at Seodin was founded, Africans had proven themselves open to new ways to cultivate. On the Matlhwareng River in 1820, Campbell met a certain Seretse who cultivated maize in marshy spots independent of missionary influence.[18] Seodin became a demonstration garden for intensive cultivation, showcasing the plow, fertilizer, private property, increased effort, a new division of labor by gender, and new crops. At first, the response to the new cultivation system was curious but conservative. Specifically, missionaries encountered prohibitions on fertilizing with manure, for there was some thought that this would harm cattle.* [19] There were some reservations about the new crops, but fewer toward species that resembled local ones, such as melons and pumpkins.[20] Although unfamiliar, maize and tobacco overcame these hesitations. Planting maize was a labor-saving innovation because leaves covered its ears, and, unlike sorghum, it did not require attention to scare birds from the ripening crop. Previously, people traded for tobacco from the Hurutshe to the east, who claimed exclusive rights to cultivate it, but Tlhaping and Tlharo cultivators could not resist cultivating their own supply. Fresh fruit must have been an equal delight. The problem with these crops was that, unlike sorghum, they required an augmented water supply in all but the rainiest years. They could not be merely inserted into existing fields, so adopting them required that cultivators start gardens in river valleys. Becoming dependent on an augmented water supply was a step toward intensive cultivation. Some seeds could be sown in damp spots along the river, but if cultivators wanted to provide the right amount of water to a greater amount of land, they needed to invest labor in construction of water-delivery systems. Additionally, unlike the fields farmed on fallow lasting an indefinite period, the permanent gardens required fertilizer. The adoption of wheat, a winter crop, was especially revolutionary. Growing it made sense, for constructing and maintaining irrigation works required significant labor, and double cropping bolstered the yields from fields, but this in turn taxed the fertility of the soil and increased the need to apply fertilizer.

Missionaries reported success in 1825. They began plowing land for Chief Mahura, who "manifested considerable pleasure" at the offer, although perhaps he was more pleased about their apparent clientage than about his ostensible improvement.[21] Additionally, common people were planting tobacco and maize.[22] The first baptism followed in 1828. People became Christian because the message fulfilled spiritual needs, but the attractions of irrigated production also would have influenced many people or at least put them in a position to listen to the message. Moreover, many people were open to missionary innovations because of factors destabilizing the extensive production system. Violence, drought, and stock disease all provided incentives to join the missionaries and farm as they suggested.

The 1820s were a decade of drought. Drought is a dominant theme in the environmental history of the thornveld and a problematic one. There is a widely held belief that the weather became increasingly drier between 1800 and the 1820s.[23] Southern Africa, like other parts of the world, experienced the "Little Ice Age" from the fourteenth century to the early seventeenth century, with wetter and cooler conditions.[24] After this interval, during the period of historical

---

* In a sense, this was true, for spreading manure could also spread anthrax.

record, there is only weak evidence for progressive cumulative climate change. There are no rainfall records and no dendrochronological studies, and accounts of desiccation are anecdotal, such as Tswana elders testifying that rivers ran stronger and deeper in their youth.[25] There is, for example, a fantastic tale of women who were gathering on the far side of the Kuruman River and were stranded when the waters came up, forcing them to take different husbands and begin new lives.[26] In fact, this is not evidence of a wetter past; anyone in Tlhaping or Tlharo territory could have walked around the Kuruman Eye, the source of the river, in a few days. These memories of damper past are problematic because they telescope longer periods, idealize the days of youth, and express hyperbole. In contrast to folk belief, climatological research discussed in Chapter 1 suggests rainfall cycles rather than desiccation. In that light, the 1820s were a trough in the rainfall cycle, probably a very deep and prolonged trough.

Bovine botulism, also known by its folk name "lamsiekte," and anthrax, two diseases principally affecting stock, provided another reason for people to be open to irrigation. These diseases pollute the environment itself, and in this region the environment exacerbates their effects.[27] The causative agent of anthrax, the bacterium *Bacillus anthracis*, is transmitted by bacteria or spores, which multiply in the blood of the host. The bacterium produces toxins that cause death by shock and renal failure. The spores remain infectious after many years in the soil or in tissue, and animals contract the disease by ingesting them. In the case of bovine botulism, animals living on phosphate-deficient grasses, such as those that occur on the dolomite bedrock on the Ghaap Plateau, contract it because they ingest bones of carrion to assuage their cravings for phosphate. This behavior is not in itself unhealthy, except when the bones are infected with the bacterium *Clostridium botulinium*. It produces a toxin in the course of infection. Minute amounts of toxin ingested by the animals can cause death through respiratory paralysis and suffocation.[28] It is difficult to distinguish anthrax and botulism in the documentary record – the most obvious difference is that anthrax causes boils and affects people as well as stock.

The bacteria of these diseases have not been omnipresent in southern Africa, but have established themselves in specific areas, remaining for long periods. It is impossible to determine precisely when the contamination occurred, but, very possibly, it happened through accumulation of stock after the founding of the Tlhaping and Tlharo chiefdoms. Treating, trading, and transporting hides, as the Tlhaping did, would have spread anthrax.* [29] Moffat calls anthrax "Hottentot's sore," suggesting a Khoikhoi origin, probably through oxen trade. The process

---

* Humans may contract anthrax through contact with contaminated animal products such as meat, feces, or hides. In contrast, handling toxic carcasses will not spread botulism.

of contamination may have been still underway in the early nineteenth century. In 1801, Molehabangwe told Somerville that the pastures at the Kuruman Eye were "healthier" than those at Dithakong. However, Kuruman did not remain healthy. Anthrax was the possible cause of death for Chief Mothibi's son and heir Petlu, in 1825, and both cattle and human disease were said to have induced the Tlhaping move from the area in the late 1820s.[30] The problem did not improve. In 1834 the visiting doctor Smith gave a description of "kwatsi," which left swollen black spots on the skin of people who ate contaminated meat, including the Moffats, and in 1836 Mothibi declined to return to Kuruman because "his cattle did not increase" there.[31] Missionaries in the area in the 1840s and 1860s continued to report that the area was unhealthy for cattle.[32] Presumably because of stock disease, people who remained in Kuruman saw the wisdom in irrigating.

Violence was another incentive to join missions. Kuruman came into the orbit of the "mfecane," a situation of deprivation and violence in part caused by the expanding Cape frontier. The violence near Kuruman was notorious, and historians have had heated debates about the 1823 engagement of the Griqua, Tswana, and missionaries against the "Mantatees" at Dithakong, over whether it was a battle with hostile invaders, a slave raid, or a defense against hungry refugees.[33] Further violence followed. From 1824 to 1828, raids by "Bergenaars," bands of Khoikhoi, Griqua, and Boer frontiersmen caused prolonged chaos and fed Cape slave markets.[34] The violence of the 1820s, like that in earlier decades, powered the downward side of the ecological cycle and ruined many people. In 1829 drought exacerbated the problem, causing the Tlhaping to abandon the capital to forage for food. The upheaval also caused the Tlharo to lose cattle, fields, and homes.[35] Some of the people who scattered as *balala* no doubt were also captured as *batlhanka* and sold into slavery at the Cape.

The Tlhaping capital had always moved frequently, but between 1827 and 1829, under the accumulated pressure of stock disease, drought, violence, and LMS presence, the Tlhaping chiefdom fragmented, and its chiefs moved east, out of the Kuruman area. Chief Mothibi moved to a succession of sites on the Vaal River, and his brother Mahura's faction moved first to the old capital at Dithakong and later to Taung in the Harts Valley. The Tlharo people remained in the lower Kuruman Valley and the Langeberg Mountains, but their chiefs were not as strong or their population as large as the Tlhaping. After 1830, the LMS was the most powerful political force in Kuruman.

The upheavals displaced many people, and Seodin became a place of refuge for them. The mission offered *balala* opportunities for independence from chiefs and gave them an alternative to foraging and captivity. There are clues that many of the converts were *balala*. Refugees from as far away as Matabele and Sotho areas settled on the mission, a variation on the *balala* custom of attaching themselves to successful producers.[36] "Poor Bootchuana" worked as interpreters for the missionaries at Griquatown, and through their work, they accumulated a few cattle.[37] Moffat recorded that "poorer" people at the mission had "learned a little of wagon driving, and other useful things, so that we could occasionally get some assistance from them."[38] In 1828 Moffat reported that Seodin residents were "chiefly poor, but industrious and with the assistance of fruitful gardens are better off than the more affluent natives, whose dependence is essentially on their flocks."[39] One resident of the mission, had been "deprived of his all" around 1824, but by 1833 had become "comfortable."[40] Moffat believed poverty led people to seek employment with him.[41] By 1828 poor people had begun to grow and trade tobacco for cattle, karosses, and other items.[42] As those working the land became richer, they also began to employ their poorer neighbors.[43] Settling on the mission evidently became a means for recovery in the ecological cycle.

The gendered response did not mirror that of class – the disadvantaged group was *not* the one most attracted to the new opportunities. Because missionaries did not make new forms of cultivation available to women, the innovations in cultivation passed the chief cultivators by. Missionaries believed women properly remained in the domestic sphere and so targeted men as the preferred cultivators.[44] In 1829 they boasted: "Many of the men are becoming industrious and will eventually prove good laborers."[45] However, one man's industry is another's drudgery. Why were Tswana men willing to cultivate in river valleys when they never had done so on dry lands? *Balala* had few other options and may have converted to the new cultural and production system because it provided a decent food supply. Alternately, if men remained invested in agropastoral wealth, the use of cattle masculinized cultivation. Moreover, irrigation produced high-value crops. Tobacco was especially valuable because it could be transformed through trade into stock. For that reason, men, having more power and social permission to seek to improve their position, were drawn to appropriate production of this valuable crop. Perhaps the missionary message of personal improvement or the new wealth helped mitigate the burden of increased drudgery. At any rate, if cultivation practices in later years are any indication, men relied on the labor of women for most tasks apart from plowing.

Statistics from 1834 record 326 male and 401 female residents with eleven wagons and three plows. Crops included wheat, sorghum, maize, tobacco, potatoes, and 828 fruit trees.[46] (See Figure 3-2.) Other reports from the 1830s and 1840s list rice and a wide variety of exotic fruits: quince, pomegranates, plums, apricots, pears, grapes, peaches, nectarines, apples, oranges, and lemons.[47]

Figure 3-2 Wheat at the Kuruman LMS mission, 1870s. (Photograph courtesy of the MacGregor Museum in Kimberley.)

From the late 1820s through the 1840s, missionaries pushed ahead with further irrigation development, and converts dug smaller furrows for their own fields.[48] A visitor in 1834 reported that irrigated wheat fields of the Tswana were vying in size with those of the missionaries.[49] Moffat was probably magnifying his achievements when he wrote his memoirs in 1842, but this is how he recalled the early 1830s:

> The ancient ramparts of superstition had been broken through by our converts, and many others, who could see no reason why the production of their fields and garden labour should be confined to . . . only vegetables cultivated by their forefathers. . . . Ploughs, harrows, spades and mattocks were no longer viewed as the implements of a certain caste, but as the indispensable auxiliaries to existence and comfort. The man who before would have disdained to be seen engaged in such an occupation and with such a tool, was now thankful to have it in his power to buy a spade.[50]

Even if it was not as Moffat remembered, the Christian culture of the river valleys clearly held the potential to transform thornveld society and culture. However, until this point, the practice was limited to marginal people in mission gardens in one river valley. Frontier innovations in relations with the environment became significant only as they became more widespread.

AFRICAN INITIATIVE IN RIVER VALLEYS

Missionaries do not deserve all of the credit for spreading irrigation beyond Seodin. On their own initiative, African evangelists in the 1840s began irrigation works at other springs.[51] Some of the reasons that people living under the jurisdiction of the Tlhaping and Tlharo chiefdoms began to irrigate are similar to the reasons that induced people to irrigate at Seodin – to meet the challenges of production. Yet not all irrigators were destitute *balala*. People under the jurisdiction of Tswana chiefs remained invested in agro-pastoralism, and when they adopted irrigation, they did not abandon extensive production, but adapted it to their own production methods.

In the 1850s, irrigation dramatically increased throughout the southern Tswana region, including in the Kuruman Valley below the mission.[52] John Smith Moffat, who was born at Seodin and returned after an eleven-year absence in 1858, reported that the water "was now turned to full account, not only by the missionaries, but by the people who had gathered round them. . . . The marshy valley had been well drained and had become a fruitful field."[53] As in the 1820s, in the 1850s a combination of factors created a sharp increase in irrigation. The immediate cause for the shift to more intensive agriculture was a drought. Of course, people in the thornveld had learned to adapt to its cyclical droughts, but during this drought they developed a new adaptation. As before, people scattered from towns and cattle posts across the veld to ease pressures on meager supplies of grass, edible plants, and water. However, the 1850 drought marked a watershed: for the first time people from southern Tswana chiefdoms coped by settling at springs and along rivers and beginning irrigated cultivation. Missionaries from around the region reported increased cultivation and irrigation, even among the most powerful in Tlhaping society.[54] Inspired by this development, missionary Holloway Helmore began work on an irrigation project on the Harts River. He died before it was completed, and his dam remained half built until the Apartheid state constructed irrigation works for poor whites on the site.[55]

While botulism and anthrax were endemic, an epidemic, bovine pleuropneumonia or lungsickness, gave people a further impetus to irrigate at this time. Lungsickness, unknown in South Africa until 1853, is caused by an airborne microorganism and is highly contagious. Animals will appear healthy during the incubation period of five to eight weeks, but susceptible herds may eventually develop almost 100 percent infection rates, with high mortality. The infection impedes breathing, and in acute cases, death may occur in a few hours. Carried by transport oxen, lungsickness raced through the subcontinent, killing over 100,000 cattle in two years.[56] Most notoriously, it was the immediate cause for the apocalyptic killing in 1856–7 by the Xhosa of their surviving cattle, with disastrous repercussions for their society.[57] Robert Moffat recorded its arrival in Kuruman in 1855: "Already hundreds in neighbouring towns have by this disease been deprived of every head of cattle they possessed, and if it continues to rage as it has done, the whole country will be swept of that which constitutes the prosperity of the natives, as this part of the country is unfavorable for sheep."[58] As it happened, the effect was not quite so dire. In 1859, the Moffats' son John Smith Moffat estimated that the cattle population was half of what it was before the epidemic, but that those surviving were "seldom so fine."[59]

Coming on the heels of drought, lungsickness provoked a food production crisis and provided a further spur to the spread of irrigation. As before, people would have increased foraging when food production failed, but as the use of firearms increased, game became more wary and harder to hunt without a gun. In 1858, a missionary considered guns necessary for subsistence hunting and petitioned Governor Grey at the Cape for ammunition for drought relief.[60] Since rain-fed cultivation, herding, and foraging were all affected in this food production crisis, the utility of irrigation became apparent. Moffat claimed, perhaps with some exaggeration, that even during the cattle epidemic at Seodin "the inhabitants may be said not to know hunger."[61]

Although it was not a problem in Kuruman, Boer expansion was a further cause for irrigation among the Tlhaping. By 1850, Transvaal emigrants were pressing against the eastern borders of the Tlhaping. In 1858, they attacked Taung, taking cattle and children as "apprentices." Missionaries reported that increased irrigation resulted from the Boer threat because it provided an alternative food source and more secure tenure.[62] The last spur for the shift toward irrigated agriculture was the weakening of the Tlhaping polity and chiefly authority and the ambition of men who found clientship restrictive. The will and power of the chief had been critical forces uniting the large Tswana towns. Countering the centripetal pull of the chief were centrifugal tendencies of those who wished to be free of him, and the Tlhaping polity existed in the tension between these forces. By the 1850s, the inward pull was weakening; the chiefdom had splintered into several branches, and the power of the chiefs suffered under challenges from both missionaries and Boers. The food production crisis gave added force to the outward pull. Just as among the fishing Nunu in Central Africa, where migration to different microenvironments helped clients establish an independent base, in this area cultivation in the river valleys gave common men a stronger position against chiefs.[63] Those who scattered to procure food took the opportunity of irrigated agriculture to establish a base away from the chief and town. When the rains returned, many people remained at the springs, providing a sore spot to chiefs in later decades.[64]

Irrigation spread throughout the area between the 1840s and the 1880s. People at Lower Metswetsaneng, below Bothetheletsa on the Matlhwareng River, were said to have irrigated before 1845 when the spring had been occupied by "bushmen." Bothetheletsa was irrigated in 1858. Ga-Tlhose, previously a bushman stronghold, was settled by Tlharo in 1862, who began irrigating soon after Robert Moffat visited them in 1867. Batlharos residents drained swamps in 1867. The spring at Konong had furrows prior to 1870. Manyeding, a village on a large spring, was irrigated "some years" before 1872. Mapoteng was a cattle post until 1874 when the volume of water from the spring increased and residents began irrigating. Other places that were irrigated at some point before the 1880s include the spring at Kathu; the river valley below Seodin; several places on the Matlhwareng River; and Vlakfontein, also known as Kagung (or Grootfontein or Metsematshwe), east of Kuruman closer to Taung. Just below the Kuruman Eye was a Tlhaping village, Gasegonyane, that was a cattle post in the 1810s, but whose inhabitants cultivated in 1885.[65] (For a map, see Figure 4-1.)

Missionaries associated irrigation with a new dispensation, but descriptions of the fields themselves reveal that this was not the case. As J. E. G. Sutton has argued, it is misleading to present intensive and extensive systems in Africa as dichotomous. He made the point that isolated cases of irrigation and terracing, often taken as hallmarks of intensive use, are not necessarily evidence of such, but rather of environmental adaptation that maintains "its essentially extensive character through local specialization."[66] Similarly, studies by Anderson and Adams have shown that irrigation development in East Africa has not entailed a linear progression toward a more intensive form of cultivation, but that production has fluctuated between irrigated cultivation and pastoralism, which operated as complementary systems of production, depending on economic and ecological circumstances.[67] These understandings of intensive and extensive land use advise against thinking of irrigation as the imperfect adoption of an intensive foreign practice. Rather, we should consider the actual practices in the context of existing farming methods.

The techniques of irrigation reveal that producers had not abandoned extensive food production. Despite use of the furrow and even the plow, gardens still exhibited the logic of shifting cultivation, for people were not attempting to significantly increase output per acre. Furthermore, cultivators were still unskilled with the technology of intensive agriculture. Although missionaries were pleased that people irrigated, they had little praise for their techniques. Their criticisms yield insight into the logic of cultivation. "Impossible things are often attempted; and what is accomplished is done in a slovenly manner.

The water-furrow is usually more or less of a zigzag instead of a straight line; and the gardens and arable land are laid out in a manner which offends the eye of a European."[68] Kuruman had the "best-kept" gardens in Bechuanaland, "but even here the 'straight-line' in fence and furrow is not always what it ought to be."[69] In their discussion of irrigation, the Comaroffs explain the missionary criticism of "arc-shaped" curvilinear forms with reference to aesthetic and cultural differences.[70] Farmers are not devoid of aesthetic influences, but, more to the point of cultivation, the difference between straight lines and curves is one of intensive and extensive land use. With zigzags, farmers expressed their preference to conserve labor rather than land or water. Straight lines indicate an attempt to make efficient use of land and water by planting close rows through thoroughly cleared fields and delivering water by the shortest route. Curved lines, arcing around trees, large rocks, and bushes, or the siting of furrows and fields on natural grades indicate a hesitancy to reshape the landscape to produce greater yields, an efficiency in human labor rather than land.

A veteran missionary's disdain regarding the southern Tswana "indolent" approach to cultivation reveals missionary prejudice, but also an ethic of low consumption and labor conservation, hallmarks of extensive production:

> They live most emphatically to themselves. When they have supplied their few wants, which they can generally do with little effort, they have done all that they think is binding upon them, and the world is little benefited by their presence in it. . . . Accustomed from infancy to habits of endurance, their wants are few.[71]

Indeed, it would have been difficult to extract large cultivated yields because soil in this region is extremely low in phosphate. A measurement at Ncweng in 1997 showed the phosphate concentration to be one milligram per kilogram, compared with the seventeen milligrams per kilogram desired for maize culti-vation.* Cultivation in this environment could not bring bountiful yields. The reluctance to intensify is evident throughout the nineteenth century; the devas-tation caused by rinderpest in 1897 shows that pastoralism remained the basis of the economy and diet and that people were not maximizing their cultivation in the river valleys. In summary, the southern Tswana practice of irrigation did not amount to an imperfect imitation of the intensive cultivation preached by missionaries. Rather, they adapted the technique in a time of stress to help them better exploit the microenvironment in river valleys, and they inserted this specialized land use into their extensive agricultural system.

---

* This information was reported in a meeting with agricultural officials at Ncweng, March 12, 1998.

COMMERCIAL HUNTING AND WOOD CUTTING: PROFIT
AND EXTENSIVE PRODUCTION

Missionaries were not the only representatives of colonial society on the frontier. Traders were also present, and they, too, had an environmental impact. In contrast to missionaries, the land uses they promoted, hunting and woodcutting, did not require intensification. These uses entailed less labor, less risk, and quicker rewards than irrigation. Also, in contrast to irrigation, they provided cash. For these reasons, men responded enthusiastically to the opportunities presented by traders. However, as heavy exploitation diminished the resources, these extensive uses became unsustainable.

Before contact with the Cape frontier, hunting had been a sport, a source of meat and the recourse of *balala*, but commercial hunting was as much an innovation as irrigation because it introduced cash. The earliest barter between the Tlhaping and travelers was of ivory for tobacco and beads.[72] By the 1830s, the trade brought consumable goods of European manufacture, clothing, coffee, sugar, tea, and cash. People spent cash earned in hunting on clothes, wagons, plows, tools, and consumables. In the late 1830s, some Seodin residents donated cash for construction of the church.[73] Ivory was a valuable resource, and the first traders from the Cape who tried to gain access to northern sources encountered resistance from the Tlhaping.[74] After the 1820s, the Tlhaping and Griqua lost their monopoly over trade with the Cape, but they continued to supply the market, even after hunting out their own lands. A trade in guns from the Cape Colony into Tswana territory began in the late 1850s and accelerated into the 1870s. Wealthy Tlhaping men purchased wagons and guns and took winter trips to northern hunting grounds.[75] The expeditions could last from two to three months, which was time enough to travel far; Kuruman people were observed collecting ivory in wagons in northern Bechuanaland and Matabeleland in 1866.[76] The adoption of cash was motivated both by a movement toward the culture of consumption introduced from the Cape and by the ability of cash to procure stock, the ancient form of wealth.

As the hunting frontier pushed to the north, Kuruman remained a depot in the trade. For example, John M. MacKenzie's history of hunting in southern Africa reviews the biographies of nine important hunters, seven of whom traveled through or very near this area, including Frederick Courtenay Selous, arguably the best-known nimrod of nineteenth-century Africa.[77] The first trading store in Kuruman, belonging to David Hume, opened in 1838 and soon had competition from other whites who bought from Tlhaping traders, including Robert Moffat, Jr., the missionary's son, and the Chapman family. An English-owned trading store even operated in the remote Langeberg Mountains in 1872.[78] Hume provided huge amounts of ivory to the auction at Grahamstown: for example, he brought 2,000 pounds in 1844, 9,000 pounds in 1849, and 22,500 pounds in 1851.[79] Ivory exports from the Cape peaked in 1858. Ostrich feathers were "almost the only article of trade" by 1864.[80]

The result of fauna becoming a commodity was its disappearance from most areas of the subcontinent, including Kuruman.[81] Although one hunter considered game abundant in 1844,[82] this was not the case during Selous's 1871–2 journey through the area. After praising the grass and landscape, he complained: "The only drawback is that there is no game whatever, not even springbucks, the Kafirs having hunted everything into the interior; so now there is more game within five miles of Cape Town, than here more than six hundred miles up country."[83] The hunter Andrew Anderson, who had seen blesbok, springbok, hartebeest, quaggas, wildebeest, steinbok, lions, "wolves" (hyenas), and jackals in 1865, lamented in the late 1880s: "All this state of things has passed away. The game has been shot and driven away more into the desert, wolves nearly all poisoned, and in crossing any of those extensive plains and open flats, a few hundred may be counted, where before tens of thousands covered the veldt in all directions."[84] Reports of the total destruction of game are exaggerations; small game certainly survived and larger animals remained in the southernmost Kalahari into the 1880s.[85]

A new opportunity to acquire cash came with the 1867 discovery of diamonds six days' journey southeast of Kuruman. By the 1880s, Kuruman was no longer a source of feathers or ivory.[86] In 1871, the British annexed Kimberley and the surrounding area as the Crown Colony of Griqualand West, whose border ran just forty kilometers south of the Eye of Kuruman.[87] The new colony needed food, fuel, and workers, so as hunting was decreasing, mining became a way for men to earn cash.[88] However, the number of Tlhaping working in Kimberley was smaller than that of many more distant societies. The disinclination of Tlhaping men to join the labor force in large numbers vexed missionaries and labor recruiters, who saw the problem as a failure of efforts at "civilizing" them.[89] In fact, Tlhaping men preferred trading with Kimberley to working there. People at Dikgatlhong, nearer to Kimberley, sold food there.[90] Nearer to Taung, men such as Masse, the Christian son of chief Mahura, were enthusiastic irrigators and possibly sold to Kimberley.[91] People exchanged some sheep, goats, and cattle for manufactured goods and cash.[92] However, in contrast to the rich documentation of the wood trade, there is very little reference to agricultural trade from Kuruman to Kimberley and it does not seem large. For example, Selous often had difficulties for food on his trip in 1872.[93]

The wood trade echoed the trade in ivory, furs, and feathers by identifying a new commodity and exhausting the resource. People turned to their forests to earn cash in Kimberley. The Tlhaping provided the markets with acacia wood for fuel and mine braces:

> A large trade has been developed in wood. The country is being denuded of its trees and bush to supply the fires in Kimberley and its neighbourhood. And Natives in large numbers have been carriers. Every man who has had a waggon and oxen and the inclination has been able to turn in money in this way. Even here, though we are 120 miles from the market, wood waggons have been constantly passing and repassing.[94]

A missionary indicated the extent of the trade when he reported eighty wagons at the annual Kuruman church meeting in 1883, many of which cost £150 to £200.[95]

Men were drawn to wood selling because, like hunting, it provided cash for less labor, less risk, and quicker rewards than irrigated cultivation. Trading natural products relied on an extensive use of the environment, and therefore, people preferred them to more labor-intensive practices. Over the long term, however, as fauna and forests declined, commercial hunting and woodcutting ultimately promoted more intensive uses, including more intensive cultivation. Early visitors believed that abundant game posed a disincentive for agriculture, but by 1883 an observer believed the decimation of game had encouraged an increase in cultivation.[96] However, profits encouraged overuse, and both woodcutting and hunting were unsustainable. The Cape frontier delivered possibilities to exploit the biophysical world for the market, and ultimately, this made extensive subsistence less sustainable.

THE SOCIAL IMPLICATIONS OF IRRIGATION AND COMMERCE

Irrigation and commerce brought new social opportunities with the potential for new asymmetrical relationships. Men who irrigated, hunted for profit, and sold wood gained an advantage relative to chiefs and *balala*. Missionary letters note an irrigating "farming class," "possessors of considerable property," who paid wages to their workers.[97] Emphasizing these developments, John and Jean Comaroff argue that a missionary-generated capitalist "agrarian transformation" increased stratification, since irrigation reduced those who could not irrigate to client status.[98] However, the practice of irrigation was decidedly conservative, a specialized adaptation in one microenvironment. Since irrigation did not involve a fundamental transformation of production, it had limited power to erase the social divisions of agro-pastoralism. The social asymmetries on the Cape frontier were largely continuations of pre-existing ones, and people irrigated to improve their positions in the older framework.

Clearly, irrigation was disadvantageous to chiefs and headmen, and they recognized it. Missionary John Mackenzie attributed the relative weakness of southern Tswana chiefs in the 1880s to altered cultivation and settlement patterns. Population dispersion from the capital to river valleys lessened their power, and by 1878 Mackenzie reported that they were attempting a rear-guard action against irrigation.

> The fountains of Bechuanaland have already been opened up and led out by the people. Indeed Bechuana society had reached an interesting crisis before the war. The people who were devoting more and more of their time to farming were constantly harassed by their chiefs who wished them to live together in the towns, in the old style.[99]

He stated that chiefs also opposed migrant labor, but with little success.[100] Mackenzie may have exaggerated the obstreperousness of the chiefs; however, he was correct that these changes were not in their interest. The power of the chiefs was dependent on their wealth in a society practicing extensive agro-pastoralism. Despite the chief's complaints and the potential of irrigation, however, in this period stock keeping remained the most profitable activity, and there was no revolution in the social arrangements of herding. People still practiced *mafisa*, and chiefs retained rights to *sehuba*. In 1887, a missionary described other chiefly prerogatives enduring from agro-pastoral society: "The chief's control over the property of his subjects, is further shown by the fact that no man, however high his position in the tribe, may remove his cattle to go to live under another chief."[101]

The lower classes also were not transformed by the changes in production. Observers still encountered *balala* and *batlhanka*.[102] As before, these were not ethnically distinct, but were a lower class of the dominant population. It was noted that local bushmen were "of a darker colour and different in form to the Cape Bushmen."[103] A frustrated labor recruiter who visited Taung in the 1870s guessed that the chiefdom had 20,000 "serfs" tending stock and cultivating fields.[104] *Batlhanka* endured even under colonial rule. In 1894, the following case appeared before the Kuruman magistrate: Thipa, headman of Batlharos, charged that a farmer named Botha had kidnapped bushmen children, whom he claimed as his slaves. These children appear to have been Khoisan, for they did not speak the Tswana language and one spoke Nama.[105] Missionaries took pains to explain that such people were not "slaves,"[106] but a colonial official did not take the same care with vocabulary: "The slaves are treated fairly well. . . . They share with their masters and consequently are better off there than if left to their own recourse . . . and it strikes one, that they feel lost, unless they work under the order of someone whom they can look up to for guidance."[107]

The poorer classes provoked particular anxiety among one missionary after the 1878 Griqualand West uprising, because "there are so many Bushmen and Bechuana of the low servant class, who have now lost their Masters and who have no longer settled homes."[108]

Although servile classes remained in existence, after the mid-nineteenth century full-time foragers became less evident. Robert Moffat's 1842 work *Missionary Labours and Scenes in Southern Africa* claims bushmen had disappeared, an assertion repeated at intervals throughout the next decades.[109] Depletion of game made the foraging life less viable, and so more *balala* may have lived as clients and fewer as foragers. Yet during times of stress, such as a drought at Dikgatlhong on the Vaal in 1877, the hungry still foraged.

> Those who have waggons and oxen are riding for wood to the Diamond Fields and buying food with the money. Fathers are working for the Europeans, but the great mass of the people will have to suffer great hunger. Even now some of them are living on roots, and it is said that in the neighbourhood of [Taung] some have died of starvation.[110]

As Boer settlers entered the region, they gave a new name to these people: "vaalpense,"* Afrikaans for "gray bellies," but their social position and poverty were the same as had held for *balala*.[111] Many European observers, who would have recognized wage labor when they saw it, testified that capitalist relations had not displaced the master–servant relations of agro-pastoral society.

The continuing responsibility of women for cultivation is another indication that frontier innovations were adopted selectively, limiting their social impact. We do not know the proportion of fields plowed by men or hoed by women. Men were involved in cultivation, but this was clearly not the norm.[112] In the 1870s, missionaries were still repeating fifty-year-old pronouncements that men were entering into cultivated production, hardly evidence of a sharp upward curve![113] Half a century after the founding of the demonstration garden at Seodin, two missionaries separately testified that women remained the principal cultivators, sometimes aggressively so.

> Nearly all the actual labour that is done is done in raising food, and this is regarded as women's proper work. During the last few years many ploughs have been introduced into the country, and the men seem to take kindly to this new work. Those brought under religious influence will often be found helping their wives in garden work and house building, as they never could have done in their heathen state. Still this is only the work of a few days and a few people.[114]

---

* This was a general term for poor people in different areas of South Africa.

[T]he gardens belong to [females]. The cattle, sheep and goats belong to the men. Well, amongst the Batlaro it seems some of the cattle had been troublesome in wandering into the gardens and destroying the women's corn. Accordingly, they determined to kill everything found in their lands. In doing this they were following a law to that effect made by a Batlaro chief; and for which also some women were cut off the church by Mr. Moffat. Numbers of cattle were hacked and killed in a most horrible manner, the women of the church taking a prominent part in the work.[115]

When men plowed the fields, women remained responsible for practically all other tasks. Unfortunately, we do not know how women perceived the advantages and disadvantages of men cultivating. Reasonably, they may have thought that it threatened their control over the supply of food to their households.[116] Alternately, they may have believed that increasing food sources within the household was desirable, even if it meant a greater workload for them and relative benefits to men.[117] A gendered division of cultivation in irrigation is not a zero-sum equation. Women could and did continue to hoe on dry lands, even as men took interest in the river valleys. It is important to recognize that the division of labor and power between men and women may not have been entirely rigid. For example, Mareinaye, sister of Chief Mahura, served as "headman" at Maropeng in the late nineteenth century.[118]

AN ECOLOGICAL REVOLUTION?

Merchant has argued that change in environmental history occurs through "Ecological Revolutions," points of radical change in human relations with the nonhuman world.[119] The missionary Campbell drew on similar usage when he called for a "revolution" through the intensification of agriculture,[120] and Chief Mothibi also recognized the potential when he worried that missionaries were attempting to bring about a change in the "whole system."[121] As of 1884, the outcome would have relieved Mothibi and disappointed Campbell. At this point, the ecological revolution was incomplete. Irrigation and commercial hunting did bring new possibilities, but people managed to be selective about them. Those who irrigated and traded did not abandon the values of extensive production and thus, the social impact of the innovations was limited. However, the eclecticism brought tensions. Commerce in natural products was not sustainable, and the paradox of irrigation in a basically extensive system would not survive under European rule.

4

Colonial Annexation: Land Alienation and Environmental Administration, 1884–1894

> Now you see the coming wave of white men. They seek land – they seek fountains. Where they find open country they will build and put in the plough and tell you that the unoccupied country is God's and not yours.[1]

ALTHOUGH the Cape frontier did not bring a revolution to environmental and social relations, colonial rule did. It inserted a new group, whites, at the top of the power structure and on the land and imported a new tool, the modern state, with which to exercise their power. Yet, the revolutionary impact of colonial rule was delayed after its imposition in 1884. Extensive production continued much as it had for over a decade and the interventionist potential of the modern state became clear only in the twentieth century. Still, later disruptions had roots in the land alienation and environmental administration of the period immediately following annexation, and thus we now consider the portentous character of early colonial rule.

By considering the importance of land alienation and environmental administration, this chapter raises issues of comparative environmental history. In much comparative world environmental history, "colonialism" and "imperialism" have served as synonyms for white settlement. According to this view, European imperialism was "biological expansion" consisting of "people, plants and pathogens."[2] "Ecological imperialism," as defined by Alfred Crosby, denotes demographic takeover in temperate zones. Since Europeans were not able to settle their colonies in tropical Africa in significant numbers, to Crosby, this continent was "within reach" but "beyond grasp" of a force which transformed the world. Southern Africa, with greater European immigration and with a history of land alienation, is a partial exception to Crosby's observation that ecological imperialism bypassed the continent. Thus, in comparative world environmental history, South Africa occupies a middle ground as a settler society, but not a "land of demographic takeover."[3] How South Africa fits in the colonial environmental history of tropical Africa is a more difficult question. Despite having analyzed cases showing common processes, historians have not yet theorized about the meaning of colonial rule in African environmental history. Part of the difficulty arises from the disparate forms of colonial rule. Another problem of generalization lies in the environmental diversity of the African continent and in the varied ways humans use it. Yet despite local variations and the lack of white settlement, Europe was a huge force in tropical African environmental history. Contact with Europe promoted and spread Christianity, industrial technology, capitalism, conservation, and the modern state. These developments led Africans to adopt farming methods from Eurasia and crops from the Old and New World. They also had the effect of impeding disease control, extracting natural resources for export, diminishing the efficacy of subsistence production, and representing Africans as unworthy neighbors, much less stewards, of the continent's flora and fauna.[4]

Although Europe's expansion in tropical Africa was not biological, there were commonalties in the environmental impact of colonial rule throughout the continent, including South Africa. I argue that one basis for generalization is the administrative policies of the colonial state. In recent years, Africanist historians have recognized that consideration of the state is a route to a clearer understanding of people's experiences; as Ivan Evans wryly observes, "Black South Africans are depressingly familiar with the phenomenon of *administration*"[5] At first glance, the state may seem an inappropriate centerpiece for environmental history. Environmental history explores people's relations with the environment more than relations with institutions, but throughout colonial Africa, the state arrogated power to itself and became an active partner in environmental relationships. Mahmood Mamdani's work in *Citizen and Subject* is helpful in showing the force of administration on rural producers. Although he does not explicitly consider environmental issues, he does reveal the impact of the state on rural people's relations with the environment. Throughout the continent, the state used colonial communal tenure and Indirect Rule to intervene into farming and herding. The colonial construction of communal tenure and Indirect Rule may be the key to generalizing much of colonial African environmental history.

Governance by headmen or magistrates is the operative difference between Direct and Indirect Rule. The primary characteristic of Direct Rule is that government administrators ruled indigenous people under colonial law. Associated characteristics included paternalism, individual tenure, and forced assimilation of indigenous people into colonial working classes. Colonized people could only receive political rights by becoming "civilized" in the European sense. In contrast, Indirect Rule consisted of governance under customary law by chiefs whose legitimacy ideally rested on some claim to traditional authority. In reality, this legitimacy was often dubious. Associated characteristics of Indirect Rule were communal tenure, racial segregation of territory, and tribal divisions. Indirect Rule forced Africans to relate to the state according to African custom (as read by colonizers), not European "civilization."[6] Both Indirect and Direct Rule involved outsiders taking control over territory and how people lived within it. Both made indigenes vulnerable to losing their land, but Indirect Rule made people more vulnerable to losing the ability to determine what they did on the land they kept.

Direct Rule and Indirect Rule stand at the poles on a continuum of methods of subjugation in colonial Africa, and colonial states developed administrations that fit somewhere between these ideal types. Direct Rule was an early tendency in French and British colonialism that shifted toward Indirect Rule at the turn of the twentieth century. As an ideology, Direct Rule was never as well developed or as widely implemented as Indirect Rule, but it made a strong appearance in the Cape Colony in the nineteenth century. In the 1850s, George Grey, governor of the Cape, worked to bring chiefs in annexed regions under the power of colonial magistrates; to provide land for white settlement; and to assimilate the Xhosa into colonial society, most often as unskilled laborers. As it was, Grey's vision was only partially implemented: private tenure was not established, chiefs remained powerful among the Xhosa, and the dense agro-pastoral population prevented the expansion of white settlement. Still, by relying on magistrates to represent the state to both whites and blacks, the Cape retained vestiges of Direct Rule for 100 years.[7] Regarding Indirect Rule, the earliest indication of what later became known by that name occurred in Natal in the 1850s under the leadership of Secretary for Native Affairs Theophilus Shepstone. As elucidated in the 1910s by the first governor of Nigeria, Frederick Lugard, it came to be the policy for British Africa in the twentieth century. Mamdani argues that Indirect Rule, "decentralized despotism" to use his term, was universal in and specific to late colonial Africa. Consequently, his definition of Indirect Rule is more inclusive than some others, and this has prompted criticisms of his work.[8] My point is not to argue the universality of Indirect Rule in Africa, but to use Mamdani's insights to identify common environmental policies in situations where Africans were governed as tribal subjects.

The case of Kuruman illustrates the evolution of the colonial state, the development of its interventionist role in environmental history, and the accrual of power by Europeans. This chapter describes the earliest colonial dispensation in colonial Kuruman. First, it explains the process of land alienation which was justified by misreading the level of intensification. Next, it details the initial system of Direct Rule through magistrates. Finally, it details imperial debates about individual or communal land tenure and argues that colonial communal tenure, under governance of chiefs or magistrates, opened Africans to state intervention. Still, in this period the typical twentieth-century patterns of colonial environmental administration were still forming and the impact of European annexation was not yet clear. In Kuruman, the first ten years of colonial rule were an interregnum between the adaptive possibilities of the frontiers and the poverty and racial disinheritance of twentieth-century rural South Africa.

CHANGING CUSTOMS OF TENURE ON THE CAPE FRONTIER

Shifting cultivation, especially as practiced by the Tlhaping with indefinite fallow, and pastoralism required only loose rights over land. In agro-pastoral society, the chief allocated land, and people held rights to the particular parcels of land they used, but they could not profit from the disposal of their rights. A few outside observers believed that land had little value and individuals had no property rights over it, but others recorded that people had rights over their cultivated fields. Rights to grazing lands are less well documented, but access to grass and water was regulated. The chief probably had special rights to land, particularly for grazing. New practices arriving with the Cape frontier had some influence on customs of land ownership, although no market for land developed. The dispersed settlement patterns of irrigated cultivation challenged the power of the chief, and permanent settlement may have given people more established rights over their fields.[9] By the time of colonial annexation, Tlhaping and Tlharo custom recognized a priority of rights over improved land. It was common to plant trees to strengthen the hold on fields, but planting trees did not give a family rights to dispose of their land through sale.[10] The evolution toward some permanent private rights was to the benefit of those who hoped to use irrigation to establish themselves as independent producers and to the disadvantage of people who remained invested in the hierarchy of the thornveld society. Chiefs reportedly attempted to compel their subjects to leave their farms to live in towns.[11]

The sharpest conflicts over land rights involved missionaries. As described in the previous chapter, in 1824 Moffat and Hamilton had received permission to use the valley after making gifts to Chief Mothibi valued at about £5. The LMS evidently felt insecure about its claim, because in 1850 Robert Moffat, Jr. surveyed and mapped the mission. His map, however, claimed that missionaries had exchanged goods worth £50 (rather than the contemporary valuation of £5) for the mission's 223 hectares of land! Missionaries obtained the signature of Gasebonwe, chief Mothibi's son, on the document, but evidently, Gasebonwe did not understand the transaction as a transfer of title.[12] By 1858 Gasebonwe challenged the claim on the basis of Tswana tenure customs. "Gasebone [sic] said though it was said his father had sold the land to the Missionaries, they were now a fresh race sprung up and they had gotten no profit from the sale. [His generation] too wished to see guns, etc., as the price of the lands and they would not believe Moffat had bought them."[13] How the missionaries placated Gasebonwe is not clear, but they retained their hold on the land.

Another controversy about land tenure arose over the Eye of Kuruman in the 1870s. As early as 1828 Joseph Arends, an escaped slave from the Cape, settled at the Kuruman Eye.[14] His family became commercial hunters, and a bad hunt in 1876 put them in debt for £110 to a trader. John Smith Moffat, now his father's successor at the mission, realized the potential value of the Arends' property and the harm possible if speculators gained control over the LMS water source. Although there was no registered title, he paid the debt in exchange for the Arends' land rights.[15] The LMS Bechuanaland contingent became deeply divided over whether the Arends, having recovered financially, should be allowed to redeem the mortgage.[16]

In a final disagreement over land, in 1874–8, a serious conflict between missionaries and tenants at Seodin resulted from the placement of a seminary, the "Moffat Institute," on the site of a village on the east bank of the river. Up to that point, all buildings had been on the west bank. Mackenzie, who viewed the land as mission property, evicted the residents, claiming that the evicted villagers were "cheerful"[17] about the changes. Yet John Smith Moffat, who grew up on the mission and claimed the confidence of its residents, records a contingent of angry men coming to him for justice and threatening to burn down the seminary.[18] It would soon become clear that tenants were not cheerful about a system of tenure that allowed evictions. The struggle over the Moffat Institute came shortly after the British annexation of the Kimberley diamond fields in the colony of Griqualand West, which lay just to the south of Kuruman. (See inset on Figure 4-1.) In 1878, discontentment among Griqua and Tlhaping led to rebellion in Griqualand West, and its partisans fled over the colonial border. Although Kuruman was still independent, some local people supported the rebels, in part because of resentment over the Moffat Institute affair. Missionaries feared harm from Seodin residents and sought refuge in the newly constructed seminary until British forces under Lieutenant-Colonel Charles Warren "relieved" the mission.[19] The occupation dislocated many people, and the army confiscated 3,000 head of cattle and several thousand sheep and goats.[20] Although they had no legal authority, Mackenzie and Warren took action against the Tswana tenure system. They confiscated irrigable land from rebels, settled refugees on it, and even granted titles to those they considered loyal.[21] However, Britain did not annex the region and in 1881 the occupiers left.[22]

THE SCRAMBLE FOR KURUMAN

The irony of imperial annexation of Kuruman is that it came only as the area was losing its importance as a trading and missionary outpost. By 1880, it was no longer on the main road north into the interior.[23] Drawn to higher populations elsewhere, the LMS never established a seminary in the Moffat Institute. An LMS inspector reported in 1884: "Don't say much in terms of eulogy of satisfaction about Kuruman in our report or I shall be tempted to laugh."[24] However, despite its declining strategic value, the region became the spoils of a broader competition, leading to its incorporation into the British Empire. The political history of the transformation of southern Tswana lands into British Bechuanaland has been told many times, and an environmental history requires only a brief review of events.[25] The initial white incursion came from the Transvaal. From the 1850s to the 1870s, the border between the Tlhaping and the Transvaal had migrated behind the line of Boer settlement into the eastern reaches of Tlhaping territory. In 1881, Transvaal emigrants moved deep into Tlhaping territory around contemporary Vryburg and Mafikeng. War ensued, and the "freebooters" founded the "Republic of Stellaland" near Vryburg and the "Republic of Goshen" near Mafikeng. The battles continued until 1884, when the British annexed Stellaland, Goshen, and the remaining independent southern Tswana territory, including Kuruman, as a British protectorate.

The politics of the British and Cape colonizers involved a struggle between two camps: on one hand were those with assimilationist goals, and on the other were those more concerned with strategic issues, claiming territory, and procuring a labor supply. The first commissioner for the new protectorate was the LMS missionary Mackenzie, the assimilationist. As a missionary, Mackenzie had worked for a quarter century to induce people to change not only their religion, but also their way of producing – from herding to peasant production. Mackenzie shared Robert Moffat's vision of Tswana people tending a fruitful garden: "I have in my mind's eye a garden which contains apples, pears, plums, peaches, apricots, nectarines, Seville and Mandarin oranges, two kinds of figs, lemons, loquats, quinces, pomegranates, grapes, almonds and walnuts."[26] However, more than the senior Moffat, who had encouraged irrigated cultivation as a practical measure which was conducive to a Christian lifestyle, Mackenzie was a partisan of the ecological and political revolution. He recognized that pastoral production sustained a centralized system of patronage and clientship and that cultivated production for the market would disperse Tswana society and weaken chiefly control. Furthermore, granting private titles after the 1878 uprising challenged chiefly prerogatives, which served his vision. He reassured chiefs that it would be possible to accept as tribute a peasant's grain in place of a herder's *sehuba* (the brisket of all cattle due to the chief), yet the new relations of production would have ensured that this was only a symbolic offering. His plans for Tswana lands included white settlement, but he believed that increased cultivation would prevent industrious Africans from losing their lands to settlers. He recorded describing "the coming wave of white men" to a chief, but assured him that permanent settlement and intensive production would protect Africans' hold on the land.[27] Mackenzie was in favor of assimilation of Africans into colonial society as farmers and workers, believing that Christianity and the adoption of European ways were necessary to "elevate" Africans gradually to the position of whites.[28] In his vision, Africans who had taken on European ways should live as equals to whites with title to farms. Yet, he argued, Africans' titles should be inalienable to frustrate speculators and avert massive land loss.[29]

Mackenzie was influential in the decision to annex the territory. On a furlough in London in 1883 he had lobbied for the proclamation of a protectorate over the Tswana. When the British colonial office came around to his position, it appointed him its first administrator. Mackenzie's three-month-long administration was largely ineffective. Violence between Boers and Tswana continued and he became embroiled in local conflicts, causing his recall in August 1884.[30] His successor in the post of commissioner for the protectorate was none other than Cecil John Rhodes. By 1884, the Cape Colony had annexed Griqualand West, and Rhodes, the director of the diamond conglomerate De Beers, had become the member of the Cape Parliament for Kimberley. He had an interest in the territory north of Griqualand West, for it held "the Road to the North," funneling labor to the diamond mines. Rhodes lobbied against Mackenzie's administration and thus became his replacement, but he was also unable to control the situation and served only two months. Continuing fighting ended his administration in September 1884.[31] The Colonial Office appointed Charles Warren, now a general, as special commissioner for the protectorate. He returned to the southern Tswana territory in 1884 with 5,000 soldiers and Mackenzie as an advisor. Contrary to Colonial Office expectations, Mackenzie and Warren set about making treaties with northern Tswana chiefs who had experienced no Boer occupation. In September 1885, when Warren and Mackenzie were promising more than the Colonial Office cared to deliver, it recalled Warren and divided the Tswana territory. Rolong, Tlhaping, and Tlharo land became the southern Crown Colony of British Bechuanaland (now in South Africa's Northern Cape and North–West provinces) and the northern areas became the Bechuanaland Protectorate (now Botswana).

THE BRITISH BECHUANALAND LAND COMMISSION
AND THE ALIENATION OF PASTURES

In 1885 the British Bechuanaland Land Commission (BBLC) was appointed under the chairmanship of Sidney Shippard, later administrator of the small colony. The BBLC's task was to rule on a host of land claims by Tswana indigenes, by Boers in eastern Bechuanaland, and by random claimants of individual grants throughout the territory. Furthermore, the BBLC was to provide for future white settlement. Its mandate demanded the impossible: "The objects sought to be attained are Native protection combined with European expansion, in other words, the security of Native rights and interests, provision being at the same time made for the beneficial occupation of *waste lands* by Europeans."[32] The BBLC traveled through most of British Bechuanaland from October 1885 to May 1886, taking a census, investigating land claims, and exploring ownership. To determine indigenous population and needs, the BBLC counted the number of huts and multiplied it by five. It estimated the total population of what would become the Kuruman District (excluding the Langeberg Mountains and Kalahari) at 11,755. The BBLC gave only eight percent of the total colony to the Africans as reserves.[33]

Around Taung and Mafikeng, Boer emigrants received arable land, but in Kuruman, Africans retained possession of almost all settlements, springs, and river valleys, including Bothetheletsa, Manyeding, Vlakfontein, Ga-Tlhose, Maremane, Smouswane, Konong, and Tlharing. (See Figure 4-1 and Table 4-1.) The BBLC did not travel west of the Kuruman Hills and left the demarcation of reserves in the Langeberg Mountains and Kalahari for a later date. Of the major springs, only Gasegonyane (the Kuruman Eye) was not granted to African users as a native reserve. The Land Settlement of 1886 designated the area just downstream from the Kuruman Eye as a town site. Some 27,677 hectares, extending approximately fifteen kilometers downstream from the Eye, were designated a Crown Reserve. The Kuruman Crown Reserve was not to be divided into private farms. Like "native reserves," it was to remain under control of the government, but not for African use. The BBLC envisioned it would be used for future expansion of a town, as a public park, and as common grazing land. The land remaining after the proclamation of the reserves and the recognition of Boer titles, that is, seventy-nine percent of the colony, was declared "waste land" to be disposed of by auction.[34]

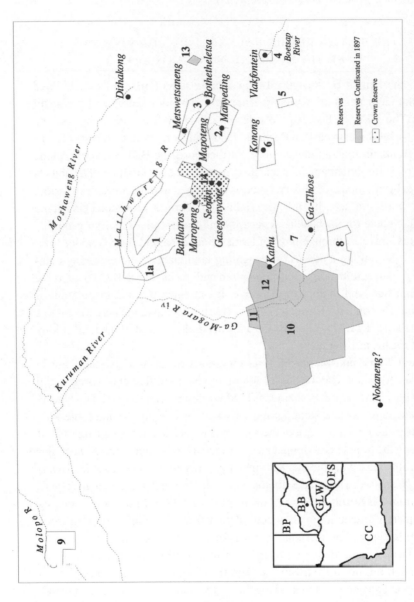

Figure 4-1 Kuruman crown and native reserves. For key to numbered reserves, see Table 4-1. Based on 1:250,000 topocadestral sheets 2622 Bray, 2722 Kuruman, 2724 Christiana, 2822 Postmasburg, 3634 Vryburg. From the Chief Directorate of Surveys and Mapping in South Africa. Reproduced under Government Printer's Copyright Authority No. 11012 dated 9 October 2001. The dot on the inset map shows the location of Kuruman town. (Abbreviations are explained on page xxi).

Table 4-1. *Kuruman Crown and Native Reserves*

	Reserve	Hectares	Established/Confiscated
1	Lower Kuruman	71,114	Established 1886
1a	Extension to Lower Kuruman	12,879	Established 1908
2	Manyeding	18,733	Established 1886
3	Bothetheletsa	14,582	Established 1886
4	Vlakfontein/Kagung	5,006	Established 1886
5	Smouswane	2,770	Established 1886
6	Konong	10,711	Established 1886
7	Ga-Tlhose	47,308	Established 1886
8	Maremane	11,383	Established 1886
9	Khuis	16,331	Established 1895
10	Langeberg	178,761	Confiscated 1897
11	Debeng	5,125	Confiscated 1897
12	Kathu	19,576	Confiscated 1897
13	Tlharing	2,676	Confiscated 1897
14	Kuruman Crown Reserve	27,677	Established 1886

Although the BBLC claimed to reserve for the southern Tswana all land they used, it had the power to define "use," and unfortunately, for these pastoralists, it defined it as cultivation only. The reserves did include pastures, but the BBLC greatly curtailed them. The BBLC was clearly prejudiced toward cultivation rather than stock keeping among Africans. Its report describes the situation at Konong as bucolic.

> Koning [*sic*] . . . derives its importance from its fountain, the suitability of the valley for agricultural purposes, and the wood on the surrounding hills. The fountain is situated in a vley [marsh] largely used for watering cattle. The water runs thence for about half a mile along a narrow valley. The valley then opens out and the water is led along its sides in two furrows, the ground between them being well and carefully cultivated. Besides the large fountain there is a smaller one just below where the valley opens out. On both sides of the valley there are rows of fruit trees bearing quantities of fruit, and close to the huts . . . there are some seringa trees giving a grateful shade. Koning is decidedly the prettiest and one of the most productive farms I have seen in Bechuanaland.[35]

The BBLC rewarded such productivity by designating the land as reserves. In demarcating reserves for Africans, the BBLC considered "the necessity of making ample provision for them, the desirability of making the Reserves *as compact as possible*, and the inadvisability of removing Natives from places long occupied and *cultivated* by them."[36] Granting well-watered parts of semi-arid lands to Africans departed from the southern African precedent.[37] However, the parcels could be small because the commission expected increased intensive production by Africans.

The reasoning behind the alienation of grazing lands had been well rehearsed elsewhere: European imperialism the world over resulted in massive land alienation and was supported by an ideology that superior rights accrued to those who practiced a "higher" use. Europeans justified their rights to claim territory on other continents through a belief that more intensive use represented a higher and better exploitation of the environment. For instance, in North America, some thinkers dismissed Native American rights on the grounds that a few nomadic foragers had no rights to keep legions of European farmers out of a territory.[38] Influenced by this logic, the BBLC recognized and protected what it considered the higher form of land use, irrigated cultivation, and ignored, discouraged, and hindered pastoralism. As discussed in Chapter 3, "intensive" practices introduced through the Cape frontier represented an adaptation to a system whose rationale remained that of extensive production. Unfortunately, for people living in the thornveld, the BBLC did not recognize or respect this. Not coincidentally, the land settlement, limiting Africans to river valleys, provided for the most typical white use of grazing lands. In the late nineteenth century, white land use in southern Africa was extensive, consisting of herding and hunting.[39] Preserving cultivation, but not stock keeping, among the indigenous people in the new colony was thus highly convenient, opening territory to the most common use of land among whites, while claiming to protect indigenous people's rights to their "highest" use, cultivation.

There were objections that the land settlement indulged Africans. Shippard reported that "Many Dutch farmers were indignant at seeing the large extent of the best-watered and most productive land in the country set apart for natives, who, they contended, would thus be encouraged in idle habits, instead of being compelled to work for their living like the vast majority of white men."[40] The BBLC, however, made the point that the settlement would not allow reserve inhabitants to subsist from extensive food production: "We feel confident that if [Africans] work industriously, and develop the resources of the land allotted to them by the Land Commission they will find it more than sufficient for their support."[41] Not only working in irrigated gardens, but also laboring in the colonial economy served as an antidote to African "idleness." Shippard was an old ally of Rhodes[42] and shared the industrialist's anxiety about the labor supply rather than Mackenzie's vision of an African peasantry. Although the BBLC documents do not refer to labor issues, they were a consideration in its deliberation. Shippard wrote his superiors in the Colonial Office a telling letter:

> Strict adherence to the limits of the Reserve fixed by the Land Commis-
> sion may also be regarded as desirable in the best interests of the natives
> themselves in as much as it must have a direct tendency to compel the
> surplus native population – instead of leading a life of degrading idleness
> on the Reserve – to earn money for themselves by working at the Diamond
> Fields or the Gold Mines or the European farms.[43]

Evidently, Shippard perceived extensive food production as an underutilization
of human resources as well as land and, therefore, argued that obliging Africans
to work was in their own best interests. The land settlement alone would not
force men into the labor market, but it was one of the cumulative shocks ending
extensive production.

THE BRITISH BECHUANALAND LAND COMMISSION
AND LAND TENURE

The BBLC did not share Mackenzie's assimilationist agenda and was not wed-
ded to granting individual title to land. Rather, it justified its tenure decisions
on its reading of Tswana custom, a problematic undertaking. Understanding
Tswana tenure laws and translating them into the colonial context was a difficult challenge, and the BBLC leaned on the official interpretation of Tswana
land customs developed in the older British colony of Griqualand West. In
Tswana practice, rights over cultivated fields had amounted to a largely secure
individual usufruct tenure, but because property was not a disposable commodity with any sort of title, Griqualand West officials largely overlooked any
private rights in favor of chiefly authority.[44] The introduction to the BBLC
report firmly associated land rights with chiefly trusteeship.

> With regard to the question of native tenure of land and of the ultimate
> destination of native Reserves, we entirely endorse the views . . . according
> to native customs, the land occupied by a tribe is regarded as the property
> of the chief, but that in relation to the tribe, he is a trustee holding it for the
> people who occupy and use it in subordination to him on the communistic
> principles.

The report continued: "We are unable to recommend that anything like a general
system of dividing native lands and securing rights of individuals by separate
title deed should be decided on at present for this territory."[45]

Regarding British Central Africa, Martin Chanock shows the irony of "customary communal tenure," since administrators and influential Africans rein-
vented custom and decisively subordinated communities to chiefly authority.

Colonial powers conceived of an African system of rights to land "flowing downward" from the political authority to the community in an "odd system with its mixture of chiefly powers, communalism, individual use and security, but no ownership."[46] "Customary" communal tenure was actually colonial communal tenure, with African custom rendered impotent. It misinterpreted African practice in many ways, in terms of denying any individual rights, placing control in the hands of the chiefs, and defining access to land by group membership.[47] Furthermore, customary tenure and governance did not take into account the role of the *kgotla* or council, a check on the role of the chief. In contrast, in the Bechuanaland Protectorate the role of *kgotla* was institutionalized under colonial rule, and its consent was required for many of the chief's decisions, although certainly this consent was vulnerable to colonial pressures. However, in 1891, the *kgotla* of the Kwena forced Chief Sechele to rescind a grant of land to white settlers.[48]

Specifically regarding the western region around Kuruman, the most arid and least attractive district in British Bechuanaland to white settlers, the findings were somewhat inconsistent with the rest of the report. The BBLC denied most claims by whites in this region. Transvaal emigrants had not occupied this area, but scores of white claimants sought title to farms they claimed chiefs had granted to them. Because these claimants had not managed to occupy the land, and because the river valleys were home to Tlhaping and Tlharo cultivators, the BBLC denied the majority of these claims. Here, its reading of custom contradicted the passage from the report's introduction quoted two paragraphs previously by downplaying chiefly power, recognizing a role of the *kgotla* (referred to by the Afrikaans term "raad") in Tswana governance, and showing sympathies for individual tenure.

> We have come to the conclusion that to grant farms in severalty was altogether contrary to the custom of the Batlapin [*sic*]; but that the Chief and also the minor Chiefs to a less extent have sometimes with, sometimes without the consent of their respective raads [counsils], given to foreigners permission to reside in their country. . . . Since the Batlapin have become less nomadic than formerly, and taken to agricultural pursuits, garden grounds and fountains have gradually come to be regarded as property of the families using them.[49]

Apparently, contradictions were already evident between the colonial construction of communal tenure and the BBLC's own observations about individual land rights among the southern Tswana.

The decision for strictly communal holdings is puzzling in light of the BBLC's own observations. Clearly, political interests tempered legal logic. This is not surprising. The interesting question is: Whose interests was communal tenure meant to serve? The Glen Grey Act of 1894 would show that individual tenure was not incompatible with the policy to raise a labor force,[50] yet, the interests behind communal tenure in the 1880s were more likely those of white settlers. According to Chanock, the recognition of communal tenure validated land alienation: "The summoning into existence of the customary regime was hugely convenient, for to treat indigenous rights as if they were the equivalent of rights recognized in English law would have created a plethora of embarrassing problems."[51] Shillington also stressed the convenience of the British Bechuanaland land settlement for whites, noting that communal tenure made it possible "to fit the greatest number of Africans into the smallest acceptable area."[52] The BBLC recommended that the colony should eventually issue individual titles within the reserves.[53] In 1889, a proclamation did provide for the colonial government, rather than headmen, to distribute arable plots and grant individual title in reserves, but the provision for titles never took effect.[54] This nonenforcement fit into a wider colonial pattern identified by Chanock – there was an "overall failure of the colonial states in Africa to survey land and introduce land registries. . . . [This] left Africans essentially without creating the basis for the kind of legal land regime that at the outset had been believed to be both desirable and inevitable."[55]

LAND DISPUTES UNDER DIRECT RULE

John Smith Moffat, retired from mission work and serving as a resident magistrate in Taung, reported after the BBLC ruling that the mood was one of relief, for the inhabitants of British Bechuanaland retained larger holdings than had their relatives in Griqualand West.[56] The BBLC itself believed that it had done a great service to the Tlhaping: "The Batlapin are indebted to the British Government for whatever ground is still left them."[57] Not surprisingly, protests did arise, mostly from chiefs and rich men who complained that they had not received individual tenure to farms. For example, Luka, son of Jantjie and grandson of Mothibi, who farmed at Manycding, complained to Shippard: "I let the Chief know of my murmuring with regard to the country, because now there are no black men who have obtained farms, only white men." Shippard responded that if he farmed successfully Luka could buy more land.[58] Although colonial rule constricted African access to the environment, the policy was not official territorial racial segregation, as it would develop in the twentieth century. The BBLC defined communal land according to a status as "natives," but no law prevented "assimilated" indigenes from purchasing private land on the same terms as whites. Yet this amounted to *de facto* segregation. Because of poverty, the purchase of land by Africans in British Bechuanaland was extremely rare.

Reserve inhabitants sought redress against white encroachment in colonial law and found some success if their cases involved upholding the findings of the land commission.[59] As it was, the land settlement had a delayed effect. Unlike Taung and Vryburg, where the reserves were smaller and the population larger, there is little evidence of overcrowding in the early years of colonial rule.[60] By 1891, Kuruman had only 166 white residents.[61] With such a small settler population and huge expanses, there was little reason to keep Africans off the "waste lands."[62] Complaints about land did come as the reserves were surveyed and their actual size became clear. After 1890, surveyors demarcated Bothetheletsa, Manyeding, Konong, the Lower Kuruman, and the Langeberg Reserves, as well as the Kalahari Reserve at the village of Khuis on the Molopo River in the Gordonia District.*[63] With the survey, protests arose over the extent of grazing lands. The petition from fifty-three inhabitants of Bothetheletsa to Queen Victoria read: "Queen! We are in great straits, for there is no place for an ox to graze, or a goat, or even a kid. . . . We are in the very centre of the valley. . . . There is no place where we can get firewood or grass."[64] Inhabitants from several other reserves also submitted petitions for larger reserves.[65]

The government of British Bechuanaland did not respond to petitions about land until 1895, when controversy arose over the new western boundary of the Langeberg Reserve. The BBLC of 1885 had not visited the Langeberg Mountains, leaving the definition of a reserve there for a later date. The boundary defined in 1895 had a devastating impact because it cut Africans off from several ravines containing springs. It prompted a petition by Langeberg residents to the administration of British Bechuanaland in Vryburg. The administration responded by appointing a body, the Matthews Commission, to investigate land holdings in the Langeberg Reserve and on the Kuruman Crown Reserve around Gasegonyane and the Upper Kuruman valley, where land holding was also uncertain.[66] The instructions to this commission upheld the notion that cultivating was a more deserving use than herding. "Whilst the Government are at all times willing to recognize the just claims of the natives to land occupied and cultivated by them previous to the annexation of the country, they should not be allowed waters and lands used merely as cattle post at a distance from their location."[67] Following these instructions, the Matthews Commission restored cultivated areas to the Langeberg Reserve, but withheld those springs used for

* Khuis was established through the British Bechuanaland Proclamation 220 of 1895. Since it was the only African reserve in the Gordonia District and was closer to Kuruman than to Upington, it was administered from Kuruman.

cattle posts. The Kuruman Crown Reserve was a more difficult issue. Africans had lived and cultivated at Gasegonyane and other springs on the Crown Reserve for many years. Given the policy of reserving land in areas of agricultural use, people on the Crown Reserve had a strong claim to their gardens. The commission considered this issue and agreed, but rather than adding the area of the Kuruman Crown Reserve to the native reserves, it devised a compromise solution. It ruled that those people who had cultivated its land before imperial takeover could remain as rent payers, but with no claim to the land.[68]

In the end, the imperial land settlement granted Africans in the Kuruman district only 4,117 square kilometers, eleven percent of the district's total 36,053 square kilometers, divided into thirteen units.[69] Thus, colonial policy consistently upheld the 1886 land settlement, to respect more intensive uses and to give no consideration to future needs. This policy would have drastic consequences for land use on reserves.

DIRECT RULE AND ENVIRONMENTAL ADMINISTRATION

Following the BBLC report, the administration of British Bechaunaland operated largely according to policies of Cape Direct Rule although with communal tenure. Magistrates held judicial authority, but the inspector of native reserves relied on headmen and chiefs to govern the reserves.[70] Most importantly, the institution of the *kgotla*, which had held chiefs accountable to the community, was not preserved under Direct Rule. Since inhabitants of communal reserves had little voice, unilateral interventions in land holdings by magistrates or by headmen were possible. Interventions by chiefs or magistrates differed according to their relationships with the governed. It is telling to compare Peters's characterization of the Tswana chief as a hero, the embodiment of the people holding privileged material rights,[71] with Evans's description of paternalism among Cape magistrates. According to Evans, paternalism cast subordinates as immature junior partners and gave the senior partner responsibility gradually to fulfill a civilizing mission, despite customary conditions. This does not mean that senior partners were beneficent. By definition, paternalism did not entail self-actualization for the junior partners, yet it sought some form of consent from them.[72]

The distinction between the privileged community leader and the "civilizing" outsider explains differences in interventions into land use. During this period, headmen acted to acquire more land for themselves and magistrates acted to promote more intensive use. In the Kuruman District, the inspector of native reserves assumed power to reallocate unused lands after two years. A man who owned a plot described as "half-drowned in water" and who reportedly spent nine months a year at Kimberley protested strenuously when the resident magistrate confiscated his land on the basis of underuse, for he had been leasing his land out for others to cultivate.[73] At the same time, the village of Batlharos near Kuruman was the scene of disputes between the headman and those who did not have land. One magistrate claimed the village was divided along religious lines: "The bulk of the ploughing lands in Thipa's location is allotted to Christians, and almost all the heathens are left out in the cold."[74] Another magistrate defined the land dispute as a matter of class: "The Headmen and councilors have got the best ground and the others must take what they can get or none at all."[75] Before colonial annexation, commoners had also been vulnerable to appropriation of resources; yet in failing to institutionalize the *kgotla*, colonial law gave new opportunities to headmen to act with less restraint. Colonial administrators recognized that vesting authority over land in chiefs and headmen disadvantaged commoners:

> Especially in the Reserves were [*sic*] there is a liberal supply of water, and a large extent of irrigable soil, radical changes are urgently required. Until now the headmen and those in their favour are the real owners of the soil, while the poor and those dependant on them are the serfs. A petty chief will take away from the rightful occupier a plot of ground which has been well worked and manured and give it to a friend or cultivate for his own benefit, pointing out a waste piece of ground or an old neglected garden for the unfortunate but more industrious poor man to break up and cultivate.[76]

Proclamation 62 stipulated Direct Rule by magistrates in land issues, but to what extent they asserted themselves against chiefs and headmen in these cases is not recorded.[77] They were more concerned with documenting the headmen's interference than their own. At this point, neither headmen nor magistrates undertook radical interference, but the potential of more extreme intervention under communal tenure would become clear as colonial administration developed into Indirect Rule in the twentieth century.

WORKING THE LAND AND WORKING FOR CASH

In the first decade of colonial rule, people maintained the largely extensive land use system that included some irrigation, but cultivation for the market did not flourish. In Vryburg, the capital of British Bechuanaland, meat was plentiful, but fruits, grains, and vegetables, "which might be largely grown in the neighbourhood," were imported on the railway network and were in short supply.[78] Kuruman, with its irrigable valleys, also imported food. A report from

1888 noted that:

> Here in the most fruitful valley of Bechuanaland, as I am assured very frequently, the garden an oasis in the desert, the natives as I write are entirely out of grain, and nearly all the waggons in the place are away to fetch some to supply the wants of the population; and this with hundreds and hundreds of acres of land lying idle and uncultivated.[79]

Different households farmed differently, and the description of Konong* by the BBLC suggests that some cultivators were working the land in a manner acceptable to European observers. Mackenzie specified: "There are two styles of agriculture in Bechuanaland. First there are 'rain-lands' or cultivated lands, which were entirely dependent on the rainfall of the country. This was the old agriculture. Then there was the higher agriculture connected with irrigation."[80] A new technology, the "American plow," or the "number 75," was increasingly in use. As early as 1852, imported American plows were available in Port Elizabeth for £4 per plow, and in 1890 "light American ploughs" could be purchased in Vryburg for an ox per plow.[81] The number 75 had an iron disk and was considered a "strong, but badly constructed heavy single-furrow plough."[82] In Kuruman, the number 75 and the hoe constituted the chief agricultural implements as late as the 1910s and 1920s.[83]

However, European observers still criticized underutilization of land and casual cultivation techniques. Underutilization was a relative condition, informed by European perceptions of proper use and their need to defend colonial land policy. For example, when Luka Jantjie complained about losses through the land settlement, Shippard lectured him about the deficiencies of his cultivation techniques: "Your own place [Tlharing] is almost waste. If you cannot cultivate the land you have, how can you ask for more?"[84] When Luka moved to the Langeberg Reserve, the surveyor general attributed his migration to wanderlust rather than any real need.[85]

Despite these biases, it is possible to read through the writers' prejudices to discern the enduring logic of extensive cultivation. The preference for extensive production among Africans was still evident: "strong commercial instincts they have, but hitherto these have lain fallow, or have been exercised in the way of barter and exchange of cattle, ivory, and other spoils of the chase."[86] Even in Konong, where the BBLC praised the picturesque farming scene, it suggested that the works could be re-engineered to deliver the water to a larger area.[87] In 1889, the magistrate described the plot he confiscated near Gasegonyane as "a small piece of mealie land miserably worked, not enclosed and half drowned in water, from which I should say that not more than 3/4 a bag of mealies could

---

* See page 85.

have been reaped."*[88] A later official's testimony indicates that, in general, irrigation on African reserves was not intended to maximize crop production: "Generally only such portions as are easily irrigable are cultivated while large tracts of ground are lying idle."[89] White observers only had eyes for the water and did not note dry land cultivation.

Farmers evidently had their own perspectives on how to use river valleys, and they continued with extensive methods of production because they entailed less drudgery. To the farmers this was a proper and practical use of land and labor. Moreover, by this time there were new forces making maximizing production in the river valleys difficult. Fields had been cultivated for over sixty years with little fertilizer. If people did want to apply manure, it was widely distributed throughout the veld and required much energy to collect. If gardens were exhausted of organic material and phosphates, cultivators would have needed frequent and long fallow that outsiders interpreted as neglect. It is also possible that perceptions about the insecurity of tenure provided a new disincentive to intensify production. John Smith Moffat argued that hesitation to develop the land was due to a general insecurity of tenure in the wake of land alienation:

> There is a rooted sense of insecurity on the land which is a bar to progress. If the native be asked why do you not make a well or a dam here by your village instead of letting your women go a couple of miles or more to draw water, the answer is 'What is the use? As soon as we have done this thing of which you speak, will not the white man come and take it away from us?'[90]

One disincentive to invest more labor in fields resulted from better economic opportunities available elsewhere. During this period there were continuing opportunities to earn cash as migrant laborers in the Cape Colony. The majority of migrant workers seem to have been young men who were probably working to establish their own households and who were not essential to their parents' herding or cultivation. In Taung, as early as 1887, "even the chiefs' sons" were going to work at Kimberley; earning cash was evidently attractive, even to those with more resources.[91] Male wage labor had the potential to detract from irrigated cultivation: "It appears it is the custom for residents of reserves to leave for an indefinite time, say from two to ten years and longer, handing over their lands to some relative to look after during their absence, in the majority of cases this land is left unoccupied and uncultivated."[92]

Selling wood, stock, or agricultural produce continued as a source of cash. Some agricultural trade did exist; people brought fruit to farms and reserves

---

* "Mealies" or "mielies" is South African English for maize.

94

in Griqualand West to barter for sheep, goats, and skins, but evidence for sales of produce and stock from Kuruman to the Kimberley market remains scant.[93] Writing of British Bechuanaland as a whole, the colony's Inspector of Native Reserves, Charles St. Quintin, reported that changing terms of trade affected this:

> They experience great difficulty in getting hard cash. Their only chance of procuring this is to send their children or to go themselves to the Diamond Fields to work for a few months. They complain that there is no money to be earned in this country, and if they offer stock or produce to the Storekeepers or traders they only receive goods in return – in former days it was the custom to give half cash and half goods for produce.[94]

People used cash to purchase plows, clothing, stock, and other goods.[95] With cash, people paid their taxes, although taxation does not seem to have been a great burden. In early years, people could avoid the tax collector by staying off the reserve in the open veld. The tax collector reported that he was lenient in difficult years and that it was possible to collect back taxes in good years.[96]

COLONIAL ENVIRONMENTAL ADMINISTRATION

Alfred Crosby has provided us with an evocative term for the biological expansion of Europe: "Ecological Imperialism." However, historians have no similar shorthand for colonial environmental impact outside the "neo-Europes." In Africa, raising questions about "environmental administration" may help us recognize common processes. Customary communal tenure and Indirect Rule underlay many of these processes in the twentieth century. This is not to say that environmental administration was uniform or static. Administration in nineteenth-century Kuruman was through Direct Rule, and there was some sympathy among colonizers toward individual tenure, although communal tenure became the legal system. Colonial annexation did not disrupt production, but it entailed two environmentally portentous developments. People lost much land, and the land they kept was held under poorly defined rights. Yet before these developments would be felt, the environment itself delivered harsh blows to southern Tswana society. Of course, the environment had delivered setbacks before this, but now the colonial situation prevented recovery. Under colonial rule, environmental trauma delivered the people of Kuruman from extensive subsistence production to a dependence on remunerated labor.

Environmental Trauma, Colonial Rule, and the Failure of Extensive Food Production, 1895–1903

I have to inform you that we are well, but we are in great straits through hunger. It is not hunger, it is death.[1]

THE environmental history of Kuruman reached a turning point in 1895. In that year, the Cape Colony annexed British Bechuanaland, and a period of critical change began. The nonhuman world and how people related to it are absolutely central to events of this period. However, the radical transformation did not result from simple environmental disaster. Before this time, people had suffered from, and coped with, drought and disease, sometimes compounded by violence. The difference now was that colonial rule interfered with the ability to survive environmental disaster. Moreover, the colonial state capitalized on developments to procure a labor supply for mines. The case of Kuruman may be exceptional in that the failure of extensive subsistence production can be dated to a few years at the turn of the twentieth century. There, a trauma between 1895 and 1903 was so severe that it claimed human lives and brought subsistence through extensive production to an end.

ENVIRONMENTAL CHANGE OVER THE LONG TERM

Longer term environmental changes had been unfolding throughout the nineteenth century. These slow changes were not always evident, and it is difficult to assess their importance. Yet these changes set a new context for production and colonial rule. The first alteration was a relative increase in the amount of bush and a decrease in the amount of grass.

More than any other environmental phenomenon, the huge expanses of grass made a great impression on the first literate travelers in the early nineteenth century. Burchell, an 1812 visitor, recorded that the country was "abounding in tall dry grass, of so great a height that the oxen were half hid as they passed through it; and our party had exactly the appearance of riding through fields of ripe corn."[2] In 1813, Campbell recorded "thousands of acres of long grass, or hay, reaching sometimes as high as the backs of the oxen."[3] Travelers until the mid-nineteenth century found the grasslands amazing, describing, for example, "long coarse grass, which being dry, gave to the plains the delusive appearance of ripe corn-fields"* or "miles of grass up to one's waist, and the hills rounded off with masses of unwanted vegetation."[4] It is clear that travelers were describing a savanna dominated by grass, not strictly a grassland, for they also noted large *Acacia erioloba* (camelthorn; Tswana *mokala*)[5] and *A. haematoxylon* (gray camelthorn; *mokholo*) scattered across the region.[6] Camelthorns near settlements were largely reduced to stumps and were slow to regenerate.[7] Other species included *Tarchonanthus camphoratus* (vaalbush; *mohatlha*), "the prevailing shrub in these places."[8] Smaller acacia shrubs and bushes do not dominate these accounts of veld composition, yet tendencies toward thickets were evident. There are reports that "straggling thickets" slowed the first visitors from the Cape in 1801.[9] Burchell noted unspecified acacia at water sources, and Moffat noticed "small acacia" around abandoned settlements.[10] Another traveler records that *A. erioloba* and *A. mellifera* subsp. *detinins* (blackthorn/swaarthaak; *mongana*) slowed his journey in the 1830s.[11] David Livingstone, who lived in Kuruman from 1841 to 1843, listed *A. mellifera* as a major species on rocky soil.[12] Burchell's account gives good internal evidence that there were few bushes. Before arriving in the thornveld, he gave *A. mellifera* subsp. *detinins* its scientific name, "detinins," conveying that it detained him. South of the Orange River, he had been caught in a thicket and freed only by cutting loose his clothes. "In revenge for this ill-treatment, I determined to give to the tree a name which should serve to caution future travellers against allowing themselves to venture within its clutches."[13] Someone so intimate with the species would have reported it as he saw it, and he described *A. mellifera* subsp. *detinins* only once in the Kuruman region, in a footnoted list of species in the area. This is strong evidence that the bush did not dominate the veld in this region.[14]

The use of travelers for evidence can be problematic, for it has been observed that their writings, including nature writing, are fraught with skewed representations of "the other."[15] This becomes a pertinent question to the history of vegetation change if there was a cultural pressure to exaggerate descriptions of grass. It was observed in the late eighteenth century that bush could replace grass in areas of heavy use,[16] but there is only one indication that visitors attributed greater meaning to the proportion of bushes and grass in the veld.

* By "corn" the writer means wheat.

The missionary Campbell found the unclaimed wealth of the land disheartening, writing in 1813: "It is grievous to see so much of the world remaining in a wilderness state, and so much of the annual productions of the ground perishing without being useful either to man or beast... I hope better times are coming to this miserable land."[17] Missionaries did believe the landscape was in need of redemption. Foremost in the missionary efforts to redeem the environment was Robert Moffat, yet the proportion of grass and bushes was not an issue for him. Rather, he believed that cutting of large acacias had caused desiccation, and as evidence for this he cited geomorphology rather than the amount of grass or bush.[18] Although observers did not approach the landscape neutrally, there was no consistent meaning for grass in these writings and no force to underreport bushes and trees.

It is a logical supposition that the veld was grassy at this time. Compared with what was to follow, the environment in the early nineteenth century was grass-friendly. Before being wiped out by commercial hunting, elephants and giraffes impeded tree growth. Furthermore, in the early nineteenth century, human and domesticated stock populations were low, so their impact was also diffused. Communal ownership of pastures also enabled the growth of grass, because men could move their herds and flocks to new fields as seasonal water supplies dried up, thus giving grazed land a chance to replenish itself. There were frequent, perhaps annual, burns (some man made), which could slow bush growth.[19]

By the 1860s and 1870s, there was an indication of greater thicket formation in the thornveld. In fact, *A. mellifera* thickets provided a dramatic obstacle to travelers. The experience of Gustav Fritsch is unlike any recorded in the thornveld until then:

> This type of umbrella-shaped acacia, which is between two to six feet tall, is decorated with pairs of hooked thorns, whose sharpness and strength has no equal in the plant world.... As we gradually lost our way and the thorns pressed nearer and nearer, our hopeless struggle began to resemble a droll play, lacking only an audience....
>
> So we pressed through by performing caprioles and a bit of bloodletting, until the falling darkness made the struggle too uneven and we outspanned, still encircled by a terrible row of thornbushes. As morning broke, I rode back to Griqua Town and by full daylight we found a tolerable way out of the cursed bushes.[20]

South of Kuruman, Fritsch missed a waterhole, until a passing Griqua man pointed out the obvious markers, the *A. karoo* (mimosa; *mooka*) and other water-dependent bushes. Thereafter, Fritsch noticed other acacia in river valleys. North of the Kuruman mission, however, the landscape began to resemble the savanna seen by previous travelers.[21] In the 1880s, another traveler, Parker Gillmore, also described dense bush. Approaching Kuruman from another Griqua town, Boetsap, to the southeast he found:

> The early part of the route is most uninteresting, the track being surrounded by the most dense description of thornbush, in which three persons who left the path (either in pursuit of game or otherwise) have never since been heard of.... After leaving this impenetrable bush the country becomes open, undulating and park-like; water, although scarce, is not absolutely wanting.[22] *

The comparison of these accounts with earlier ones strongly suggests that change in veld composition had occurred along roads. It seems that Fritsch and Gillmore saw less grass and more bushes on the open veld than earlier travelers did. It is a reasonable hypothesis that by the 1860s and 1870s bushes were increasing in areas of higher population and along roads, which were areas of highest seed distribution. Factors developing toward the end of the nineteenth century made bushes more prominent in this environment. The disappearance of elephants and giraffes meant fewer animals were eating trees and bushes.[23] The many different wild grazers and browsers were replaced by growing populations of three species, cattle, sheep, and goats, whose grazing impact was more concentrated than that of a similar-sized, but mixed population.[24] Cutting large trees for Kimberley aided other woody species in the savanna competition. Additionally, on the reserves colonial officials decried the "pernicious" practice of annual burning,[25] and responded by criminalizing man-made fires and extinguishing natural ones, which allowed more shrub growth. Because bush growth is localized and gradual, it is unwarranted to argue that the entire region had become bushier; however, because of their restriction to river valleys, African herders found themselves in the environment most prone to bush growth. The colonial land alienation put the majority of the population on river valley reserves, where moist soils favored bushes more than on the dry veld.† There is some evidence that at the turn of the century the veld on the reserves was less dominated by grass: an 1891 tree list gives prominence to small thirsty trees such as *A. mellifera* subsp. *detinins*, *A. karoo*, and *Terminalia serica* (yellowwood or silver cluster; *magonona*).[26] There are also reports of

---

* The story of people disappearing in the thickets is somewhat fantastic, but Gillmore suggested that lions were responsible.
† For a discussion of photosynthesis and the reasons bushes survive better on wetter soils, see pages 120–2.

nonpalatable exotics that were introduced around the turn of the century, and their existence presented difficulties for herders in the area.[27] An 1899 report states the situation succinctly: "The best waters appear to be in possession of the natives, but by compensation of nature [this is] the inferior veld. The best veld appears to be where there is no surface water."[28] The combination of bush encroachment and restriction of African herders to river valleys made their grazing environment less grassy and therefore less desirable for cattle.

Another alteration in environmental conditions was a continuation of, and perhaps an increase in, stock disease as herds and flocks concentrated on reserves. These included "horsesickness" (possibly the old scourge anthrax), a reappearance of lungsickness in 1890, and foot and mouth disease in 1892.[29] The diseases harmed production, and quarantines against them hindered trade. Bovine botulism may have worsened in the early colonial period. It did become more evident after 1895, possibly because available phosphate in vegetation fell during drought, prompting animals to eat more bones. As the disease became more serious, the healthier conditions in the Langeberg Mountains and the Kalahari, which do not have dolomite bedrock or phosphate-low grasses, became apparent.[30] The case of Luka, chief of one section of the Tlhaping, illustrates the difficulties of herding and dry land farming on the Ghaap Plateau. Luka, whom Shippard had accused of neglecting his land,* explained that he did so because keeping stock and dry land farming were too difficult. The irrigated gardens provided maize, but Luka did not consider this adequate.

> Let it be known that I have not forsaken Manyeding. Let it be known that I am still paying taxes for Manyeding. . . . Let it be known that when I left Manyeding I left it because of sorrow. My people sorrowed because they lacked cattle and sheep and goats and kaffir corn, as it is a land which soon becomes burnt up in the plains. When I was there I ate nothing but mealies like a pig and a horse. I ate them with salt and water.[† 31]

Since it is on the Ghaap Plateau which has a phosphate deficiency, Manyeding is notoriously bad cattle country.[‡ 32] By 1892, Luka was living in the Taung Reserve, which was becoming crowded. He claimed he would like to return to Manyeding, but could not because there was no place for his cattle. He declared his intention to "get land in the Langeberg," the healthiest veld and most remote reserve.[33] Luka was one of thousands drawn west. By early

---

* See exchange between Luka and Shippard on pages 89 and 93.
† As a chief, Luka had rights to both Manyeding and Tlharing.
‡ Manyeding is close to the village of Kikahela. That name is derived from "*kika*," the pounding block used to chop meat, and "*hela*" or "only." "Kikahela" connotes an unhealthy environment for cattle, meaning "all the cattle are dead and the pounding block remains without meat."

1894, "at least 3400" people had migrated from Taung to the northern hills of the Langeberg Range, the Korannaberg.[34] Luka was attempting to purchase a private farm with money collected from his subjects. In July 1894, Luka paid £115 to C. B. Scholtz, the resident magistrate of Kuruman, for a farm in the Korannaberg. The land, given to the Bechuanaland Railways as a subsidy for railroad construction, was not yet available for purchase. Scholtz deposited the money in his own account. When the matter came to light in February 1895 the magistrate claimed "the matter was delayed longer than I expected, but my intention was always that as soon as the farms were advertised I would apply to the Government for permission to assist Luka in purchasing a farm." In the meantime, Luka and his people moved to the Langeberg Reserve, waiting to take possession of any farm the government granted them. However, there were no provisions to allocate farms in this area, and the authorities took steps against "squatters."[35] The worsening environmental conditions on reserves and dissatisfaction set the conditions for a crisis, yet Luka denied any allegations of disloyalty: "It was said that I was raising an army; but I have no power to think of such a thing. . . . Let it be known that if I had any such thoughts I would have imitated the Batlaros [*sic*] who have fled."* [36] Rebellion awaited greater catastrophe.

EPIZOOTIC AND VIOLENCE, 1895–1897

Once started, the decline of extensive production was rapid, the cumulative effect of several environmental and human factors. The first was a familiar visitor – drought. The mid-1890s marked a shift in the cycle between wet and dry years. The first half of the decade, particularly the season of 1893–4, had seen heavy rains.[37] However, the summer beginning in late 1894 marked the beginning of several years of drought, and very quickly the lack of rain threatened food supplies. Already in January 1895 a missionary reported "a state bordering on starvation."[38]

The best-known environmental repercussion of imperial takeover in Africa was rinderpest. Rinderpest, German for "cattle plague," is a viral disease that strikes ruminants, both cattle and game such as buffalo, wildebeest, and large antelope such as eland and kudu. It causes inflammation and hemorrhage of the mucus membranes, as well as diarrhea and death. The virus is airborne with an incubation period of three to nine days. It is highly contagious; commonly reported infection rates in virgin soil outbreaks are morbidity near 100 percent and mortality around ninety percent. Death occurs after a sickness of seven to twelve days, but those cattle that do survive are immune to further infection.[39]

---

* The Tlharo Luka mentions are followers of Morwa, who moved to Namibia after British annexation of the area.

The disease had been endemic in Asia since ancient times, and Italian invaders inadvertently introduced it into Somalia in 1887 by importing oxen from India. It then swept through the rest of the continent, from the Horn south to the Cape of Good Hope and west to Cape Verde. It remained north of the Zambezi River until March 1896, but thereafter it spread remarkably quickly toward Mafikeng at an average of twenty miles per day.[40] The disease followed the old missionary, trader, and migrant laborer route south through the northern Tswana chiefdoms to British Bechuanaland. In April and May 1896, missionaries in Kuruman were waiting apprehensively for the "fearful scourge."[41] Authorities took action to control the situation. They restricted travel and shot infected cattle as well as and those presumed to have been exposed.[42]

Quarantine regulations further undermined the food supply by preventing imports with ox wagons. The resident magistrate described how people were coping with a difficult situation on Manyeding in August 1896:

They have no grain of any kind. . . . They have no money to purchase any even if attainable and in consequence of the stringent Rinderpest regulations they cannot fetch mealies from elsewhere. Many of the men have gone to Kimberley in search of employment and those still here remain for the protection of the women and children and to work their lands.[43]

Not everyone was destitute, but in the second half of 1896 local shops were unable to supply the needs of all who came with cash to purchase food.[44] Foraging was, of course, a traditional recourse of hungry people. However, annexation to the Cape brought stricter game protection laws.[45] Missionary J. Tom Brown, a resident in Kuruman from 1886 until 1918, appealed for a revocation of game laws so hungry people could hunt, but he found little cooperation from the Cape government.

For about 3 months your secretary has known that these people have been in a hungry state, whole families have been living on the roots of grasses and trees. Whenever an edible root was to be found it has been dug up for food. The country is stocked with game. Between here and Motito springbok, hartebeest, etc. roam over the unoccupied farms. God's providence for man's wants are by man's laws forbidden to be used. What are the natives to think but that, as they say, "It is the purpose of the Government to wipe them off the country?" What am I to say to them in reply to their complaints? Must I be plain and say, "Yes the Government knows you are hungry but cares not." I am ashamed to return to those people with no answer.

When I am asked as I have been lately if the Government has conquered God, what reply am I to make?[46]

The harvest of wheat in November offered some hope of lessening hunger, yet the spring planting of maize was in danger because of a lack of seed. The magistrate repeatedly appealed for mules for transport, as well as for maize for food and seed. When the government hesitated, the LMS guaranteed repayment.[47] Seed maize arrived only in December, too late for planting, and covered with weevils.[48]

Despite the hardship, the quarantine measures were well advised, for they slowed the plague. It appeared in British Bechuanaland in April, struck Vryburg in May, and was in Kimberley and other Griqualand West districts by October. However, missionary reports from Kuruman and Taung testify that those areas remained free of the disease in August. By October, Taung herds had succumbed, and the government gave up prevention efforts.[49] In that month, a group of herders in the Langeberg Reserve murdered a constable appointed to enforce rinderpest regulations. Throughout all this, rinderpest hovered on the edges, but did not overtake Kuruman, and quarantine regulations remained in effect.[50] Given the relative success in containing the disease, the resident magistrate expressed cautious optimism in early December:

> For several weeks we have had the plague on our very borders in different places, yet were fortunate enough to keep it out, and there is no reason why we should not be able to further remain free, if the farmers and natives cooperate with us, which on the whole, they very cordially do.... I had a long conversation with Toto the paramount chief of the Batlaro [*sic*] and he is now in favour of stamping out the disease by shooting infected kraals until such time as we find that the pest has got beyond our control. I told him the destruction of such cattle would be stopped if it came so far.[51]

Toto's purported willingness to see cattle shot may not have been a genuine feeling, expressed freely.

The inspector of native reserves described continuing success in limiting the disease at end of the year:

> On the 24th October last, the Rinderpest appeared in a very virulent form on ... the north bank of the river Mashowing, which is the boundary between the Vryburg and Kuruman districts. The disease spread rapidly along the north bank of the Mashowing and it was not until the 9th December that it appeared at Batlaros [*sic*] in the Lower Kuruman Native Reserve in this district. Since that time it has spread over a distance of about eleven

miles and only on the side unprotected by the Cape Police. In that area there are about 2,300 cattle of which up to date 101 have died and about 16 salted [immune].[52]

In late December the resident magistrate held a meeting with Boer, English, Tlhaping, and Tlharo farmers to discuss policy for containing the disease. Apparently, the English farmers supported a policy to shoot healthy cattle that had been exposed, but "Dutch farmers and some of the natives" opposed it.[53] In Kuruman, as elsewhere in southern Africa, Africans believed that whites had introduced the disease to undermine them. In 1991, I was told that a Mr. Liebenberg, "an Englishman, not a Boer," brought a bottle of rinderpest to Heunig Vley, in the Kalahari, and contaminated the water supply.[54] This folk explanation echoes suspicious of an earlier century.

Violence elsewhere ended peace in Kuruman. Although the official policy was no longer to shoot apparently healthy cattle, police did so in Taung in November. This exacerbated tensions, and in late December violence erupted between the police and some residents of the Taung Reserve. In early January the murder of a white trader on the Mashoweng River provoked retaliation against people there. Fugitives and refugees from both altercations fled to the Langeberg Reserve, and government forces followed. The Langeberg Reserve was an unlikely spot for a rebellion. Langeberg people were not particularly anti-British. In fact, they had escaped many difficulties of the other reserves; there was relatively little land alienation, little stock disease, and no weakening of the chiefship as among the Tlhaping. Furthermore, Chief Toto had been cooperating with the government on rinderpest control. However, he was fearful of retribution for the October murder of the rinderpest constable in his territory. There was also resentment regarding the 1895 land survey and the enforcement of the reserve boundaries.[55] One Tlharo sub-chief, Khibi, remained loyal to the Cape government, but the rest supported Toto, who harbored the fugitives. When Toto did not surrender the rebels from Taung, his people suffered attack from the Cape government. From February until August 1897, Cape forces fought and raided communities in the Langeberg Reserve and also at Ga-Mopedi in the Lower Kuruman Reserve. Finally, heavy artillery defeated the few rebels and many bystanders, and the war ended.[56]

Ironically and tragically, the retaliation against those who had resisted rinderpest measures elsewhere finally spread the full-blown epidemic throughout Kuruman, when colonial troops and their draft animals entering the Langeberg Reserve broke the quarantine.[57] According to Cape Colony estimates, in the financial division of Vryburg, which included Kuruman, the disease took 80,664 cattle of a total of 86,964, almost ninety-three percent. Perhaps because of their communal lands and shared water sources, African areas were harder hit than white ones. For example, Mafikeng lost ninety-seven percent of its cattle, while Gordonia, to the southwest, the only district of British Bechuanaland without a significant Tswana population, lost only twelve percent.* [58]

The loss of stock was only one result of the war. The state considered rebellion treasonous, and 1,896 Langeberg residents were sentenced *en masse* to five years' indentured servitude on western Cape farms. Technically, the accused had been given a choice of standing trial for treason or accepting indentured servitude, and as a test of the mass sentence, two men, with the support of John Smith Moffat, went to trial. Their case was dismissed for lack of evidence, but that decision did not affect the status of other indentured people. [59]

The most permanent retribution was that the Cape government decreed that rebels had forfeited their right to land. The largest and healthiest reserves for cattle, the Langeberg and the adjoining reserves Kathu and Dibeng, were confiscated and made available for white settlement. (See Figure 4-1.) The collective punishments for the rebellion – land confiscation and indenturing – support Mamdani's observation that colonial powers had "a notion of community rights so one-sided as to be at loggerheads with any meaningful understanding of individual rights." [60] The Cape prime minister justified the harsh punishment:

> It is of the first importance in a Colony where the black population enormously outnumbers the white that the natives should clearly understand that rebellion entails the forfeiture of their right of occupation of the land. Human life is of small account with the natives so that the loss of a few hundred lives in a rebellion makes but little impression upon them. The loss of their cattle is more serious, but even that is soon forgotten. The one punishment that endures is the loss of their land, for it compels them to scatter and seek a livelihood by honest work. [61]

The Cape government also confiscated reserves in Vryburg and Taung where people had rebelled. These confiscations were complicated by the terms of the annexation of British Bechuanaland to the Cape Colony. British Bechuanaland Proclamation 220 of 1895 required that any further land alienation receive the approval of the secretary of state for the colonies, but obtaining it did not provide much of a hindrance. [62]

Only the group of pro-Cape Tlharo under Chief Khibi was given land to replace what they lost in the confiscated Langeberg Reserve, a parcel taken from rebels at Ga-Mopedi in the Lower Kuruman Reserve. Other Langeberg residents who had not been indentured were left to their own devices to find a home

---

* Since there had been no census before the epidemic, these numbers are only rough estimates.

and a livelihood in the remaining reserves. During these upheavals, the Cape government took the opportunity to abolish the smallest British Bechuanaland reserves, including Luka's farm at Tlharing.[63] The approximately 250 residents of these reserves had not participated in the war, but the Cape government decided to "concentrate" African lands. This provoked criticism from Shippard, former chairman of the British Bechuanaland Land Commission and administrator of the Crown Colony before its annexation to the Cape: "I should be glad to know, as a matter of curiosity, where the Cape Government proposes to locate even the natives who at present occupy the numerous small reserves which it is intended to sell to white farmers. . . . So far as I can see, there only remains the Kalahari."[64] The confiscation of these parcels was the first demonstration that communal tenure made Africans vulnerable to losing the land "reserved" for them. Communal tenure had enabled the state to punish the entire Langeberg community collectively for the rebellion and eased the confiscation of the smaller reserves, because the state needed to accomplish only a single eviction to remove an entire group.

The fighting and its aftermath caused extreme population loss, but exactly how much is hard to determine. The official estimate of war dead was 1,200 to 1,500 people, including Chief Luka Jantjie. Chief Toto's fate is not documented, but the Tlharo today remember that he was taken to Robben Island. The resident magistrate estimated that between 1896 and 1897 the population on district reserves underwent a decline from 12,650 to 6,280, nearly fifty percent! There had been no precise count, however.[65] The Langeberg war claimed thousands of casualties and prisoners, but halving the population of the entire district is probably an exaggeration. In 1897, many of the people who had lived in the Langeberg Reserve were surviving as refugees and were probably overlooked in the count. Also, more men were going to the mines, and they might have been overlooked. Yet, by the end of 1897, the human population, land base, and cattle herds had all been devastated with a blow so severe that subsistence production and the social organization dependent on it would not recover.

FAILURES OF PRODUCTION AND DISTRIBUTION:
FOOD SHORTAGE AND FAMINE

The combination of rebellion, retaliation, and rinderpest worsened the already severe food shortage. The Native Affairs Department (NAD) report for 1897 summarized the situation and how people sought to remedy hunger.

> The food supply is very bad. This year the natives have ploughed more than usual. They have to look forward to their ground supplying them with

food and necessaries on account of rinderpest having swept off most of their cattle. There are a great many natives in a very bad condition.... The crops are very promising, but if the drought continues the crops will fail, which means starvation.[66]

People recognized that cultivation, even intensified cultivation, was their best option. Not only did reserve dwellers plow more than usual, but they constructed new furrows.[67] Missionaries found tenants for all plots at the LMS mission at Seodin and added approximately thirty-five more acres to rental land. Despite this, they reported five applicants for every mission plot.[68] In response to the need, the resident magistrate granted new fields in the Kuruman Crown Reserve to landless, hungry people in 1896 and 1898.[69]

Even in this crisis people continued the eclectic combination of irrigation and extensive cultivation. Despite the food shortage, the costs of intensification remained high. There were ditches providing water to some fields, but other fields were simply laid out on damp ground. Also, sections of the valley above and below the mission were swampy. Digging more furrows and draining swamps might have made more land available for cultivation. Despite this apparent potential for increasing irrigable acreage, many of the plots granted to indigent households on the Kuruman Crown Reserve were entirely dry, suitable only for cultivation of sorghum.[70] The resident magistrate believed that if only cultivators would invest more labor in their fields they could prevent famine:

> In spite of the drawbacks occasioned by War, Rinderpest and drought there is hope that starvation will not be so bad as some anticipate for it must be remembered that along the valley's [*sic*] the lands can be irrigated. If the Inspector of Natives will use his energy in this direction he should have no difficulty in succeeding to instill into the minds of the natives less slothful and lazy habits and then more land would be cultivated than is brought under cultivation at present.[71]

Sloth was hardly the cause for underutilization. In fact, people had less ability to intensify after the famine than they had had before. Intensification did not occur for many reasons a lack of physical energy during the food shortage, capital, and skill. The death of the cattle eliminated the prime source of fertilizer and the source of draft power.[72] A culture of "belt-tightening" during hard times and preferences for certain types of food may have also played a role. Irrigation provided maize and wheat, which Luka disdained as pig and horse food, unsatisfactory replacements for milk, meat, and sorghum in the diet.* Furthermore,

---

* See quotation on page 100.

people who invested labor and capital in their fields were vulnerable to their harvests being stolen.

Government relief supported 870 hungry people in 1898,[73] but hunger continued. Especially hard hit were refugees from the Langeberg Reserve, whose social network had been destroyed: "The old men, women and children who were released from amongst the Langeberg prisoners and remain in this district are now in a semi-state of starvation. Their friends are no longer able to support them, most of the natives are not able to work."[74] Langeberg refugees were in the worst situation; by 1898 some had died.[75] The severity of the crisis strained reciprocal customs: "The shortness of food is beginning to be felt among the natives owing to the number of starving friends they have had to support. In a short time many natives will be in a state of starvation," even though "most of the able-bodied men are away working."[76]

A letter written in February 1898 by one Mmusi Seburu to missionary Roger Price provides rare African testimony about the plight after rinderpest. He reported that deaths through starvation were beginning in the Kuruman Valley and that work in a garden was vulnerable to thieves. Seburu poignantly suggested that those indentured after the rebellion were fortunate.

> I have to inform you that we are well, but we are in great straits through hunger. It is not hunger, it is death. At Maroping [*sic*] . . . people have died of hunger but they are not all. In the Matlhoaring [Matlhwaring] Valley three have died of hunger – I mean people whom I know. The theft is such as I have never seen since I came to this part of the country in 1885. It may be said that everybody steals, although everybody, as a matter of fact, does not steal. We have no longer anything in our lands. Anything that has born fruit in our gardens, they take it at once, however much we watch our gardens. Some have now been seen eating a dog, they being in a very bad state through hunger. Although rain has fallen it helps nothing. This is the thing which I said: of those who are taken to the Cape Colony and those who remain, those who are taken to the Cape Colony will live. But some people say it is better for them to stay.[77]

Seburu mentions two options to procure food when production failed: foraging, which as in earlier years was only roughly differentiated from stealing, and working elsewhere. During the famine, people turned to foraging, an old survival technique which may have delayed entry into the labor market.[78] However, those who foraged on "waste lands" found that white settlement was increasing, and the government was now enforcing the land settlement. In 1898, there were several cases against "vagrants," people searching for food on private property or on the confiscated reserves.[79] The second option, working elsewhere, was more common – the number of men working as migrants in the Kimberley diamond mines increased significantly after rinderpest.[80] In fact, some whites who had been frustrated by labor shortages before rinderpest self-servingly saw this as a bright side to the huge losses of cattle. "In several ways rinderpest has not been an unmixed evil. The wealthy Bechuanas leading indolent lives have learnt the value of labour. The northern locations are beginning to be better tapped, and are becoming what they should be, i.e. valuable labour reserves."[81] The trend toward wage labor did not enrich people. A storekeeper reported that his business suffered because his customers were "too few and too poor to support a store any longer."[82] In 1899, the Langeberg refugees were still dependent on government aid and food prices were very high.[83]

The onset of the South African War prevented recovery. Very soon after the confiscation from the Tlharo, significant numbers of Afrikaners, attracted by the healthy conditions for cattle, had settled in the Langeberg, becoming the first significant white population in the district. In 1899, these Boers rose up in rebellion in aid of their compatriots in the Transvaal.[84] Already reeling from rinderpest, violence, and land loss, Africans in Kuruman, especially those in Seodin, suffered further during this war. Boer rebels besieged the "town" of Kuruman in October 1899, although it still was not much more than a mission station, a government office, and a few shops. It fell to the Boers on January 1, 1900. They commandeered Tswana stock and plundered loyalists' stores and farms. Hungry people turned to the missionaries for support, and the missionary Brown expected famine.[85] The British dispatched Charles Warren, now a lieutenant general, on his third and last expedition to the region. The Boers gave him no resistance, and he secured Kuruman without a fight on June 24, 1900.

Continuing harassment by Boer commandos and the demand for food by the British garrison put further pressure on the food supply at Seodin.[86] Additionally, the drought cycle continued and rain came too late to sow unirrigated lands in the summers of 1899–1900, 1900–1, and 1901–2.[87] Moreover, in 1901 locusts took their toll on the crops.[88] It is hard to imagine that matters could be much worse, but the siege of Kimberley cut off opportunities to work from October 1899 to February 1900, and even after the mines opened, Boer raids made travel unsafe.[89] Brown described the serious situation in February 1901. His letters are deeply critical of the British occupation:

There is not much news to send. We are still cut off from the world and are in a much worse state as far as food is concerned than we were last year. The military commandeered *all* the foodstuffs in the place in December and since then no one has been able to purchase any. Every European family in the neighbourhood except ourselves is being supplied with food by the Government (military). Coffee, sugar, tea, soap, rice and milk can no longer be had. There is still meal and biscuits and plenty of meat. But the natives and Bastards [*sic*]* are feeling the strain. The latter more especially as they were not able to plough last year owing to Boer occupation. Our old people to whom coffee and tea have become necessities are feeling the lack of these beverages: The strain is terrible. We are helping the needy out of our own small supply, but cannot continue to do so. To add to our anxiety we have the horribly inhuman treatment measured out to the poor natives by the Boers in the field. There is no doubt left in any of our minds that natives are being cruelly murdered.[90]

People responded by putting more land under cultivation. On the Kuruman Crown Reserve the magistrate again granted plots for hungry people to grow food.[91]

Brown himself established relief operations, but found the British occupation was a great drain on the food supply.

[The Commander] said he heard I had mealies. I said, Yes, I had. 'Then I want them to feed the hungry people' was his next word. I told him they were the Society's mealies and that I was selling them to the people who were without food and that I wished to keep some for seed for the people.... He replied he would feed the people and so I agreed to let him have them ... I told him I should expect market rates for the mealies. The next day he sent for the mealies and received from me 1740 lbs. weight. He has refused to pay market rates and altho' I was offered by a trader £2.10 per 200 lbs. and which you will see is the market rate.... He would only pay £17 for the lot. Instead also of feeding the people who were starving he sold the mealies to his friends for food for the horses, and I have been compelled to send starving people from my door.[92]

Possibly, the Seodin community, under occupation and siege, suffered more from the war than people on the remote reserves. Starving people figure prominently in Brown's letters in late 1901: "Whole families are literally starving – children are going about crying for bread;" and "Our school has had to be closed on account of famine."[93] Compounding the problem was anthrax: "Sickness is very prevalent. Anthrax – caused by eating diseased meat – has made its appearance, and I am afraid it will carry off many of our people, for many have

---

* By "Bastards" (usually written "Bastaards") Brown means people of mixed African and European heritage, primarily Griqua.

no other food than the carcasses of horses, donkeys, cattle and sheep and goats that have died of disease."* [94]

Apart from a few settlements, including Kuruman, Boers controlled the entire northern Cape Colony (essentially the former colony of British Bechuanaland) until the end of the war.[95] In late 1901 their renewed attacks further depleted the food supply, perhaps also among Tlhaping and Tlharo communities farther afield, but events in remote areas are not as well documented as those at Seodin. At first the Boers reportedly respected African neutrality and did not raid Tlhaping and Tlharo stock, but at the end of the war, an LMS teacher recorded, "Without rhyme or reason, the Boers come to the Batlapin outposts, and sweep off hundreds and hundreds of head of stock."[96] Conditions continued to worsen as the war came to an end: "Especially towards the end the Natives experienced great hardships and were on the verge of starvation."[97] In May 1902 the British accepted the Boer surrender. The end of the war did not end the food crisis, for the drought continued, and at harvest in May 1903 there was again "a total failure of crops."[98]

WAGE LABOR AND GOVERNMENT INTERVENTION
DURING THE 1903 FAMINE

In 1903 the magistrate in Kuruman conflicted with the Cape government over the response to this famine. The disagreement is important because it revolved around the role of the state in economic and environmental recovery. The outcome made clear the government's preferred response to famine – increased migrant labor. The colonial state did not force men into wage labor; they found this solution on their own, and earning cash had its advantages. Yet state involvement would determine the relative importance of wage labor and local production over the long term. The state was the only entity that could pay the costs of intensification, the only one that could regulate food production and establish practices suited to the new conditions on the reserves. It had shown the potential of intervention in production arrangements before. However, it was not willing to undertake this, for reasons very familiar in South African history.

In the interests of survival, people had taken action. Male migrant labor had become so important by 1902 that "under ordinary conditions," one-third of the men were away working.[99] Permanent emigration of entire families also continued.[100] Even this could not prevent the food production crisis from becoming a famine. Some households turned to old patterns of famine relief, foraging. As the resident magistrate said, "Many are living on roots," and he speculated

---

* Merely coming into contact with contaminated flesh can cause anthrax. Its reappearance suggests that measures to prevent infection were dropped during the famine.

that poor people would become nomads in the Langeberg and Korannaberg Mountains.[101] The Kuruman resident magistrate at the time, M. J. Lyne, appears to have been a capable and compassionate man. With the inadequacy of wage labor and foraging to meet the immediate needs of the population, he sought to provide assistance to increase food production among hungry people. However, Lyne and Cape Colony administrators differed on this. Again reporting a "total failure of crops," Lyne telegraphed the Cape government on May 2, 1903, petitioning for assistance. He divided needy people into three groups: widows and aged men without land and supported by charity; wives and children of migrant laborers; and men who for unspecified reasons were unable to work at mines, but were capable of other labor.[102] One hundred and ninety members of the first group were already receiving relief, and the NAD increased the stocks of maize to distribute to this group. Lyne expected that the second group would also require straight charity. The NAD took another course, requesting that De Beers arrange for monthly remittances to the families of men at the diamond mines, but the company demurred. For the third group, the NAD arranged a local road construction project that began on May 27, 1903.[103] A commission investigating poverty among whites in the northern Cape Province in 1899 had declared that new road construction was essential to the economic development of Kuruman, so this project was beneficial on several fronts.[104]

Public work projects were not the government's preferred solution, since southern African mines were experiencing a shortage of labor. Colonial perceptions of an inferior Tswana work ethic justified a hesitance about work projects. Conventional wisdom among employers was that good help was scarce due to "the natives having few wants and what they have are easily supplied."[105] An earlier Kuruman magistrate had reported that "the Bechuanas will not work unless driven to it."[106] John Smith Moffat had been scathing about such thinking: "When there is work with money in it, they will do it, just as readily as men of other races. The cant about 'teaching the native the dignity of labour' is cant and nothing more."[107] Moffat's views did not prevail, and officials suspected that public work projects harbored malingerers who would be more beneficially employed in mines. Just one month after the beginning of relief works, uneasiness regarding the road-building project surfaced.[108] Officials demanded the magistrate ensure that its employment schemes were absolutely necessary. For example, when the daily wage was cut from two shillings three pence to two shillings, seventy-eight men quit the road project. A NAD representative admonished Lyne:

> It is absolutely necessary that only men who have no other way of providing for their families should be taken on. . . . You say 78 men have left owing

to reduction of wages. The natural inference therefore is that these men were not in distress otherwise they would not have thrown up work for the sake of an extra threepence.[109]

Lyne held his ground on the need for local work projects:

The great majority are those who would not ordinarily leave locations and who have postponed working as long as possible. Their presence in such numbers is sufficient indication of distress. The working class proper find employment in De Beers where they are better paid and general conditions are better than on the road and those who have refrained from going to Kimberley have done so out of consideration for families whom ordinarily they leave with sufficient food to last until their return, a feeling which it is undesirable to discourage. . . . They will now go to mines. . . . There is absolutely nothing in location and many are living on roots. After going into matter with Inspector it is considered that work should be found at once for two hundred and fifty men at least in addition to the one hundred now employed.[110]

Despite this plea, the project ended and the employed men were dismissed, even as Lyne continued to plead for local employment for an estimated 530 needy men. His correspondence expressed that his motivation to keeping men near home was to restore food production, while the response of the NAD makes it clear that the Cape government did not share this concern.

When the funds for road building ran out, the Public Works Department offered men work on the railroads elsewhere in the Cape Colony for two shillings per day. Lyne objected; in the wake of the 1897 indenturing and subsequent seizure of the Langeberg Reserves, there were strong suspicions against government schemes that involved leaving home. Furthermore, leaving Kuruman would interfere with cultivation.[111] The NAD dispatched its chief inspector to explore options. His report does not indicate that he visited the reserves; nonetheless, he flatly and confidently contradicts Lyne on the severity of the food shortage and on the ability of migrant labor to alleviate hunger without hindering cultivation. The report is fixated on migrant labor and attributes low food production to a familiar cause: indolence. Because it reveals much about government thinking during the food shortage, I quote it at length.

I do not agree with the representations 'that if the men at present on the Reserve leave, no ploughing can be done, and the distress will continue next year.' As a matter of fact, a large number of men have been away working for some time past, these are now returning with the accumulated wages, and will certainly not go to work again this year, hence it follows, that there will always be a sufficient number of men on each Reserve to carry on ploughing. On my way up, I passed two lots of Natives returning to Kuruman from Kimberley, these men have been working four months and have been receiving 4 shillings per diem, the great part of which they had with them, and I find on enquiring at the Chief Registrar's Office, here, that sixty left the Mines for home this morning. With the frequent return of Natives and constant influx of money to the Reserves, I cannot conceive that any great distress can exist amongst the people. Moreover, as an illustration that money is not scarce with them, I may state, that the largest trader at Kuruman informed me, that his business with the Natives during the past six months has been greater than during any time previously and further, that this increase was not caused solely by purchase of grain, but included luxuries, such as meat, coffee, condensed milk, cloth-ing, etc.

To the suggestion 'that pauper relief will have to be afforded to many women and children' (presumably the wives and families of about 350 men remaining in the reserves waiting for grain) I am absolutely opposed, if carried out, it would mean an expenditure of about £1200. At no time during the present year was there any necessity for a single sixpence to be expended in the shape of relief excepting to the Widows and decrepit already referred to, but even if these were, that necessity has now, ow-ing to a fortuitous circumstance ceased, due partly to the arrival on the scene of Captain Goodyear, representing the Witwatersrand Native Labour Association, and partly to a number of the men who were discharged hav-ing left for Kimberley. Captain Goodyear has agreed to pay an advance of one bag of mealies per month or cash equivalent to signers on. Capt. Goodyear signed on 52 men on one day and expected 50 more.

Subsequent to the general meeting, I held a meeting of the Headmen and elicited from them, that it was not so much the scarcity of food, that was causing anxiety, but scarcity of seed, Kafir corn, and mealies, and they all agreed that if 100 bags of good seed (for which they are prepared to pay) were supplied by government, the agitation in connection with distress would cease.

The Bechuana is probably the worst class of Native we have to deal with. In a good season he barely works, but lives in what to him is the 'lap of luxury' and in time of drought he flies to government for relief. It is an erroneous idea to think that the Bechuana have no stock, their stock has been greatly reduced by rinderpest and other causes, but many are still in possession of sheep and goats, but not many cattle, but it is mainly due to their indolent habits that they are poor in stock. The residents of Barkly

West (to mention one district out of many) also suffered great loss by the same causes, but they now own fairly good herds and flocks.[112]

Lyne pleaded with the NAD to disregard this report. He charged that the chief inspector had not adequately investigated conditions in Kuruman and that his recommendations were "the merest hazard."[113] He had made his own tour of the reserves by September 1903 and offered alternative programs to mitigate the distress. He argued that merely feeding hungry people did not address the deeper problem. It was also not sufficient to promote migrant labor, because as even the chief inspector had noticed, men who were able were already away working, but people were still hungry. In the most extreme case, in Bothetheletsa, only the headman and one or two others of the population of sixty-seven men were not away working. The famine, Lyne argued, was the result of deep flaws in the local economy, "the general unfavorable economic condition of the natives rather than an improbable contingency, and to minimize the risk of a recurrence of the present distress, it is advisable to improve such conditions." As a remedy, Lyne proposed government intervention to intensify food production by improving irrigation, sinking wells for stock, and offering loans for stock purchase.[114] However, these requests prompted no action.

This discussion has focused on government officials, not only because they dominate the written record, but also because they exercised the power to promote migrant labor instead of food production. The real story is about the black people who coped with these hardships. The surviving testimony from them is sparse but piercing: "It is not hunger, it is death" and "Has the government conquered God?" It requires extraordinary empathy but little historical specificity to imagine how starving people came to terms with their hunger. We can better assess how survivors reckoned their options for mine labor, road work, or farming. As both parents and grown children, men and women of working age would have had responsibilities to provide for others. Women did what they had always done – farmed as best they could and foraged. Men, who had lost their cattle and the ability to plow or provide milk, had the new option of going to Kimberley, and they did in large numbers to obtain food. This decision signaled that plowing would become a secondary activity for these men. Those men who resisted going to the mines may have been the most ardent farmers or may have been unfit for mine work. Their decision to leave the public works after the wage cut in order to work in the mines or to have no employment at all must have been agonizing. This collective step from extensive production to wage labor was portentous. In the future, people would not continue to practice extensive cultivation, and they could not afford to invest the labor necessary for intensification.

ENTITLEMENTS UNDER COLONIAL RULE

All around the world, from Ireland in the 1840s to Bengal in the 1940s, colonial rule provoked food crises of unprecedented severity.[115] In North America, environmental historians have observed that indigenous ecologies and subsistence systems collapsed because of colonial transformation.[116] Throughout southern Africa, the simultaneous occurrence of rinderpest, drought, and violence brought trauma during the onset of colonial rule. Charles Ballard emphasized this in the history of Natal and argued that the effect of rinderpest and drought was so severe because colonial rule impeded processes of coping and recovering.[117] This appears to be true for Kuruman as well. Although the production crisis was extreme, the drought, violence, and cattle disease that provoked it were not entirely unprecedented. A long-term transformation resulted from this crisis because it occurred under colonial rule. Under the new circumstances of colonial rule, their entitlements, the resources they had to get food, failed; they could no longer produce enough for themselves, and distribution from elsewhere was inadequate.[118] In Kuruman, people could not return to the subsistence production practices they had followed before. Laws barred them from leaving the reserves to forage, to clear new fields, to herd their sheep and goats, to find healthy pastures for the cattle that survived, or to hunt the fauna that remained. In southern Africa, when farming entitlements failed, entitlements gained by selling labor became more important. Faced with starvation during the crisis at the turn of the twentieth century, Kuruman people responded to the option of labor in the colonial economy. In other parts of southern Africa, people became dependent on wage labor more gradually and less dramatically than in this area, but the changing conditions of production under colonial rule always played a role.[119]

6

The Environmental History
of a "Labor Reservoir," 1903–1970s

> Even if life was difficult for you [at work] everything you were
> getting was fair because of the struggles of how they were living at
> home . . . because of the children at home and how they were living.[1]

B Y 1903 extensive production could no longer provide for the population. Such transitions from independent food production to wage labor
by Africans, according to Colin Bundy, lie "at the core of South Africa's social history."[2] That this transition occurred, however, should not obscure the
continuing historical dynamic, including the environmental dynamic in the increasingly dependent rural reserves.[3] The collapse of indigenous production
is also a major theme in environmental history, but in contrast to temperate
regions of the New World, in South Africa the indigenous population remained
the majority. They did not lose all their land and they remembered how to
farm. In Kuruman, the history of indigenous food production continued after the collapse of subsistence and peasant production. Even as people became
more dependent on remunerated labor, they continued to work the environment.
Even though people in the twentieth century gained part of their livelihood by
selling their labor, the study of environmental history continues to illuminate
changes in their lives. The environmental history of this period revolves around
the overlapping interactions between humans of different categories, the nonhuman world, the state, and the cash economy. Incorporating environmental
factors into this history does not entail arguing that they are the determinant
forces. Although Kuruman people live in a dry and bushy veld, its harshness
did not drive them into the cash economy, and their irrigable valleys did not
protect them from impoverishment. Through small stock herding, dry land and
irrigated cultivation, seasonal maize harvesting, and tributary asbestos mining,
people had increased power to choose where they worked and for what sort
of remuneration. The enduring significance of local production challenges the

characterization of such areas as "labor reservoirs," and the variety of activities suggests that through the first half of the twentieth century, at least, dependence on cash was mitigated by other forms of remuneration. After the mid-twentieth century, cash became increasingly dominant, and supplementary production began to drop off.

The complex interactions in this history include those between people. In the nineteenth century, rich households and *balala*, as well as men and women, had different social positions and different options for food production. In the twentieth century, the failure of extensive subsistence production and the entrenchment of remunerated labor altered the social organization of food production. It was still predicated on cooperation, often unequal cooperation, but by the 1950s, the unequal rewards and obligations of reciprocity became disincentives to production. Opportunities for wage labor came to men before they did to women. Taking more responsibility on the reserves, women took over tasks previously limited to men, and the fundamental divisions by gender were somewhat blurred. In food production women continued to cooperate more and reciprocate more equally than men did, but the costs of cooperation pressed on them. As for class divisions, there had always been people in this society who could not produce enough food for themselves, but in this new dispensation, poorer people chose wage labor over working in the fields of their neighbors, further eroding the cooperative organization of cultivation. Finally and powerfully, race had become the key determinant in shaping how people interacted with the environment and each other. People once known to themselves and the world as the Tlhaping and Tlharo had become first of all black South Africans, and the disadvantage of this position is manifestly evident in the history that follows.

POPULATION AND PRODUCTION

Indentured servitude, famine, and violence caused the human population to drop at the turn of the century. (See Figure 6-1.) Official statistics indicate that the black population of the Kuruman District in 1904 was only eighty-four percent of that reported in 1896. It had nearly recovered by 1911, and thereafter, it rose precipitously. By 1946 it was 224 percent larger than it had been fifty years earlier. (Unfortunately, redistricting after 1950 impedes following these trends beyond that date.) This is an impressive growth, but it is hard to discern how population increased on the reserves. These statistics do not differentiate between people living in town, on white farms, in mines, or on communal lands. I found only two numbers for the population on black communal lands before 1950, and they are significantly lower than those for the population as a whole. In 1936 and 1946, roughly half of the total population was reported as living on reserves.

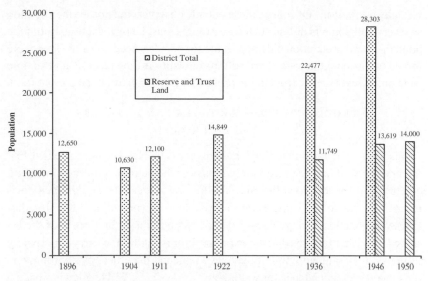

Figure 6-1 The black population in Kuruman, 1896–1950.

The problem with these numbers is that there was a possibility of undercounting rural areas, particularly migrant laborers, or of inflating urban numbers by counting migrants from elsewhere working in Kuruman mines. Therefore, the rural population was probably larger than that shown in Figure 6-1. In South Africa as a whole, the reserve population did not see the same steep growth as in the total population. In 1904, ten percent of the population lived in cities; in 1946 it was twenty-three percent.[4] Together, these statistics allow a cautious yet important conclusion: although the population was growing, increasing numbers of people found their livelihoods off the reserves. The population on the reserves was not sufficient to inflict Malthusian depravation or to induce Boserupian intensification.[5]

How did cultivation and herding contribute to the livelihood of the population? Statistics suggest that they were not nearly sufficient for the subsistence on reserves. In his study of census statistics for food production on reserves throughout South Africa, Charles Simkins estimated that Kuruman reserves produced less than twenty-five percent of their subsistence requirements between 1927 and 1960.*[6] Descriptions of the food supply support the argument that production was low. During the first decades of the twentieth century, government officials reported that the reserves were often on the brink of famine. In the early decades of the century, observers assessed the food supply as "poor"

---

* This is certainly an underestimate, since agricultural statistics did not count green maize picked before the harvest, which made up a significant portion of the crop.

virtually every year.[7] Of course, these outside observers did not see the situation as reserve inhabitants did, so such assessments must be read cautiously, but the point that local production did not provide for people's needs is valid. They were forced to make up the food shortfall through labor off the reserve, and as time went on, this work away from home prevented them from producing more food.

PRODUCING FOOD: BROWSERS AND GRAZERS IN A BUSHIER VELD

As discussed in the previous chapter, there is reasonable evidence to believe that the grazing veld had been extremely grassy at the beginning of the nineteenth century, but was less so at the end. Yet this was a localized and gradual environmental change and is therefore impossible to situate within a few decades. However, botanical change occurred and is important to the history of the reserves. If bushes increased at the expense of grass and if the carrying capacity of the veld consequently fell, it may have lessened the efficacy of herding and thus increased dependence on wage labor. In 1941, C. W. De Kiewiet made a related argument, linking soil erosion with the decline of subsistence production leading to wage labor.[8] There is little gully erosion on Kuruman soils. Yet bush encroachment is perceived to be the more significant problem in semi-arid South Africa, and its particular effects on black rural society may be similar to those of soil erosion.[9] However, the hypothesis about environmental degradation and wage labor does not hold for the case of bush encroachment in Kuruman.

The "received wisdom" of grazing science is that overgrazing the thornveld causes bush encroachment and that bushes constitute an undesirable grazing environment.[10] The most effective encroacher, the woody shrub *Acacia mellifera* subsp. *detinins*, has by one estimate reduced grass in some areas by fifty percent.[11] Other encroaching bushes include *A. karoo*, *A. hebeclada* (trassiebush; *sekhi*), and *Rhigozum trichotomum* (driedoring; *mokuburwane*). (See Figure 6-2.) Arguments about declining grazing are based on theories of ecological succession and climax. In the thornveld, grassland is most desired for cattle grazing and is also claimed to constitute the climax community. Overgrazing by stock is said to deplete the grass and to give an advantage to bushes, which is perceived to reverse the process of ecological succession.[12]

Within the field of ecology, concepts of strict succession patterns and one stable climax are increasingly being supplanted by theories with more dynamism.[13] Nonclimax models have emerged in range management as well. Recognizing that change is a natural phenomenon and appreciating variations in ecological systems has made some range scientists hesitant to attribute all vegetation change to anthropogenic "degradation."[14] Rather, they explore how rainfall levels, spatial variation, soil types and soil moisture, burning, insects,

Figure 6-2 The view from the Ghaap Plateau looking toward the Kuruman Hills, 1998. The medium-sized bushes are *Acacia mellifera* subsp. *detinins*. (Photograph courtesy of Peter Heywood.)

and other nonhuman factors may cause differences in bush and grass levels. Also important are different types of photosynthesis and different levels of transpiration. Photosynthesis and transpiration involve gaseous exchange through tiny pores called stomata: carbon dioxide (CO_2) enters photosynthesizing leaves through stomata, while oxygen (O_2) and water vapor exit the leaves through them. Most plants (including trees, bushes, and some grasses) use an inefficient enzyme to capture CO_2. Because the first detectable product of this reaction contains three carbon atoms, these are termed "C_3 plants." Stomata must open widely to provide enough CO_2 for C_3 photosynthesis, and this allows loss of water vapor through transpiration. In contrast, at least ninety-five percent of thornveld grasses are C_4 plants, so named because their first product of photosynthesis contains four carbon atoms.[15] Because C_4 grasses have a specialized leaf structure, called a Kranz anatomy, and an efficient enzyme able to bind CO_2 readily, they are able to photosynthesize effectively when their stomata are only partially opened and, therefore, do so with less transpiration. This is a great advantage in dry areas. However, on moist soils a higher rate of transpiration is less of a liability and the C_4 advantage is diminished. For this reason, C_3 plants such as bushes can better establish themselves at rivers and boreholes and near subsurface water sources. Rainfall can also be a factor in veld composition,

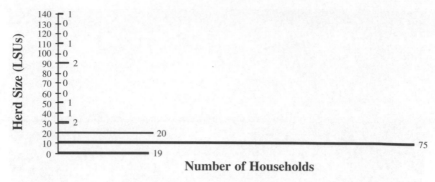

Figure 6-3 Herd size (LSUs) by number of households, Konong, 1959.

supporting bush growth at the expense of grass: wet periods allow the establishment of bushes that may survive dry cycles and greatly increase in later rainy years. These observations illustrate nonclimax thinking about environmental change and refute the notion that an increase in bushes necessarily is anthropogenic ecological degradation. One presumably anthropogenic change that has nothing to do with local herders involves the rise in atmospheric CO_2. The increase in this "greenhouse gas" is believed to have affected grass–bush ratios worldwide. In the past two centuries, CO_2 in the atmosphere has risen from 275 parts per million (ppm) to the 2000 level of 369 ppm.[16] Presumably, with high atmospheric CO_2 levels, C_3 photosynthesis is less of a disadvantage even on dry lands, and woody plants are better able to succeed against C_4 grasses.[17]

Any assessment of veld quality varies according to which animals are grazing, how many are grazing, and what people hope to gain from keeping them. Few people on reserves around Kuruman had enough animals to raise them commercially. In 1948, it was estimated that a few herders owned herds of fifty or 100 cattle, but ninety percent of the population owned from two to five heads of stock.[18] A survey of herd size by household made on the Konong Reserve in 1959 shows the situation was not quite so dire, but also that the majority of the population was stock poor. A crude conception of the total wealth may be grasped by converting all stock numbers to large stock units (LSUs). In the most simple and most common calculation, one LSU equals one cow, or five sheep or goats. Of the 123 households, ninety-four had ten or fewer LSUs[19] (see Figure 6-3).

Keeping animals, especially cattle, provided some black people with a little cash. Like white farmers, Africans sold cream. In 1947 there were eighteen producers selling cream to the local dairy, but in 1963 Africans in the district were said to own 200 milk separators.[20] Before the mid-1930s, sales of stock were small and sporadic and only to neighbors and traders. At the Kuruman stock auction which opened in the mid-1930s, racist practices, either discrimination by the auctioneer or having to wait until all whites had sold their stock, reduced proceeds for black sellers.* The market value of cattle made it difficult for cash-poor people to accumulate and retain herds.[21] Another problem in cattle keeping was that the old endemic diseases, anthrax and bovine botulism, made it difficult to rebuild cattle herds after rinderpest.[22] In 1919, the veterinary scientist Arnold Theiler discovered the cause of lamsiekte and determined that clearing fields of bones and dosing stock with sterile bonemeal were effective preventatives. However, the former requires labor and the latter requires cash. White farmers in Kuruman moved into commercial cattle raising, dairy in the 1920s and beef in the 1940s.[23] On reserves, therefore, the proportion of small stock, which were less susceptible to botulism, remained higher than on white-owned farms. In our interviews, people reported endemic problems with botulism (*magetla* or *stiefsiek*) and periodic outbreaks of anthrax.[24] The NAD subsidized bonemeal purchases, but people also administered maize and *A. erioloba* (camelthorn) pods as a remedy.

Even without a lot of cattle, people herded. In the twentieth century, a new herding system, one that was adjusted to conditions of land alienation, poverty, and grass shortage, was developed. Goats and donkeys predominated in this new dispensation. They reproduced quickly, required little capital, and thrived on the bushes. Because of the higher reproduction rates, small stock could be slaughtered more frequently than cattle and they provided an easily accessible supplement to the livelihood provided by low wages. These animals were cheaper than cattle, healthier, better suited to the environment, and reproduced well. Raising small stock and donkeys could not remedy the poverty, but could mitigate it.

Goats were useful primarily for meat and some milk, but donkeys had many subsistence uses and also provided cash.[25] London Missionary Society personnel brought donkeys to the Tlhaping and Tlharo territory by 1858 to serve as pack animals for a postal service.[26] People found little use for donkeys while the cattle economy was strong. After its collapse, several decades passed before people on reserves owned many donkeys, perhaps because of the expense of acquiring a breeding population. In 1906, nine years after rinderpest, there were only thirty donkeys along with eighty-two horses, 29,923 goats, 7,147 sheep, and 3,548 cattle on Kuruman reserves. A report in 1911 stated that "very few donkeys are owned by Natives," so the great majority of the 4,180 animals reported for the district as a whole in 1912 must have belonged to whites, who used them in asbestos mining as well as for farm work and transport.[27] The 1930 census, the first to enumerate the animals on African reserves, reported

---

* Numerous interviews confirmed that at the Kuruman auction Africans' stock were sold last.

there were 7,879 donkeys, compared with 16,272 on white farms.[28] After this point, the racial balance of donkey ownership shifted. With access to credit and state aid, white farmers were able to overcome the handicap of disease, begin water development, and improve bovine stock. Moreover, mechanization of traction and transport around mid-twentieth century gave whites less need for draft animals.[29] Thus, in 1946 there were 9,168 donkeys on white farms; in 1950, there were 4,250; and in 1960, there were only 2,145.

Because of poverty, the donkey population on black reserves did not follow this trajectory. Perhaps, as whites had less use for them, the animals became cheaper for people on reserves. They proved to be very useful.[30] The first and most obvious use of donkeys was for transport. The transformations of colonial rule demanded that people develop new techniques to negotiate time and space, and donkey carts saved human energy and time. The South African Railways operated a bus service in the region after the 1920s, but bus travel required cash and adapting to a schedule, while donkeys were nearly free and more convenient.[31] The second use of donkeys was for hauling goods. In the twentieth century, people relied on donkeys rather than oxen for carrying loads to Kimberley. A biologist from the University of Arizona, Homer Shantz, visited Kimberley in 1919 and photographed "a typical" wagon pulled by at least fifteen "burros."[32] Contemporary recollections of when donkeys became the primary draft animals vary from the 1930s to the 1950s, corroborating a report in 1953 which asserted that "the cattle which are kept in this district consist of ninety-seven percent breeding stock, with the result that donkeys are the only transport or trek animals."[33] For people living on the semi-arid lands around Kuruman, donkey carts were particularly important in transporting maize grown in the western Transvaal. After the harvest the maize had to be brought home, and those who wanted to save shipping costs of railroad transport used their own donkey carts. There were also local uses for donkey carts. People invested in specialized carts to carry water, wood, gravel, and sand for brick making. Individuals with a cart designed for moving one of these commodities gained an income by serving their neighbors. The third use for donkeys was as draft animals. Cattle had served as draft animals in the nineteenth century, but in the twentieth century donkeys took over this job. A fourth benefit to donkey keeping was that they were slaughtered for meat. Donkeys were not a favorite food, but they were eaten. Additionally, donkey dung, mixed with sand, was used in construction. A final dividend of donkey keeping was that their milk was considered medicinal for sick children. The population on reserves continued to rise, to 11,007 in 1946 when it reportedly surpassed the cattle population of 10,372.[34] (See Figure 6-4.) As explained in Chapter 8, economic change and betterment reduced donkey numbers after the 1940s.

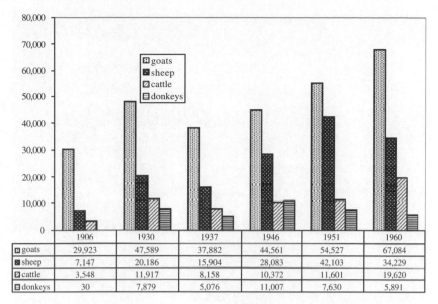

	1906	1930	1937	1946	1951	1960
▣ goats	29,923	47,589	37,882	44,561	54,527	67,084
▨ sheep	7,147	20,186	15,904	28,083	42,103	34,229
▨ cattle	3,548	11,917	8,158	10,372	11,601	19,620
▤ donkeys	30	7,879	5,076	11,007	7,630	5,891

Figure 6-4 Goats, sheep, cattle, and donkeys in selected years.

Besides being useful, donkeys were well suited to the environment. They were omnivorous: "The donkey eats everything, unlike the cattle; the cattle choose."[35] As ruminants, cattle and goats have a digestive system that effectively extracts nutrients from a high-fiber diet, although digestion slows as food becomes more fibrous. By contrast, nonruminant equines on a high-fiber diet extract fewer nutrients, but pass food more quickly through their guts. Thus, by ingesting more than ruminants can, equines maintain a sufficient rate of nutrient absorption on a poor quality diet. A study in Namaqualand, an arid region south of the Orange River on the Atlantic Coast, found that a donkey might eat as much vegetable matter as five goats, but can live on a diet that goats have difficulty digesting.[36] Donkeys and ruminants do compete for food, but their relationship is not a zero-sum equation. Donkeys consume large quantities of low-quality forage that cattle and goats avoid. Hence, in environments where low-quality forage is predominant, the sustainable donkey biomass may outweigh that of cattle and goats. In droughts frequent in this region, they were "the hardiest of all four-footed creatures."[37] Unlike their equine cousins, horses suffered disease and were expensive. In fact, the greatest utility of horses may have been in rounding up donkeys.[38] The ability to keep cattle or the reliance on donkeys was a function of economic position, which in South Africa was determined by race and class. In addition to poor/black people, the benefits of donkey keeping

125

Figure 6-5 Gladys Motshabe and friend in a donkey cart, 2001. (Photograph courtesy of Peter Heywood.)

were available to women, since donkeys were more gender neutral than horses or cattle. (See Figure 6-5).[39] However, gender neutrality made donkeys no less useful to men.

How many donkeys would a household ideally own? People told me that they might have use for thirty: three teams to rotate on a plow, two for pulling a wagon, and a few to spare. Thirty is a considerable number and reveals as much about the assessment of need as about the animals' usefulness. Most years, plowing was an economically marginal activity, but when good rains came, people did not want to be lacking donkeys. A poor household could keep so many because the costs and risks were low. Donkeys reproduced without intervention from humans and amounted to something close to a free good. People had no reason to maximize their extraction of donkey power, so they acquired more than would be considered necessary in a profit-making enterprise. Although few households achieved a herd of thirty, donkeys, which eat a lot, became numerous.

There is inconsistent evidence about grazing shortages on the reserves in this period. In 1908, to make good on promises to demarcate one more reserve, the government added an additional 12,848 hectares to the Lower Kuruman Native Reserve.[40] In 1909 the local inspector of natives believed there was an adequate grass supply.[41] However, people on the reserves complained of overcrowding, which could have many meanings, including a grass shortage.[42] Telesho Mogonarin, a reserve resident, wrote to the governor-general in 1921 to protest land alienation, stating:

> May your royal Highness know that the people live by tilling the land, we live along a river ... and whenever it was full we used to be ploughing there out in the west since our ploughing lands were there, but they have been taken by the Dutch. Moreover we are poor because even the stock which we do possess lacks pasturage.[43]

By 1924 the government land surveyor reported that because of traffic through the Lower Kuruman Native Reserve to asbestos mines and the Kalahari, grazing was "lamentably inadequate."[44] His recommendation resulted in the purchase of the "horseshoe block," between the two arms of the Lower Kuruman Reserve.[45] African testimony to the Native Affairs Commission in 1937 stressed that congestion was a problem.[46] Further land purchases, motivated by national politics rather than local needs, followed the 1936 Trust and Land Act.

Despite the evidence for shortage of pastures, limited borehole development would have kept areas away from the rivers grassy. However, borehole development after the 1940s increased moisture and grazing pressure on wider areas. In this period stock populations were also rising. Between 1927, the first year for which complete data is available, and 1969, the number of goats rose by sixty-seven percent, sheep by ninety-five percent, and cattle by 176 percent.[*] Calculated in LSUs, there was a 108 percent increase in grazers and browsers from 21,837 LSUs in 1929 to 45,551 LSUs in 1969, but insufficient evidence about how water holes and stock were distributed across the increasing land base impedes any calculation of population density and grazing pressure.

The documentary record contains few descriptions of veld composition. Local officials who did record veld quality were most concerned with poisonous plants.[47] In fact, concern about excessive woodcutting caused the government to restrict cutting of live trees. Regulations passed in the 1910s and 1920s allowed people to collect only dry wood for domestic use.[48] The ban on cutting *A. mellifera* was lifted in 1951.[49] There was an observation in 1949 that *A. mellifera* was supplanting other species: "In some regions it is so thick that it has become impossible to move from place to place in the veld."[50] By mid-twentieth century, there were certainly conditions which favored bushes over grass, on dry soils as well as moist ones. Burning remained illegal, and there were reports of "conservatives who want the veld to be burnt every year."[51]

---

[*] See statistics in Appendix B. Donkeys and horses are not included in this calculation because their numbers were only irregularly recorded.

Although both whites and blacks set fires, and some started after lightning strikes, fire was controlled and was no longer a way for humans to shape the savanna. In addition, by 1960, CO_2 levels had risen to 317 ppm.[52] Certainly, CO_2 alone would not explain an increase in bushes, but in conjunction with heavier use, periods of heavy rain, efficient propagation, and fewer fires, it could be a factor in making the veld bushier.

Determining the timing and extent of botanical change is difficult and so is assessing it. Cronon has commented, "We want to know whether environmental change is good or bad, and that question can only be answered by referring to our own sense of right and wrong. . . . Historical narratives, even those about the nonhuman world, remain focused on a human struggle over values.[53] Although we are not compelled to valorize indigenous knowledge or perspectives, we must consult the values of people experiencing this history. It is significant that people now living in this area do not consider that bushes indicate a degraded grazing environment. When asked their estimation of the proportion of grass and bushes in a relatively bushy area, a member of one group said, "It is all right for the animals. It's all right because there is grass for cattle, and bushes for goats and sheep."[54] People consistently valued grass, known simply as *bojang* or "grass," as the best grazing for cattle. However, they also valued species that were undesirable in the opinion of mainstream range management. They said *mongana* (*A. mellifera*, subsp. *detinins*), the scourge of the overgrazed thornveld, was the best fodder for goats. *Sekhi* (*A. hebeclada*), another species common in disturbed areas, was listed as the most desirable species for sheep.[55] Given the high proportion of sheep and goats owned by people on reserves, this is a strong endorsement for these species. Additionally, these and other bushes were also said to be important even to cattle herding, because the leaves stay green after the grass wilts. When asked what the ideal herding veld for all animals would be, one group responded the most important item would be *bojang*, but after agreeing on this, a woman quickly said the ideal veld must include trees, explaining "if the grass died, then trees remain."[56] Cattle may be considered grazers rather than browsers, but even bovines innovate when they are hungry, and, in a pinch, Kuruman cattle can become browsers. Since cattle herds served more as investments than as commodities to be sold in peak condition, lean but living beasts were acceptable to their owners.

These examples of the local veld-*anschauung* are key to understanding the significance of the environmental change to subsistence on reserves. Contemporary valuation of bushes provides good reason to avoid the argument that this environmental change made food production less sustainable and led to an increase in wage labor. The gradual appearance of bushes cannot compete with the imperial conquest, colonial rule, low wages, and segregationist administration as causes for poverty and economic dependence. The appreciation of bushes among contemporary Kuruman herders reveals that they were not even a contributing factor. In fact, bushes allowed people to continue the herding they could best afford. This raises a critique of the unqualified preference for grass among some range ecologists. The enthusiasm for grass conflates economic and ecological arguments, since the agenda supporting grass does not just arise from a concern about preserving the climax community, but also for promoting capitalized beef production. Since most people on communal lands did not have the means to acquire grazing cattle and would have difficulties in maintaining them, the association of grasslands and higher carrying capacity does not hold.

PRODUCING FOOD: EXTENSIVE CULTIVATION AND CASUAL IRRIGATION ON RESERVES

John Mackenzie probably would not have found the situation after the turn of the century so hopeless. The missionary, who died in 1899, had been a champion of irrigated cultivation among the southern Tswana and had long hoped that cattle would lose their importance. No doubt he would have found the suffering from 1896 through 1903 tragic, but he would have also seen a solution in irrigated farming. As was true before 1900 and is true today, different households worked their gardens according to different methods, but most inhabitants did not fulfill the dream of Mackenzie (see Figure 6-6). In 1964, officials estimated there were three dry land farmers, seventy-five irrigators (obvious underestimates), and 2,434 pastoral farmers on communal lands in Kuruman.[*] [57] Regarding the development of water resources, cultivators put in some furrows and wells, but preferred to plant damp places in the valleys over constructing irrigation works.[58] This practice minimized labor, but also kept harvests lower than they could have been if the available water had been used to bring a wider area under cultivation. In addition to the damp valleys, people continued to plow the dry veld. However, this dry land planting differed from the shifting cultivation of a century earlier. First, all indications are that people plowed rather than hoed. Furthermore, by the 1940s, maize had replaced sorghum as the staple crop. Maize had the advantages of being higher yielding, requiring less effort to protect it from birds, and allowing a variety of preparations.[59] The good reasons to choose maize did not include suitability to a semi-arid environment. In perhaps half of the summers it was too dry for people to plant maize on

---

[*] This number probably includes only those on the government projects, but the imbalance is nonetheless clear.

Figure 6-6 Exceptional irrigated gardening near Batlharos, 1998. In preparation for spring planting, Jan and Evelyn Bele have carefully constructed berms and trenches to channel water from the Batlharos Eye to their garden. Such dedicated gardening is rare today. (Photograph courtesy of Peter Heywood.)

rain-fed fields. Cultivators plowed dry lands only after sufficient rains had fallen. Even after planting, however, it was possible rains would fail and farmers would have wasted effort and seed.[60] So, growing maize on dry lands involved greater risk than growing sorghum. Perhaps the existence of remunerated labor allowed cultivators to take this risk.

As the missionaries before them, government officials were dismissive of these agricultural practices, particularly the failure to increase irrigation. For example,

> The Reserves include the best land in the territory, and there ought to be no want if even a moderate portion of the land were properly cultivated. There is an adequate supply of water and no overcrowding; yet most families frequently depend for some period of the year on locusts, berries or bulbs, and the indifferent physical condition of the people may often be attributed to insufficient food supply.[61]

Once again, these descriptions of "laziness" and "backwardness" can be read through the writers' prejudices to reveal an enduring logic of reducing drudgery:

"What can be cultivated without undue native exertion has been taken up by them."[62] According to the inspector of native reserves in 1909: "The wheat lands of the natives along the Kuruman are looking very well. It is however to be regretted that they leave so many lands uncultivated."[63] The same theme echoed through a report nearly fifty years later, when the agricultural officer reported that the gardens in Ga-Mopedi had not been plowed in three years. Animals trampled unfenced plots, and fenced plots yielded a luxurious growth of reeds. All the same, people were purchasing wire to fence off their gardens.[64] The plots must have had some value that the officials did not recognize.

Government records do not record the importance of cultivation to households, but people attest to it today. Some informants who were born as late as the 1940s claim that their fields were their most important food source and that some of their parents usually spent cash only on what they could not produce: salt, tea, coffee.[65] The ability to produce food varied widely by household. As in the previous century, there was no "peasantry" in Kuruman producing grain regularly for markets. Yet they did sell a small amount of high-value crops grown under irrigation, requiring a cooperative effort. Although it is not mentioned in the documentary record, people today recall that they grew fruit and tobacco for themselves and to trade. Of all the villages, Batlharos is most remembered for its orchards, even as "Green Batlharos," where people grew grapes, quince, figs, apples, and pears. Girls carried fruit to sell in Kuruman town, and their parents brought it by donkey cart to mining centers.[66] People also grew tobacco in the river valleys and traded it on drier reserves and on farms. The fruit trade dwindled as it became more regularly available in stores and as hawkers were required to have licenses, probably by the 1960s.[67] Finally, mines opened nearby, and women on reserves had another source of income: brewing beer, possibly from their own grain.[68] No one claims that trading fruit, tobacco, or beer was hugely profitable, but they recall that their own production provided a good proportion of their staples and also a little cash. There were also noneconomic motivations to garden. People did it because they considered it the proper thing to do, or because they enjoyed tending plants.

As in the nineteenth century, there were powerful factors working against intensification. First, environmental conditions posed constraints, for in some areas, such as along the Matlhwareng River arm of the Lower Kuruman Reserve or in Ga-Tlhose, the water supply was simply inadequate.[69] The Kuruman River arm of the Lower Kuruman Native Reserve suffered the same handicap after the municipality of Kuruman developed around the Kuruman Eye and consumed more and more of its flow (see Chapter 7). In all river valleys, 100 years of irrigated cultivation had left soil in the river valleys exhausted. Applying manure was difficult because the reserves were stock poor and animals grazed widely. Economic conditions also worked against intensification. Building irrigation works, draining marshes, and constructing furrows and dams required capital, a particularly scarce resource. Buying fertilizer seeds and plows also required money, and in 1935 an official estimated there was only one plow for every ten families.[70] At some springs, increasing the amount of land under irrigation required more advanced technology and engineering skills than the farmers possessed.[71] Next, there were already so many demands on people's labor that they simply could not take on more cultivation work. With the increase in migrancy, male labor was not consistently available at home. Only those families who had sufficient labor power to clear fields could bring new fields under irrigation.[72] Finally, since irrigation before colonial takeover had been a casual, less intensive endeavor, the tradition of extensive production would have served as a force against a more thorough practice of irrigation.

Although aridity is the overwhelming theme in the environmental history of Kuruman, deluge also hindered cultivators. In 1974, irrigators experienced a further natural trauma when tremendous rains created a stupendous flood in the Kuruman and other river valleys. In Prieska on the Orange River, 150 millimeters of rain fell in less than five hours. A frequently repeated local story, corroborated by Pieter Snyman, is that the rivers were swollen enough to allow a motor boat to travel over 100 kilometers on the Kuruman River from Kuruman to Van Zylsrus, a mind-boggling achievement to anyone who has seen the long waterless stretches of valley in a normal year.[73] The flood was devastating to those who lived or farmed in the valley. It destroyed trees, furrows, and houses. The water stayed for three or four months, and when it receded people found their topsoil gone, replaced by deep mud or exposed rock.[74] Where soil remained it was waterlogged and remained drenched by exceptionally high rainfall in 1975 and even higher amounts in 1976 (see Figure 1-3). When my research assistants and I toured the fields at Ncweng in 1997, we saw where the 1974 flood had washed out fences and furrows, cut channels, dug pits, left mounds, and exposed bare rock in the fields.[75] Many times we were told that the 1974 flood ended people's cultivation and that this natural disaster made them give up farming.[76]

Mackenzie would have been disappointed. Throughout the entire area, political, economic, cultural, and environmental forces prevented the black people of Kuruman from fulfilling Mackenzie's dream of intensive cultivation. Whatever missionaries and government officials thought about it, people in the river valleys continued to practice the cultivation they could afford. As was the case with herding, their methods did not give the highest yields or much commercial remuneration, but they did provide some sustenance.

SELLING LABOR FOR WAGES AND OTHER REMUNERATION

The story of exchanging labor for remuneration is not only of men going to mines. In the first decade of the twentieth century male migrant labor to mines was the most important form of outside labor. As the century progressed, however, men and women found other ways to sell their labor, and it is evident that they sought out remunerated labor that resembled extensive production. As maize harvesters, as tributary asbestos miners, or as asbestos cobbers, people had less drudgery, risk, and supervision than in mines, white farms, or urban households. In these jobs, they worked as family units, producing directly from the environment. None of these jobs paid wages for the amount of time worked, and some did not pay cash at all. They provide further indication that even after herding and cultivating were not able to support the population, people did not become immediately dependent on cash; they actually identified new supplements to it.

The increase in selling labor is directly related to increasing difficulties in providing subsistence. Before imperial annexation, Tlhaping household heads had shown reluctance to engage in migrant labor, preferring to sell wood (a practice which continued well into the twentieth century) or to send their sons to the mines.[77] The gendered nature of early migrancy was once assumed to result from the needs of capital. Belinda Bozzoli challenged this assumption by arguing that it resulted from the subordinate position of women as laborers in agro-pastoral societies.[78] Berger, however, has questioned this interpretation, observing that women had "a large measure of economic power with a relative lack of social power" and suggesting that it was women's economic capacity and control that may have *allowed* them to avoid migrant labor.[79] Both the environmental trauma and the response were gendered. The failure of male production brought about the large-scale entry of men, and not women, into the labor market. Since men were involved in cultivation only during plowing, donkeys could somewhat remedy both the loss of cattle and the loss of male labor.

Class divisions also influenced who migrated to work. Evidence from 1898 reveals that poorer people had fewer options than those who could produce some food:

Most of the young men of the kraals go to Kimberley to work in preference to hiring themselves out in the District. The labour supply of the Farming Community* is generally obtained from the Vaalpenses; i.e., those who

---

* "The farming community" means white farmers.

have not native reserves to live on or have been turned out of the Reserves owing to want of food to give them.[80]

Similarly, by 1911, "those with no crops" were most dependent on wages.[81] During times of low food supply, male migrant laborers and entire families sought a more secure living elsewhere. Few households could afford to be ambivalent about selling their labor.[82] In 1907, migrant labor was "the principal resource" in Kuruman, as an estimated seventy-five percent of men between the ages of fifteen and forty worked half the year at the mines.[83] The 1911 census of the black population between twenty to forty-nine years of age listed only thirty-nine percent as male, an indication that many men were away working.[84]

Men were able to choose where they earned cash, and they exhibited marked preferences. The diamond mines and nearby "river diggings," smaller alluvial diamond deposits on the Orange River, were by far the most popular destination of labor migrants.[85] Government records report that in 1908, 646 men went to the Kimberley mines, 602 went to diamond diggings on the Orange River, and forty-two went to work on farms in other districts. In 1911, 778 workers went to the Kimberley mines, 576 went to other Cape Province mines (presumably the river diggings), and none went to other cities or mines. In 1912, all 1,508 passes issued in Kuruman were for Kimberley or other Cape mines. The absence of migrants to the Witwatersrand resulted from worker preference, not mine recruiting. After the South African war, gold mines cut wages for unskilled migrant workers, and labor there had little appeal for local men.[86] In 1903, the first group to work in Johannesburg returned with negative reports of poor treatment at the mines.[87] Recorded objections included the diet and the working schedule of thirty days per month. They were concerned that Witwatersrand mines could keep men longer than their contracts, and they mistrusted the representatives of the Witwatersrand Native Labour Association.[88] Additionally, they considered gold mines dangerous.[89] Even in 1908, when a slowdown in Kimberley caused local distress, no men went to Johannesburg. Instead, they worked at river diamond diggings, where wages were only half of what gold mines paid.[90] The decision to avoid Johannesburg was a very localized one, not even common among the Tlhaping; Vryburg and Taung men traveled at least as frequently to Transvaal mines as to Kimberley.[91]

Low wages and a frequent failure to fulfil contracts with workers dissuaded people (apart from the poorest) from working on local farms.[92] Harvesting work on "maize triangle" farms was an entirely different matter. The seasonal migration to the western Transvaal and Orange Free State was a major source of livelihood for "half or more" of the people from Kuruman reserves.[93] This migration was well established by 1935, when "nearly all able-bodied men with the bulk of the wagons and trek animals" were away harvesting.[94] In 1954, a reported 2,059 adults were at the harvest, with Delareyville being the favored destination.[95] Like cultivation at home, this was family labor. Men, women, and children left the reserves for several months at harvest time. They usually kept five percent of what they harvested.[96] Maize harvesting was migrant labor, but not wage labor, for participants were paid in kind. They brought home thousands of bags of maize, sometimes enough to feed themselves for the entire year and even a surplus to sell.[97] However, this was not a balanced diet. Upon their return, many people sought treatment for pellagra, a protein deficiency disease, at the mission hospital in Batlharos.[98] The maize harvest was an important source of the staple, and it gave households a cushion against dependence on cash. It also had a powerful effect on how people farmed their own land, for it was impossible to be at two harvests at once. People in 1997 attested that the ability to produce food at home determined who went to harvest.[99] Yet regardless of the situation at home, going to the harvest made sense. It provided the benefits of cultivation in a humid environment without the risks of waiting for rain to fall on the thornveld or the costs of irrigation in the river valleys. Thus, the Transvaal harvest provided another disincentive for more intensive cultivation in Kuruman.

There was another important alternative to male migrant labor. People in Kuruman had an advantage over many black South Africans, for they could find remunerated work without leaving home by mining asbestos. Blue asbestos, or crocidolite, lies in a belt from the Orange to the Molopo Rivers.[100] In the Kuruman District, the best deposits were on the Lower Kuruman, Ga-Tlhose, and Maremane Reserves. On these reserves from the 1910s to the 1940s, people dug asbestos as tributary workers, "[winning] the material as best they may" and selling it to asbestos concerns.[101] Like subsistence production and maize harvesting, this was a household venture. Men dug the rock, while women and children were responsible for cobbing (removing asbestos from the hard rocks), smoothing the fibers, and sorting them by length and color. As a government official noted, "Probably more often as not, the family and not the individual is the unit of labor."[102]

The early asbestos industry on these reserves has been called "asbestos farming,"[103] and the expression is very telling. Like farming, asbestos mining consisted of extracting a product with family labor. In their asbestos work, people applied the logic of extensive production to a new process. This was possible because in this early period of asbestos mining, people on reserves organized their own production and controlled their own labor. Even on private lands, miners exercised so much autonomy that in 1921 seven white owners of asbestos-rich farms in the Kuruman Hills complained that "the natives working on the claims are under no control whatever."[104] Diggers did not register claims with the chief or the state, but simply dug where they chose: "A native generally does his own prospecting for the most suitable spots, or may have such indicated for him, but follows his own method of mining."[105] They had sufficient engineering skill for shallow underground workings: "These people literally burrow along seams of crocidolite into the hills. They work either open-cast or by underground methods, filling the working behind them with broken rock as they proceed."[106] Mining, obviously, has no practice of fallow, but in some ways it resembled that of shifting cultivation. People sought to conserve their labor and capital rather than maximize extraction: "The countless occurrences of fibre on many farms (or at numerous points within one farm) provide abundant opportunities of shifting development to some other place as soon as the work ceases to be remunerative."[107] Moreover, the disdain of mining officials about asbestos production methods is reminiscent of criticisms of cultivation methods: "Unless under the direction of a white man there is no attempt to develop a system, or in fact develop at all. The tendency is to work out rich patches only and discard more or less everything under half an inch in length."[108]

Tributary asbestos mining in Kuruman was similar to peasant production of food crops in other parts of the country, because households sold the product to traders. The method of payment was conducive to traders' profits, since workers received a combination of cash and goods or "good-fors," certificates redeemable only for goods at the trader's shop.[109] Payment advances perpetuated the system: "Money is advanced in the shape of stores to the native, who must accept them or starve. Once he gets behind, he is apt to remain so and the position of the native who is thus left in the hand of his employer may fall little short of slavery."[110] Mr. Seamecho, who recalled the practice from his childhood, expressed resentment against it: "It was terrible, those good-fors. You work and then you want to go and buy something, clothing or something. . . . When you get a ticket, then when you pay, you just show that. You don't get a cent!"[111] Despite the low payment and risks of debt, contract asbestos work remained attractive to household heads because they worked without white supervision and kept control over juniors' wages.[112]

The system of loose control was attractive to asbestos companies, since they paid only for the actual product. Because they bore few costs, their profits were high; in 1916 they paid an average of £18 per ton and sold for £35 per ton. Yet, tributary mining was short lived. The first decade of asbestos production suffered because of fluctuating demand, poor quality control, the 1918 influenza epidemic, and lack of good transport.[113] Furthermore, as the easily accessible seams played out, extraction required more capital.[114] By the mid-1920s, the

136

industry was becoming more profitable and capital investment increased. In 1927, the first capitalized company began to pay wages in Kuruman. It received mineral rights on the reserves and began to hire male miners as wage laborers. Tributary production continued after capitalized mining began. Even as companies became responsible for bringing asbestos-bearing rock from underground, women continued working more informally, paid as piece workers to cob fiber. Wage labor was also the system when mining of manganese (used to harden steel) began in the new town of Postmasburg, just south of Kuruman, in 1929.[115] The late 1920s offered black people around Kuruman good opportunities for wage labor very close to home.

The Great Depression had a terrible effect on these young industries and, consequently, on their workers. Manganese mines ceased production in October 1931, and virtually all workers were laid off. Unemployment on Kuruman reserves was estimated at eighty percent and that was before asbestos production ceased.[116] The Depression had an intense effect because a terrible drought coincided with unemployment. The years 1932 and 1933 are notorious in South Africa for their crushing drought. Planting in river valleys continued, but dry land cultivation was impossible, and many animals died of hunger and thirst. The Transvaal maize crop failed, so there was no harvesting. A quarantine against foot and mouth disease prevented those who had stock from trading it.[117] Even before the Depression, there were reports that men from Kuruman reserves were "not at all popular in the large labour centres," because hunger and disease had made them "unable to stand real hard manual labor."[118]

The year 1932 opened with famine. David L. Makgolokwe, a headman, described the situation in January:

> I beg to inform you of the bitter outcrying of my people. They complain about the great starvation that is amongst them. These people flock to me everyday to ask for food. Sir, please help and approach the government to help. The people are dying for lack of food. Cattle and sheep and goats have been swept away on account of starvation. Lands are dried up with no rain at all.[119]

The indigent and starving population was put at 3,000.[120] Reserve dwellers resurrected an old response to food shortages, foraging, but with a new twist as they searched asbestos mining sites for fibers long enough to sell:

> The Superintendent of Locations in inspecting asbestos workings [in the Lower Kuruman Native Reserve] came across a Native working asbestos. He states that at the price he was receiving for fibre he could only earn

about 3 pence per day and was in such a weak state due to hunger, that he could only just manage to stand erect. The time when this man was found was past 6:30 pm and he was still working.[121]

Clearly, people were dependent on remunerated labor for survival.

By February, the magistrate was recording the first deaths and predicting a need for emergency rations among seventy-five percent of the population.[122] As Iliffe observed for Zimbabwe, famine had changed by the 1930s, when relations with colonial society brought both food shortage and its relief.[123] In contrast to the 1903 food shortage, during the Depression, the failure of remunerated labor was a major cause of suffering. Also in contrast to 1903, the government had no motivation or ability to use wage labor as a relief policy, and so it began feeding the population. The ration was one pound of maize per day for adults and half a pound for children, a "borderline, bare maintenance, or semi-starvation ration" intended to encourage the recipients to search for another food source. Since people were already dependent on wage labor, government policy also differed from that of 1903 by attempting to enhance cultivation. During a 1931 visit, the secretary of native affairs had made a gift of wheat seed to Vlakfontein and the policy seemed to have worked, for even though the seed had not been equally distributed, no Vlakfontein residents applied for relief in 1932.[124]

The government response to the 1932–3 famine was very different than it had been thirty years earlier. During the turn-of-the-century crisis, Magistrate Lyne had recognized that rations provided no long-term solution to the problems creating famine. Yet the government wanted to increase the work force and did not consider his proposals to improve food production. Those who wanted a secure work force had their way, and in the twentieth century many men became migrant wage laborers. In contrast, this famine was due to the failure of both wage labor as well as food production. For this reason, the government at last became willing to invest in remedying food shortages.

Asbestos and manganese operations resumed after 1936, and then greatly expanded, because preparations for war in Europe raised demand.[125] Since unemployment was still high, in 1936 local NAD officials arranged for men to go to Johannesburg, but reported that of 100 recruited only seventeen were deemed fit enough for work.[126] The government also provided food relief during the drought of 1942, which an eighty-seven-year-old man described as "the worst the Kuruman district has ever experienced."[127] (Actually, 1933 and 1938 had received less rain.) Food shortages continued until the end of World War II. This finally convinced men to go to Johannesburg in significant numbers.[128]

Development of manganese continued, and iron extraction began at Sishen, west of the town of Kuruman, in 1950.[129] These mines drew some laborers from local reserves, but many Kuruman men avoided manganese work, in part because they disliked working deep underground.[130] By 1961, recruiting agencies were signing men for contracts on the Witwatersrand mines. Approximately 3,300 left the district, while 6,100 men migrated into the district to work in local mines.[131]

In contrast to other regions, there is no indication that African men and the colonial government cooperated to keep women at home in Kuruman.[132] More women sold their labor as the century progressed. Some women did work in cities as domestics, but large numbers worked in local asbestos mines. In fact, some informants claimed that more women than men worked in asbestos.[133] The shift from tributary to wage labor was particularly gradual for women, who continued cobbing on a piecework basis until the 1970s.[134] Women today report that they were supposed to pool their earnings with the cash their husbands brought home, yet they controlled the household cash reserves.[135] Furthermore, they continued to control the granary after harvest.[136]

The unforeseen repercussion of asbestos mining was the tremendous burden of asbestos-related diseases (ARDs). Mines operated all along the Kuruman Hills, and wind-borne fibers spread to the people living below. In one chilling example, the village of Ncweng is particularly close to sites of tributary mining. Tragically, its primary school was situated a short distance below a hillside covered with crocidolite waste (see Figure 6-7). Today, we know that exposure to asbestos can be deadly, causing three fatal diseases: lung cancer, mesothelioma, and asbestosis. There have been no epidemiological studies of ARDs in communities in the Kuruman area, but the conventional wisdom is that merely living in the villages near the mines creates a risk as high as exposure gained through risky occupations elsewhere. A rough but alarming estimate is that as many as twenty-five to fifty percent of people in these villages suffer from ARDs, depending on their proximity to the mine dumps.[137] One study by Talent et al. of 735 former asbestos miners living within 100 kilometers of Kuruman revealed that thirty-five percent had lung abnormalities. The study also indicated that among ex-cobbers seeking treatment at Batlharos Hospital, twelve of fifty-four women suffered mesothelioma, normally an extremely rare disease. Doctors at Batlharos Hospital frequently diagnosed mesothelioma, including a high incidence among people who had never worked in the mines but were exposed to dangerous levels of asbestos in their daily lives.[138] Ironically and tragically, given the terrible health repercussions of asbestos, at this time men preferred it because the process was safer than gold mining. Mr. Seamecho explained: "You die from T. B. only, but the stones don't fall."[139] Of course,

Figure 6-7 An unreclaimed asbestos mine above the Ncweng primary school, 1998. Children play on the school grounds just below an unreclaimed crocidolite mining site. Tributary miners worked the hills above the village and sold asbestos to trading stores. The government covered this mine with earth and vegetation in late 2001. (Photograph courtesy of Peter Heywood.)

asbestos inhalation does not cause tuberculosis. However, tuberculosis is also rife in this area, and ARDs are often assumed to be tuberculosis. It has been burdensome for survivors to prove that ARDs, rather than tuberculosis, were the cause of death, and therefore, many people have received no compensation.[140]

Men and women who chose to work in asbestos or manganese did so because they valued their lives at home. Working close to home allowed them to come home on weekends, stay in closer contact with their families, and participate in herding and cultivation. Not all reserves had asbestos deposits, but their inhabitants also sought out labor near home. After 1937, people in Vlakfontein found nearby employment at the cheese factory in Reivilo.[141] Unfortunately, one favored job died out after the 1950s; the increasing mechanization of agriculture reduced the need for seasonal harvesters in the Transvaal, with a dramatic drop in the 1970s.[142] By the 1960s, however, Kuruman women had taken up cash-paying seasonal work as grape and cotton harvesters on farms on the central Orange River.[143]

Exploiting its thrice-blessed bedrock (asbestos, manganese, and iron), the Kuruman economy had a modest mining boom from the 1950s to the 1970s. It hardly needs mentioning that black workers benefited less than white workers from economic growth. Black workers today testify that they needed cash and accepted what they could get.[144] Asked if asbestos wages were fair, a man recalled that working conditions were difficult and that the mining carts (coco-pans) he pushed up a track were extremely heavy, but

> Even if life was difficult for you everything you were getting was fair because of the struggles of how they were living at home . . . because of the children at home and how they were living . . . . They didn't have enough food to eat or clothes to wear, so they were forced to live under those hard circumstances. Even now I'm still having pains from those cocopans.[145]

The proximate mines did not bring prosperity to the reserves. Indeed, hunger and disease dominate Cosmos Desmond's description of Kuruman reserves in 1969.[146] Thereafter, as the dangers of asbestos became known, demand for crocidolite dropped and this source of cash failed. Production fell from the 1977 high of 200,966 metric tons to 7,320 tons in 1987.[147] By 1997, the last of the mines had closed, and many people regretted the loss of jobs in the asbestos industry, even though they were often deadly.

"IF WE WERE ALL EQUAL, THERE WOULD BE NO COOPERATION"

Clearly, race determined how people related to the environment and economy. The importance of race in twentieth-century South Africa, however, should not obscure the enduring importance of class and gender relations within African societies. Through the failure of extensive subsistence production, the agro-pastoral hierarchy had weakened at the extremes. Chiefs had lost their political and economic power, but unequal distribution of wealth continued: it was esti-mated in 1903 that "approximately seven-eighths of the stock is owned by half the residents."[148] Chiefs and headmen continued to have power to distribute land, and there were several disputes on reserves between 1908 and 1911.[149] The conflicts were between loyalist refugees from the Langeberg Reserve and longer term residents, between a headman and his sub-headman, and between family members or neighbors with opposing claims over land. Government documents record that the *kgotla* could be active in such disputes.[150] However, it is also evident from documents about Ga-Mopedi and Ga-Tlhose that land distribution was unequal and that headmen and their favorites were in the posi-tion to claim the best land.[151] Men in Ga-Mopedi told me that an earlier chief had confiscated land for his son and had given some people fields that were too far away to use.[152] Inspector of Native Reserves H. J. Purchase recorded the 1908 complaint of some people in Batlharos about Mmusi, their headman. "The burden of their cry was that they were as cattle, the Government was their master and Mmusi the lion and that their master instead of driving the lion away was driving the cattle into the jaws of the lion."[153] In 1938, an official observed unequal distribution of land and believed it resulted from when fields were allocated more than fifty years earlier. He suggested re-allotting and allocating the land.[154] There is no record that this occurred.

At the other extreme of the social scale, the classes of *balala* and *batlhanka* dissolved because of colonial law, the diminished need for client labor, and the end of full-time foraging. As in earlier times, wild foods supplemented everyone's diet,[157] but foraging off the reserves was inappropriate to the land holding and legal systems of the Cape Province. In 1913, a group of stock-thieving "bushmen" were apprehended on white-owned farms in the Langeberg Mountains, and two were killed. This was the last mention of bushmen in Kuruman.[155] By the twentieth century, the Vaalpense were increasingly perceived as living in the Kalahari, where foraging was more viable.[156] As the herding client and foraging classes disappeared, the Tswana term *balala* became more of an epithet for bad character.[158] The government ethnologist reported that by 1960 people no longer were obliged to work in the chief's fields.[159] Although the failure of extensive subsistence production leveled the richest and poorest strata to the middle levels, neighbors continued to work cooperatively in farming. It is in these cooperative relationships between households that reciprocity endured, and it remained an unequal reciprocity.[160]

Cattle keeping was the aspect of production that suffered the most in the failure of extensive subsistence. Contemporary informants in the 1990s did not recall the lending of stock in *mafisa* relationships.[161] Not only were there fewer cattle, but when so many men were occupied in wage labor, the advantages of an economy of scale became apparent.

> Even if you look after [a small herd], you will starve to death. You've got to leave it and go to work. By the minute you come back, some of it has disappeared, some of it has died, because of lack of anyone to look after them. But if you have about twenty, then it is very, very profitable and you can make a living out of it and they look after it more properly and you know, they increase, so you realize that in the country, really, the rich get richer and the poor get poorer.[162]

Under these conditions, dividing a herd between clients no longer made sense.

However, with regard to cultivation, separate households still worked the land cooperatively. The system was called *thusana*, "helping each other," or more frequently *letsema*, literally, "harvest," since working together was most common during the harvest season. My informants universally asserted that until at least the 1950s, these noncapitalist arrangements were common among all types of households. Men participated in *letsema* relationships chiefly during plowing, which remained their responsibility, while women worked together throughout the season. *Letsema* among men revolved around access to draft animals, while women shared human labor. People who spoke with me recalled that in their youth reciprocal arrangements, more than cash, circulated draft animals and equipment between richer, poorer, and those in between.[163] A male informant recalled: "If you had a lot of cattle for pulling the plow and for working the fields, people definitely come and help you, so when you are finished plowing your lands, they can take the same stock to go and plow theirs."[164] Another man also described reciprocal labor in masculine terms:

> Now, *letsema*, all that it entails is that you having no cattle or oxen, having nothing but a piece of land, you'd go and help when he is working on his land and we together would go and work on his land. When all the other people who have the means have done their fields, then they think of you, because you have been going around helping them and then they go and do your land without any charge.[165]

Cooperative work provided those without draft animals a means to plow, but there were still disadvantages for the borrowers.[166] As the grandson of a richer man recalled:

> If people had no stock at all, they would come and help my grandfather plow and then in kind, he would lend them his stock to go and plow for them. But you see, as you can guess, his lands would be plowed in good season, when the rain has fallen, when there is plenty of time for the crops to grow. But these people who came to hire or to help him, their lands are going to grow later and there will be so many of them, that they can't plow a lot of land, you see, and not at the opportune time.... Not that he is cheating them, but being the master, they help him first and only when they are finished, they go to their places. The plowing was only done when there had been rain. As soon as the soil dries up, you stop plowing. You wait for rain to come and if it doesn't come in good time, then you wait and wait and eventually you may end up having never plowed.[167]

Mr. Seamecho remembered a household that had no access to oxen and was determined to plow before the season was too late: "When I was a young boy I saw a man, a hefty man, he had nothing, no cattle or what. His wife handled the small plow and he pulled it. Nobody could lend him oxen, because everybody was busy. Now, he started himself. The climate was going."[168]

143

Apart from plowing, women were responsible for most of the tasks of cultivation. Their tasks included sowing, weeding, chasing birds away, and harvesting, and they performed these much as they had before men and plows became involved in cultivation.[169] The devotion of male energies to outside labor placed the burden of supplementary production on women, although some women worked in asbestos mining and away from the reserves. At times when it was difficult to find men to plow through reciprocal channels, women paid cash to neighboring men.[170] Perhaps because local production was only one of many sources of subsistence, there is little evidence for gendered conflict over environmental resources.[171] In fact, the blurring of gender duties begun by the introduction of the plow continued.[172] The restrictions on female contact with stock eased: girls herded animals, at least sheep and goats, and cattle if there were no boys to do so.[173] Women even plowed and milked cattle when men were scarce.[174] People agreed that gender had become less of a determinant for agricultural and domestic work. "The roles have now sort of merged."[175] Men and women both have gardens now, but usually men do the plowing and only exceptional women raise stock.

For women's production, the most important relationships continued to be those they made with each other. As in earlier times, they still worked in each other's fields and those who had land and those without continued to cooperate.[176] Women's cooperative work was different than that of men. In plowing, access to draft animals and equipment was the chief constraint on production, while in weeding and harvesting, human labor was the greatest issue. Therefore, reciprocal obligations demanded more of women's energy than among men. In all stages of cultivation, the field owners might have been expected to cook food for their helpers.[177] Some informants do not recall field owners working in each other's fields, and they state that all the helpers were landless people who received a portion of the harvest for their help.[178] Others agreed that field owners worked together, but they only shared labor and not their harvests.[179] The advantage of sharing labor with other field owners was that the harvest stayed in the household, but field owners had less motivation to work in other people's fields than landless people did.

> Formerly, anybody could call them to *letsema* – you just call them to do their work for you. And it was done, there was no payment for it, because tomorrow the others would be calling you to go and work for him. But that was a one day sort of thing, or two days at most, you had *letsema*, but if you get somebody to work for you continuously, then you've got to pay him, in kind.[180]

Having too many helpers, therefore, could be expensive. One woman recalled that she asked only two people to help in her riverbed garden, because if more came, there would not be enough food. However, since her dry fields were bigger, she needed more helpers during years when it was rainy enough to plow them.[181] Field owners established relationships with a few families who would help them year after year.[182]

A man born in 1901 recalled the dynamic:

NJ: I would like to ask you about *letsema*. . . . How did it work? . . . Did they help each other to plow?

MK: Yes, when they are going to plow, they are going to each other to help. . . . People were not equal. There were those who had cattle and those who did not. . . .

NJ: Can you explain more how poor people became poor and rich people became rich?

MK: It was God who made people unequal. If we were all equal there would be no cooperation.

NJ: Can you explain that?

MK: If I ask help from you, you would not help me because we are both rich and there would be no cooperation.[183]

Other informants, particularly those descended from successful farmers, were more moralistic about how people became rich or poor, portraying the poor as wastrels.

In my interviews, people consistently explained that these relationships were not usually based on cash. Elders recall that people without fields might receive milk, meat, or grain without the obligation of work.[184] The chief and *kgotla* also distributed food to poor people.[185] Yet people might be less willing to share with those who had not made themselves useful during harvest. An old man's recollection of "Damara" refugees who came to Kuruman after the 1906 rebellion in Namibia says much about his work ethic. He recalled a conversation with people who wanted food without giving assistance in the fields:

The Damaras, they didn't like to work for themselves. They were just going in a group, going house to house. If your house is big, he is coming to beg for food and you say, "No I've got no food. I can't feed you all." They say, "Why, your house is big, you've got lands to plow. Why do you say come and plow with me?" [So I say] "I will pay you, but I can't give you food."[186]

This man's choice of words suggests wage labor, but rather than offering them cash for their time, he was declining to grant them food without work. His sister-in-law supported the common testimony that not all payment was with cash. "[People without land] went begging. It was a sort of begging. . . . They go

145

to help, so the owner of the plot will help them with food."[187] People from land-less families describe their parents working hard, helping their neighbors, and receiving food for their assistance.[188] The cooperative effort, and therefore cultivation itself, depended on the inequality that had been present in agro-pastoral society. It does not diminish our recognition of the dominance of capitalism to say it was a lesser influence on the ways people worked together.

As dependence on cash increased, the social organization of food production became anachronistic, contributing to its decline after the mid-twentieth century. Poorer people may have opted for wage labor rather than clientage because it paid better returns. The Comaroffs argue that Tswana values put great emphasis on building wealth, social position, and influence.[189] An official exaggerated behavior, but conveyed core values when he reported: "There is no cooperation. They won't work for another man."[190] This decision not to participate in unequal reciprocal relations of cultivation may lie at the heart of the transformation toward a greater dependence on cash wages and may be a major cause of the decline of supplementary food production that became evident after the mid-twentieth century. As people became more equal, or equally impoverished of the cash they needed, they cooperated less and thus produced less food. In Botswana in the 1970s, Kgalagadi chose to work in mines as an escape from the domination by the Kwena.[191] The same ambition motivated poorer residents, some women but especially men, of the Kuruman reserves. As a headman explained with conspicuous frustration:

> They were loving each other during that time. It's not like today, if I have got a tractor, I can't help the other one. He comes to me to ask for help, you have to pay me. If I say let's work together, helping me plowing, I will help you also, he doesn't want. He thinks I try to make him a servant. People today are all high-minded.[192]

Today, *letsema* practices are a thing of the past. Cooperative cultivation (apart from among family members) is rare, and selling produce for cash is more common.[193] People consistently connect the decline of *letsema* with the mines, most specifically the new mines that opened in Kuruman after the 1950s.[194] Another economic change at this time was that mechanization began to reduce employment at the Transvaal harvest, and so the bundle of activities that provided subsistence began to fray just as new jobs more convenient to home offered cash.[195] For women, the opportunity to earn cash as asbestos cobbers became more attractive than growing crops.[196] As cash became more available, working for food in your own or someone else's field became far less attractive: "In the olden days if a person comes to help you, he didn't expect any payment from your pocket. Now because most of the people [plot holders] don't have money that's why most of them are reluctant to come and help you with plowing."[197] People in Ga-Diboye stated that *balala* disappeared as late as the 1970s when they demanded cash for their work.[198] Both men and women could earn cash, and as the amount of cash within households increased, even those who did not go out to work were less motivated to participate in *letsema*. Another development in the 1950s that may have impeded *letsema* is Betterment. Chris de Wet's research in the Ciskei shows that moving people from small clusters to platted villages had the potential to interfere with cooperative labor.[199] People told us that Betterment undermined cooperation by restricting cultivation.[200] Also, like the headman quoted above, some believed that people had cooperated simply because they "loved" each other more than people today do.[201]

A capitalist transformation in the Kuruman reserves did occur, but its completion was delayed until the mid-twentieth century brought an expansion of local opportunities to earn cash. One eventual result of the transformation was the virtual extinction of supplementary production based on reciprocity as field owners and client laborers alike invested their efforts in earning cash elsewhere. As their interest dwindled, so did cultivation. Today, the great majority of fields in river valleys lie fallow year after year, and elders regret that few farm as they used to.

However, the twentieth-century history of people interacting with their environment cannot be adequately explained through economic and biophysical factors alone. The intervention of the racial state into where blacks lived and what they did there made it impossible for many to continue the farming they could do. The state disrupted relations between blacks and their environment in two ways. Through the implementation of segregation, it directly reduced access to land and water. Additionally, conservation policies limited how people could use the land and water they retained. It also established commercial production among a very few. This was not the peasant production of nineteenth-century South Africa, but a new form that developed through the efforts of the segregationist state. The following two chapters discuss the impact of the state in the environmental history of Kuruman. Chapter 7 considers how segregating water and land affected people's relations with the environment. Chapter 8 explains the impact of segregationist conservation policy.

7

Apportioning Water, Dividing Land: Segregation, 1910–1977

Into this area where people are quite literally dying of starvation, and where T.B., scurvy and all forms of malnutrition are rife, thousands more people have been and still are to be moved for the sake of tidying up the map.[1]

IN 1910, a new country, the Union of South Africa, was created with four provinces: the former British colonies of the Cape and Natal and the former Boer republics of the Orange Free State and South African Republic. An inchoate principle of segregation underlay Union governance at the beginning, and over the next four decades it developed into more sharply defined and extreme policies. After the formation of the Union, successive generations of segregationist policy increasingly determined how people related to each other, the state, the economy, and the environment, although the last point is not often recognized. The environmental dynamic is evident in many aspects of the history of racial segregation. Because segregated spaces are lived-in environments where certain uses are possible but others are difficult, segregationists considered the quality of the environment and its potential uses when they allocated territory between races. Not just the quality of the environment, but existing uses came into consideration, and the fact that African land use was extensive made confiscation of choice lands and water supplies easier. Moreover, the outcome of segregation was environmental. Removals and resettlements forced people to adapt to different environments, and these adjustments exacted a high price from the victims. In Kuruman, environmental segregation involved the state taking from blacks well-watered parcels and sources of water and granting them to white people. The effects on the black people of Kuruman were a shift of the population toward the Kalahari, a depletion of the water supplies in the largest remaining reserves, and a further weakening of food production. The history of segregation in Kuruman starkly exposes the power behind the ways people of different categories related to the environment. In fact, these relations were articulated through violence. It also illustrates how environmental considerations greatly enrich existing historical understandings.

ENVIRONMENTAL RIGHTS OF TRIBAL SUBJECTS

Environmental segregation was predicated upon the fact that Africans related to the state as tribal subjects. Mamdani argues that the tribal definition of Africans resulted from the challenges of governing colonial possessions. Thus, colonial governments relegated Africans to a "world of the customary from which there was no escape."[2] Customary law and Indirect Rule bonded rural Africans in particular relations with the state, which were distinct from those of European colonizers or African urban elites. Two aspects of distorted tribal custom shaped the process of forced removals: communal land tenure and Indirect Rule. Communal tenure allowed the state to deal bluntly with communities rather than with individuals who held rights to negotiate for themselves. Thus, the eviction of thousands of people was inestimably easier than it would have been with individual tenure, for their collective fate could be determined by one process culminating in one decision. Communal tenure also buffered rural society from market forces and led the state to use physical force. Indirect Rule made Africans ineligible for civil rights and consigned them to an authoritarian government with little community accountability.

Thus, in order to understand environmental segregation in Kuruman, it is necessary to consider the development of territorial, administrative, and political segregation in the Union and its variations in the Cape Province.[3] The 1910 agreement that created the Union of South Africa stipulated a race-based franchise for three provinces. It restricted the Cape system of property-based franchise for Africans and rule of whites and blacks through magistrates to that province alone. Thus, its political and administrative system became an exception in a country moving toward increasing segregation and Indirect Rule. The segregationist impulse became evident already in 1913 when the Natives Land Act established "scheduled" areas where blacks could legally own land. Its strictures against land purchases adversely affected cultivation by blacks in many parts of South Africa, although not in Kuruman. Poverty had allowed very few blacks in Kuruman to acquire land – in 1911 blacks owned only four farms in the entire district.[4] As it was, in 1917 the ban on land purchase became a moot point when a court ruled that the Natives Land Act inappropriately interfered with franchise rights and its provisions were set aside in the Cape Province.[5] Because political rights in the Cape Province were acquired through land ownership, abolishing them was necessary to the process of territorial segregation. Ensuing years involved protracted negotiations and struggle between white politicians, their constituencies, the black elite, and different arms of the bureaucracy over the extent of segregation and the division of land.[6]

Administrative segregation grew with the passage of the Native Administration Act of 1927 that repudiated the paternalist consultative tradition and made customary law and government proclamations the basis for rule over Africans. It proclaimed the governor-general to be "Supreme Chief of all Natives" (in the Transvaal, Natal, and Orange Free State, but not the Cape Province) and gave him the right to rule Africans by decree. It put Africans under the jurisdiction of the Department of Native Affairs rather than under the Department of Justice. It did not establish chiefs as the lynchpin of governance over Africans, but it segregated the justice system by inaugurating customary law as the legal code for Africans and empowered African courts judged by chiefs and headmen to have jurisdiction over minor matters.[7] However, the Cape property-based franchise continued to offer an inconsistent possibility for black participation in the state. In 1936, two pieces of legislation abolished this exception. First, the Representation of Natives Act abolished the nonracial property-based franchise. With land ownership thus unlinked from the right to vote, the Native Trust and Land Act, passed at the same time, banned Africans' right to purchase private land. In compensation for the abolition of the franchise, the Trust and Land Act committed the state to increasing the area allocated to blacks from seven to thirteen percent.* [8] The Trust and Land Act also vested ownership of African land in the South African Native Trust (SANT), which became the representative of the state in matters of land and how black people used it. While the end of the franchise and private land ownership had little effect in Kuruman, where few black people owned land and voted, the *quid pro quo* for the loss of these rights transformed this region. To compensate for lost voting rights, the act mandated that the government purchase land for black use in "released" areas, and a disproportionate amount of this land was in Kuruman. The purchase of the released areas weakened blacks' hold on river valley reserves. In the coming decades, segregation would become more extreme, but these racially based constrictions of rights in the 1920s and 1930s were sufficient to give local whites an advantage over blacks in a water rights struggle and to begin the process of forced removals.

---

* This land was purchased slowly. By 1960, the trust had procured 4,107,369 hectares, with 2,102,098 hectares of released areas left unpurchased.

THE WHITES OF THE EYE

In the decade after 1910, a particular conjunction of race and space created an anomalous situation in the upper Kuruman Valley; there, people achieved a more intensive use of water through private ownership and modern engineering, but because of racial segregation, the only people who could achieve this were white. Overwhelmingly, the Kuruman Eye was the most valuable resource in the area, and, therefore, the Land Settlement of 1886 had placed a town site at the Eye. Eventually, as whites settled there, they took advantage of being racially privileged and living at the source of the largest river in a dry area. On the edge of the Kalahari, the Kuruman Eye is an impressive sight, but its flow is actually a trickle in a vast dry landscape. Unfortunately for blacks who lived downstream in the Lower Kuruman Native Reserve, as whites developed water and land upstream, they found themselves in a drier environment and were less able to practice any sort of irrigation at all. The story of how the whites of the Eye left blacks high and dry merits interrupting the narrative of the Kuruman region in general to focus on the upper river valley.

The BBLC recognized LMS water rights to the Kuruman Eye, but had reserved it and 27,677 surrounding hectares as the Kuruman Crown Reserve, awaiting future disposal by the state. It suggested that the government construct irrigation works on the Crown Reserve below the LMS property at Seodin and that it rent or sell plots to farmers of all races. However, the government of British Bechuanaland did not pursue this plan, acceding to LMS objections that the project would displace current residents.[9] As discussed in Chapter 4, people living on the Kuruman Crown Reserve had insecure rights over land. The 1895 Matthews Commission had allowed those in residence before imperial annexation to remain as rent payers, but the ultimate disposal of the area remained in question. In 1898, the Kuruman Crown Reserve was mapped, and possible projects were analyzed.[10] Still, because of ambivalence about subsidizing agriculture for poor whites, officials delayed action. The magistrate explained in 1903:

> Local conditions preclude European settlement. The market for produce is limited. Capital could not be profitably invested with the result that the only possible European . . . would be the "Poor White." . . . In a native district like this, the consequence of the introduction of that class would be deplorable. They would be surrounded by natives engaged in a similar occupation many of whom would be better off and have a higher standard of life.[11]

The Cape government surveyed thirty-one lots between the Kuruman Eye and the LMS estate; however, they remained undeveloped and available for rent on a temporary basis, with no racial qualifications.[12] A 1911 Cape Provincial commission in the person of M. C. Vos upheld the rights of residents on the Kuruman Crown Reserve.[13]

Nonracialism and ambivalence about aiding poor whites were incompatible with segregationism, and they did not survive long after the establishment of the Union.[14] The Private Locations Act of the Cape Colony (Number 32 of 1909) increased taxation and forced the mission to evict its tenants in 1910.[15] In 1913, drastic changes resulted from the creation of a Kuruman village management board with jurisdiction over 6,380 hectares on the Kuruman Crown Reserve south of the LMS. In 1916, Kuruman became a municipality with a council and mayor,[16] and this institution gave local whites a mechanism for pursuing their interests in the Crown Reserve.

The era of irrigation in the service of evangelization finally ended in 1917, when the municipality paid £9,500 for most of the LMS estate, although the society retained ownership of the church and other buildings on seventeen hectares.[17] The municipality demolished Moffat's original dam and constructed new irrigation works just below the Kuruman Eye. The first of the 130-plus lots in the municipal irrigation project went on the market in 1918.[18] Segregation of the town of Kuruman accompanied this development, and in 1918 the municipality evicted Gasegonyane, the Tswana and Coloured community at the Eye, on the grounds of inadequate toilet facilities, compensating them with £400.[19] With the center of town secured as white territory, the remaining Crown Reserve became the locus of a struggle revolving around blacks having use of it, whites wanting it, and the Union government waffling over who should have it.

The Kuruman Crown Reserve had an ambiguous status. It had many black residents, including the community of Seodin just below the pared-down mission. The Lands Department accommodated the municipality by selling it 9,105 hectares of the Crown Reserve including Seodin in 1920. When the municipality informed residents that they must accept compensation and leave, the Seodin community, aware of its rights under the 1895 Matthews and 1911 Vos rulings, refused. The municipality sued in the Supreme Court of Griqualand West in Kimberley. The LMS missionary A. E. Jennings organized a vigorous defense, and Vos, who had briefly been minister of native affairs in 1919,[20] returned to mediate a settlement in 1921. Vos had little sympathy for the municipality, saying its actions constituted "A Municipal Naboth's Vineyard, without a doubt."* [21] Canceling the sale, he allowed the municipality only 2,570 hectares of rangeland east and west of the purchased LMS estate. Blacks at Seodin and

---

* See I Kings 21: 1–2 for the story of the Israelite King Ahab arranging for Naboth's death, so he could inherit his vineyard.

along the river valley were allowed to stay. He also put the Kuruman Crown Reserve under the administration of the NAD, although the territory did not officially become a native reserve.* [22]

SEGREGATION OF THE FLOWING EYE

As land allocation was settled, the struggle over the subdivision of the environment had just begun. Residents of the Kuruman Crown Reserve had retained their rights to land, but blacks who lived downstream could not prevent whites from moving the locus of water rights and use upstream. In Kuruman, summer is the season of rain, but it is also the season of heat and evaporation. During the summer of 1923–4, heavy water use by the municipal project caused severe shortages at Seodin.[23] Before the construction of the municipal irrigation works, there had been seasonal shortages,[24] but the Kuruman Eye had been a largely reliable source of water in the northern portion of the Crown Reserve. A 1917 surveyor's map shows furrows from Moffat's dam running over one kilometer beyond the original mission boundary. Below that were another dam, a few short furrows, and cultivated lands all along the river to the northern boundary of the Kuruman Crown Reserve.[25] (See Figures 7-1 and 7-2.) The 1918 municipal irrigation project began just below the Kuruman Eye and served more gardens than the mission furrows had. Thus, the furrows were often dry at the edge of municipal property. Galeboe, the headman of Seodin, described the problem in 1941.

> In the winter there is enough water for domestic purposes and for our stock but not enough for our wheat crop. In the summer we do not get any water and we have to get water for domestic purposes from the Mission station.† . . . Before the white people got the ground that used to belong to the Mission, the water from the eye flowed right to Maroping – a distance of ten miles from here and we had enough water then.[26]

The sale of most of the mission had transferred water rights from the LMS to the municipality.[27] This transfer ignored the fact that a century of use established a claim for black cultivators. An awareness of Seodin's legal rights may have encouraged the municipality to negotiate. In 1924, it offered to share

---

* The municipality attempted to purchase the northern portion of the reserve in 1925, and the proposed 1927 Natives Land (Amendment) Bill defined it as a white-claimed area but this bill was not passed. Despite these attempts to reverse Vos's decision, his line has remained. In 1977, it became the boundary between Bophuthatswana and "white" South Africa, and since 1994 it has divided the new North–West and Northern Cape provinces.

† The mission station he refers to was a small portion of the original estate consisting of missionary houses, the school, and the church. This is the current site of the Moffat Mission that the LMS retained after the sale of the irrigated lands to the municipality.

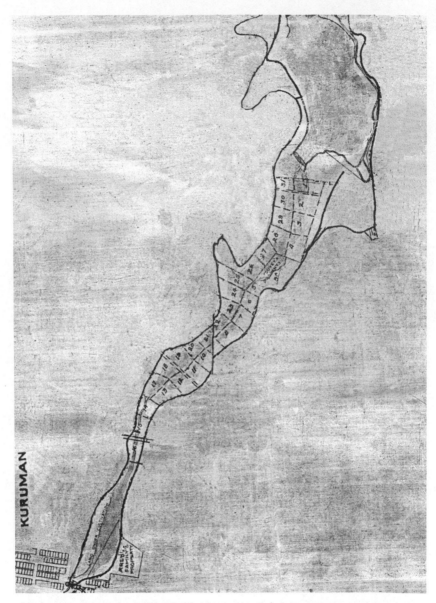

Figure 7-1 Surveyor's map of the Kuruman Eye and the upper Kuruman River Valley, 1917: This map and Figure 7-2 show the Kuruman River and existing fields along it in 1917. Note the "native village" in Figure 7-2 (Seodin on the west bank) and "land in cultivation" downstream from the mission. The dark lines in Figure 7-1 show the proposed municipal irrigation scheme that would deprive African cultivators downstream of water.

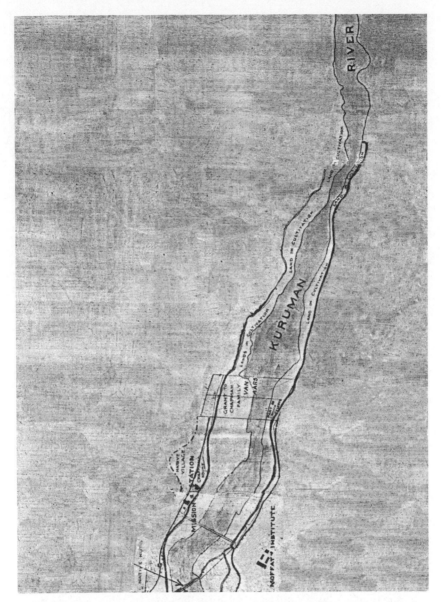

Figure 7-2 Surveyor's map of the Kuruman River Valley below the mission.

one-fifth of the water if Seodin people would share one-fifth of the costs of an improvement to prevent seepage and increase the water supply by lining the furrows with concrete.[28] Jennings objected to the scheme that "if they will pay £600 to repair other people's property, then they may be allowed to enjoy their

155

undisputed water-rights." Besides, he continued, Seodin people had "not that amount of wealth in the value of their whole live-stock."[29] They negotiated throughout the 1920s, but the water rights struggle never entered court. Government departments considered and declined to press a suit, some arguing that even if the first irrigators at Seodin had established a prior right, it was uncertain whether communal landholders could inherit water rights.[30]

The situation changed in 1939 when the northern portion of the Kuruman Crown Reserve, including Seodin, was at last designated African ground and given over to the SANT.[31] Jennings had left Kuruman in 1930, and the last LMS missionary at Kuruman, Humphrey Thompson, was not a political advocate. Recognizing that segregation was occurring on a larger scale, he was concerned about the repercussions of aggressively claiming black rights, fearing the complete removal of blacks from the upper valley. He objected to a suit over water rights and argued against a compromise of blacks claiming even one-fifth of the Kuruman Eye's output.[32]

Instead, he proposed a new solution to the struggle, neither litigation nor mediation, but a technical solution, drilling for an alternative supply of water for Seodin. The government agreed to do so. The fact that the NAD pursued this expensive solution in Seodin, where nature had provided an impressive supply of water, where downstream users had established rights, and where there was little profit to be made through cultivation, reveals the high political costs of a legal solution. Officials validated the spurious one-fifth calculus when they agreed that this was the amount due to Seodin and proposed to provide it – not from the Kuruman Eye, but through boreholes. The headman of the Seodin community objected to the abandonment of the legal claim by the LMS and the NAD:

> We get the overflow of the water from the Municipality but we do not get enough water for our lands. . . . Mr Thompson suggested to us that we should ask the Government to give us an independent supply and put down boreholes . . . but we will not be able to irrigate our lands from the boreholes and we want the Government to get us a share of the water from the "eye" to irrigate our lands. I do not remember it being said that if we got boreholes we would abandon our claim to the supply from the "eye" to avoid friction with the Europeans. We want the boreholes to ensure our domestic supplies, but we still want a share of the water from the "eye" for our lands.[33]

Despite Galeboe's objections, given the political climate, if Seodin were to receive any water it would come from engineers rather than attorneys. In 1948, a white resident was candid about the segregation of nature: "There is not enough water here for an ethical division."[34] Today people as far as Ncweng, thirty kilometers downstream, cite municipal use of water as a cause of their current hardship.[35]

Unfortunately, technology could not replace the bounty of nature. Searching for water in dolomite compartments is difficult, and it was more so in the 1940s because of the rudimentary searching techniques and because of the drought.[36] From 1941 to 1948, the NAD searched and found very little groundwater less than eight kilometers from the Kuruman Eye, sinking five failures before drilling two successful holes. Planners scaled down the projected size of the gardens from thirty to twenty-four hectares. Once pumping began, water levels in the wells dropped and the supply weakened.[37] The NAD supplemented drilling with agricultural extension, and people began to plant in straight lines, but in 1942 only one of fifty or sixty Seodin plotholders earned a living from gardening.[38] By 1959, there were only thirty-two plotholders, producing lower yields than farmers on other Kuruman reserves.[39] The technical solution was not adequate to sustain extensive or to create intensive food production.

Similarly, the investment in municipal irrigators did not create robust commercial production. From the beginning, the local produce market was small. Furthermore, lack of transport, small plot sizes, and uneven allocation of water made it possible for only a few plotholders to become commercial farmers.[40] Many plotholders made their living raising stock on the dry veld and raised the forage crop alfalfa ("lucerne" in South Africa) along the Kuruman River, but the profits from alfalfa could not have justified the cost of constructing the municipal project.

The improvement of irrigation facilities by the municipality of Kuruman illustrates some reasons for the success of white agriculture in South Africa at the time when black food production stagnated. Rather than markets, it was the state that supported and sustained white irrigation in Kuruman, awarding them land and water denied to blacks. More importantly, it enabled them alone to use it intensively. Thus, whites achieved the development that had eluded black farmers. Intensification by means of irrigation requires capital, sophisticated technology, and a central body responsible for constructing shared infrastructure and regulating water rights. These demands have caused the close historic correlation between large-scale irrigation and a strong state.[41] The extent of irrigation from the Kuruman Eye cannot compare to the huge works in ancient Asia or the modern American West, and certainly, modest irrigation such as in Kuruman has been accomplished without state intervention. However, in South Africa, the state mobilized itself to changing the racial as well as the natural landscape. The Union government developed irrigation, not on a large scale, but for a racially defined constituency, by granting land, financing development, providing expertise, allocating plots, and regulating water use. This assistance

157

permitted whites to intensify their irrigated production at the expense of black land and water rights. While earlier regimes had been ambivalent about the ability of "poor whites" to make worthwhile use of irrigated plots, by the 1920s, the Union government was investing in them and promoting their advancement relative to black cultivators.[42]

EXTENSIVE AGRICULTURE MEETS
AGRICULTURAL EXTENSION

While white people were intensifying cultivation in the upper Kuruman Valley, the status of the black area downstream from the Kuruman Crown Reserve came into question. In 1924, the magistrate proposed removing the residents of the Lower Kuruman Reserve and turning the land over to white settlers. In exchange, he suggested that reserve occupants be given dry lands suitable for grazing. He justified his proposal with the familiar allegation of underutilization on the reserves: "The natives hardly do any cultivation . . . notwithstanding the fact that they are in possession of the best agricultural land in the district."[43] The Union government did not seriously entertain this proposal. The Native Affairs Commission (NAC) turned it down with a lecture on the history of intensification.

> These considerations are not new nor are they only applicable to the Kuruman district and they have on innumerable occasions been urged in many other parts of the Union. While, superficially, they may appear attractive there are other aspects which should and must be taken into account. It is true that the Bechuanaland Native (as his brother in other parts) is a pastoralist rather than an agriculturist, a characteristic largely the result of past influences and environment but which it cannot be assumed will remain invariable in Bechuanaland. There have been brought into play forces such, for example, as the increase of population, the need for money to obtain the necessary means of existence, and education which have compelled Natives in other parts of the Union to enlarge their agricultural activities. Such forces, it is thought have not or at least to a very small extent, been felt by Natives in British Bechuanaland.

Representing the paternalist ethic, the NAC restated the old hope for intensification, asserting that government aid could improve irrigation.

> Non-beneficial occupation is not a "crime" common only to natives, and until such a crime is prosecuted with vigour in the case of every community it seems hardly defensible to eject the native for committing such a "crime" and replace him by the European agriculturist who is, and has been since

Union, supported by Government facilities debarred to natives. The large expenditure of public money spent directly upon Europeans' agricultural development compares most unfavourably with the meagre expenditure upon native agricultural needs.... Steps should be taken, not only in the Kuruman Lower Reserve, but in all native areas to urge, to teach and to encourage natives to make the most of the agricultural possibilities and to restrict their pastoral pursuits by adopting "quality" instead of "quantity" where their stock is concerned.[44]

As early as 1904, the Tswana writer Sol Plaatje urged the government to promote more intensive agriculture through investment in water supplies and extension services.[45] The first director of native agriculture, R. W. Thornton, was appointed in 1929,[46] but in the early years of the Union, land and labor hunger among whites worked against investment in food production on reserves. In the face of such pressure, it was difficult for paternalist and assimilationist arguments to establish extension service to Africans. It took the major economic and environmental crisis of the 1930s, which was large enough to raise fears about a rural collapse, to promote investment in Kuruman. The Native Economic Commission (NEC) of 1930–2 expressed concern about this possibility. In its tour of reserves around the country, the NEC observed drastic consequences of the Great Depression. It issued a report in 1932 describing low production and methods it characterized as unsound. Most importantly, it warned that bad farming could create a great migration of the black population from reserves to cities, which by definition were white-claimed areas. When Thornton warned of a "colossal poor black problem," he constructed a new motivation to invest in the intensification of African agriculture.[47]

During the 1931–2 food shortage, the state issued emergency rations. In 1932, Thornton visited Kuruman and recommended the state take action to ensure more regular food production.[48] Government water engineers had also been inspecting the reserves and assessing the potential for improved irrigation. On these recommendations, in 1933–4 the NAD constructed professionally engineered projects in Maropeng, Bothetheletsa, Manyeding, Konong, Batlharos, and Vlakfontein/Kagung. The engineers measured water flow, calculated how much land could be serviced, laid out surrounding fields according to their elevation and slope, and built concrete furrows to eliminate seepage. A favorable 1937 report claimed that the projects delivered water to 469 hectares of land. Plots measured from one-quarter morgen to one morgen,* and each project employed a black agricultural demonstrator.[49]

---

* A morgen is a Cape Dutch unit of area equaling 0.8565 hectares.

159

But yields on these irrigated plots did not compare with those on white farmers' lands or on plots farmed by agricultural demonstrators. Presumably, white farmers and the demonstrators were using more fertilizer and weeding more thoroughly, while constructing irrigation works did not create sufficient conditions for black households to practice these intensive techniques:

> In not a single instance has full advantage been taken of these schemes, simply because the natives are not capable of making full use of irrigable ground. Possibly when they become better nourished they will be able to bestir themselves out of the mental torpor into which they have sunk. To quote an instance, in the Manyeding location we saw the canal flowing brim-full but practically no use is made of the water, which is allowed to flow on the veld. . . . Last year the natives at Manyeding Location harvested about 10 bags of wheat and under 100 bags of maize off 60 morgen. Mr. Wessels, who has the adjoining farm, Magapere, on 10 morgen reaped 300 bags of wheat, 180 bags of potatoes and 155 bags of mealies.[50]

By 1939, the reported area under irrigation had dropped to 197 hectares.[51] In 1940, one NAD agriculture official contrasted the success of agricultural demonstrators and reserve householders: "The demonstrators succeeded to obtain an average yield of 5 bags of maize per acre while on the neighbouring plots, worked according to Native methods the yield averaged 2 bags per acre. The Natives begin to realize the necessity to work the plots properly and in this connection there is great improvement."[52]

Intensification did not happen because the forces that operated against it in earlier decades were still strong. These forces included a lack of capital for fertilizer necessary on the poor soil, a shortage of labor, and insecure tenure. Government extension policy also contributed to the failure by directing itself toward cultivation for subsistence. The official expectation was that irrigation would increase the food supply, diet, health, and, therefore, the energy and productivity of the population. So, the state promoted vegetable growing on the projects, despite the fact that "they say it pays them better to grow tobacco . . . [and] the people do not appear to like eating anything but cabbage."[53] Read today, officials' dedication to growing vegetables is dogged but misguided:

> The natives grew the vegetables for a season but would not eat them. When they found there was little demand for vegetables they refused to grow them again and put in tobacco for which they found a ready market. This little incident is significant of their lack of appreciation of anything done for the ultimate benefit for themselves and their families.[54]

160

In contrast, tobacco was bartered with people on white farms and in more arid reserves. As in the 1820s, growing tobacco and exchanging it for stock was a way to transform perishable harvests into durable wealth.[55] Even if cultivation was less productive than agricultural officials would have liked, irrigation contributed to the supplementary subsistence of Kuruman people. People in Batlharos told us that the community involved itself in maintaining the irrigation project and that the headman controlled water allocation.[56] The tobacco and fruit trades were very important to household budgets, and cultivators grew some grain as well.

A 1944 report on natural water sources on reserves restated the theme of underutilization and misuse and proposed further development of springs, "gems of the desert," for irrigation and as a clean water supply for people and stock.[57] In 1951, a committee investigating irrigation projects in Kuruman presented another bleak assessment, that irrigators had inadequate supervision and thus farmed as they always had. Posing the familiar contrast between proper irrigation and "neglect," it emphasized lost opportunities: "It is extremely regrettable that the great improvement presented by the irrigation schemes to the natives in this arid region finds itself in a neglected condition."[58] In this last delivery of the old paternalist sermon that Africans should convert to intensive cultivation, the committee kept the faith that the state could induce the change.

As in earlier decades, officials believed extensive agriculture was a cause rather than a symptom of poverty. In many ways, this discussion about the cause (laziness) and the consequence (poverty) of extensive cultivation was a reprise of white response to African cultivation during the trauma at the turn of the twentieth century. In the eyes of white observers, the neglect by Africans of irrigable resources had always been a failing. Missionaries believed it had moral consequences and paternalist administrators fretted over economic consequences, but the segregationist state would differ from its predecessors by punishing the failing. As segregation intensified, the missionary/paternalist agenda of intensifying production receded. As the Apartheid state began practicing forced removals and implementing Betterment, the contradiction between segregation and intensification in the river valleys was becoming clear. A 1952 memo states: "It cannot be said that maintaining such small irrigation schemes fits with planning rural villages on Trust lands, where superfluous natives will be settled."[59] The magistrate's 1924 argument for removing Africans from river valleys and resettling them on the dry plateau, cited at the beginning of this section, was gaining acceptance. In the Apartheid period, government interventions into relations between blacks and the environment were overwhelmingly directed toward promoting pastoralism and achieving greater segregation. Extensive cultivation bore the cost, and several river valley reserves were the casualties.

ESCHEWING THE TRUST

The Native Trust and Land Act mandated that the Union government purchase 6,209,625 hectares of land to be added to African areas, including 1,384,104 hectares in the Cape Province. In Kuruman, the trust initially proposed acquiring 399,384 hectares. Thus, an astonishing forty-three percent of the released areas in the Cape and six percent of those in the country were in Kuruman, where the 1936 census counted only three-tenths of a percent of the total black population.[60] The fact that the NAD sought so much land in Kuruman is curious, to say the least. Even the NAC, which held hearings on the issue in 1937, expressed puzzlement over the reason, and we can only speculate about the motivation. Perhaps the trust sought so much land in Kuruman because it was cheaper in the thornveld than in areas with more precipitation and more overcrowding. Alternately, the motivation might have been to relieve unsuccessful white farmers in Kuruman of financial hardship, but, if so, the unintended consequence of releasing their farms for purchase for black occupation was to reduce the market value of the land. Burdened by the possibility of a SANT purchase, white farmers in released areas petitioned that their land be bought immediately.

In 1938, the NAC made the obvious recommendation to reduce the released area in Kuruman and to use the funds to purchase more land in the eastern Cape, where the need was greater.[61] In Kuruman between 1939 and 1941, the SANT purchased ninety-three properties comprising 104,493 hectares.[62] Thereafter, land purchases proceeded at a slower rate, and by 1963 the trust had acquired 124,676 hectares, supplementing 267,776 hectares in reserves, crown land, and the "horseshoe block" farms.[63] By 1964, the countrywide total acquisition of released areas had been 4,469,992 hectares, with 641,562 hectares in the Cape. Thus, with approximately three percent of all SANT land purchases in the country and nineteen percent of those in the Cape, Kuruman remained overrepresented in released areas.[64] Most of the purchased farms lay on the Ghaap Plateau in the northeast portion of the district and linked the Lower Kuruman, Manyeding, and Bothetheletsa Reserves. These SANT lands ultimately provided the space to resettle communities from reserves in the southeastern part of the district and from reserves in neighboring districts, enabling the shift of the black population of Kuruman toward the Kalahari.

Although people on Kuruman reserves had petitioned for more land, and their herds were growing, they failed to take advantage of the new territory available to them. In 1941, only twenty families lived on the 104,493 hectares purchased by the trust.[65] In fact, so few settled on the SANT lands that in the early 1940s the NAD offered to subsidize settlement by people from overcrowded areas in the Ciskei, but the government-sponsored delegation that visited Kuruman gave it an unenthusiastic recommendation and only two or three families applied.[66] An official, explaining the reluctance of Kuruman people to move to the farms, explained: "They seem beaten by the country like all other people."[67]

There were significant disincentives for people to move from reserves to the SANT farms. The first reason was environmental, a lack of irrigable land. Also, the state mandated greater restrictions on land use on SANT lands than on reserves. A ban on dry land plowing, which did not apply to the reserves (see Chapter 8), was a major factor discouraging voluntary movement to the SANT farms. Larger scale stockowners had other reasons for hesitating: only the first twenty-five LSUs could be grazed without charge, and unlike on reserves, fees were due for larger herds. However, most households did not have twenty-five LSUs (as illustrated in Figure 6-3). Smaller scale herders would have been very reluctant to threaten the viability of their herds through sales and, therefore, would have felt little pressure to keep them in peak condition, fattened on SANT land for the market. Herd composition was also a factor in allowing people to stay on the reserves. Since browsing goats and sheep far outnumbered grazing cattle, even if river valleys were bushier than SANT lands, most stockowners would not have felt a strong impetus to seek grassier pastures. In 1927 the ratio of cattle to sheep to goats was 1:2.9:7.3. In 1946 it was 1:2.7:6.5, and in 1969 it was 1:2:4.4.[68] The continuing dominance of goats and increasing usefulness of donkeys allowed people to live in a bushy landscape. Moving from reserves to SANT farms had costs: leaving relatives, communities, schools, churches, and river valley gardens. The benefits to herding could not outweigh these costs.

Since Kuruman people were not motivated to move to trust lands, and people from other places were not motivated to move to Kuruman, the government had a problem. SANT land purchases were intended to provide space for segregation on a larger scale. In the long term, their settlement required the clearance of "black spots," small reserves in areas designated for whites only. In the meantime, the lands and their grass did not go to waste. The terrible drought of 1942 prompted the NAD to lease unused SANT farms in Kuruman, Vryburg, and Mafikeng to white stockowners, and in 1946 there were more white-owned than black-owned animals on trust farms. Kuruman SANT lands became a regular source of grazing, often at bargain rates, for white farmers until the 1960s.[69] Some white farmers lobbied to buy these farms, and NAD officials expressed concern that Africans must use or lose them.[70]

The development of segregationist policies put new pressures on inhabitants of the river valley reserves in Kuruman. The portentous developments by the 1940s were that the state had become less interested in promoting intensive land use among Africans and that the SANT had acquired a huge territory suitable for extensive pastoralism and intended for Africans. Kuruman blacks had become vulnerable to being gathered from their well-watered environments and spilled out onto the southern Kalahari. The most important step in the intensification of segregation came after the 1948 election of the National Party on the platform of Apartheid. The Afrikaner Nationalist vision was validated in 1961 when the country became the Republic of South Africa, superseding the Union of South Africa, which had been a British dominion. Around that time, segregation policy moved into its final and extreme phase, Separate Development.

REMOVALS FROM BLACK SPOTS AND WHITE FARMS, 1943–1963

Forced removals in Kuruman are a most egregious example of the segregationist state intervening into environmental relations. They show the lack of constraints on the state, which removed people without regard for their desires, well-being, or property. They also show a dramatic impact on the victims. The amount of coercion necessary to relocate people varied, but it was necessary in every case. In the cases of Smouswane, Dikgweng, and workers from white farms, more tolerable conditions after the removal alleviated the process. In other cases, such as Konong, Kagung/Vlakfontein, Ga-Tlhose, and Maremane, the threat of violence terrorized people, compensation was desultory, and assistance in their new location was inadequate. The process of removals was manifestly an environmental one. Blacks lost possession of desirable river valley parcels in exchange for particularly inhospitable environmental zones. The environmental differences between the land taken from or relegated to blacks contributed to the ongoing weakening of supplementary subsistence cultivation. Yet forced removals have a significance that goes beyond their effect on food production. By disrupting people's lives, sense of home, and relations with particular environments, the racial state both exerted and gained power over black people.

In Kuruman, forced removals were a huge undertaking that rearranged the entire map. In fact, of all the river valley environments allocated to blacks by the 1886 Land Commission, only three – the Lower Kuruman Reserve, Bothetheletsa, and Manyeding – survived the segregationist era. In Kuruman, the segregationist state abolished seven black reserves and villages on the Kuruman Crown Reserve – Smouswane, Dikgweng, Khuis, Konong, Vlakfontein/Kagung, Ga-Tlhose, and Maremane – and forcibly removed 8,500 people to SANT farms, according to official statistics, although the actual number could be twice that (see Figure 7-3 and Table 7-1). In addition, approximately 12,000 people from communities in other districts were also resettled on Kuruman trust lands.[71] Finally, thousands from white farms across the region moved to reserves.

Historians recognize that segregation predated the National Party victory in 1948, but not always that pre-Apartheid segregation also involved removals. In June 1942, forty-five families comprising 268 people left the Smouswane Reserve for a desirable SANT farm parcel, the stretch of the Matlhwaring river valley between Bothetheletsa and the eastern arm of the Lower Kuruman Reserve, called New Smouswane or Ellendale, after the farm purchased by

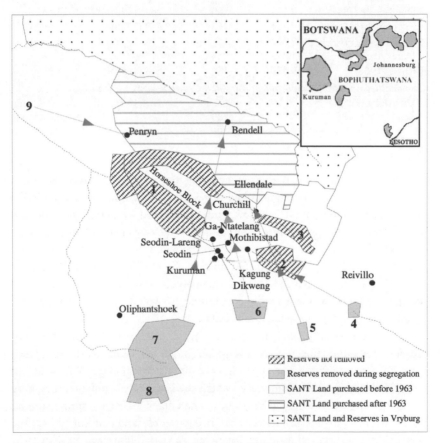

Figure 7-3 Segregation of land in Kuruman. For key to numbered reserves, see Table 7-1. Based on 1:250,000 topocadestral sheets 2622 Bray, 2722 Kuruman, 2724 Christiana, 2822 Postmasburg, 3634 Vryburg. From the Chief Directorate of Surveys and Mapping in South Africa. Reproduced under Government Printer's Copyright Authority No. 11012 dated 9 October 2001.

Table 7-1. *Segregation of Land in Kuruman*

Reserve	Size in hectares	Population in 1936	Last Recorded Population (Year)	Removed to
Reserves not removed				
1 Lower Kuruman	83,993	5,918	—	
2 Manyeding	18,733	630	—	
3 Bothetheletsa	14,582	665	—	
Removed reserves (year removed)				
4 Vlakfontein/Kagung (1966)	5,006	329	492 (1960)	New Kagung
5 Smouswane (1942)	2,770	200	268 (1942)	Ellendale
6 Konong (1959)	10,711	363	679 (1956)	Churchill
7 Ga-Tlhose (1976–7)	47,308	1,700	6,340 (1969)	Bendell
8 Maremane (1976–7)	11,383	946	with Ga-Tlhose	Bendell
9 Khuis (1968)	19,576	189	618 (1959)	Penryn
Communities removed from portion of Kuruman Crown Reserve allocated to whites				
Dikgweng (1953)			127 (1947)	Ga-Ntalelang
Seodin (1962–8)		809		Seodin-Lareng

the trust.[72] They told AnCRA researchers that they used their own donkey carts to move and that the government had provided no temporary accommodation or monetary compensation. The new land was favored with good transport and open water and people adapted well; although they wished they had received more services from the government, they believed that their life in the new territory had actually improved over that in the Old Smouswane Reserve.[73] They were fortunate that the old and new parcels were both river valleys and that the new one was not extremely remote. It would be more difficult for people experiencing subsequent removals.

Another community that experienced removal before the implementation of Apartheid was the village of Dikgweng, on the section of the Kuruman Crown Reserve allocated to the Kuruman municipality as commonage. While Seodin struggled with the municipality over water, the issue between the municipality and Dikgweng was the right to herd stock. The village was near a spring feeding a small tributary to the Kuruman River. Once its people irrigated, but by 1911 the spring had gone dry, and thereafter, many people worked in town.[74] Vos's 1911 ruling upheld the village's right to remain on the Kuruman Crown Reserve, and its residents occupied 557 hectares, about one-fifteenth of the commonage.[75] In 1941, when the commonage was proclaimed a cattle improvement area, the municipality demanded that Dikgweng's "scrub" bulls be castrated and threatened that noncompliance would result in removal of the entire village. However, Dikgweng people had already castrated their bulls and sought stud service from neighboring farmers' bulls, so the native commissioner believed the bull issue was a canard to remove blacks from the commonage.[76] Harassment of stockowners continued in 1944 when the municipality impounded horses and donkeys that ostensibly posed a traffic hazard.[77] Despite promises of pastures, schools, and compensation, the community continued to resist removal and hired a Vryburg attorney, but when they ran out of money to pay for representation, they gave up. Like the people of Smouswane, they received a relatively desirable piece of the available real estate, moving in March 1953 to Ga-Ntatelang on the portion of the Kuruman Crown Reserve given to the SANT.[78] They received monetary compensation and poles for rebuilding their houses.[79] The town, of course, still needed a labor supply, and the municipality built a coloured township, "Vaaldraai" (later "Wrenchville"), on the cleared site. This foreshadowed the 1963 removal of the Kuruman urban black township to Mothibistad on the former Kuruman Crown Reserve.[80]

Beginning around this time was a less unified exodus from white territory throughout South Africa, as many black laborers left white-owned farms. Because this decades-long migration consisted of thousands of separate movements from many points in white territory to many points in black territory, it is difficult to summarize. The process had begun by 1949, when the LMS Church at Danielskuil reported it was losing members who were moving from white farms to trust lands.[81] The SANT lands and reserves also attracted people from farms in the nearby districts of Postmasburg, Kimberley, and Hay that did not have extensive communal lands. I found many former farm laborers in Ga-Sebolao, a village in the Lower Kuruman Reserve on sandy veld five kilometers from the river west of Batlharos, who explained their experience to me. Ga-Sebolao had been a cattle post until the 1960s when the government offered lots there. The exodus from farms was not "forced" as the removals from reserves were, but increasing pressure on farms put people under economic duress and often forced them to choose to leave.[82] Several people reported they, their parents, or their grandparents left the farms because owners demanded they sell their stock. "At the farms, you can't own ten goats," one man said.[83]

The next forced removal occurred in 1959, after the implementation of the policy of Apartheid, and was on a much larger scale, entailing a greater threat of violence. The Konong Reserve was favored with many springs, including the closest rival to the Kuruman Eye.[84] It had a government-built irrigation project, an investment that suggested permanence, but its agricultural value and the extensive production of it residents brought its status into question. In 1935 and 1946, neighboring farmers tried to buy land on the edges of the reserve, and in 1948, the Kuruman Farmers Union urged removal of the reserve.[85] The matter came to the NAC in 1949, when liberal members voted against removal but the majority passed a motion to compensate Konong residents with "twice as much land with good water," which Chairman D. L. Smit called "a pious hope."[86] When the task of acquiring adequate land delayed the removal, white farmers again raised the issue, making the argument that the conditions of extensive agriculture – small population, veld burning, and herding rather than cropping – legitimized removal.[87] Of course, proper agriculture is in the eye of the beholder. Our interviews conveyed that people at Konong had grown grains, fruits, vegetables, and tobacco and did not consider their farming to be underproductive.[88] One woman recalled the 1959 removal with a story that evokes the coercion and violence of the process:

> On that day the first lorries to come were three so they stood before the other house, then they asked the people of the house, did they know that they were moving on that day? The people said they didn't know. They said when you see these lorries you are moving now, right now. Then the lorries crossed the river to the other side of the village. My house was the first one that side of the village. They found me at the fountain drawing water. They said to me, for what are you fetching water, because you are going? So I never said anything just stood like this, and the chickens remained there. I wanted to take them but they ran away, but they said they couldn't wait for me to take my chickens out of the bushes. They took my roofing into the truck, and they started chasing the people into the lorries, and they pushed the walls of my house down.[89]

Many livestock were left behind or died on the journey, but when their owners returned for possessions and animals that had been left behind, they were arrested for trespassing.[90] People arriving at SANT farms found that Betterment planners had not yet laid out streets and plots, so they organized their own. They told us that the resettlement area had no houses, little water, an unhealthy environment for stock, no schools, and no transport services and that they considered the compensation inadequate.[91] After 1960, Konong was divided into twelve farms and sold to whites.[92] As one resident remembered, "The reasons we were given for the removal was that the officials wanted to start a diamond mine . . . and a coal mine, but no mining ever took place; the land was just given to the white farmers. We believe the reasons we were given were not true."[93]

During this period one reserve managed to reverse its definition as a black spot. Actually in the Gordonia District, Khuis was the northernmost reserve administered from Kuruman. The village straddled the dry Molopo River, the border between South Africa and the Bechuanaland Protectorate. The expense of transportation and drilling for water in the Kalahari made this reserve especially troubling to the NAD.[94] In 1953, it proposed that Khuis people on the South African side of the border move to trust lands, but they refused, comparing the proffered horseshoe block to a penal colony.[95] Evidently, neither removal nor water development were worth the effort, because in 1959 government officials dropped the issue of relocation, but also halted drilling.[96]

SEPARATE DEVELOPMENT AND REMOVALS, 1963–1977

In 1960, an argument could have been made that the process of segregation in Kuruman was complete. After SANT farms had linked up the central reserves – the Lower Kuruman, Botheletsa, and Manyeding – land acquisition slowed.[97] There were reasons to think the four remaining satellite reserves might remain. The idea of removing Khuis had been dropped. Maremane and Ga-Tlhose in the southwest were very large (61,829 hectares), and in 1953 the Secretary of Native Affairs confirmed that Vlakfontein/Kagung in the southeast did not qualify as a black spot.[98] Despite this, the ideology of segregation had changed greatly by 1960, and the new policy of Separate Development provided a force for further removals. Separate Development was the grand version of segregation that sought ethnic as well as racial separation. While earlier policies had stressed protection of white privilege, Separate Development claimed as its ostensible goal self-determination by Africans and this changed blacks' experience of segregation. Eventually, Separate Development resulted in granting a sham "independence" to ethnically defined "Bantustans," including Bophuthatswana, "The Land of the United Tswana."* [99] Bophuthatswana consisted of nineteen reserves, and because even a masquerade of an autonomous nation-state required somewhat contiguous territory, these were consolidated through land acquisition and removals into seven parcels by 1977.[100] The process connected all remaining reserves in Kuruman and Vryburg and gave the final northward push to the black population.

Prime Minister H. F. Verwoerd, the architect of Separate Development, seems to have played an active role in determining the division of land between blacks and whites in Kuruman. In 1962, he dispatched the successor to the NAC,

---

* Separate Development ideologues borrowed "Bantu," a language group name, as a generic term for black South Africans. Since it was ascribed by Apartheid authorities, it was considered objectionable.

the Bantu Affairs Commission,* to investigate the possibility of further land purchases there.[101] Following this, he chaired a key meeting in October 1963 that reorganized black and white areas in Kuruman by mandating the purchase by the SANT of farms north of the Lower Kuruman Reserve, including some on the Vryburg boundary that had not been included in the original released area. It also excised unpurchased SANT farms linking Vlakfontein/Kagung with the core reserves from released areas and made the decision to remove Vlakfontein/Kagung, Maremane, and Ga-Tlhose to the northern trust farms.[102] The result was large removals to the most inhospitable areas.

Like Konong, Vlakfontein/Kagung was on an impressive spring, the source of the Groot Boetsap River that flowed southeast into first the Harts and then the Vaal Rivers. Nearby was a small white town, Reivilo, home to a cheese factory that processed milk sold by mostly white dairy farmers across a wide area.[103] Not sharing the luck of the Kuruman municipality, Reivilo did not control its water source, and in 1954, it petitioned for the removal of the reserve.[104] The government held meetings with blacks on the reserve in 1963, but people told us that these were not open discussions. "We didn't agree. We were oppressed. We were forced." "If at that meeting you had a lot to say, questions to ask, you were asked to sit down."[105] People were warned to salvage building parts from their houses before the government broke them down. The removal trucks came on October 15 and 16, 1966. Some residents chose to go to the Taung Reserve, and some went to the new Reivilo township, where they could continue working in the cheese factory, but most people went to the settlement provided by the government, also called Kagung, on trust land east of the town of Kuruman. The advantage of this site was that it was on the main road between Kuruman and Vryburg. The resettlement of Kagung was relatively well ordered, and the trauma of setting up the new community seems to have been less than in the removals of Konong or Ga-Tlhose and Maremane. The government gave compensation according to the type of house. Streets had already been platted, lots were allocated, and temporary housing in tents was provided. Animals trekked to the new site, but the move and new location on the Ghaap Plateau inflicted a high mortality.[106]

Khuis again became a matter of concern to officials in 1965, not coincidentally, the year before Botswana received independence, as politicians became concerned about a village straddling a border with an independent black country. It was reported that "foreign Bantu" were crossing at Khuis to seek

---

* Because more "African" nomenclatures were seen as appropriate, the NAC became the Bantu Affairs Commission (BAC). Likewise, in 1958 the NAD became the Department of Bantu Administration and Development (BAD – also known by its Afrikaans initials, BAO).

work in South Africa.[107] By this time, a stock quarantine fence along the Molopo River had divided Khuis people from the Botswana side of the village. Although village residents could still move between the countries, the fence constricted pastures and access to water. Barred from half of their herding environment and from drawing on herds across the river, the fence posed a serious problem, and its construction resigned people on the South African side to removal. The move was voluntary only in that it allowed them to recognize necessity. As the headman explained:

We have long heard that we must move but we never complained of troubles here. The authorities saw it wise for us to move from here. . . . But we will follow what the Law says, as we are children of the Law. If we refused to go where the Law says, we will be in more troubles. . . . I have given up. I now agree. The trouble we have here is the quarantine here. If we leave from here we will live better and God will help us with more rain.[108]

In March 1968, Khuis people were moved to Penryn and other settlements on SANT lands between the northern border of the Lower Kuruman Reserve and the southwestern border of the Vryburg District. In a symbolic yet strategic move, the South African police put a border post on the emptied reserve.[109]

The territory and population of Maremane and Ga-Tlhose were by far the largest of all that suffered removals in Kuruman, with a population estimated at between 10,000 and 20,000 people by the Surplus People Project, a nongovernmental organization that documented removals.[110] Probably because of the scale of this removal and the challenging environment of the resettlement area in the Kalahari, the government delayed the removal of these reserves until 1976–7.[111] Planners had trouble obtaining sufficient water and laying pipes from the few sources to the many supply points. The settlements, the largest of which was Bendell, on 79,502 hectares required approximately 100 kilometers of new roads, but building them in sand was difficult.[112]

A removal of this magnitude showed the high price the state was willing to pay for segregation, but the people of Ga-Tlhose and Maremane bore most of the costs. When they arrived at their new homes, they suffered food and water shortages and found that facilities were not complete and schools were not ready.[113] The relocation to an underdeveloped desert camp took a high toll. Thirty-five children perished during resettlement. In addition to poor water and sanitation, people at Bendell and neighboring communities blame their health troubles on a parasitic worm infesting the sands of the new location, but medical professionals have not identified the worm.[114] The Surplus People Project made a visit to the Bendell area in 1982 and asserted "some of the

171

most depressed areas in the country are found north of Kuruman. The Wyks, Bendell, Deerward,* and the Batlharos are poverty-stricken, dry, dusty, isolated and forgotten by the rest of the country. Obtaining water is an all-consuming struggle." Surplus People Project researchers were struck by a "huge graveyard" in Bendell.[115] Because of the number of people affected, inadequate preparation by the government, and the harsh Kalahari environment, the removal of Ga-Tlhose and Maremane took the highest toll, including human mortality, of all the removals in Kuruman. After the removals, the South African Defense Force received the former reserves as a military base, Lohatlha.

ENVIRONMENTAL HISTORY AND RACIAL SEGREGATION

The case of Kuruman reveals environmental factors in the history of segregation. Studies of other regions in South Africa and elsewhere will reveal further ways that the specific character of the environment influenced the process and the outcome of segregation. However, that environmental factors must be incorporated into our understanding of segregation is only the most basic lesson of this chapter. The most important conclusion to be drawn from this chapter concerns social categories, social institutions, and power in environmental history. These factors have been evident since the earliest discernable history of the thornveld, in the division of production privileges between chiefs, common men, women, and *balala*. The restrictions in that system made Cape frontier innovations attractive to men constricted by their chiefs. Colonial rule had introduced people of European descent and the modern state to southern Africa. From the beginning of colonial rule, the potential for environmental intervention existed, and people differentiated by race had different abilities to create propitious relations with water and land. In twentieth-century South Africa, segregation between whites and blacks became the major preoccupation of the state. In the service of segregation, it developed and exercised its interventionist muscle, remaking blacks' relations with water and land. In the process of forced removals, the state exerted the most concentrated power in the environmental realm to date for the benefit of white people.

---

* Deerward was the resettlement spot for the Di Takwanen Reserve in Vryburg, removed in 1973. The Wyks was a resettlement spot for people from Ga-Tlhose and Maremane.

8

Betterment and the Bophuthatswana Donkey Massacre: The Environmental Rights of Tribal Subjects, 1940s–1983

> It is true that the cattle and the land should be cared for. We are the
> government's cattle. We give the Government milk. The tax money
> is the milk. The Government should give green pastures to its cattle
> otherwise they will dry up.[1]

FORCED removal was an obvious and particularly blunt form of state intervention into black people's relations with the environment, but it was not the only aspect of segregation with environmental implications. Blacks who retained their land also suffered a constriction of their rights, including environmental rights, as they became subjects of state intervention. After the 1930s, the state operated conservation programs and became an active and usually unwelcome partner in blacks' relations with the environment. On African reserves, conservation was part of development programs generally known as "Betterment." Betterment entailed comprehensive and coercive transformations of the ways Africans lived on the land. Initially legislated in 1939 and refined in 1949, it was the policy of "planning" African areas according to the modern principles of agricultural production and conservation science. It characterized African farmers and herders as wastrels destroying soil, forests, and grazing veld. Highly technocratic, Betterment gave officials in the Native Affairs Department (NAD, later the Bantu Administration and Development [BAD] Department) authority to remedy putative abuses by planning land use. It was also intended to support segregation by maximizing the use of communal lands. This involved relocating people into compact platted villages, demarcating and fencing specific areas for cultivation and grazing, enforcing soil conservation measures in cultivated areas, and calculating a carrying capacity (determined in large stock units) for the grazing veld. Most important to affected people, Betterment involved the culling of stock to reduce numbers to the calculated carrying capacity.[2]

Although a rural program, Betterment had great significance for metropolitan society, and many histories of Betterment examine its national context by discussing the forces behind and repercussions of the program. National forces included the need for political control and cheap labor, as well as the ideology of the threat of degradation.[3] These policy considerations give insight into the motivations behind Betterment, but the conditions that made radical intervention possible deserve more comment. Therefore, I will explore the national context of segregation and Indirect Rule. I will discuss countrywide matters, but more than focusing on the goals of policy makers, I will concentrate on the relationship between the state and rural blacks. In this chapter, I will also explore the local effects of Betterment. A few authors have emphasized the ways Betterment changed people's lives, including Isabel Hofmeyr who explores its effect on oral narrative and Chris de Wet who discusses the ways it affected community relations. Like these, my own discussion of Betterment will focus on the environmental, agricultural, and social impact.[4]

This chapter begins with developments under the Union and Republic governments and follows further developments in a black homeland. Compared with the rest of South Africa, conservation in Bophuthatswana was especially draconian and even violent, culminating in the 1983 donkey massacre. It was particularly extreme near Kuruman, where the Bophuthatswana army and police killed as many as 10,000 donkeys. For many people in this area, it was the most traumatic experience of Apartheid. Although it targeted animals, it was a violent demonstration of the power of the state over poor and disenfranchised people. Occurring in the violent 1980s, the donkey massacre was an extreme but not exceptional conservation measure. It was executed through the government structures that implemented Betterment and was based on its principles. Just as homeland governments developed from colonial structures, conservation in Bophuthatswana was an outgrowth of Betterment.

INDIRECT RULE AND ENVIRONMENTAL RIGHTS

According to Mamdani, Betterment is only one of many forceful actions by African colonial states against rural producers. He argues that customary land tenure provided some protection from market forces, causing the colonial state to turn to coercion to realize its development agenda. The definition of rural Africans as tribal subjects made the forceful exertion possible. Mamdani's observation is vital for colonial African environmental history because he exposes a common logic behind different environmental interventions by the colonial state: cultivation, soil conservation, agricultural development, and animal culling.[5] To understand the interventions of Betterment, it is necessary to explore the creation of this customary world for tribal subjects. In South Africa, it was imposed as part of the larger push toward segregation.

Colonial communal tenure had been in place since the 1880s, but Indirect Rule was instituted in a slow process in the fifty years after the Union of South Africa was founded in 1910. Between 1910 and 1936, the Cape Province was an exception in the Union of South Africa because it retained a property-based, rather than racially based, franchise. With the goal of implementing segregation, the Union government eradicated this potential for equal political participation and abolished the Cape system, which tended toward Direct Rule, in favor of Indirect Rule. The 1927 Natives Administration Act was an important step in the process, although it did not completely bring the Cape system in line with the rest of the country.

Implementing rule through chiefs was a problem in Kuruman because the district had none. After the 1897 rebellion, the Cape government abolished the institution of the chieftaincy among the Tlharo. The Tlhaping chief had moved from Kuruman to Taung in the 1820s, and although he officially had authority over all Tlhaping, he was notoriously weak. Because chiefs did not exist, it was necessary to invent them, and the government created a Tlhaping chief for the Kuruman district in 1944 and re-appointed a Tlharo chief in 1945.[6] In reconstituting the chieftaincy, the government chose descendents of nineteenth-century rulers, but did not devise any official role for the *kgotla*, the assembly of all men. The government also created structures for nontraditional community leaders. In 1948, a local council, consisting of both Tlhaping and Tlharo representatives, was created for the district. Officials appointed three members, and six were elected from newly formed districts. Chiefs and headmen held no official position in the council, although they were likely to be members.[7] The local council brought Kuruman into conformity with the system in the more populous Xhosa areas of the Cape Province, but this local government was not based on traditional structures. In contrast, the ethnic ideology of Afrikaner Nationalists, who took power in 1948, required tribal institutions. The growing forces of Apartheid soon challenged the council system.[8]

The next step in the nationwide process of establishing administrative segregation, the passage of the Bantu Authorities Act of 1951, occurred in part because of problems in implementing conservation. After 1944, all SANT lands automatically were subject to Betterment regulations, but the implementation of Betterment on the older reserves (as opposed to the recently purchased SANT lands) required a formal request by the community. However, this is not to say that reserve inhabitants chose this option freely.[9] Not surprisingly, many people were often unhappy about and opposed Betterment measures, especially stock culling. It provoked significant resistance in several rural areas: in 1943 in the Pedi territory in the northern Transvaal, in 1950 in Witzieshoek on the northern border of Lesotho (later the homeland of Qwa Qwa), and in 1960 in the Transkei.[10] The state's response was to strengthen its presence on reserves through Bantu Authorities – the co-option of chiefs into the structures of Indirect Rule. The intent was to use chiefs to communicate about and to organize the community for Betterment changes, and it involved subjecting Africans to a further restriction of rights. Opposition to Betterment was not the only force promoting Indirect Rule – there was a preexisting vision of self-determination by "tribes" – but in the 1950s Betterment created an immediate need for stronger representatives of the state on reserves. The result was the Bantu Authorities Act of 1951. It inaugurated three levels of government for black South Africans. In 1959, the Promotion of Bantu Self-Government Act invested them with powers of self-government.[11]

The lowest level of Bantu Authorities was the basic building block of Indirect Rule: Tribal Authorities, councils of salaried members appointed by local chiefs and magistrates.[12] In 1955 and 1956, Kuruman received Tlhaping and Tlharo Tribal Authorities. The Tlhaping authority had jurisdiction over Manyeding, Bothetheletsa, Seodin, part of the Lower Kuruman Reserve, and SANT lands where Smouswane people had been relocated. The Tlharo tribal authority had jurisdiction over most of the Lower Kuruman Reserve, Ga-Tlhose, Maremane, Khuis, and remaining trust lands. The Tribal Authorities differed from the local council system because Tlhaping and Tlharo structures were separate. Tribal Authorities provided basic services to rural communities and imposed voluntary levies for school administration, clinics, and Betterment projects such as fencing, road building, stock improvement, and water development. They had difficulty collecting levies, however, so the South African Native Trust bankrolled the programs.[13] At the next level were Regional Authorities that had power to administrate education, public works, health care, and agricultural extension for tribal clusters. In 1958, the Seokama Dichaba Regional Authority was created, uniting all Tlhaping and Tlharo Tribal Authorities in the Kuruman and Vryburg Districts under Tlharo Chief Robanyane Toto as chairman.[14] In 1962, all Tswana-speaking groups in the Republic of South Africa were united at the third level by the Tswana Territorial Authority, which took over many of the responsibilities of the Regional Authorities, including agricultural services and planning.[15] Despite these interventions, local chiefs remained relatively weak.[16] Tlhaping and Tlharo leaders did not become engines driving Betterment. Union and Republic government officials played that role, but they tried to use Tribal Authorities to communicate with and to obtain the consent of reserve inhabitants.

THE IDEOLOGY OF BETTERMENT IN THE THORNVELD

Betterment began with an official ideology about environmental change, its causes and its effects. To understand the specifics of Betterment in Kuruman, it is necessary to discuss its local variant of conservation ideology. In twentieth-century Africa, official environmental ideology often developed into a "received wisdom," and scholars now examine it critically, arguing that knowledge about the environment and its proper uses takes on the authority of a discourse as understood by Michel Foucault.[17] Assertions of degradation were often based on selective evidence and were usually ignorant of indigenous understandings. Depictions of degradation rested on colonial power relations – on which party had the authority to determine and communicate truth. In South Africa after the 1930s, the official position on conservation was that soil erosion on African reserves posed a considerable threat. Beinart has shown that concerns about environmental degradation in South Africa were first directed toward settler agriculture and only later toward African reserves. An important landmark was the 1923 Drought Investigation Commission that warned that pastoral overuse on white-owned farms created desert conditions.[18] In the wake of the North American "dust bowl" in the 1930s, officials developed an acute preoccupation about soil erosion in African areas and paid more attention to international alarms than to local environmental conditions. This conservationist discourse developed as segregation was intensifying, but Beinart argues that conservation was not merely a segregationist reflex; it had international origins, a biophysical awareness, and a technical momentum.[19]

By condemning African land use practices, the conservationist discourse was an outgrowth of earlier opinions among missionaries or paternalist administrators about African farming and herding. However, unlike its predecessors, segregationist conservation did not claim to intervene for the sake of Africans' moral or economic advancement, but because it feared that a Malthusian agricultural collapse would have repercussions for urban and white-claimed South Africa. As the motivation switched from "improving" Africans to protecting whites, agricultural extension on reserves used fewer carrots and more sticks.[20] Because it privileged the group over individuals, the ideology of ethnic self-determination supported a more extreme intervention than was possible under the earlier paternalist ethos. Paternalism was not in accordance with the ideology of extreme segregation, self-determination, and cultural protection and did not survive long after the implementation of Apartheid in 1948. Its demise is evident in Kuruman, where government support for irrigation schemes fell out of favor and stock culling began. While the forces behind Betterment should not be reduced to segregation, the intensification of segregation at this time certainly eased the introduction of coercion into agricultural extension.

The power/knowledge dynamic is manifest in the colonial discourse about soil erosion on reserves, because those with expertise and authority formulated the "received wisdom" and implemented policy with minimal consultation of Africans and little research into actual environmental conditions. The national and international obsession with soil erosion did not import easily into Kuruman, which is flat with sandy and stony soils and thus has no gully erosion. Nonetheless, experts constructed two aspects of semi-arid land use, donkey keeping and dry land plowing, as local causes of erosion, but the links were tenuous. Policies against these economically marginal activities developed without inquiry into their utility or environmental impact.

For many reasons in addition to their impact on the soil, the official verdict on donkeys was overwhelmingly negative. This required denying the many ways poor blacks found donkeys useful, for travel, transport, plowing, and food. Their reputation was so dire that one official warned of "the donkey menace."[21] A 1932 memorandum details how they were considered a problem, stating that their carcasses went unclaimed and harbored botulins, thus making the environment unhealthy for cattle. They destroyed the veld by digging and trampling the grass; they reproduced quickly and had no marketable value; they were worth less than the crops they damaged; people did not claim them when they did damage; and they consumed large amounts of fodder on overstocked pastures.[22] Only rarely did white officials recognize the practicality of donkeys, as in this report in 1950:

> As Kuruman is essentially stock country, it is surprising how few cattle the natives own and how many donkeys (approximately 10,000) there are. It would appear that cattle owing to the need for continual dosing with bonemeal . . . are a risky proposition and need attention e.g. food and water regularly. The donkey on the other hand requires no attention, is a useful draught animal and if he dies, his meat would be eaten as readily as in the case of an ox.[23]

Rather than considering why they were suited to people's needs, officials blamed both donkeys and people for their prevalence. In later years, as motorized transport became common, another issue arose: donkeys are recklessly resolute in the face of oncoming traffic. Peta Jones has reconstructed the encounter from a donkey's point of view.

> Once a donkey gets used to motor vehicles, it realizes that they can steer and stop, just as a donkey can. As donkeys will always stop and steer

around a stationary object, a donkey will expect vehicles to do that when the stationary object is itself – usually standing in the middle of the road because the view is good from there. What it does not seem to realize is that motor vehicles are actually going faster than donkeys can, and are therefore less efficient at steering and stopping and are also controlled by humans with unreasonable notions about rights of way. Sadly, it is a lesson many donkeys learn only in the instant they are killed.[24]

Indeed, the hazard donkeys posed to traffic was one ostensible cause for the removal of Dikgweng.[25] Assertions that the animals were feral and Africans were apathetic established a need for intervention.

The second problem identified by conservation officials was dry land (rain-fed or nonirrigated) plowing. Ever since the agro-pastoral revolution, Kuruman people had recognized that herding was more propitious than cultivation. By investing their energies into the maize harvest in the western Transvaal rather than planting at home, twentieth-century reserve inhabitants affirmed that sensibility. However, they did not cease all cultivation in irrigated gardens or, in years with sufficient precipitation, on rain-fed fields. In response, officials asserted that dry land plowing was destructive and that disturbed dry soils were dangerously vulnerable to wind erosion. A 1947 memorandum detailed the problem with plowing.

> Firstly, it leads to soil erosion (wind erosion), secondly no crops are ever reaped and thirdly the Native settlers destroy all vegetation through ploughing virgin soil at liberty all over the farms. I have noticed that sand dunes have formed next to dry lands which were denuded of all earth and only boulders and outcrops of rock left.[26]

Alerted to the danger, the NAD senior agricultural officer made an inspection. He reported that leaving land fallow during dry seasons resulted in "a dust bowl and we actually saw such a land which was plus/minus 6 inches lower than the surface of the ground immediately around it, and the sand . . . had formed a complete wall around it."[27] These are eyewitness descriptions of degradation; yet, as with bush encroachment, it is difficult to determine to what extent local evidence indicates a wider problem. The NAD contended that the region faced a problem reminiscent of the American Dust Bowl in the 1930s. In 1951 its annual report described dust storms strong enough to derail a train in Taung![28] "Soil erosion happens,"[29] but so does exaggeration. A crisis of this magnitude requires confirmation, and I found no corroboration of these extreme conditions in the 1951 report of the Kuruman native commissioner or in the report of the agricultural officer. P. H. R. Snyman's local history also omits mention of dust storms.[30] We do know that local farmers disagreed with the NAD about the threat of desertification. As one official notes: "Native and European farmers have little understanding" that dry land plowing turns "the land into a desert."[31] The lack of corroboration suggests that the alarm about a general crisis was not based on local conditions.

The last important aspect of Betterment ideology was primarily economic and only secondarily environmental. Originally, the vision was to restrict farming rights to a limited number of "economic units" that would have the resources, including freehold private tenure, to farm commercially. The economic unit was defined as the amount of arable land or the number of stock deemed necessary to produce commercially. Kuruman was considered pastoral, and the economic unit was twenty-five LSUs.[32] The theory was that full-time farmers would develop the understanding and investment in the land to practice conservation. Of course, this restriction was dependent upon finding another means of support for the surplus people who would be relegated to "rural villages" with no farming rights. The idea was most clearly developed in the report of the Tomlinson Commission (1954–5), whose recommendations would have pushed many people off the land.[33] It recommended granting the farming class private tenure for their land, but the Verwoerd government refused to do so on the basis that "individual tenure would undermine the whole tribal structure."[34] The commission had also called for massive investment to provide jobs for the nonfarmers, but the Verwoerd government declined to make the recommended investment in industrialization on the reserves. Thus undermined, the Tomlinson Commission recommendations are significant by showing the limits of Separate Development. Although planning for economic units fell out of political favor, Betterment officials did not give up the idea of promoting commercial production. The concept remained alive, and the concomitant limitation of farming rights reappeared in the 1983 donkey massacre.

Thus, the dominant ideology became that donkeys and dry land plowing caused soil erosion, and this conviction provided a justification for the radical intervention that promoted two changes in Kuruman. It hindered the supplementary subsistence farming in favor of commercial production. Additionally, it redeveloped the landscape. Over time in both cases, environmental justifications for these actions receded in favor of political and economic ones, and the planning process acquired its own momentum.[35]

REDEVELOPING THE LANDSCAPE

Essentially, in Kuruman, Betterment involved real estate development in a most improbable location. In the 1960s and 1970s, Betterment was less oriented toward protecting the land and more toward accommodating people who suffered removals. This brought revolutionary changes by creating intensive land use, a possibility that had so long eluded people in Kuruman. Through investment of capital by the state rather than labor by the inhabitants, the environment was reshaped to support a larger population. This was not intensification through changing the techniques of cultivation, but by creating an infrastructure that maximized pastoral use and allowed for denser human settlement. The system of rotational grazing and the technologies of well drilling and road building were powerful tools that allowed planners to work with little regard for environmental conditions. Redeveloping the landscape was a huge task, presenting acute organizational challenges. Perhaps because the undertaking was so large, or perhaps because of the bureaucratic momentum, the planning process is the best-documented aspect of the history of Betterment. It is evident that local environmental and economic conditions did not motivate the development, since there is little discussion about them. For example, a 1956 report gives two perfunctory paragraphs on climate and veld type. The remaining seventeen pages qualify as an example of "detailed" planning, with technical information organized into points, subpoints, and tables.[36] The report describes the development of 41,424 hectares near the Vryburg boundary for 1,658 people and 3,999 LSUs. The report lays out a system of rotational grazing, giving the miles of barbed wire needed as well as the number of boreholes, handpumps, windmills, watering ponds, and gates, complete with costs.[37] A 1969 report on the development of 79,503 hectares near Bendell for the removal of Ga-Tlhose and Maremane is even more detailed. It types the veld according to Acocks's classification and describes parcels as being in a subclimax or climax condition. It also is explicit about Betterment plans. It includes a map showing the placement of twenty-seven proposed villages, with roads connecting them. It also makes accommodation for people who were denied farming rights, although the policy to restrict rights was never implemented in Kuruman.[38] These rich technical records of real estate development are of limited usefulness because they do not record the impact on the landscape and in the lives of the people inhabiting it. Answers to these questions must be sought in other sources, particularly the memories of those who lived through Betterment.

Betterment demarcated separate residential and productive spaces. The most intrusive aspect of the spatial reorganization was relocating people to "live in streets," as they put it, on one-quarter or one-half morgen plots in platted villages. I heard differing accounts about the relocation process; sometimes the government provided trucks, sometimes people used their own donkeys.[39] I learned only one instance of compensation: £4,000 for the people of Seodin.[40] Some people did not cooperate, and their houses were destroyed.[41] Artificial water sources were critical to the redevelopment. Both the number of wells and the efficacy of drilling techniques rose dramatically during Betterment. Only six wells existed on Kuruman reserves before 1930. Sixty-four were added in the 1930s (perhaps half of which yielded water); 156 were added in the 1940s (perhaps two-thirds of which yielded water); eighty good wells were added in the 1950s; and seventy-two good wells were added in just two years in 1960–1.[42] Some of these wells were in the new villages, where they sustained increased human settlement, but many were distributed across the veld, where they significantly increased the grazing range.

Since the entire communal area was subject to Betterment, it is a reasonable assumption that between the 1950s and 1970s, virtually every rural black household (except those whose houses happened to fall within the new grid) was forced to relocate. Every village I saw, on reserves or land, had been reorganized on a grid by 1965.[43] I was told that before Betterment, people lived "according to their family names, like the Tshetlhos would stay in this portion, another family in another portion."[44] The homesteads had been widely spaced, as far as fifty to 200 meters apart from each other, and officials criticized this arrangement on the grounds that foot traffic between homesteads caused erosion, an implausible assertion in this flat underpopulated region. Segregation was a more obvious impetus for developing platted villages than soil erosion. The largest new settlement, Mothibistad, established east of Seodin in 1960, received most of its population from the Kuruman municipal "location" that was removed in 1963.[45] Segregation was also the immediate cause for the relocation of the people of Seodin to a Betterment settlement called Seodin-Lareng. Between 1962 and 1968 they were forced to move from their scattered houses because the Group Areas Act mandated a buffer zone between their village and the municipality boundary.[46] Even where people were not evicted from newly declared white spaces, their relocation supported segregation – consolidating the population to create larger settlements and providing room for newcomers from black spots and white farms. Closer settlement also facilitated political control, evident in the bright spotlights on high poles illuminating Mothibistad at night.

Betterment provoked sharp resistance in other areas, and the government ethnologist, P.-L. Breutz, reported: "The population is usually opposed to any kind of Betterment scheme, owing to the influence of the propaganda from the towns."[47] Kuruman people, however, did not offer much resistance. This was, after all, the district described by a proud missionary as "the most law-abiding Native area in the Union,"[48] and it was characteristically quiescent about Betterment. Perhaps the experience of the 1897 rebellion had made Kuruman people cautious. As Chief Toto, a descendent of the vanquished rebel, commented on Bantu Authorities, another institution that provoked resistance in other areas:

> If this act has been passed we have very little to say. . . . The land which used to be ours in the by-gone days, today it's not. We have to accept this as most have it already in force. We have tried several times to reject things but that has helped us nothing. Let us die with the rest.[49]

This is not to say that everyone was fatalistic. Of the 115 families on the Vlakfontein Reserve, twenty-eight left for other reserves after hearing Betterment proposals.[50]

Betterment stripped black people of the land they used and of the right to buy land. In the early 1960s, only one black man, Jacob Oss, owned land in the Kuruman released area.[51] After the Tomlinson Commission recommendations on private tenure were rejected, the BAD declined to entertain offers from blacks to buy private farms on trust land. The redevelopment was entirely predicated upon communal tenure, and Betterment relocations give evidence of its constricted rights. The BAD had moved far from the conviction of missionaries and earlier administrators that intensive cultivation on private land was the highest form of land use. For example, E. Mantanga had drilled a well in his garden on a farm, but was forced to give it up without compensation when he was assigned a plot in a different area.[52] When another black man who aspired to own property argued that private ownership would encourage people to make improvements to the land, an official scolded him: "I must point out that it is a poor tenant who does not improve the land he occupies so as to get the most of his opportunities."[53] Such moralizing was an ironic contradiction to the experience of people who lost their homes, wells, and gardens without compensation, both in Betterment relocations and in forced removals.

Villagization challenged community relations, as De Wet puts it in his book title, "moving together, drifting apart." Some people told me that living in streets had the advantage of proximity to schools, churches, hospitals, and shops.[54] Also, it was easier for people to visit each other.[55] However, the more crowded settlements provoked quarrelling.[56] One man explained the problem: "When you move to a new structure, and the person you may be living next to may not be humanely tempered, may not look after your things, may be cruel to animals, and may not be tempered to live with other people."[57] Furthermore, the new residential patterns raised problems for food production: People objected when their neighbors' chickens and goats ate food intended for their own animals, and the new settlements put people farther away from their fields and pastures, where stock theft became more of a problem.[58]

Table 8-1. *Rotational Grazing*

	Camp 1	Camp 2	Camp 3
First year	Spring and winter	Summer and winter	Autumn and winter
Second year	Summer and winter	Autumn and winter	Spring and winter
Third year	Autumn and winter	Spring and winter	Summer and winter

In addition to remaking residence patterns, Betterment also stipulated how people could use productive spaces. Because of the semi-aridity of the area, herding became the only approved land use, except in irrigable lands, and the only approved method of herding was a rotational camp system. The ostensible reason for the camps was soil conservation, but as with the case of villagization, other considerations tempered environmental ones. Officials made no survey of veld conditions and no inspections to determine how sustained "overuse" was possible. In fact, they rarely reported about environmental conditions.[59] As discussed in Chapter 6, certain pressures made the veld bushier at mid-century, but the stated goal of rotational grazing was to prevent erosion, the national concern, not bush encroachment, a local process.[60] Besides demarcating pastures, Betterment also imposed controls on the number of animals that could use them. The number of animals permitted in each system was determined by multiplying the size of the grazing area by the set carrying capacity, which was one LSU on every ten or twelve morgen, depending on rainfall levels. Range scientists now believe that "there is no single biologically optimal carrying capacity," that different economic objectives – for example, whether an animal is fattened for market or kept for bridewealth – allow for different stocking levels.[61]

Apart from residential areas and cultivated fields on the river valley reserves, the entire veld came under the spatial and temporal discipline of the camp system. Before Betterment, people kraaled their animals at the homestead at night, and Betterment separated humans and animals into different spaces. Animals moved to large fenced enclosures where they needed no herders. A three-camp, three-year system of seasonal rotation, as depicted in Table 8-1, dictated their movements through pastures. The logic of the camp system was to prevent any area from being intensively grazed for two seasons and to allow pastures a period of "rest." The theory was that this prevented animals from selectively overgrazing desirable grasses and thus forestalled both bush encroachment and erosion. A ranger, paid by the government but appointed by the chief, supervised the camps.[62] I found no record of conflict over the camps system in Kuruman, where after the initial protest over demarcation of the reserves in the 1890s, people requested that fences be erected and maintained, especially on boundaries where white farmers encroached. In interviews, I learned that they appreciated camp fences because they made it easier to find animals that strayed.[63] When people criticized camps, it was for being too small and restricting the amount of pasture.[64]

HINDERING SUBSISTENCE, PROMOTING COMMERCIAL PRODUCTION

In addition to redeveloping the landscape, Betterment, like colonial agricultural planning throughout Africa, hindered supplementary subsistence farming. In Kuruman, the state targeted donkey herding and dry land plowing, although irrigated cultivation also came into question. By restricting the number of productive activities, the NAD effectively restricted the number of people who worked the land, and by banning some subsistence activities, it opened more of the landscape to commercial production. The NAD also inaugurated programs that promoted commercial stock production. Thus, the goal of the Tomlinson Commission to restrict farming rights to a minority was achieved with less investment and without legal intervention.

The first development was the banning of "indiscriminate" dry land plowing in Betterment areas in Kuruman in 1949.[65] Since all SANT farms came under Betterment regulations, residents were entitled only to a small "garden." Of all aspects of Betterment, this ban was the greatest point of contention between Kuruman blacks and the government. Africans knew that environmental conditions were the same on their reserves and private lands, and whites were able to plow as they pleased on privately held farms in the Kuruman District. Furthermore, plowing was legal on reserves in neighboring Vryburg. Pointing out these inconsistencies to the NAD had limited effect. By the mid-1950s, soil erosion was becoming less of a matter for concern to officials and was replaced by an economic consideration – generating income.[66] As it gained power, developers even became critical of plowing on irrigated lands that were in no danger of wind erosion, proposing that vleys might be more valuable as grazed than as cultivated spaces.[67]

Throughout the 1950s, people objected and attempted to secure plowing rights.[68] Cultivators had gained some advantage by May 1960, when Betterment on reserves was raised for approval of the Tlharo Tribal Authority. By then, the agenda of political restructuring outweighed conservationist concerns, and resistance to Betterment had raised fears in the government that heavy handedness would be counterproductive.[69] Furthermore, consent was necessary to implement Betterment, and after the creation of Tribal Authorities, the consultation about implementing Betterment became more meaningful. The Tlharo Tribal

Authority did not oppose fencing and branding, but it did express concern about stock culls and did refuse to yield on plowing rights.[70] Pushed on this point, a frustrated official admitted the ban on plowing was not environmentally necessary: "To argue further with the Bantus is a waste of time. I've been doing it for the past two years. . . . The reserves here are not more liable to wind erosion than those in Vryburg and Lichtenburg, where plowing is permitted. It can be effectively combated with proper windbreaks."[71] The government agreed to concede on this issue, and in 1962 the Lower Kuruman, Maremane, and Ga-Tlhose became Betterment areas without loss of dry land plowing rights.[72] However, developers did reduce dry land plowing areas by placing residential areas on plowed fields.[73]

The vision of stock production as a commercially viable undertaking required forming a link between Africans' herds and markets. The first link was dairy production, and the NAD established a demonstration dairy herd in 1942.[74] Milk production was well suited to Betterment because it was both pastoral and commercial, and diary cooperatives were established on several reserves in 1951. Men retained ownership of their cows, but milked them at a central location. The cooperative recorded each member's production, sold the milk, and disbursed monthly payments.[75] Dairy production allowed developers to make a case against supplementary subsistence production, and they suggested that people plant fodder crops rather than maize on irrigated lands.[76] The experiment, however, was not a success. Since 200 blacks in Kuruman owned cream separators (as noted in Chapter 6), the problem must have been with the cooperative, not with commercial milk production itself. Private sales of milk ended in 1975, when the local butter factory closed. The stronger link to the market was through stock sales. The NAD also held auctions that yielded significant wealth, for example, £23,224 in 1953 and 28,428 rand in 1965, and black men also sold stock at the Kuruman public auction. Commercial stock production was a very significant economic development, but unfortunately, it was not recorded how many people were selling cattle or how many animals were sold.[77]

The men selling cattle at the auction kept and disposed of them according to their abilities and circumstances. The vision of restricting farming rights to a limited number of farmers who were allowed only twenty-five cattle never took effect in Kuruman.[78] Already in 1955, developers declined to restrict farming rights because of the problem of what to do with the surplus nonfarming population.[79] Preparations in 1959 to resettle people of the Konong Reserve on the Churchill block of farms evoked a remarkable expression of doubt on this subject from within the bureaucratic ranks. The proposal bears a margin note in Afrikaans with an illegible signature: "I think there was not cattle limitation in Kono [*sic*] Reserve. . . . There will be cattle limitation in the new Kono reserve. I think it is bad enough that these people will be moved out of water-rich Kono to a desert and now to place this additional burden on them will bring only bitterness. These are defenseless people, and this is no way to treat defenseless people." The handwritten response (also in Afrikaans) summoned the environmental received wisdom to justify stock reduction: "If farming practices are not correct, we can really make that world a desert, and then I would like to see how satisfied the Bantu are with their removal."[80] The provisions were not implemented, but officials continued to think of commercial production as the ideal, and in Kuruman and elsewhere "planners still persevered in thinking in terms of economic units."[81]

The most notorious aspect of Betterment was stock reduction. Africans in Kuruman were stock poor, and the reserves were usually described as understocked. Therefore, concerns about the carrying capacity did not motivate stock culling. Instead of culling excess animals, the state culled "inferior" animals, and in contrast to cattle, which consisted of "scrub" and "improved" breeds, the entire species of donkeys was considered inferior. Donkeys and Betterment were incompatible because the state aimed to support efficient, modern, and market-oriented production by a few, while donkeys helped many with supplementary subsistence.

Officials reported an extremely high donkey population, noting that forty percent of all animals on reserves in the Kuruman District were horses or donkeys and that there were nearly four donkeys per person in Vlakfontein/ Kagung.[82] The first cull in the district was in 1949, and like those that followed, it involved sale, not slaughter. In 1950, officials arranged for sellers in Vlakfontein to receive ten shillings per animal from the National Bonemeal Factory, but that price did not draw sellers. When Vlakfontein residents did agree to limit donkeys voluntarily, they set the number at eight per household, with an extra eight allowed for wagon owners, an offer that officials disparaged as no reduction at all. In 1953, a proclamation declared all reserves in the district (even those not under Betterment regulations) to be areas of donkey limitation. The first major cull after the proclamation claimed 177 horses and 969 donkeys.[83] The culling procedure was to brand animals deemed valuable and to arrange for sale or slaughter of the surplus. Perhaps because a paternalist ethos endured from Cape Colony administrative traditions, these donkey controls sought consensus from owners. Paternalism was not free of violence and coercion, but imagining the colonial endeavor as a civilizing mission mitigated some extreme tendencies.

Although there was no overt opposition, a common response to culling programs was noncooperation. Officials believed that people hid their animals during culls and asked chiefs to work to reduce the population in their villages, resulting in more frustration in government offices than action on the reserves.[84]

These responses underscore the value of donkeys. Auctioning surplus animals could have been helpful for cash-poor households, but people did not always come forward to sell. For example, in three auctions in 1967 only sixteen donkeys were offered, suggesting there were not many surplus or feral donkeys. Evidently, live donkeys were worth more to people than what was being offered.[85] Officials threatened drastic measures, but after 1953 there was little culling. The donkey population on reserves dropped after the 1940s, but not as drastically as on white farms – from 11,007 in 1946 to 5,891 in 1960.[86] The drop was probably due in part to Betterment intervention and in part to a diminishing use of wagons and plows.

There is little direct evidence about what people affected by culls thought about them. Minutes of official district "Meetings of Chiefs, Headmen and People" preserve some rare popular commentary on donkey limitation. Some men defended the animal, which entailed defending plowing.[87] Yet participants at these meetings were not unanimous defenders of donkeys. The group voted sixty-six to six in support of the 1953 donkey limitation proclamation. Minutes of meetings from 1951 and 1952 record strong criticism of donkeys:

A donkey is no good. It is only of use if you use it for draught purposes. If the donkeys are decreased, it will be better for the cattle in this area;

Donkeys are useless and are despised;

There are more than 1,000 donkeys in my area which have no owners. When a donkey does damage we cannot find the owner;

Donkeys are ruining the Kuruman District. This law is just the right thing to decrease the number of donkeys. We will be allowed a number of donkeys each. The donkeys in my area are roaming about and have no owner. It will be a good thing if all donkeys are branded;

The donkeys use all the water and nothing is left for our other stock. These donkeys cause a lot of trouble amongst us.[88]

In later meetings some men complained about donkey limitation, but in contrast to the ban on plowing, others supported donkey reduction. There are several possible reasons why men in these meetings took a stand with the colonial state against donkeys. Tswana culture had a high regard for cattle, while ownership of donkeys, the poor person's animal, carried no prestige. If donkeys were perceived to be in competition with cattle, there would have been sentiment against them. Moreover, women, who found donkeys useful and were barred by custom from owning cattle, did not participate in the meetings. Additionally, government officials and Apartheid structures cowed dissent. Most important, later developments imply that the anti-donkey sentiment was rooted in the interests of the nascent class of commercial beef producers, who would have been the chiefs, headmen, and leading men participating in these meetings. This group was made up of the "progressive farmers" who could benefit from Betterment and were able to accumulate cattle. These were the sellers at stock auctions, and they would have been sympathetic to the idea that the veld be used to support cattle rather than donkeys. Interested in maximizing commercial production and profit, they were more likely to see donkeys as underutilized, surplus, or wild. The class divisions over donkeys and cattle are not explicit in the documentary record of this period, but it may be inferred that aspirant beef producers were among those speaking against donkeys.

There is another reason why the people at the meeting may have agreed to donkey limitation: even those people who used the animals also believed that too many of them could cause damage. Certainly, it would be an overcorrection to deny that humans and domesticated animals can damage the environment. People had the motivation and ability to accumulate large numbers of donkeys, and donkeys are voracious eaters. It is possible that as numbers grew, the toll on the land became clear even to subsistence herders. Two recent South African studies differ on whether rural blacks who use donkeys also perceive that they can be destructive. In interviews for the Namaqualand study, people reported that donkeys eat more than goats do, waste fodder, and have a higher impact on the remaining vegetation. Informants expressed concern that donkeys, particularly feral ones, impaired subsistence goat keeping. A countrywide survey in 1994 of over 500 respondents by the South African Network of Animal Traction contradicts this finding. It found no negative assessments of donkeys among rural black people.[89] Unfortunately, it is now probably impossible to determine to what extent people in previous decades believed that donkeys were capable of environmental degradation. Colonial control over the documentary record and the politicization of memory after the donkey killing in 1983 have obscured voices from that period.

THE EFFECTS OF BETTERMENT: EVIDENCE FROM ABOVE

The analysis of Betterment thus far has been based on verbal evidence, as recorded in documentary sources and offered in oral testimony. It is possible to triangulate these sources with other, nonverbal evidence – black and white aerial photographs, available at the office of the surveyor general. Airplanes flying east–west transects photographed the Kuruman District in 1958, 1965, 1972, and 1981. I acquired photographs from each of these years from two roughly congruent east–west strips chosen as samples of the communal areas. I chose as my first sample the strip beginning in the west at the Kuruman Hills in the

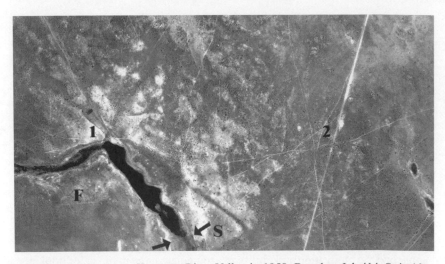

Figure 8-1 The Lower Kuruman River Valley in 1958. Based on Job 414, Strip 10, Photographs 7709 and 7707 from the Chief Directorate of Surveys and Mapping in South Africa. Reproduced under Government Printer's Copyright Authority No. 11012 dated 9 October 2001.

southern portion of the Lower Kuruman Native Reserve, extending over SANT farms to Bothetheletsa in the east. The second sample lies across the northern portion of the Lower Kuruman Native Reserve, beginning at the confluence of the Kuruman and the Matlhwareng Rivers in the west extending over the Matlhwareng Valley and neighboring SANT farms to the east.[90] Because reading aerial photographs is a specialized skill, I contracted a consultant, Kim Euston-Brown, to interpret them. She identified cultivated fields, thickets, settlements, heavily grazed pastures, pasture fencing, and mines on the photographs; located them on maps; and provided me with a description of landscape features at different moments that I will discuss in the context of the documentary and oral history.[91]

The southern swath recorded in these aerial photographs shows the most heavily populated part of the district, just north of the town of Kuruman, including the lower river valley, the southernmost portion of black communal areas, and the Ghaap Plateau to the east. The first set of pictures from 1958 and 1981 show the southern river valley. (See Figures 8-1 and 8-2). This set of photographs illustrates differences in white and black land use, the removal of Seodin, and the construction of Mothibistad. Although the photographs are not congruent, the major feature of the river valley and the points marked "1" and "2" provide orientation.

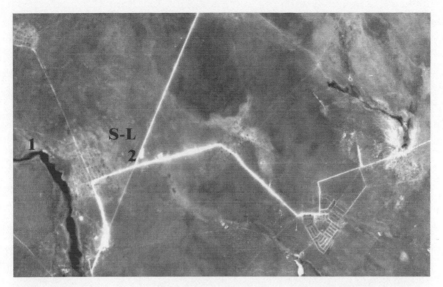

Figure 8-2 The Lower Kuruman River Valley in 1981. Based on Job 854, Strip 12, Photograph 441 from the Chief Directorate of Surveys and Mapping in South Africa. Reproduced under Government Printer's Copyright Authority No. 11012 dated 9 October 2001.

The southern boundary of these photographs touches the white-occupied valley to the north of town. In Figure 8-1, the boundary between black and white zones is discernable (marked with arrows). Because of the more intensive cultivation, white-owned gardens appear as a dark rectangle in the lowest part of the river valley (at the very bottom of the photograph). Immediately over the boundary in the reserve the shade lightens, as the vegetation thins on the Lower Kuruman Reserve. In 1958, the homesteads and kraals of the original Seodin (marked as "S"), just north of the reserve boundary, are visible in the bright reflections where vegetation is thinner and the calcrete surface was exposed. The Kuruman River is full behind a dam. Cultivated fields are visible along the river valley and away from the valley on the veld (marked as "F"). Changes on the 1981 photograph in Figure 8-2 include the streets of the new settlement of Seodin-Lareng (marked as "S-L") crisscrossing what had been empty veld. Also, the platted grid largest black settlement, Mothibistad has appeared six kilometers east of the river valley.

The next set of aerial photographs shows the transformations of Betterment in the horseshoe block. We see the effects of Betterment in 1965 in Figure 8-3. New Betterment villages, Bylfontein and Hertzog, named for former

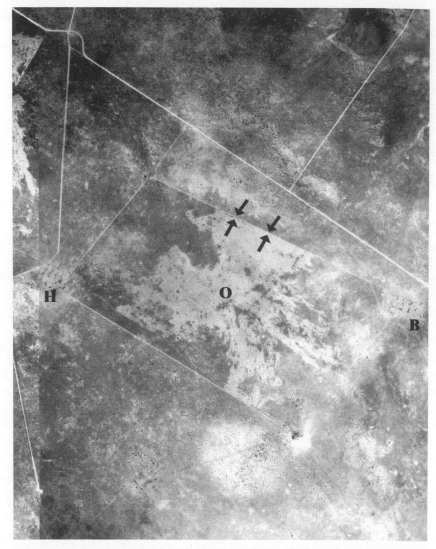

Figure 8-3 The Horseshoe Block in 1965. Based on Job 537, Strip 2, Photographs 068 and 069 from the Chief Directorate of Surveys and Mapping in South Africa. Reproduced under Government Printer's Copyright Authority No. 11012 dated 9 October 2001.

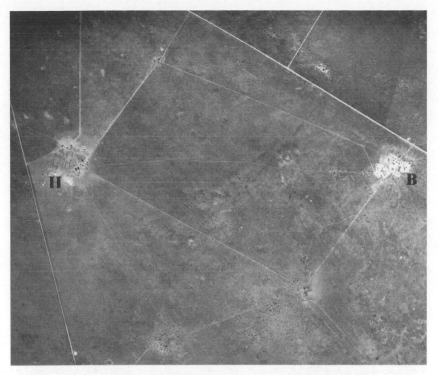

Figure 8-4 The Horseshoe Block in 1972. Based on Job 700, Strip 3, Photographs 9391 and 9392 from the Chief Directorate of Surveys and Mapping in South Africa. Reproduced under Government Printer's Copyright Authority No. 11012 dated 9 October 2001.

white-owned farms on the horseshoe block (marked "B" and "H"), are evident. The bare patch around Bylfontein shows more intensive land use, but Hertzog looks less disturbed. A large blotch in the camp between Bylfontein and Hertzog suggests overgrazing (marked "O"), and sharp edges on the perimeter (marked with arrows) indicate thicker vegetation in neighboring camps protected by fencing. Figure 8-4 shows that by 1972 grazing pressure has equalized between the camps, but that the impact of the settlement at Hertzog has increased. The higher altitude of the 1981 flights provides a wide perspective on the horseshoe block (see Figure 8-5). Roads extend like spider webs, and Betterment villages perch at crossroads like fat white spiders. The 1981 view of the wider area shows many such settlements, regularly spaced, joined by gravel roads and far from urban centers or ancestral lands. Sharp fencing lines (marked by arrows) show that the camp system controls grazing pressure.

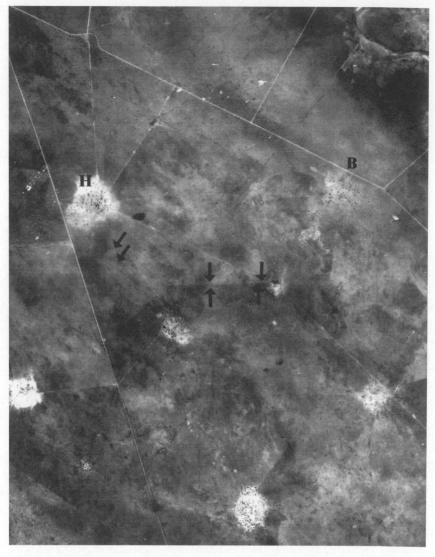

Figure 8-5 The Horseshoe Block in 1981. Based on Job 854, Strip 1, Photograph 528 from the Chief Directorate of Surveys and Mapping in South Africa. Reproduced under Government Printer's Copyright Authority No. 11012 dated 9 October 2001.

The most dramatic changes appear between 1958 and 1972 northeast of the Matlhwareng Valley in the southern Kalahari. As in earlier sets, the photographs in Figures 8-6 to 8-8 are not congruent, but the points marked "1," "2," and "3" provide orientation, as do the dolaritic dykes, which appear as dark lines. In 1958 (Figure 8-6), this land is owned by whites, who cultivate fields. There are few roads, and the impact of grazing is even and not interrupted by fencing. The most striking feature is the bushes clustered along the dolaritic dykes, where the water collects underground, and the bushes in dark patches on the veld. By 1965 (Figure 8-7), the SANT has purchased the land.[92] Plowing was of course, illegal on trust lands, and the fields are fading into the veld. Otherwise, the area remains undeveloped, a remote corner of underpopulated veld. By 1972 (Figure 8-8), the situation changes dramatically, as the area is prepared to receive the residents of the Di Takwanen Reserve in Vryburg, which will be removed the following year. (The photograph in Figure 8-8 was taken at a higher altitude and covers a larger area to the south of the earlier photos in Figures 8-6 and 8-7.) Most incongruously, gravel roads on a grid measuring one and a half kilometers on each side have been put down on the former cultivated field. This is the future site of the village of Deerward, awaiting both houses and people. Additionally, to the south a giant triangular cul-de-sac connects the main road to two former farm homesteads, where the villages Elston and Ga-Ramatale will be constructed. The aggressive development of the bare veld comes as a shock. Nothing in the earlier photographs has suggested that this region could attract dense human settlement. The only reason for the road is to service the new villages, and the only reason to situate villages in the southern Kalahari is because the South African government wanted them nowhere else.

THE GREAT BOPHUTHATSWANA DONKEY MASSACRE

If Bantustans were to pass as modern nation states, as the policy of Separate Development stipulated they must be, they could not be governed only through tribal structures. And so, Separate Development in South Africa departed from Indirect Rule elsewhere when it invested tribal structures with the trappings of a modern state, superimposing a bureaucracy and a weak parliament on colonial institutions. In 1968, the Tswana Territorial Authority received a bureaucracy, including an agricultural department, whose white officials provided continuity with the previous administration.[93] An appearance of political modernization came through elections in 1971, but chiefs retained reserved seats in the Bophuthatswana Parliament. In 1972, Bophuthatswana received self-governing status with Lucas Mangope, chief of the Bahurutse ba Manyane, as president. Bophuthatswana became the second South African black homeland to receive

Figure 8-6 The Kalahari Northeast of the Matlhwareng River in 1958. Based on Job 414, Strip 4, Photograph 2802 from the Chief Directorate of Surveys and Mapping in South Africa. Reproduced under Government Printer's Copyright Authority No. 11012 dated 9 October 2001.

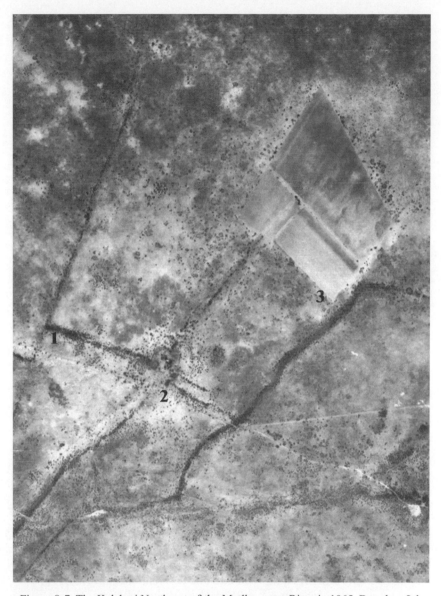

Figure 8-7 The Kalahari Northeast of the Matlhwareng River in 1965. Based on Job 537, Strip 2, Photograph 062 from the Chief Directorate of Surveys and Mapping in South Africa. Reproduced under Government Printer's Copyright Authority No. 11012 dated 9 October 2001.

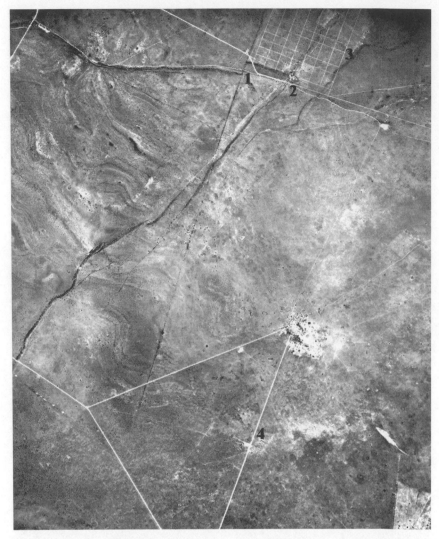

Figure 8-8 The Kalahari Northeast of the Matlhwareng River in 1972. Based on Job 700, Strip 3, Photographs 9386 and 9385 from the Chief Directorate of Surveys and Mapping in South Africa. Reproduced under Government Printer's Copyright Authority No. 11012 dated 9 October 2001.

"independence" in 1977. These homelands were not independent of Pretoria, but the South African government did devolve some control. There were elections, but less than half the seats in Parliament were open to popular contest and the voting was frequently fraudulent.[94]

Although they were created in the service of racial segregation, these institutions acquired the ability to act in their own interest on behalf of their own members. Indirect Rule and communal tenure had long since exposed rural blacks to intervention by the state. Under the Union and the Republic of South Africa, government officials never managed to implement the policy that farming rights be limited to a restricted number of households who would farm for commercial profits. However, in Bophuthatswana state intervention was unfettered by an ideology of self-determination of an ethnic unit. The state was undemocratic, and the governing elite competed directly with the governed for resources. Thereafter, donkey control under Bophuthatswana became extremely virulent. Furthermore, since 1960, governance in South Africa as a whole had become much more repressive.

Although it transcended race, the anti-donkey tendency remained embedded in class. Compared with the elite in other African colonies, the officials who acted against donkeys had relatively great power and material benefits. Furthermore, there was little holding them accountable to homeland residents. Corruption and patronage characterized Bophuthatswana governance. In fact, in July 1998, Mangope was convicted of 102 counts of theft totaling over 3.5 million rand and three counts of fraud involving 1.2 million rand.[95] Mining and maize production fueled the Bophuthatswana economy, but in the driest, western reaches around Kuruman, cattle ranching provided the greatest wealth, and the state funneled much of this wealth to the elite. The position of chiefs was ambiguous. The state provided them with considerable material benefits, including parliamentary salaries, the ability to monopolize land, and a cut of government contracts. Yet Mangope's relations with the chiefs were strained, and some were among his strongest critics and opponents. Even before the donkey killing, Tlharo Chief R. B. Toto, who had been the original Bophuthatswana minister of agriculture, fell out with Mangope and became a leader in the Sebuasengwe opposition party.[96]

In the 1970s, there were accusations that government cattle breeding projects in Kuruman favored rich and well-connected purchasers by selling stock directly to them rather than at public auction. Moreover, in preparation for independence, Bophuthatswana acquired additional land that was not included in communal territory, but was made available as private farms. Leases for these farms frequently went to chiefs, cabinet members, or to the president and his circle, and most commercial beef production took place on these farms rather than on communal pastures near villages. Beef producers received assistance through funds provided by Pretoria to the Bantu Investment Corporation (BIC). After 1973, the BIC guaranteed a floor price for every animal sold at auction in Bophuthatswana, and in 1975–6, twenty-two percent of them were purchased

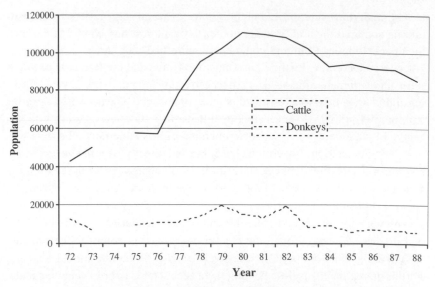

Figure 8-9 Cattle and donkeys in the Tlhaping-Tlharo District.

with its funds.[97] Additionally, the BIC provided commercial farm loans through the Bophuthatswana National Development Corporation and, after 1981, through the Agricultural Bank of Bophuthatswana. The Department of Agriculture gave increased assistance with marketing through Agricor, its extension program founded in 1979. Concerning cultivation in wetter areas of Bophuthatswana, the government made clear its vision of proper traction, importing 200 tractors from Austria in 1982. Agricor was rewarded for its efforts to commercialize in 1983 when a trade adviser to President Ronald Reagan visited and complimented its agricultural development work, promising to seek markets for Bophuthatswana produce.[98]

Because of these efforts to develop the commercial beef industry, the cattle population rose steeply after Bophuthatswana became self-governing: it was 43,607 in 1972 in the Tlhaping-Tlharo District (composed of land formerly in the Districts of Kuruman and Vryburg), but by 1981 it had reached 109,894 (see Figure 8-9). The Tlhaping-Tlharo District brought together areas that had previously been in the Kuruman and Vryburg Districts, so the number of cattle cannot be correlated to earlier statistics from Kuruman, but the changes in the proportions of cattle and donkeys is noteworthy: in 1946 there had been slightly more donkeys than cattle in the Kuruman District, but in 1981 there were eight times as many cattle as donkeys in Tlhaping-Tlharo. In the year ending in September 1982, Tlhaping-Tlharo producers earned 80,795 rand in stock sales, a large proportion of the 103,769 rand earned in Bophuthatswana as a whole.[99] Territorial authority meetings continued to discuss donkey numbers in the 1970s, agreeing to limit untaxed animals to six per owner, but subsequent enforcement is not recorded. After independence, warnings about the high donkey population continued, with Tlhaping-Tlharo cited as having the greatest problem. In regional council and National Assembly meetings some men defended donkeys as necessary for plowing and petitioned for cultivation rights.[100]

The majority of rural people engaged in supplementary subsistence production and did not participate in commercial cattle raising or cultivation with tractors. Certainly, many people owned both donkeys and cattle, and small farmers could benefit from some of the new programs, but Agricor aimed to help commercial farmers, as acknowledged in a 1986 Agricor report: "The land can support only a small portion of the population through involvement in farming."[101] However, access to land remained communal, so physical, not market, forces were required to put production in the hands of commercial farmers.[102] Because "customary" institutions had little community accountability, physical force was feasible.

The immediate cause for the state to act against donkeys and their owners was the weather. Unfortunately, the early 1980s saw a devastating drought, and, as usual, bovines were most vulnerable to shortages of fodder and water. Under this pressure, Bophuthatswana acted to reserve grazing for them. In May 1983, a governmental decree announced that all "surplus" donkeys were to be exterminated, but people who proved their animals were "necessary" could keep four. What followed grew out of the precedent of earlier donkey control, but it had an astounding and unparalleled vehemence. The contingencies that transformed this cull into a near-extermination campaign are not clear. Bophuthatswana Department of Agriculture and Agricor reports from 1983 do not mention the donkey killing. E. M. Mokgoko, the minister of agriculture, delivered an official explanation in a speech to the Bophuthatswana National Assembly. He echoed the received wisdom on the destructiveness of donkeys, claiming that since 1978 the state had attempted to reduce numbers, and referred to the seriousness of the drought.[103] However, there were no scientific studies on the impact of donkeys, and it is impossible to determine what their environmental impact was during the drought. In any case, the drought cannot explain the violence and repression in the action. Perhaps the savageness of the massacre was politically motivated, intended to terrorize people and preempt opposition. Increasing repression by the South African government at the time must have given the Bophuthatswana regime confidence to act brutally.

Government records for this year are not yet open, so the role of Pretoria cannot be determined; white soldiers did participate in other parts of Bophuthatswana, although no one reported their presence around Kuruman.[104] The word on the street, recalled W. J. Seremane, a Bophuthatswana dissident, was that President Mangope had nearly collided with donkeys on the highway and this turned him against the entire species.[105] Whatever the immediate cause, the difference between donkey control in 1983 and earlier years was not due to a change in the donkey population or their environmental impact. Instead, it was due to changes in the state and the economy.

Based on interviews in Ncweng, Ga-Mopedi, Kagung, and Seodin, villages near Kuruman, I have reconstructed the donkey killing in that area.[106] Sometimes accounts are contradictory, as they were regarding the warnings people received. Some people reported that the cull had begun like earlier ones, with meetings on reducing the population. People then tried to sell, but found no buyers. Others recalled hearing on the radio about the plan to reduce donkeys or from those who had already experienced the culling. Some people had enough warning to send their donkeys to two small villages that were never removed from white South Africa and hence were not under Bophuthatswana jurisdiction. Others sent animals to relatives who worked on white-owned farms.[107] In each village, some people were taken by surprise.

Members of the Bophuthatswana Police Force and the Bophuthatswana Defense Force arrived in trucks or in "Hippos," the troop carriers that would become infamous patrolling black urban townships during the 1980s. At the small village of Ncweng, people remember that they gathered their animals in preparation for counting, as in previous culls. They hardly expected the immediate shooting of most donkeys. They soon learned their error, because soldiers shot donkeys from their vehicles. When soldiers arrived, they did not explain the procedure or count the assembled animals, but simply opened fire. Some people expected only jennies to be culled, but soldiers shot jacks and jennies alike. After shooting the gathered donkeys, soldiers fanned out across the veld. Searching the streets, the river valley, and the grazing areas, they shot the donkeys they saw. A few people, realizing the danger, hid donkeys in their houses. This worked if neighbors did not tip off soldiers to search the house, as they sometimes did. In Seodin, the headman reported that an intervention temporarily halted the shootings. Thereafter, soldiers and police proceeded less randomly, paying greater attention to how many donkeys were permitted per household.[108]

Although no people were killed, the violence of the shootings was extremely traumatic for witnesses. The last armed clash between people and the state in this region had occurred in 1897. Before 1983, most Kuruman people had never seen troop carriers or heard gunfire. Moreover, the soldiers explicitly threatened people who complained about the shooting. There is strong consistency in the interviews about the brutality of the shootings and how it provoked revulsion: "The soldiers did not take aim, but shot animals anywhere, as often as it took to kill them."[109] Every interview indicated that these were inhumane killings. "We were very disturbed about the actual way in which the donkeys were killed, because they were not put to death – they were savaged. Others were shot in the eye, different parts of the body, and the feet, and this made the actual killing gruesome because they had to suffer too much pain, unlike if they were shot once in the head."[110] People told me that the soldiers were not local men, who might have been sympathetic, but were from other parts of Bophuthatswana. One man reported that his cousin had participated, but he later suffered nightmares and left the army.[111]

Many, many donkeys died. Some people reported losing their entire herd of donkeys, up to eighteen animals. Even donkeys in harness were not safe from shooting. One man was using his donkeys when they were shot:

> When the soldiers came in, I was riding in my cart, on my way to fetch building soil. They met me on my way, and never asked where I was going, or how many should they kill. They just mowed down the whole four, and I had to ask people to come and help me take the cart home and take the other two carcasses home and the other two I left them for people who wanted their meat. I was very heartbroken. What was surprising about the soldiers is that they never asked how far I was staying in order that I could maybe take the cart home, but they just shot the donkeys.[112]

A woman explained her feelings at seeing the blood and carcasses lying on top of each other: "It was like they were people."[113]

Donkeys were worth about fifteen rand per animal,[114] but no compensation was offered. Dead donkeys had value as meat, and the shock of the killings did not prevent people from taking advantage of the opportunity for a substantial meal. I asked one group, "What did you do after the soldiers left?" "We ate," they shrugged.[115] The government made no provisions to move the carcasses, and eventually, many donkeys rotted in the field and stank. The shootings stopped without explanation, but Seremane believed that pressure from the government in Pretoria, possibly motivated by fear of an outcry by white animal lovers, stopped the donkey killings.[116] It is impossible to say how many donkeys were killed, but the Bophuthatswana agricultural census reports show a steep decline in the population. The given number for Bophuthatswana as a whole dropped from 47,927 in 1982 to 28,835 in 1983. Over half the reported missing donkeys were from the Tlhaping-Tlharo District, where the count of 19,047 plummeted to 8,599.[117] Conceivably, not all of these animals died; presumably, many people would have been wary of census takers and would have hidden their surviving donkeys from government eyes.

Like other Betterment practices, the donkey killing "led to the impoverishment of affected people."[118] Many claimed that they had earned an income from transporting goods with their donkey carts or that the death of donkeys forced them to pay cash for services they could previously provide for themselves. The death of the draft animals made it more difficult to plow. An older woman believed the killing was especially disadvantageous for women: "Widows and divorcees who had donkeys, those donkeys acted as their husbands. . . . Since then their suffering was exacerbated, and they are still suffering even now."[119] It was expensive to replace donkeys after the shootings because their price rose.

As for the cattle, killing donkeys did not improve conditions enough to save them. These species existed in overlapping but different biological and geographical niches. The patterns of land ownership determined that donkeys and cattle raised for market had not been in direct competition for the same pastures. Donkeys grazed near villages, on highly populated communal lands, where more animals competed for grazing, and theft was a greater risk. With or without donkeys, these were not ideal areas for commercial beef production. Furthermore, donkeys were adapted to a wider range of possible fodder than cattle, including drought-resistant bushes. True, donkeys did eat the grass that survived the drought, and they ate proportionately more than cattle or goats did. Nevertheless, killing them did not equip cattle to survive in a bushy, diseased, and drought-prone environment. Statistics show that the Tlhaping-Tlharo District was not able to sustain the high cattle numbers of the early 1980s. The numbers dropped from 102,253 in 1983 to 92,763 in 1984 and 84,971 in 1988 (see Figure 8-9). As a means of ensuring the sustainability of beef production, the donkey killing was a failure.

COERCION AND CONSERVATION

There were strong motivations behind the use of coercion in Betterment. Yet, coercion in conservation was more than just a means to an end. Conservation served different ends at different times: to prevent degradation, to establish segregation and political control, and to promote the economic interests of the homeland elite. In fact, De Wet believes that during the 1950s and 1960s, bureaucratic-technocratic problem solving gained enough momentum to promote conservation for its own sake.[120] Throughout the continent these different purposes were reconciled with the use of force. The needs of segregation were not the primary cause for coercive conservation, because even in British colonies that did not share the South African segregationist agenda, implementing conservation involved coercive action. Even within South Africa, the use of force served differing ends. For example, retaliation by the state against anti-Betterment revolts in Pondoland and Tembuland in 1961–2 was intended to reassert political control and also to enforce the Betterment regulations that provoked the revolts.[121]

Rather than asking what intentions motivated the use of force, I have asked what conditions made it possible. The use of coercion in conservation reveals something more fundamental about the South African state than its dedication to particular outcomes; it exposes the environmentally abusive possibilities of Indirect Rule. Although technocratic and "scientific," the interventions were predicated upon racial segregation; it is inconceivable that the state could have made such drastic interventions on lands occupied by whites, who had greater political rights and held their land under private tenure. In contrast, blacks had little representation among decision makers. Like other coercive conservation programs, Betterment related to Africans as tribal subjects, and thus, it never aimed to respond to local concerns and was never consensual. The fact that land was held communally was an important condition enabling intervention. Because "communal" tenure was not connected to community institutions, people had limited participation in decisions about how to use the land. Additionally, the colonial creation of tribal structures set the stage for the use of force. The resistance to the ban on dry land plowing suggests that local Tribal Authorities retained some sense of accountability to the people, but the Bophuthatswana government felt no such restraint. The donkey massacre was more drastic than earlier conservation programs. This was not because of the material interests of the Bophuthatswana elite. Their interests were no more compelling than the need of the central government to keep political control or enforce segregation. The difference was that in the homeland of Bophuthatswana the authoritarian potential of colonial institutions was more fully developed. It was the increased concentration of power in the state and the lack of political and civil rights among its subjects that sustained coercion in conservation, including the donkey massacre, probably the most repressive conservation program in South African history.

9

Retrospectives on Socio-Environmental History and Socio-Environmental Justice

L IKE a photographic print in the processing bath, an unrecognized history in Kuruman comes into sight when human society and the biophysical environment are mixed in the developing solution. It emerges that the quiet thornveld and quiescent people there share a complex history. For more than 200 years, people interacted in varying and changing ways with the landscape and each other. The point of this book, however, has not been to vindicate Kuruman as a scene of dynamism. More importantly, this history of the edge of the Kalahari yields new perspectives on the wider field of southern African history. We have seen that the environment is a locus of struggle between people. Moreover, the different ways people relate to biophysical conditions and processes help shape structured inequalities in society. Images developed through the socio-environmental approach to the history of Kuruman will be reflected in histories of other places – in southern Africa and in other parts of the continent. These include Bantu speakers consigned to a foraging class; agro-pastoralists who are receptive to, yet discriminating of, innovations introduced from Europe; Africans being transformed into colonial subjects through environmental processes; migrant workers who herd and garden; and an environmentally interventionist state acting on the food production of the colonized.

As a retrospective on the larger meanings suggested by a socio-environmental study of Kuruman, I will comment on several points it raises about the interpretation of South African rural history. First, the collapse of the extensive subsistence system around 1900 and the gradual abandonment of supplementary production in the mid- to late-twentieth century raises the question of whether the disappearance of old ways led to a declining quality of life. The second point involves assessing the inability to intensify. The perseverance of extensive techniques and the attrition of food production raises the question of to what extent extensive production was a shortcoming. The final point has the greatest scope: certain people in every period held power, sought to increase it, and exercised it

in the realm of how they and others interacted with the environment. This raises
the question of power in environmental history. In answering it, I will begin
with explanations given by people in Kuruman and then close with my own.

HISTORIES OF DECLINE AND ADAPTATION

NJ: Do you think there is a future for people who are not plowing?
IS: There is no future for us. If the mine shuts down what are you going to do? You
can't depend on the mines, but plowing is from Adam and Eve to today.[1]

What we are telling you here is what our mothers used to do. As we grew
things changed and our lives got better.[2]

The first environmental histories of colonized peoples tended to emphasize the decline of their culture, population, autonomy, and ways of living in
the environment. *The Roots of Dependency*, by Richard White, describing the
collapse of indigenous systems of environmental management in the United
States, was a powerful influence on my early thought. In fact, initially, I envisioned my study of Kuruman ending with the collapse of extensive subsistence
production at the turn of the twentieth century. It became clear, however, that
environmental history continued after that collapse and that people adjusted
in interesting ways worthy of consideration. Additionally, the critique of the
"received wisdom" on degradation alerted me that where colonial observers
saw environmental degradation and destruction, it was possible to see innovation, such as in the adaptation to bushes and use of donkeys. It was clear
that even after the collapse of indigenous environmental management, people
were engaged in specific and deliberate practices to mitigate their poverty and
dependency on the cash economy, for example, in the Transvaal maize harvest,
and tributary asbestos mining. This is not to say that colonized Africans exercised agency without constraints or that all their activities were environmentally
friendly; the point is that they worked creatively and deliberately to mitigate
their circumstances and to persevere. Their efforts, and the measure of success
they found, are worthy of consideration. In Kuruman, these innovative relations
with the environment showed that black rural areas were not stagnant in the
wake of a process of underdevelopment. Eventually, however, food production
supplementing wage labor also diminished. Despite this broad trend, even today, some people who do not qualify as cattle barons still raise animals – a few
cattle or more goats and some donkeys. Some people even cultivate, showing
that people responded to the disincentives to food production in varied ways
that belie inexorable decline.

Social stratification is another factor arguing against a declensionist interpretation. *Balala* lived in very hard circumstances and would not have mourned the passing of the old order as a loss. In fact, by irrigating and leaving to work in mines, they contributed to its end. Eventually, the prescriptions about the ways men and women related to the environment receded, and so today some widows control their families' herds. Emphatically, gender remains a critical social factor, but gendered distinctions in the sphere of relations with the environment have receded. In the twentieth century, racial categorization had a totalizing effect on people's experiences, but even within the category of blacks, some people benefited as class divisions reappeared. Different categories of people experienced the transition from one dispensation to the next differently, so describing a universal trajectory of decline flattens the variety of experience.

Clearly, Kuruman people experienced trauma and loss, as they did at the turn of the twentieth century. At times, they had very little room to maneuver and were victims more than agents, as when they suffered forced removals. Changes in their environment, such as increasing stock disease, the growing density of bushes, and the loss of water to the municipality, made it difficult to continue cultivation and cattle herding as they had. Hard times, however, do not dictate that history be about decline, degradation, or victimization. As might be expected, some older informants, such as Isaac Seamecho, quoted at the beginning of this section, stressed the deterioration from older days, but others, such as a woman in a group interview, also quoted above, considered that their lives were easier since they found new ways to support themselves. People held differing opinions on which ways to support themselves were the best. In one interview, my research assistants asked a group to make a matrix showing change over time in ways of working for a living, including food production. Interview participants showed stock keeping and cultivation declining in importance after the 1930s, with cultivation declining to the point of becoming negligible. Working in mines and as domestic servants peaked in the 1960s and declined thereafter. The jobs that became more prevalent in the 1980s and 1990s were sewing, harvesting grapes on Orange River farms, selling beer, making bricks, and trading hides. When asked to rank the jobs according to their advantages and disadvantages, individuals gave different answers. Some people preferred the independence of farming, selling beer, or sewing, because miners were vulnerable to retrenchment. Others preferred the regular salary of a steady job. One woman preferred grape harvesting, simply because that was what she knew best.[3] These different experiences, perceptions, and priorities warn against overgeneralization in the evaluation of well-being.

People expressed these differences of opinion and experience when they postulated overall historical trends. Many people had a nuanced interpretation of enhanced or eroded well-being. Understandably, they communicated discouragement about the currently high levels of unemployment, and some people conveyed perceptions of general impoverishment over time.[4] Nurses who had worked at the Batlharos hospital before the 1960s, however, recalled severe malnutrition at that time, especially during drought, and stated that nutrition had improved with increasing education.[5] A group of women who lived in Ga-Mopedi contradicted this, asserting that their health and nutrition were better when they produced more themselves, but they understood that things had improved for people who lived near the hospital and schools or had jobs.[6] Some told us that the hardship of poor people was relatively greater now than it had been, but understood that class stratification had always existed and that not everyone was now poor.[7] Also I was told that the physical demands of food production were high. A woman whose parents had worked in others' fields recalled: "It was no joke that they had difficulties. It was really tough during those days."[8] They also had mixed memories of the diet of past days. People today still eat *veldkos*, but one man explained why he preferred the taste of foods from the shop: "Wild foods have a disadvantage in the sense that if you eat them you will get sick and sometimes they taste bad. Unlike before, they didn't taste bad. Maybe that is because of civilization."[9] Even though people regretted the loss of old ways, many conveyed that the changes entailed differing costs and benefits for different people.

THE ENDURANCE OF EXTENSIVE PRODUCTION

Regarding the ways people related to their biophysical environment, I have stressed that production was extensive. To do this, I have relied upon European sources criticizing African production; however, by no means have I characterized extensive production as backward or the absence of intensification as a failure. At first, people did not intensify because they had no reason to do so and many good reasons not to. Later, they simply could not. Before 1800, the recent establishment of agro-pastoralism, the small population, and the low rainfall all worked to make food production reliant upon wide areas and low labor inputs. The Cape frontier introduced new types of land use, irrigation, and commercial hunting, and people adapted these to their existing ways of working the environment. The tragic irony of this history is that colonial land alienation created pressures to intensify only as impoverishment and political disinheritance made it impossible for people to do so. As supplementary food production decreased by the mid-twentieth century, low production became an excuse for the segregationist state to deny black people their land and water. Under Betterment, the state imposed more intensive habitation and pastoralism by investing capital to develop the necessary infrastructure. Empty expanses were populated with people and stock, even as the percentage of people who practiced food production declined. The decrease in the farming population would not be a problem any more than it was in affluent societies in the developed world, except that many nonfarmers in Kuruman had an insecure claim on entitlements.

What is the future of human interactions with the environment on communal lands in the southern Kalahari? Would some form of intensive land use provide more people with more of their sustenance? Many black people in the Kuruman River Valley hope that water from the Kuruman Eye will be restored to them and dream of intensive cultivation. Some gifted gardeners still do remarkable work. I recall a beautifully manicured plot in Seodin-Lareng and seeing many well-tended vegetable gardens on a walk along the river to Batlharos. In Ga-Mopedi, we saw a wheat field guarded by a woman and her children against birds, and in a nearby field donkeys and young male relatives plowed for an older woman. There was a veritable orchard next to the bone-dry river in Sedibeng, and even in Betterment villages, we saw a few healthy kitchen gardens watered by private boreholes.

If we agree with Ester Boserup, who argued that population growth is the major condition for agricultural growth, then we would expect intensification to occur if enough people need to produce more food.[10] However, Boserup identifies the logic of agricultural growth – labor aversion offset by the need for higher yields – more convincingly than she does its conditions. A more realistic assessment of agricultural growth acknowledges that in any given environment, certain human uses are possible and others are not. Few people would argue that semi-arid environments can sustain the same intensification as humid ones, and perhaps in spite of its eyes, the semi-arid thornveld will not see more intensive land use. The extremely low level of phosphates in the soil and the high price of fertilizer, not to mention the lack of water, suggest that cultivation will not be a cost-effective option in the near future. Rather than widespread capital- and labor-intensive production, the concern should be sustainable and affordable production. Sustainable production might involve sorghum, goats, and donkeys, even if they are not valuable enough to merit intensive commercial production.

INDIGENOUS THEORIES OF ENVIRONMENTAL JUSTICE

We are afraid to go to the trust farms because there will not be any work for our children and the graves of our grandfathers are here at Dakwen. The drought is being caused by white people.[11]

I was once asked at work by a white man why it was that when the white men became rich he gave his donkeys to blacks, but why when blacks were rich, they did not give the donkeys to people who are poor, but they decided to kill them?[12]

My final, farthest-reaching question addresses the role of power. Concentrations of power create structured inequalities between people in different racial, class, and gender categories, and this history has shown that the inequalities between these categories are fundamental to the ways people relate to the environment. Thus, power is a necessary consideration in environmental history, and in order to understand the historical dynamic between people and the biophysical environment, it is necessary to identify influence, authority, and material advantages in society. However, the consideration of power is more than a historical exercise; it is a moral process, involving reflection about how humans should live on this earth. Among environmental thinkers in the northern industrial world, moral reflection raises issues of the human impact on ecosystems and species and the disproportionate distribution of pollution among poor people and people of color.

Likewise, human–environmental relations provoked moral consideration in my interviews, and my informants explained past environmental relations with theories about the exercise of power and its repercussions – theories about environmental injustice and justice. This was particularly evident in two spheres. First, people frequently testified that drought has become more common in the thornveld and suggested that the improper exercise of power has caused drought. Thus, people's assertion of progressive desiccation, while reflecting a near-universal tendency to romanticize old times, also provides commentary on the rank abuses of power in their lifetimes. Second, people conveyed a well-defined populist vision of the propriety of donkey herding, maintaining that proper environmental relations must be democratically determined and must bring benefit to poor people.

In my interviews, people asserted with a nearly unanimous voice that progressive desiccation has occurred in Kuruman, although meteorological records indicate that this is not the case. A group who had lived at Konong even asserted that they had no droughts in their old home.[13] Even as they described the decline of *letsema* and the economic developments that discouraged plowing, they still maintained that a major reason more people did not cultivate or keep many animals today was the decline in rainfall. "The reason we buy food from the shop is that there is no more rain and we don't have seed to plant. In the olden days our parents never bought food from the shop but only coffee and salt."[14] Of course, there is a tendency of popular memory to idealize the past.* [15] As with other sources, historians who use oral data must critique, but not dismiss, stories of a halcyon past, including the humid conditions. However, climatological records do not indicate that Kuruman experienced progressive desiccation in the period of historical record. Furthermore, in 1997, when I was told that rainfall was declining, the area had seen six years of increasing rainfall. Although the early 1980s had been terribly dry, the average annual rainfall for the decade 1987–8 to 1996–7 was 444 millimeters, above the yearly mean of 416 millimeters for the period beginning 1931–2 (see Figures 1-4 and 1-5). Under these conditions, what led people to say that rainfall had decreased?

One possibility is that the incidence and severity of drought have remained constant, but that people cannot adapt to it as they once did. Herding remains the most significant economic activity in this environment, but the vegetation has changed. When people compare the amount of grass to that present in earlier times, then the effects of drought seem all the more acute if the veld is bushier than it was. Stock populations are also much higher than they once were, and when it withers, there is more competition for the grass that remains. During drought people must purchase more fodder, the cost of which they feel acutely. Because human populations are large, access to the open veld has shrunk and people cannot gain much sustenance from foraging in hard times. Additionally, because of taste preferences and new demands upon household labor, maize replaced sorghum as the staple, although it is more sensitive to drought and more difficult to cultivate in this area. Therefore, people who cultivate maize today will be more frustrated by drought than sorghum farmers in the past. In one interview, a matrix on the history of rain showed many droughts in the past, yet people asserted progressive desiccation as a cause for the cessation of cultivation. I asked how this could be: if droughts in the past did not keep people from plowing, why did they do so today? I was told that drought was more serious today because other factors compounded it: "In the olden days even if you had no rain, you had enough stock.... Today it is difficult. Even if you have stock you worry people will steal it."[16] Because of historical changes, droughts have a sharper impact on food production than they once did, even if they become no more frequent or severe. Another factor contributes to the discrepancy between memories of rain and records of the rain gauge; people believe that human disharmony, which they have witnessed in abundance, can cause drought.

Among Tswana people, *pula*, or rain, is a metaphor for blessings. This connects to a metaphorical aspect of testimony about increasing drought. I came

---

* Already in the 1880s, John Mackenzie warned that oral testimony on desiccation should not be taken uncritically.

to believe that people used "drought" as a code for hard times of social and environmental origin. But, drought is more than a symbol; it is believed to result from social hardship. In a neat reversal of environmental determinists who would attribute their level of development to the dry thornveld environment, my informants suggested that discordant social relations *created* the increasingly dry thornveld. Steven Feierman's elucidation of the ideas of *kuzifa shi* and *kubana shi* in Shambaai, Tanzania, provides a related example of social determinism. The concepts *kuzifa shi*, "healing the land," and *kubana shi*, "harming the land," describe social and political behavior with climatological and environmental repercussions. People in Shambaai believe the land is harmed when the king does not maintain proper relations with the people and when his power is inadequate to repel harmful forces, leading to drought and famine. The land is healed when proper relations between the king and his subjects are restored or when competition between the ruler and challengers is ended, restoring rainfall and plenty. Other scholars have observed similar beliefs among Tswana people that human, particularly chiefly, behavior will affect rainfall.[17]

Conceptions in Kuruman of social relationships and proper behavior are not as centered on the ruler as they are in Shambaai, but there is a related concept of "moral ecology." For example, a group of women told us that when they were girls they climbed Ga-Mogana, the conical hummock in the Kuruman Hills, and saw rocks that looked like breasts. But, they said, white people cut the breasts in half, causing the land (not just this particular stream) to dry up.[18] In the first epigraph opening this section, Dikgweng people, resisting removal in 1948, also blamed whites. The Khuis headman, in agreeing to removal in 1967, suggested that difficult relations with the government were the cause of drought and that assenting to removal would restore the rain: "If we refused to go where the Law says, we will be in more troubles.... If we leave from here we will live better and God will help us with more rain."[19] Statements about people causing drought also appear in remembrances of 1983. People regularly claimed that it became severe only after the donkeys were killed and then was "the worst of our lives." Moreover, some asserted that the terrible drought finally lessened only after many cattle succumbed, a clear statement on environmental trauma as a cost of social transgression.[20] In a variation on the theme of biophysical repercussions, one man recounted, to gales of laughter, that a police officer who had been particularly brutal to donkeys had suffered a condition that caused his skin to peel off.[21] Perhaps these reflect a particular African concept of environmental injustice.

The idea that the proper way for people to live together and the proper way to live in the environment are linked becomes even clearer in beliefs about donkeys and their impact. After 1983, the donkey killing was thoroughly politicized, becoming a cause against Bophuthatswana and Apartheid. Today, in the Kuruman area there is a strong pro-donkey position that extols their moral significance to poor people, Christianity, the environment, and democracy. Donkeys carry a profound load in the way people speak about the world. Like that on drought, the testimony about donkeys shows a belief in the relationship between human behavior and environmental conditions. People not only assert that the donkey killing caused drought, but that donkeys are valuable morally as well as economically. On this basis, they refute arguments for donkey control. I consider this environmental populism, the similarly problematic antithesis of the colonial received wisdom. The state never managed to suppress this discourse, although the pro-donkey position remained a social production subject to political forces.

It is difficult to trace the history of the popular position on donkeys. Unfortunately, few statements by people who benefited from them have been preserved in the documentary record from previous decades. As discussed in Chapter 8, there was some pro-donkey testimony at the "Meetings of Chiefs, Headmen and People" in the early 1950s. Some members of the Bophuthatswana National Assembly spoke in favor of donkeys before 1983, and despite the autocratic government, there were vehement objections during the cull.[22] However, the massacre promoted an extreme valorization of donkeys, as killing them became identified with Bophuthatswana and Apartheid.

Although donkeys eat proportionately more than ruminants and there were a lot of them in Kuruman to do the eating, in my interviews, people held that donkeys had virtually no negative impact, environmental or otherwise. They refuted each reason given for killing them. They denied that there were any feral donkeys or that the grass shortage was particularly severe before the massacre. Furthermore, they disagreed that donkeys eat a large amount of fodder. They recalled other justifications used by the Bophuthatswana government – that donkeys had especially toxic urine and sharp hooves that destroyed grass – and also denied these. They rejected even the most moderate reasons to control donkeys; one man dismissed a concern that would be familiar to anyone who has used motorized transport in the region. Emphasizing the responsibility of drivers, he mused, "You need a license to drive; a donkey doesn't get a license."[23]

While denying any negative impact, people explained that using donkeys was a veritable Christian responsibility and salubrious for society. A very high proportion of the population in Kuruman is Christian, and people often asserted that the donkey killing was a serious moral transgression because of the biblical significance of donkeys. Referring to Jesus on Palm Sunday, a man explained to me, "We must understand that God wanted us to use the donkeys, because there is a quote in the Bible which states that you would find the donkey tied to a pole and bring it to me."[24] It is very significant that this belief predated the donkey massacre; in 1981, a member of the Bophuthatswana National Assembly made much of Jesus' selection of a donkey. "Our Lord Jesus Christ had to make use of the services of a donkey because he was not used to riding a horse, even then if he had a horse, he could have been thrown by the horse and could also have been forced to train this horse to be ridden."[25]

In addition to the Christian significance, people emphasize the special relationship between donkeys and common people. There is a wide understanding of the donkey killing as a class-based injustice. As one member of the National Assembly said in 1983, "People now think the donkeys are being killed because the Government is rich. It is the rich people who have decided that the donkeys should be killed."[26] The interviews showed the class analysis to be ubiquitous. One man theorized that donkey and cattle ownership defined classes:

> The situation of our people in the Kudumane [Kuruman] area is like this: we have different peoples who lived differently. People who own cattle, you find that most do not own donkeys. They only farm cattle. These people who own donkeys are the people who live a very low life. They do not even have a motor car – a donkey to them means a lot. With it they do most of their work, transport for water, bricks, gravel, sand, wood . . . mostly for building. Since we have such a high rate of unemployment, some with these donkeys, they can help the others who do not have donkeys to draw water for them and bring them wood when they build their houses and in return they got paid and that is how they create life. So these are the two different types of people we have in our area.[27]

Others supported him in blaming the class of cattle owners for the event: "What actually disturbed me most was that the people who made the decision do not have donkeys. Although they know the importance of donkeys in our lives, they themselves have cows and sheep."[28] "I started not to trust anybody who is a wealthy cattle owner, because they could take any decision that would affect even the lives of ordinary donkeys."[29] One informant asserted that ungrateful "faceless" people motivated the government to shoot donkeys: "Even though those faceless people used donkeys to reach the standard where they are having cows and horses, they have actually forgotten that."[30] Consider the second epigraph opening this section: "I was once asked at work by a white man why it was that when the white men became rich he gave his donkeys to blacks, but why when blacks were rich, they did not give the donkeys to people who are poor, but they decided to kill them?"[31] Thus, a man contrasted the way capitalizing white and black farmers treated donkeys, implicitly criticizing the blacks.

Of course, whites had private tenure and political rights, which protected them from coercive conservation. In fact, during the same decade as the massacre in Bophuthatswana, two white municipalities erected monuments to the animals.[32] In 1984, the Municipality of Upington erected a bronze statue of a donkey attached to a pump, a perfectly lifelike animal that stands frozen in its step on a circular path around the machine. In 1986, the Pietersburg District Agricultural Union erected a statue of a donkey at repose. In Upington, donkey-powered machines allowed white farmers to pump water for commercial fruit production, while in Pietersburg, donkeys carried rock during the late nineteenth-century gold rush. Both statues have inscriptions acknowledging donkeys' hard work and contribution to the human economy. The recognition by these white communities of donkeys (and not of black workers!) at about the same time that Bophuthatswana massacred donkeys is a remarkable expression of the pervasive irony of South African history. The great discrepancy in these treatments of South African donkeys results from divisions of both race and class among humans. In Upington and Pietersburg, donkeys grazed on privately held farms, where owners had rights over the land and its use. A white owner had the right to decide whether a donkey should be destroyed or put out to pasture. Furthermore, donkeys in Upington and Pietersburg contributed to capitalization, while donkeys in Bophuthatswana supported those who could not capitalize. The memorialized donkeys aided those who had power and did so on terms set by the powerful.

The issue of good government and democracy is closely linked to memories of the donkey massacre. The significance of the donkey killing was not lost on the political opposition, weak as it was, in Bophuthatswana. After the killings, J. B. Toto, the chief of the Tlharo people and a member of the opposition Sebuosengwe Party, made the donkey killing an issue and thus became known as "Rra-Ditonki" or "Mr. Donkeys."[33] In addition, an African National Congress (ANC) partisan and protest singer, Blondie Makhene, wrote a song about the donkey killings. It describes ghosts of donkeys haunting Mangope and goes on to urge people to join Umkhonto we Sizwe, the military wing of the ANC.[34] Thus, in contrast to the monuments in Upington and Pietersburg, a song of revolution commemorates donkeys in Bophuthatswana.

Mangope resisted the 1994 transition with violence. The March riots in Mafikeng/Mmabatho were publicized worldwide, but protesters also took to the streets in Batlharos and Maropeng, chanting "give us back our donkeys." The police responded by shooting and killing one protester.[35] The contrast between donkey-killing Bophuthatswana and a democratic ANC government was not lost on those who spoke with us. Prompted by the subject of the donkey killing, a young woman spoke with great emotion when she contrasted Bophuthatswana rule with that of the ANC:

> We were very happy in 1994 that we voted in the government of the people by the people, a democratic government.... Unlike if you have something that does not satisfy you, then you are not in a position to say it. During Mangope's reign, there was no cooperation. Even though they called themselves democrats, they did not practice democracy. The only thing they knew was to oppress people, as they were pawns of the Apartheid government which used him to oppress other people.[36]

An older woman who had one surviving donkey was still fearful: "The small donkey that survived has reproduced and I am so afraid that I do not even trust the present government. I am always afraid that it will do the same."[37]

Not everyone in Kuruman ascribes to the tenets of donkey populism. Mangope is now the leader of the United Christian Democratic Party (UCDP) and has some supporters in the area. In the 1999 elections, the UCDP received eighteen percent of the vote in the communal areas north of Kuruman town.[38] In my interviews I did not hear his supporters defending Mangope's donkey policy. My research assistants and I witnessed the pressures for conformity with the populist position when we held our interviews after one community meeting. When the assembled people heard that we wanted to discuss the donkey massacre, there was a public discussion of whether we should be allowed to hold interviews on such a sensitive subject. To address their concerns, we met with the headman and a few leading men to explain my purpose and hear their statements. Thereafter, we were allowed to proceed and it was resolved that people should talk freely. All the same, I noticed one Mangope supporter fleeing the scene. I was not successful in my attempt to interview this man or Agricor officials; their continued reticence and my impending return to the United States made it prohibitively difficult. Clearly, like official colonial positions, populism is capable of waging campaigns against alternative perspectives. Environmental historians must account for the social dynamics that feed it, and they should consider social divisions in relations with the biophysical world, but populism requires the same critical examination as given the official received wisdom, and we must maintain a critical distance from its values and proposals.[39]

SOCIO-ENVIRONMENTAL HISTORY AND
SOCIO-ENVIRONMENTAL JUSTICE

Men move boundary stones; the pasture flocks they have stolen. They drive away the orphan's donkey and take the widow's ox in pledge. They thrust the needy from the path and force all the poor of the land into hiding.

Like the wild donkeys in the desert, the poor go about their labor of foraging food; the wasteland provides food for their children. They gather fodder in the fields and glean in the vineyards of the wicked. Job 24: 2-6 (NIV)

Land alienation, loss of stock, foraging by the poor, labor in others' fields – this passage from Job encapsulates much of the environmental history of the thornveld. Like Kuruman people, Job has a moral assessment of how people influence others' relations with the environment. No stranger to suffering himself, Job speaks plainly: the perpetrators of environmental injustice are simply "the wicked." Wickedness, however, does not offer strong enough explanatory power to sustain the conclusion of an academic study. That is not to say that social scientists are morally detached from their subjects. Both North American environmental and South African social historians write of injustice by those holding power, in destruction of the biophysical world and exploitation and repression of people. Abundant examples in both fields qualify as good history after Cronon's observation: "At its best, historical storytelling keeps us morally engaged with the world by showing us how to care about it and its origins in ways we had not done before."[40]

As Cronon notes, historians explain change, but also evaluate it. The preceding chapters describe environmental and social change. Much of the story has turned on the exercise of power, and the evaluation has rested on questions of inequality and justice. The evaluation of ecological change is particularly difficult. As a subject of others' power, the environment has in some ways been resilient, but in other ways it has been transformed. Following the lead of disequilibrium range ecology, I have been cautious about describing change as ecological degradation. The thornveld became bushier, but tendencies toward bushiness always existed, and herders were not entirely responsible for the change. Whatever the cause, it will qualify as degradation if it is irreversible and involves a loss of biodiversity. That question is for researchers in other disciplines to determine experimentally. This history included other changes in the biophysical world. The eyes continued to flow; however, people now capture streams as they emerge from the earth, and a major anthropogenic change in the biota of the river valleys has resulted. Probably, the wild animals once inhabiting the thornveld have lost the most in this history. Large herbivores and carnivores are gone, and the loss of wetlands must have reduced birdlife. Donkeys, although they are domesticated, also suffered as a species at the hands of people. Today, there is a protected space for wildlife, but that is not to say that local people co-exist with other species. The luxury "private desert game reserve 'Tswalu' " covers 1,000 square kilometers in the Kalahari northwest of Kuruman. At 4,000 rand per night per person, it caters to a market few can afford, let alone black residents of communal reserves who might like to view the local fauna.[41]

Despite the drastic changes suffered by plants and animals, in this book I have been more occupied with changes in the ways different categories of humans interacted with the environment. Class, gender, and racial categories are unequally sized receptacles of power, all of which determine different people's relations with the biophysical world. Social power has a reciprocal relationship with the environment. People both gain power from and use the biophysical world as an instrument of power over others. This study upholds C. S. Lewis's assertion, quoted in Chapter 1, that "Man's power over Nature turns out to be a power exercised by some men over other men with Nature as its instrument."[42] On the agro-pastoral frontier, chiefs confiscated stock, pelts, and wild plant food to maintain their advantage in the ecological cycle. The colonial state hindered Africans' food production by restricting their land in order to secure a labor force. The twentieth-century state, both the central government and Bophuthatswana, assailed black people's relations with the environment, in part, to maintain control as it implemented the plan of segregation. However, the environment was more than an instrument in this history; it provided a material base for the power to dominate others. At the same time it gave power to endure domination.

I do not mean that immediate relations with the environment are the ultimate source of power. For example, divisions by gender arise from cultural norms while expressed and realized in environmental relations. Although, white South Africans' power over blacks rested on their control over the bedrock, water, and topsoil, the inequalities of colonialism and segregation arose from many factors in the long history of interactions between Europe and Africa. In the modern world, people from different continents and countries interacted according to many contingencies, including religions, political systems, economies, and racial prejudices, as well as the environmental relations of the parties.[43] Environmental interpretations are necessary but not sufficient explanations for the acquisition of power in chiefdoms, colonies, or capitalist economies. That said, South African historiography has not sufficiently integrated the necessary environmental explanations.

Has environmental injustice been more severe in some dispensations than in others? Were there times when people in Kuruman lived with fewer environmental inequities? Imbalances of power always existed in the ways people related to the environment. On the agro-pastoral frontier, rich men had advantages over women and *balala*. Yet women retained control over one form of production, and while *balala* may have had the harshest physical existence of anyone in this history, they had more freedom when they avoided towns, and had a remote possibility of rising to the level of the powerful. On the Cape frontier, the introduction of irrigation and trading opened new routes to the accumulation of wealth and power. In the period before the imposition of colonial restrictions, male *balala* and food-producing male commoners had new opportunities to establish themselves, but women did not. A few men who took up irrigation independent of chiefs or hunted commercially paid wages to workers, but reciprocal and client labor remained the rule. In this period, capitalist inequalities did not replace those of the agro-pastoral society.

In the colonial period, the locus of power shifted from those defined by their gender and class to those defined by their origins, culture, and race, and Europeans gained power over Africans. The subjugation of Africans expressed itself in their inability to continue their production practices, and they became more dependent on the cash economy than on the environment. This dependence on the white-controlled economy entailed a collective subordination to another race. Yet European rule not only lowered but also leveled African society. When imperial annexation undermined indigenous ways of governing, of accumulating wealth and power, the result was some flattening of class and a blurring of gender. After the collapse of subsistence production, the thornveld on communal lands and the river valleys became less of a basis of power for one class or one gender. Rather, relations with the local environment came to mitigate the inequalities that people of a marginalized race experienced in national society.

The economic and political subordination of one race is not the same as segregation, the policy that exacerbated and hardened differences. Racial segregation concentrated power and made weaker people subject to new levels of abuse. Like earlier imbalances of class and gender, the aggregation of power in racial categories was expressed in the ways people related to the environment. Under segregation, those who had once functioned as men and women, fully entitled Tlhaping and Tlharo or *balala*, Christians, commercial hunters or woodcutters, colonial subjects, migrant laborers, asbestos producers, herders, and farmers became first of all black South Africans. Thus classified, their ability to act according to any other identity and to exercise power accruing to any other category was limited. Racial classification was totalizing and brought extreme restrictions to the ways blacks interacted with the nonhuman world. Many actually lost the right to stay in their homes and were deposited in harsher environments. However, forced removals are not the only environmental expression of racial imbalance. Through the policy of Betterment, segregation also restricted how black people could use the environments they were allowed to live in. The irony of this racially driven policy was that it redeveloped class as a receptacle for power, as the donkey massacre shows. Thus, even in Apartheid South Africa, race was not the only salient division in the ways people related to the environment. The inequalities and injustices were undoubtedly most extreme in the segregationist period, when more wealth existed and the mechanisms of disenfranchisement were strongest. There were high physical and emotional costs for the black people of Kuruman, including the lives of children at Bendell. Nevertheless, toward the end of that period, food security improved. There had been famines throughout the early nineteenth and twentieth centuries, but the last one was in 1941. The transition from seasonal hunger to chronic malnutrition is a familiar one among the disadvantaged in southern Africa, but senior Batlharos nurses we interviewed in 1997 believed that malnutrition had also decreased since the 1960s.[44] This does not mean that every individual had secure entitlements, but that someone was sharing his or her wages or pension with family in Kuruman. Although unemployment caused hardship, people in the 1990s were getting by, perhaps better than many before them had. The AIDS pandemic will make this more difficult.

The political liberation of 1994 was a cause for joy and some improvements. In its wake, there have been projects to improve the infrastructure, and people who suffered forced removals have filed land claims. However, majority rule will not necessarily redeem the history of Kuruman from environmental inequalities. What it provides is an opportunity to mitigate the ill effects of the colonial heritage. Mamdani has observed that in much of independent Africa, the colonial institutions of Indirect Rule in the countryside have not been democratized and "customary" tribal structures have not been opened to community participation.[45] Unless this occurs in South Africa, people on communal lands in Kuruman and elsewhere will remain vulnerable to unjust state intervention, however progressive the national constitution. The political will to develop democracy and invest in poor rural people remains to be demonstrated. Moreover, because South Africa is a poor country with underdeveloped traditions of participation, the necessary resources for these developments are scarce. Future sustainable development in Kuruman will involve the following specific improvements: restoring people to or compensating them for land they lost during segregation; encouraging small stock ownership among the many rather than cattle production among the few; cleaning up the deadly asbestos litter; distributing the water from the Kuruman Eye equitably; and helping people with affordable, small scale cultivation – possibly of sorghum – on dry lands. Most fundamentally, however, it is necessary to recognize that environmental and social justice are linked and that power imbalances will determine the ways men and women, rich and poor, and blacks and whites live with each other and the natural world.

Appendix A

South African Census Statistics on Human Population

Kuruman Human Population

	White Males	White Females	Total Whites	Coloured Males	Coloured Females	Total Coloured	Black Males	Black Females	Total Blacks	Source
1904	704	526	1,230	533	537	1,070	4,942	5,668	10,630	CPP G 19 - 1905
1905										
1906										
1907										
1908										
1909										
1910										
1911	2,060	1,774	3,834	793	798	1,591	5,632	6,468	12,100	UG 32 F - 1912
1912										
1913										
1914										
1915										
1916										
1917										
1918										
1919										
1920										

(continued)

Kuruman Human Population (continued)

	White Males	White Females	Total Whites	Coloured Males	Coloured Females	Total Coloured	Black Males	Black Females	Total Blacks	Source
1921	2,430	2,283	4,713	899	933	1,832	7,156	7,693	14,849	UG 15 - 1923
1922										
1923										
1924										
1925										
1926										
1927										
1928										
1929										
1930										
1931										
1932										
1933										
1934										
1935										
1936	3,588	3,442	7,030	2,354	2,432	4,786	11,327	11,150	22,477	UG 50 - 1936
1937										
1938										
1939										
1940										
1941										
1942										

Year										Source
1943										
1944										
1945										
1946	3,459	3,284	6,743	1,295	1,182	2,477	14,319	13,984	28,303	UG 51 - 1949
1947										
1948										
1949										
1950										
1951	2,191	2,327	4,518	846	856	172	10,775	11,304	22,079	UG 42 - 1955
1952										
1953										
1954										
1955										
1956										
1957										
1958										
1959										
1960	3,048	2,742	5,790	1,554	1,480	3,034	22,592	19,904	42,496	RP Special Report No. 234

Appendix B

South African Census Statistics on Stock Population

Stock Population on African Reserves in the Kuruman District

	Cattle	Goats	Sheep	Donkeys*	Horses	Source
1904						
1905						
1906	3,548					G 36 - 1907
1907				30	82	UG 32 - 1912
1908						
1909						
1910						
1911						
1912						
1913						
1914						
1915						
1916						
1917						
1918						
1919						
1920						
1921						
1922						
1923	5,829					UG 25 - 1925
1924	7,456					UG 4 - 1926
1925	7,608					UG 13 - 1927
1926	8,598					UG 24 - 1928
1927	7,197	52,560	20,638			UG 37 - 1928
1928	8,775	53,426	22,566			UG 41 - 1929
1929	8,232	45,376	16,050			UG 35 - 1930
1930	11,917	47,589	20,186	7,879		UG 12 - 1932
1931						

Stock Population (continued)

	Cattle	Goats	Sheep	Donkeys*	Horses	Source
1932						
1933						
1934	5,074	26,793	12,140			UG 44 - 1935
1935	6,495	40,715	10,815			UG 54 - 1936
1936	7,809		13,711			UG 59 - 1937
1937	8,158	37,882	15,904	5,076	1,313	UG 18 - 1939
1938	8,340	40,317	16,493			UG 31 - 1940
1939	7,877	37,037	16,398			UG 27 - 1941
1940						
1941						
1942						
1943						
1944						
1945						
1946	10,372	44,561	28,083	11,007	2,215	UG 77 - 1948
1947	9,744	61,128	38,170			UG 57 - 1949
1948	10,121	45,790	28,418			UG 30 - 1950
1949		51,559	45,150			Special Report Series 1 No. 4
1950	9,920	54,743	34,521			Special Report Series 1 No. 24
1951	11,601	54,527	42,103	7,630		Special Report Series 1 No. 5
1952		51,667	26,609			Special Report Series 1 No. 7
1953	10,211		34,425			Special Report Series 1 No. 8
1954	11,313	64,409	31,948			Special Report Series 1 No. 7
1955	1,594	65,162	34,735			UG 49 - 1958
1956	12,709	67,572	36,348			UG 56 - 1959
1957	15,738	69,174				UG 67 - 1959
1958	2,970		55,143			UG 70 - 1960
1959						
1960	19,620	67,084	34,229	5,891	4,242	RP 10 - 1964
1961	19,716	66,854	31,674			RP 40 - 1964
1962	26,438	65,816	22,711			RP 64 - 1965
1963	23,482	50,185	29,877			Report No. 06-01-01
1964		54,861	28,597			Report No. 06-01-03
1965						
1966						
1967						
1968						
1969	19,903	87,999	40,243			Report No. 06-01-06

* Donkey statistics before 1950 are from CAR NTS 8331 14/350, December 23, 1950.

Appendix C1

1991 Individual Interviews

Interviewee	Date	Venue	Interpreter(s)
Molema, John-A	7 June 1991	Bothetheletsa	Rosey Molokoane, Peter Mokomele
Keupilwe, James Letileng	11 June 1991	Batlharos	
Boihang, Boihang	14 June 1991	Seodin-Lareng	Rosey Molokoane
Mogodi, Mr. and Mrs.	14 June 1991	Batlharos	Rosey Molokoane, Peter Mokomele
Moeti, Simon	14 June 1991	Maropeng	
Setungwane, Prince	14 June 1991	Manyeding	Rosey Molokoane, Peter Mokomele
Seamecho, Isaac-A	15 June 1991	Ga-Mopedi	
Gaelijwe, M.	18 June 1991	Mothibistad	
Motate, Kgakgolo	18 June 1991	Logobate	Constance Paul
Toto, Bogosing James	18 June 1991	Batlharos	Constance Paul
Marele, Mrs.	18 June 1991	Batlharos	
Kgokong, Mosiane-A	18 June 1991	Batlharos	Constance Paul
Pelele, Sannah	20 June 1991	Logobate	Rosey Molokoane
Gaetsewe, N. Mrs.	21 June 1991	Maropeng	Rosey Molokoane, Peter Mokomele
Seipotlane, Mr., Baruni, B., and Block, Mr.	21 June 1991	Batlharos	Rosey Molokoane
Seamecho, Isaac-B	21 June 1991	Ga-Mopedi	
Ditshetela, M.	24 June 1991	Mothibistad	
Itumeleng, Johannes	24 June 1991	Batlharos	
Lekalake, M.	24 June 1991	Mothibistad	
Moholeng, Evangelist	24 June 1991	Seodin	Richard Mogwera
Kgokong, Mosiane-B	26 June 1991	Batlharos	Rosey Molokoane, Peter Mokomele
Molema, Irene Nomanthamsanqa	10 Aug. 1991	Bothetheletsa	
Riekert, Don-A	20 Sept. 1991	Kuruman	

Interviewee	Date	Venue	Interpreter(s)
Lombard, Larry	23 Sept. 1991	Kuruman	
Van der Merwe, J. J.	24 Sept. 1991	Kuruman	
Wing, Joseph	25 Sept. 1991	Kuruman	
Molema, John-B	25 Sept. 1991	Bothetheletsa	
Riekert, Don-B	26 Sept. 1991	Kuruman	
Seamecho, Isaac-C	26 Sept. 1991	Ga-Mopedi	
Seipotlane, M.	26 Sept. 1991	Batlharos	Rosey Molokoane
Seamecho, Marry Magdalene	26 Sept. 1991	Ga-Mopedi	
Olivier, Gert	27 Sept. 1991	Farm Avontuur	Johan Olivier
Mokgoje, Mr. And Mrs. M. J.	28 Sept. 1991	Manyeding	Julius Mogodi
Mogodi, Julius	28 Sept. 1991	Manyeding	
Van Wyk, Eddie	2 Oct. 1991	Kuruman	
Snyman, P. H. R.	26 Nov. 1991	Pretoria	
Van Wyk, Eddie	5 May 1994	Kuruman	

Appendix C2

1997–1998 Individual Interviews

Interviewee	Date	Venue	Interviewer(s)	Interpreter(s)	Content of Interview
Barnette, Benjamin	15 Oct. 1997	In car	Jacobs		General history
Plaatjie, Anna	21 Oct. 1997	Bathlaros	Waples	None	Life history
Koikanyang, White	22 Oct. 1997	Bathlaros	Waples	None	Life history
Tshebedi, Muriel	23 Oct. 1997	Bathlaros	Russell	Mosala	Life history
Mabahanyane, Olebile	23 Oct. 1997	Bathlaros	Jacobs	Tshetlho	Life history
Mabilo, Peace	23 Oct. 1997	Bathlaros	Jacobs	Tshetlho	Life history
Orapeleng, Violet	27 Oct. 1997	Bathlaros	Russell	Tshetlho	Life history
Kopman, Joseph	28 Oct. 1997	Sedibeng	Jacobs	Tshetlho	Life history
Motshabe, Gladys	28 Oct. 1997	Sedibeng	Mosala, Russell, Waples	Mosala	Life history
Mosikatsi, Ascersion	29 Oct. 1997	Batlharos	Russell	Mosala	Life history
Barnette, Emma, Sana, Elizabeth, Jane, and Nokiya Plaatjie Jacobeth	29 Oct. 1997	Batlharos	Russell	Mosala	Life history
Tanke, Emma	30 Oct. 1997	Sedibeng	Mosala, Russell, Waples	Mosala	Life history

230

Mokosi, Gladys	30 Oct. 1997	Sedibeng	Mosala, Russell, Waples	Mosala	Life history
Motlhatlane, Edward	30 Oct. 1997	Ncweng	Mosala, Waples	Mosala	Life history
Molema, John-C	3 Nov. 1997	Bothetheletsa	Jacobs, Russell	Mosala, Tshetlho	General history
Ditlholelo, Vivian	7 Nov. 1997	Ncweng	Jacobs	Tshetlho	Life history
Tshupologo, Timothy	7 Nov. 1997	Ncweng	Jacobs	Mosala	Life history
Diewee, Kenalemang Martha	8 Nov. 1997	Ncweng	Tshetlho	r.a.	Life history
Koikanyang, Private	8 Nov. 1997	Ncweng	Mosala	Mosala	Life history
Albutt, Vera	1 Dec. 1997	Kuruman	Jacobs	r.a.	Health/nutrition
Gaobuwe, Shakerboy Kaotsane	21 July 1998	Batlharos	Kotoloane	r.a.	Life history
Ilanka, Rose Peme	23 July 1998	Batlharos	Jacobs, Tshetlho	Tshetlho	
Setlhodi, Mr. Agisanang David	27 July 1998	Seodin	Jacobs, Chirwa	Chirwa	Donkey killing
Seremane, W. J.	31 July 1998	Pretoria	Jacobs	r.a.	Donkey killing
Makhene, Blondie	27 Nov. 1998	Telephone interview	Jacobs	r.a.	Donkey song

Appendix C3

1991 and 1997–1998 Group Interviews

Interview	Date	Venue	Interviewer(s)	Interpreter(s)	Number of Participants	Type of Interview
Heuning Vlei	28 Sept. 1991	Heuning Vlei	Jacobs	Julius Mogodi	3	
Manyeding	30 Sept. 1991	Manyeding	Jacobs	Moabi Kitchen, Peter Mokomele	4	
Ga-Mopedi-A	6 Oct. 1997	Ga-Mopedi clinic	Jacobs, Kristin Russell, Megan Waples	Bhangi Mosala, Kgomotso Tshetlho	65 women	Mapping exercise
Batlharos-A	8 Oct. 1997	Batlharos Anglican Church Meeting Hall	Jacobs, Russell, Waples	Mosala, Tshetlho	3 men	Mapping exercise
Ga-Mopedi-B	9 Oct. 1997	Ga-Mopedi clinic	Jacobs	Mosala, Tshetlho	25 men (kgotla)	Group interview centered on a map
Batlharos-B	10 Oct. 1997	Batlharos Anglican Church Meeting Hall	Waples	Tshetlho	5 women	Mapping exercise and group interview
Ga-Mopedi-C	11 Oct. 1997	Ga-Mopedi	Jacobs	Mosala	5–6 women	Transect walk
Ncweng-A	12 Oct. 1997	Ncweng school	Jacobs	Mosala	45	Mapping, question and answer
Ncweng-B	11 Oct. 1997	Ncweng school	Waples	White Koikanyang	10, mostly men	Transect walk
Sedibeng-A	12 Oct. 1997	Fields of Sedibeng	Jacobs	Mosala	15 women	Mapping, interview
Batlharos-C	13 Oct. 1997	Batlharos Anglican Church Meeting Hall	Jacobs, Russell	Mosala	5 women	
Ga-Mopedi-D	13 Oct. 1997	Ga-Mopedi clinic	Jacobs	Mosala	5 women	Food listing
Ncweng-C	14 Oct. 1997	Ncweng Agricor office	Mosala	Mosala, Tsholo Steenkamp	25	Mapping, interview
Ncweng-D	14 Oct. 1997	Ncweng Agricor office	Steenkamp	Mosala, Steenkamp	25	Modified food matrix ranking
Batlharos-D	15 Oct. 1997	Tour of West Batlharos	Jacobs	Mosala	3 men	Tour, question and answer
Ga-Mopedi-E	16 Oct. 1997	Ga-Mopedi clinic	Mosala	Mosala	14 men	Veld species matrix ranking
Batlharos-E	17 Oct. 1997	B. Barundi's home, Batlharos	Jacobs	Mosala	5	Life history
Batlharos-F	18 Oct. 1997	Kagelelo Andreas's home	Russell, Waples	none	7–8 women	Wealth ranking, nutrition discussion
Ncweng-E	20 Oct. 1997	Ncweng clinic	Mosala	Mosala	23	Fodder matrix ranking

Code	Date	Location	Facilitators	Community members	Number	Activity
Ga-Mopedi-F	20 Oct. 1997	Ga-Mopedi clinic	Tshetlho	Tshetlho	7 women	Food matrix ranking
Ga-Sebolac-A	22 Oct. 1997	Ga-Sebolao	Jacobs	Benjamin Barnette	Large group	Question and answer
Ga-Mopedi-G	22 Oct. 1997	Ga-Mopedi clinic	Jacobs	Mosala, Tshetlho	25 men (kgotla)	Veld species matrix ranking
Ga-Sebolac-B	22 Oct. 1997	Ga-Sebolao	Mosala, Tshetlho	Mosala, Tshetlho	5 women	Mapping, question and answer
Batlharos-G	24 Oct. 1997	B. Barundi's home, Batlharos	Russell, Tshetlho, Waples	Tshetlho	15	Timeline interview
Ga-Tlhose	25 Oct. 1997	John Pasediwe's home, Kagung	Jacobs	Mosala	5	Mapping, removal dicussion
Ncweng-F	27 Oct. 1997	Ncweng Agricorp office	Mosala, Waples	Mosala	5	Timeline interview, wealth ranking
Ga-Mopedi-H	27 Oct. 1997	Ga-Mopedi clinic	Russell, Tshetlho	Tshetlho	9 women	Wealth ranking
Ncweng-G	28 Oct. 1997	Ncweng	Jacobs, Russell	Tshetlho	9	Transect walk
Sedibeng-B	28 Oct. 1997	Sediberg, outside of Kgotla	Jacobs	Tshetlho	30	Fodder matrix ranking, rainfall comparisons
Ga-Sebolac-C	29 Oct. 1997	Ga-Sebolao	Jacobs	Tshetlho	8	Rainfall ranking, question and answer
Ga-Sebolac-D	30 Oct. 1997	Ga-Sebolao	Waples	Steenkamp	4	Wealth ranking
Ga-Mopedi-I	30 Oct. 1997	Ga-Mopedi clinic	Tshetlho, Jacobs	Tshetlho	3 men	Detailed discussion of veld species
Maiphiniki-A	31 Oct. 1997	Maiphiniki	Jacobs, Mosala, Russell, Tshetlho, Waples	Mosala, Tshetlho	7	Rainfall ranking, livelihood ranking
Batlharos-H	2 Nov. 1997	Andreas' sisters home, Batlharos	Russell, Waples	none	5 women	Informal interview, health discussion
Maiphiniki-B	4 Nov. 1997	Maiphiniki	Mosala, Russell, Tshetlho, Waples	Mosala, Tshetlho	9	Stock matrix ranking, informal interview
Ga-Diboye-A	5 Nov. 1997	Mr. Ituraleng's home, Ga-Diboye	Russell, Tshetlho, Waples	Tshetlho	30	Livelihood ranking
Ga-Diboye-B	5 Nov. 1997	Mr. Ituraleng's home, Ga-Diboye	Jacobs	Mosala		Question and answer, veld species matrix ranking
Ga-Lotlhare-A	6 Nov. 1997	Ga-Lotlhare school	Mosaia, Russell	Mosala	10	Stock matrix ranking
Logobate-A	17 Nov. 1997	Logobate school	Jacobs	Karabo Noko	3	Question and answer
Logobate-B	17 Nov. 1997	Logobate school	Waples	Afrikander, Tsatsimpe	25	Milk and meat ranking, question and answer
Ga-Lotlhare-B	18 Nov. 1997	Ga-Lotlhare school	Waples	Poppy Afrikander	17	Gender discussion
Ga-Lotlhare-C	18 Nov. 1997	Ga-Lotlhare school	Jacobs	Tsatsimpe	16	Livestock/disease discussion
Ncweng-H	19 Nov. 1997	Ncweng Agricorp office	Jock McCulloch, Jacobs	Karabo Noko	8	Asbestos question and answer
Ncweng-I	20 Nov. 1997	Ncweng	McCulloch, Jacobs	Noko	4 men	Tour of asbestos mines

(continued)

233

Group Interviews (continued)

Interview	Date	Venue	Interviewer(s)	Interpreter(s)	Number of Participants	Type of Interview
Churchill-A	24 Nov. 1997	Churchill primary school	Russell	Victoria Tsatsimpe	6	Question and answer re: removals
Churchill-B	24 Nov. 1997	Churchill primary school	Tshetlho, Waples	Tshetlho	21	Question and answer re: removals
Kagung-A	24 Nov. 1997	Kagung school	Russell	Afrikander, Tshetlho	10	Question and answer, wide variety of topics
Seodin-A	24 Nov. 1997	Seodin tribal offices	Jacobs, Waples	Tsatsimpe		Question and answer re: removals
Batlharos-I	25 Nov. 1997	Batlharos Anglican Church Meeting Hall	Afrikander, Russell, Tshetlho	Afrikander, Tshetlho	3 women	Question and answer, removals and Betterment
Maiphiniki-C	25 Nov. 1997	Maiphiniki	Waples	Afrikander, Tshetlho	8	Listing stock diseases
Ga-Diboye-C	25 Nov. 1997	Mr. Itumaleng's home, Ga-Diboye	Afrikander, Russell, Tshetlho, Waples	Afrikander, Tshetlho	11 women	Gender discussion, livelihood ranking
Churchill-C	1 Dec. 1997	Churchill primary school	Russell	Victoria Tsatsimpe	15	Livestock vs. wage labor ranking
Churchill-D	1 Dec. 1997	Churchill primary school	Tshetlho, Waples	Tshetlho	14	Wealth rankings
Seodin-B	3 Dec. 1997	Seodin, tour of old areas	Jacobs	Tshetlho	10	Tour, question and answer re: removals
Kagung-B	20 July 1998	Kagung middle school	Jacobs, Russell	Afrikander	20	Question and answer re: donkey killings
Kagung-C	20 July 1998	Kagung middle school	Jacobs	Tshetlho	7	Question and answer re: nature
Kagung-D	20 July 1998	Kagung middle school	Jacobs	Tshetlho	7	Question and answer re: donkey killings
Kagung-E	20 July 1998	Kagung middle school	Peter Heywood	Stephen Kotoloane	9 men	Question and answer re: donkey killings
Kagung-F	21 July 1998	Kagung middle school	Heywood	Kotoloane	9 men	Question and answer re: environmental attitudes
Kagung-G	21 July 1998	Kagung middle school	Jacobs	Tshetlho		Question and answer re: donkey killings
Ga-Mopedi-J	22 July 1998	Ga-Mopedi	Jacobs	Tshetlho	7	Question and answer re: donkeys and environmental attitudes
Ga-Mopedi-K	22 July 1998	Ga-Mopedi	Heywood, Kotoloane	Kotoloane		Question and answer re: water
Ncweng-J	22 July 1998	Ncweng	Heywood, Kotoloane	Kotoloane	31	Question and answer re: environmental attitudes
Ncweng-K	24 July 1998	Ncweng	Jacobs	Kopano Chirwa	10	Question and answer re: donkey killings
Seodin-C	27 July 1998	Seodin tribal offices	Jacobs	Chirwa	14	Question and answer re: donkey killings
Seodin-D	27 July 1998	Seodin tribal offices	Heywood	Kotoloane	20	Question and answer re: donkey killings

Appendix D

A Note on Archival Sources

In addition to the oral evidence described in Chapter 1 and published primary and secondary sources, in this research I made extensive use of archival sources. The primary archives where I worked were the Council for World Mission Archive at the School of Oriental and African Studies (SOAS), London; the Public Records Office in London (PRO); the Cape Town Archives Repository in Cape Town (CTAR); and the National Archives Repository in Pretoria (NAR). In addition to these, I visited specific collections at the National Archives of Zimbabwe (ZAR) and the University of the Witwatersrand. The small but interesting collection at the Moffat Mission in Kuruman was also helpful.*

At SOAS, I read incoming letters from London Missionary Society (LMS) missionaries in Tswana areas from 1815–1910. These letters are not indexed by subject, so I read them page by page. For the first eighty-five years, these letters gave good details about environmental and social aspects of missions among Tswana-speaking people. For the missionaries, the existence of oppressed classes and extensive production were evidence of African depravity, and methods of food production were integral to their conception of themselves and the Christian message. By the 1870s, they made a link between Christianity, imperialism, intensive production, and land tenure, so their commentary on these subjects provided good evidence on the period of imperial annexation. At the turn of the century, missionaries described and expressed concern about rinderpest, violence, and famine. Therefore, these were extremely rich sources, but as discussed in Chapter 1, they required careful, critical reading. Only rarely in these letters did Africans speak for themselves. All the same, evidence presented with a consistent bias is better than the lack of it as in LMS letters

---

* On these holdings, see Kristin Russell and Megan Waples, "The Kuruman Moffat Mission Trust Archives Unearthed, *South African Historical Journal* 40(1999): 239–46.

after 1900. It seems that mission work among independent and recently colonized agro-pastoralists required more inquiry into socio-environmental matters than working among dependent migrant laborers did. After 1900, missionaries had less to say about food production or social organizations.

The next set of records, colonial documents, are held at the PRO in London and the CTAR in Cape Town. At both archives, the holdings are computerized and I identified documents through keyword searches. At the PRO, I read the Colonial Office Series (CO), covering the Griqualand West and British Bechuanaland from 1871–95. At the CTAR, I read records of the Crown Colony of British Bechuanaland (BCC), including the very useful evidence gathered by the Land Commission of 1884–5 (BBLC). After 1895, this area was annexed to the Cape Colony, whose records are also held at the CTAR. Of those records, I also read correspondence from Kuruman officials to the Native Affairs Department (NA), the Lands Department (LND), and other departments. I also found many of these letters in the Kuruman Magistrate's Correspondence Series (1/KMN) and in the Kuruman Native Commissioner's Correspondence Series (2/KMN). The 1/KMN and the 2/KMN series contain documents from the Cape Colonial Administration, the Union government, and the Republic of South Africa and were extremely useful for my research. These early colonial documents offered rich descriptions similar to those in missionary letters and required similar critical reading.

The final set of records, correspondence from Union and Republic officials, is held in the NAR in Pretoria. NAR holdings are also computerized, and I searched hundreds of files on the Kuruman District from the correspondence series of several departments. Most important were those of the Native Affairs Department, later known as Bantu Administration and Development (NTS and BAO, in their Afrikaans abbreviations). Other useful departments were Irrigation (IRR), Lands (LND), and Commissioner General Mafikeng (KGM), which contains records from the Tswana Territorial Authority.

Paternalistic officials in the twentieth century were interested in how people related to each other and the environment, because they intended to "improve" upon it. However, like the LMS records, the quality and quantity of social and environmental information in official correspondence, both in the CTAR and NAR, drops eventually. Compared with earlier officials, those working under Apartheid had far less interest in how black people were living or in the impact of policies. More and more, government records document the implementation of government programs without much reference to the people affected by these programs. Even records of Betterment and forced removals have little to say about socio-environmental history. A critical reading of these documents yields an understanding of the state and its ideology, but disappointingly little about how people related to the government. Therefore, it was absolutely necessary to have oral evidence for this period. Fortunately, people who remember it are still alive and able to tell their stories. Without their memories, future historians may have a harder time researching the experiences of black South Africans in the mid-twentieth century than in earlier periods.

Notes

CHAPTER 1

1. Dan Jacobson, *Electronic Elephant: A Southern African Journey* (London: Hamish
    Hamilton, 1994), 125. "Bygone road to Africa" is the translation of the title of
    P. H. R. Snyman, *Kuruman: Vervloë Pad na Afrika* (Pretoria: Human Sciences
    Research Council, 1992).
2. Herman Charles Bosman, "The Homecoming," in *Selected Stories* (Pretoria:
    Human and Rousseau, 1980), 38.
3. P. D. Tyson, *Climate Change and Variability in Southern Africa* (Cape Town: Oxford
    University Press, 1987), 68. See also Coleen Vogel, "160 Years of Rainfall of the
    Cape – Has There Been a Change?" *South African Journal of Science* 84(1988):
    724–6.
4. Mark Majodina, "Report on Rainfall Variability Over Kuruman, May 1998."
    Mr. Majodina's report is available in the Robert Moffat Library in Kuruman.
5. Town Council of Kuruman Information Office brochure, "Kuruman," n. d. [1994–
    7]. For a web version of this brochure see http://www.epages.net/kuruman. Regard-
    ing the springs south and southeast of Kuruman, including those at Manyeding and
    Konong, see J. Smit, "Groundwater Recharge in the Dolomite of the Ghaap Plateau
    near Kuruman in the Northern Cape, Republic of South Africa," *Water South Africa*
    4(April 1978): 81–92. Interview with Eddie van Wyk, Assistant Director of Water
    Affairs, Kuruman.
6. For the impressions of a recent traveler to Kuruman see Jacobson, *Electronic
    Elephant* (1994), 112–47.
7. Reuters Library Report, March 10, 1988; Snyman, *Kuruman* (1992), 5.
8. Carol Morello, "South Africa's Blacks Never Knew that Asbestos was Killing
    Them," *USA Today*, February 10, 1999, 8A–9A. Also on asbestos-related disease
    in Kuruman, see Lundy Braun et al., "Asbestos-Related Disease in South Africa:
    Opportunities and Challenges Remaining Since the 1998 Asbestos Summit," report
    presented to the South African Parliament Portfolio Committee on Environmen-
    tal Affairs and Tourism, October 12, 2001. http://www.brown.edu/Departments/
    African_American_Studies/Asbestos/.
9. J. P. H. Acocks, *Veld Types of Southern Africa*, 3rd ed., Memoirs of the Botanical
    Survey of South Africa No. 57 (Pretoria: Botanical Research Institute, 1988): 44–9.

The Kalahari Thornveld is type 16 in Acocks's classification. The subtypes found in this region are 16.a.4 (the Kalahari Thornveld proper, northwestern subdivision) and 16.b.1 (Vryburg Shrub bushveld subtype, Tarchonanthus subdivision).

10. The new survey identifies four veld types in this area: Kalahari Plains Thorn Bushveld (30), Kalahari Mountain Bushveld (31), Kimberley Thorn Bushveld (32), and Kalahari Plateau Bushveld (33). Noel Rooyen and George Bredenkamp, *Vegetation of South Africa, Lesotho and Swaziland: A Companion to the Vegetation Map of South Africa, Lesotho and Swaziland*, 2nd ed., A. Barrie Low and A. G. Rebelo, eds. (Pretoria: Department of Environmental Affairs and Tourism, 1998), 35–7. For a general description of the environment, see also Snyman, *Kuruman* (1992), 8–10.

11. Andrew Smith, "Kuruman: Bad for Farming, Good for Flying," in *Cross Country*, n. d., 41. I found a reproduction of this article at http://www.paragliding.co.za.

12. Belinda Bozzoli and Peter Delius, "Radical History and South African Society," in *History from South Africa*, Joshua Brown et al., eds. (Philadelphia: Temple University Press, 1991), 17–20; Michael Williams, "The Relations of Environmental History and Historical Geography," *Journal of Historical Geography* 20(1994): 3.

13. C. W. De Kiewiet, *A History of South Africa: Social and Economic* (London: Oxford, 1941); William Beinart, *The Political Economy of Pondoland, 1860 to 1930* (Cambridge: Cambridge University Press, 1982); Jane Carruthers, *The Kruger National Park: A Social and Political History* (Pietermaritzburg: University of Natal Press, 1995); and Charles van Onselen, *The Seed Is Mine: The Life of Kas Maine, a South African Sharecropper, 1894–1985* (New York: Hill and Wang, 1996).

14. Madhav Gadgil and Ramachjandra Guha, *This Fissured Land: An Ecological History of India* (Delhi: Oxford University Press, 1993), 12.

15. These groundbreaking works of social history include Robin Palmer and Neil Parsons, eds., *The Roots of Rural Poverty in Central and Southern Africa* (Berkeley: University of California Press, 1977); Colin Bundy, *The Rise and Fall of the South African Peasantry* (Berkeley: University of California Press, 1979); Timothy Keegan, *Rural Transformations in Industrializing South Africa: The Southern Highveld to 1910* (Johannesburg: Raven, 1986); and William Beinart, Peter Delius, and Stanley Trapido, eds., *Putting a Plough to the Ground: Accumulation and Dispossession in Rural South Africa, 1850–1930* (Johannesburg: Raven, 1986), which defies its title by rarely discussing the act of plowing. On the liberal and revisionist schools of South African historiography, see Christopher Saunders, *The Making of the South African Past: Major Historians on Race and Class* (Cape Town: David Philip, 1988), 143–97. For an environmentally aware neoclassical economic history, see William Duggan, *An Economic Analysis of Southern African Agriculture* (New York: Praeger, 1986).

16. See all articles in Special Issue on Politics of Conservation in Southern Africa, William Beinart, ed., *Journal of Southern African Studies* 15(January 1989).

17. William Cronon, "Modes of Prophecy and Production: Placing Nature in History," *The Journal of American History* 76(1990): 1129. On North American social and environmental history, see Alan Taylor, "Unnatural Inequalities: Social and Environmental Histories," *Environmental History* 1, 4(1996): 6–19. For a

class-based environmental history of United States conservation and land use, see Karl Jacoby, *Crimes against Nature: Squatters, Poachers, Thieves, and the Hidden History of American Conservation* (Berkeley: University of California Press, 2001).

18. Richard White, *Roots of Dependency: Subsistence, Environment and Social Change among the Choctaws, Pawnees and Navajos* (Lincoln: University of Nebraska Press, 1983).

19. White, "Environmental History, Ecology, and Meaning," *The Journal of American History* 76(1990): 1115; John M. MacKenzie, "Empire and the Ecological Apocalypse: The Historiography of the Imperial Environment," in *Ecology and Empire: Environmental History of Settler Societies*, Tom Griffith and Libby Robin, eds. (Edinburgh: Keele University Press, 1997), 220.

20. James Fairhead and Melissa Leach, *Misreading the African Landscape: Society and Ecology in a Forest-Savanna Mosaic* (Cambridge: Cambridge University Press, 1996). See also essays in Melissa Leach and Robin Mearns, eds., *The Lie of the Land: Challenging the Received Wisdom on the African Environment* (Portsmouth: Heinemann, 1996). On this point, see also the first synthesis of the environmental history of sub-Saharan Africa, James McCann, *Green Land, Brown Land, Black Land* (Portsmouth: Heinemann, 1999).

21. For such works, see Helge Kjekshus, *Ecology Control and Economic Development in East African History: The Case of Tanganyika, 1850–1950*, 2d ed. (London: Heinemann, 1977; Athens: Ohio University Press, 1996); Leroy Vail, "Ecology and History: The Example of Eastern Zambia," *Journal of Southern African Studies* 3(1977): 129–55. For a critique of this tendency, see Julian Koponen, *People and Production in Late Precolonial Tanzania: History and Structures* (Upsala: Scandinavian Institute of African Studies, 1988), 367.

22. Robert Harms, *Games Against Nature: An Eco-Cultural History of the Nunu of Equatorial Africa* (Cambridge: Cambridge University Press, 1987).

23. White, "Environmental History, Ecology, and Meaning," *The Journal of American History* 76(1990): 1116.

24. Bozzoli and Delius, "Radical History and South African Society," in *History from South Africa* (1991), 21. For a work inverting the emphasis of structuralist analyses, see Patrick Harries, *Work, Culture and Identity: Migrant Laborers in Mozambique and South Africa, c. 1860–1910* (Portsmouth: Heinemann, 1994).

25. Cronon, "A Place for Stories: Nature, History and Narrative," *The Journal of American History* 78(1992): 1347–76.

26. James C. Scott, *Seeing Like a State: How Certain Schemes to Improve the Human Condition Have Failed* (New Haven: Yale University Press, 1998).

27. Phillip Curtin, "Epidemiology and the Slave Trade," *Political Science Quarterly* 83(1968): 190–216, and *Death By Migration: Europe's Encounter with the Tropical World in the Nineteenth Century* (Cambridge: Cambridge University Press, 1989); Jan Vansina, *Paths in the Rainforest: Toward a History of Political Tradition in Equatorial Africa* (Madison: University of Wisconsin Press, 1990).

28. Steven Feierman, *Peasant Intellectuals: Anthropology and History in Tanzania* (Madison: University of Wisconsin Press, 1990); Elias Mandala, *Work and Control in a Peasant Economy: A History of the Lower Tchiri Valley in Malawi, 1859–1960* (Madison: University of Wisconsin Press, 1990).

29. John Iliffe, *Africans: The History of a Continent* (Cambridge: Cambridge University Press, 1995). For another depiction of Africans in a hostile environment, see Harries, *Work, Culture, and Identity* (1994), 1–17.

30. Kjekshus, *Ecology Control* (1996); Vail, "Ecology and History: The Example of Eastern Zambia," *Journal of Southern African Studies* 3(1977): 129–55.

31. James Giblin, *The Politics of Environmental Control in Northeastern Tanzania, 1840–1940* (Philadelphia: University of Pennsylvania Press, 1992). See also essays in Gregory Maddox, James Giblin, and Isaria Kimambo, eds., *Custodians of the Land: Ecology & Culture in the History of Tanzania* (Athens: Ohio University Press, 1996).

32. Alfred Crosby, *Ecological Imperialism: The Biological Expansion of Europe, 900–1900* (Cambridge: Cambridge University Press, 1986); Carolyn Merchant, *Ecological Revolutions: Nature, Gender and Science in New England* (Chapel Hill: University of North Carolina Press, 1989); Donald Worster, *Rivers of Empire: Water, Aridity and the Growth of the American West* (New York: Pantheon, 1985); and White, *Roots of Dependency: Subsistence, Environment and Social Change among the Choctaws, Pawnees and Navajos* (1983).

33. On levels of analysis in environmental history, see Worster, "Transformations of the Earth: Toward an Agroecological Perspective in History," *Journal of American History* 76(1990): 1090–1; Merchant, *Ecological Revolutions* (1989), 5–26.

34. Earlier agricultural histories of Tswana-speaking people in similar environments include Duggan, *An Economic Analysis* (1986); Gary Okihiro, "Hunters, Herders, Cultivators, and Traders: Interactions and Change in the Kgalagadi in the Nineteenth Century," Ph.D. dissertation, UCLA, 1976.

35. Mandala, *Work and Control* (1990), 8–12.

36. J. E. G. Sutton, "Editor's Introduction: Fields, Farming and History in Africa," Special volume on the History of African Agricultural Technology and Field Systems, *Azania* 24(1989): 7. "Towards a History of Cultivating the Fields," is the title of Sutton's article, see pp. 98–112.

37. Ester Boserup, *The Conditions of Agricultural Growth: The Economics of Agrarian Change under Population Pressure* (New York: Aldine, 1965). For a helpful discussion of Boserup's ideas, see Randall Baker, *Environmental Management in the Tropics: An Historical Perspective* (Boca Raton: CRC Press, 1993).

38. Cited in Frank Ellis, *Peasant Economies: Farm Households and Agrarian Development* (Cambridge: Cambridge University Press, 1988), 102–19.

39. Sutton, "Towards a History of Cultivating the Fields," *Azania* 24(1989): 98–112; Thomas Spear, *Mountain Farmers: Moral Economies of Land and Agricultural Development in Arusha and Meru* (Berkeley: University of California Press, 1997).

40. Giblin, *The Politics of Environmental Control* (1992).

41. Harms, *Games Against Nature* (1987).

42. Henrietta L. Moore and Megan Vaughan, *Cutting Down Trees: Gender, Nutrition and Agricultural Change in the Northern Province of Zambia, 1890–1990* (Portsmouth: Heinemann, 1994).

43. James Webb, *Desert Frontier: Ecological and Economic Change along the Western Sahel, 1600–1850* (Madison: University of Wisconsin Press, 1995).

44. Kevin Shillington, *The Colonisation of the Southern Tswana, 1870–1900* (Johannesburg: Raven, 1985); Jean Comaroff and John L. Comaroff, *Of Revelation and Revolution*, Vol. 1, *Christianity, Colonialism and Consciousness in South Africa* (Chicago: University of Chicago Press, 1991); and John L. Comaroff and Jean Comaroff, *Of Revelation and Revolution*, Vol. 2, *The Dialectics of Modernity on a South African Frontier* (Chicago: University of Chicago Press, 1997).

45. Mary Louise Pratt, "Scratches on the Face of the Country; or what Mr. Barrow Saw in the Land of the Bushmen," *Critical Inquiry* 12(1985): 119–43. Regarding these travelers' depictions of people, Beinart has questioned Pratt's argument about their ethnocentricity and masculine bias. Beinart, "Men, Science, Travel and Nature in the Eighteenth and Nineteenth-Century Cape," *Journal of Southern African Studies* 24(1998): 775–99.

46. Moore and Vaughan, *Cutting Down Trees* (1994), xi–v; Fairhead and Leach, *Misreading the African Landscape* (1996), 55–70.

47. Moore and Vaughan, *Cutting Down Trees* (1994), iii.

48. Transcripts of these interviews are deposited at the Moffat Mission Trust library in Kuruman.

49. David Henige, *Oral Historiography* (New York: Longman, 1982), 49–51.

50. As an RRA guide, I used Robert Chambers, *Rural Appraisal: Rapid, Relaxed and Participatory* (Brighton: Institute of Development Studies, 1992).

51. Martin Hall, *Farmers, Kings and Traders: The People of Southern Africa, 200–1860* (Chicago: University of Chicago Press, 1990), 32–45.

52. See Martin Legassick, "The Griqua, the Sotho-Tswana and the Missionaries, 1700–1840: The Politics of a Frontier Zone," Ph.D. dissertation, UCLA, 1969. See also, Leonard Thompson and Howard Lamar, eds., *The Frontier in History: North America and Southern Africa Compared* (New Haven: Yale University Press, 1981).

53. Legassick, "The Frontier Tradition in South African Historiography," in *Economy and Society in Pre-Industrial South Africa*, Shula Marks and Anthony Atmore, eds. (London: Longman, 1980), 44–79.

54. Nigel Penn, "The Orange River Frontier Zone, c. 1700–1805," in *Einiqualand: Studies of the Orange River Frontier*, Andrew B. Smith, ed. (Cape Town: University of Cape Town Press, 1995).

55. Crosby, *Ecological Imperialism* (1986); Griffith and Robin, eds., *Ecology and Empire* (1997).

56. For one exception, see Martin Melosi, "Equity, Eco-Racism and Environmental History," *Environmental History Review* 19, 3(1995): 1–16.

57. Andrew Hurley, *Environmental Inequalities: Class, Race, and Industrial Pollution in Gary, Indiana, 1945–1980* (Chapel Hill: University of North Carolina Press, 1995). See also all articles in a special issue "Environmental Justice in the City," *Environmental History* 5(2000).

58. Mahmood Mamdani, *Citizen and Subject: Contemporary Africa and the Legacy of Late Colonialism* (Princeton: Princeton University Press, 1996), 21.

59. C. S. Lewis, *The Abolition of Man: Reflections on Education with Special Reference to the Teaching of English in the Upper Forms of Schools* (London: Geoffrey Bles, 1943; 2nd ed. 1946), 40. On previous uses of this quotation by other environmental historians, see Taylor, "Unnatural Inequalities Social and Environmental Histories," *Environmental History* 1,4(1996): 16.

CHAPTER 2

1. John Campbell, *Travels in South Africa Undertaken at the Request of the Missionary Society* (London: Black, Perry, 1815; reprint ed., Cape Town: C. Struik, 1974), 186.
2. For a good introduction to the history of Khoisan and Bantu settlement in southern Africa, see Leonard Thompson, *A History of South Africa* (New Haven: Yale, 1990), 1–30.
3. Hall, *Farmers, Kings and Traders* (1990), 47.
4. For an introduction to the issue, see John Lamphear and Toyin Falola, "Aspects of Early African History," in *Africa*, 3rd ed., Phyllis Martin and Patrick O'Meara, eds. (Boulder: Westview, 1994), 86–94.
5. Vansina, "New Linguistic Evidence and 'The Bantu Expansion,'" *Journal of African History* 36(1995): 173–95.
6. Vansina, "New Linguistic Evidence and 'The Bantu Expansion,'" *Journal of African History* 36(1995): 193.
7. Tim Maggs and Gavin Whitelaw, "A Review of Recent Archaeological Research on Food-Producing Communities in Southern Africa," *Journal of African History* 32(1991): 3–24. This fluidity is a strong theme in archeological findings throughout the region. See also James Denbow, "A New Look at the Later Prehistory of the Kalahari," *Journal of African History* 27(1986): 3–28; John Parkington and Martin Hall, "Patterning in Recent Radiocarbon Dates from Southern Africa as a Reflection of Prehistoric Settlement and Interaction," *Journal of African History* 28(1987): 1–25; and Alan G. Morris, *The Skeletons of Contact: A Study of Prehistoric Burials from the Lower Orange River Valley, South Africa* (Johannesburg: University of the Witwatersrand Press, 1992).
8. Regarding archeological research into agro-pastoralist sites near Kuruman, see Maggs, *Bilobial Dwellings: A Persistent Feature of Southern Tswana Settlements*, South African Archaeological Society, Goodwin Series (1972), 54–64; A. J. B. Humphreys, "Note on the Southern Limits of Iron Age Settlement in the Northern Cape," *South African Archaeological Bulletin* 31(1976): 54–7; and Anne Thackeray, J. F. Thackeray, and P. Beaumont, "Excavations at the Blinkklipkop Specularite Mine Near Postmasburg, Northern Cape," *South African Archaeological Bulletin* 38(1983): 17–25.
9. George Stow, *The Native Races of South Africa* (London: Swan Sonnenschein, 1905; reprint ed., Cape Town: C. Struik, 1964), 432–59; George Theal, *The Yellow and Dark-Skinned People of Africa South of the Zambezi* (London: Swan Sonnenschein, 1910; reprint ed., New York: Negro Universities, 1969), 152–3; and Simon Molema, *The Bantu Past and Present: An Ethnographical and Historical Study of the Native Race of South Africa* (Edinburgh: W. Green and Son, 1920), 38–40.
10. Saunders, "Early Knowledge of the Sotho: Seventeenth and Eighteenth Century Accounts of the Tswana," *Quarterly Bulletin of the South African Library* 20(1966): 60–70.
11. Morris has compared these accounts in *The Skeletons of Contact* (1992), 47–54.
12. Hendrick Jacob Wikar, *The Journal of Hendrick Jacob Wikar (1779)*, A. W. van der Horst, trans., E. E. Mossop, ed. (Cape Town: Van Riebeeck Society, 1935), 143–71.

13. R. J. Gordon, *Cape Travels 1777 to 1786*, vol. 2, E. Raper and M. Boucher, eds. (Houghton: Brenthurst, 1988) 300–54.

14. L. F. Maingard, "The Brikwa and the Ethnic Origins of the Batlhaping," *South African Journal of Science* 30(1933): 597–602.

15. For statements by Tlhaping and Korana about their early connections, including the settlement at Nokaneng in the Langeberg, see testimony in "The Bloemhof Blue Book," *Evidence Taken at Bloemhof Before the Commission Appointed to Investigate the Claims of the South African Republic, Captain N. Waterboer, Chief of West Griqualand, and Certain other Native Chiefs, to Portions of the Territory on the Vaal River now Known as the Diamondfields* [The Bloemhof Blue Book] (Cape Town: Saul Solomon, 1871), 187, 281, 289, 292.

16. Maggs suggests Nokaneng may have been at 28° 13′ south latitude and 22° 30′ east longitude, a spot marked with that name on some modern maps. T. M. O'C. Maggs, *The Iron Age Communities of the Southern Highveld*, Occasional Publication of the Natal Museum, Number 2 (Pietermaritzburg: Natal Museum, 1976), 277, note 1. No stone ruins are known at this spot. Humphreys, "Note on the Southern Limits of Iron Age Settlements in the Northern Cape," *South African Archaeological Bulletin* 31(1976): 55.

17. Records by Barrow, Borcherds, and Somerville of the Truter–Somerville expedition did not use the name "Tlhaping." Barrow and Truter differentiated between the "Booshuanas" at Dithakong and the "Baaroloos" (Barolong) further north. John Barrow, *A Voyage to Cochinchina* (London: Cadell and Davies, 1806; reprint ed., Kuala Lumpur: Oxford University Press, 1975), 387, 403–4. (Barrow edited "An Account of a Journey to the Booshuanas," by J. Truter, his father-in-law, for inclusion in this book on his own travels in Asia.) See also Petrus Borcherds, *An Autobiographical Memoir* (Cape Town: A. A. Roberts, 1861; reprint ed., Cape Town: Africana Connoisseurs, 1963), 123; and William Somerville, *William Somerville's Narrative of His Journeys to the Eastern Cape Frontier and to Lattakoe 1799–1802*, Frank Bradlow and Edna Bradlow, eds. (Cape Town: Van Riebeeck Society, 1979), 123.

18. W. H. C. [Henry] Lichtenstein, *Foundations of the Cape and about the Bechuanas*, O. H. Spohr, ed. and trans. (Cape Town: Balkema, 1973), 63–4, 66.

19. Andrew Smith, *The Diary of Dr. Andrew Smith, Director of the "Expedition for Exploring Central Africa, 1834–36*," vol. 1, Percival R. Kirby, ed. (Cape Town: Van Riebeeck Society, 1939), 359.

20. John Campbell, *Travels in South Africa Undertaken at the Request of the Missionary Society* (1974), 206–7. A different genealogy often cited in the Tlhaping tradition is given by John Mackenzie, *Austral Africa: Losing It or Ruling It*, vol. 1 (London: Sampson, Low, Marston, Searle and Rivington, 1887), 43. See also William Burchell, *Travels in the Interior of South Africa*, vol. 2 (London: Longman, Hurst, Rees, Brown and Green, 1822–4; reprint ed., London: Batchworth, 1953), 374.

21. J. Tom Brown, *Among the Bantu Nomads* (London: Seeley Service, 1926), 206. Brown had long experience among the Tlhaping, but he does not record where he heard this story. This tradition influenced F. J. Language, who maintained that the Tlhaping were an offshoot of the Rolong who gained independence under the political leadership of a talented chief. Language also constructed and dated

genealogies for Tlhaping chiefs. F. J. Language, "Herkoms and Geskiedenis van die Tlhaping," *African Studies* 1(1942): 117.

22. P.-L. Breutz, *The Tribes of the Districts of Kuruman and Postmasburg*, Republic of South Africa, Department of Bantu Administration and Development Ethnological Publications, no. 49 (Pretoria: Government Printer, 1963), 38, 154.

23. Martin Legassick, "The Griqua, the Sotho-Tswana and the Missionaries," Ph.D. dissertation, UCLA, 1969, 66. His emphasis.

24. Legassick, "The Griqua, the Sotho-Tswana and the Missionaries," Ph.D. dissertation, UCLA, 1969, 60–71. He does not address the Briqua tradition, but it fits into his explanation for multi-centered origins.

25. See Campbell, *Travels in South Africa Undertaken at the Request of The London Missionary Society; Being a Narrative of a Second Journey into the Interior of that Country*, vol. 2 (London: London Missionary Society, 1822; reprint ed., New York: Johnson Reprints, 1967), 73–130, see especially pp. 107–8; Brown, *Bantu Nomads* (1926), 223–5; Breutz, *The Tribes of Kuruman* (1963), 38, 92; Burchell, *Travels*, 2(1953), 376. Korana presence is also indicated in a map by Lichtenstein, *About the Bechuanas* (1973), 83. It refers to them as "*Ma*tsaro*qua*." Interestingly, "ma" is a misrepresentation of "ba," the Tswana plural prefix, while "qua" is a Khoisan suffix for group names. Thus, Lichtenstein combined Tswana and Khoisan nomenclature for the Tlharo.

26. *Evidence Taken at Bloemhof* [The Bloemhof Blue Book] (1871), 187, 281, 289, 292.

27. Lichtenstein, *Travels in Southern Africa in the Years 1803, 1804, 1805, and 1806*, vol. 2, A. Pumptre, trans. (London: Henry Colburn 1815; reprint. ed. Cape Town: Van Riebeeck Society, 1930), 371.

28. J. Englebrecht, *The Korana: An Account of Their Customs and Their History with Texts* (Cape Town: Maskew Miller, 1936), 76–9.

29. Legassick, "The Griqua, the Sotho-Tswana and the Missionaries," Ph.D. dissertation, UCLA, 1969, 48, described the late eighteenth century as a period of amalgamation. Neil Parsons wrote of "Tswana wars" between 1770 and 1820, *A New History of Southern Africa* (New York: Holmes and Meier, 1983), 48–50. See also Neil Parsons, "Prelude to Difiqane in the Interior of Southern Africa c. 1600–c. 1822," in *The Mfecane Aftermath: Reconstructive Debates in Southern African History*, Carolyn Hamilton, ed. (Johannesburg: Witwatersrand University Press, 1995), 323–49; Andrew Manson, "Conflict in the Western Highveld/Southern Kalahari c. 1750–1820," in Hamilton, ed., 351–61.

30. See Burchell, *Travels*, 2(1953), 378 for reports of theft by "bushmen" near Tlhaping territory. In contrast, Borcherds reported that bushmen did have "the least tendency to steal" from the Truter-Somerville expedition. Borcherds, *Memoir* (1963), 114.

31. Burchell, *Travels*, 2(1953), 377.

32. Robert Moffat, *Missionary Labours and Scenes in Southern Africa* (London: Snow, 1842), 12. Also on the Thamaga, see the letter by Robert in Robert and Mary Moffat, *Apprenticeship at Kuruman: Journals and Letters of Robert and Mary Moffat, 1820–1828*, I. Schapera, ed. (London: Chatto and Windus, 1951), 102, note 81, 126; Burchell, *Travels*, 2(1953), 336, 352–3; Campbell, *Travels* (1974), 214; Campbell, *Second Journey*, 2(1967): 6–8; Stephen Kay, *Travels and Researches in Caffraria* (New York: B. Waugh and T. Mason, 1843), 190.

33. Campbell, *Travels* (1974), 186.
34. Elizabeth Eldredge, "Slave Raiding Across the Cape Frontier," in *Slavery in South Africa: Captive Labor on the Dutch Frontier*, Elizabeth Eldredge and Frederick Morton, eds. (Boulder: Westview, 1994), 101–14.
35. Maingard, "The Brikwa and the Ethnic Origins of the Balthaping," *South African Journal of Science* 30(1933): 599.
36. Parsons, "Prelude to Difiqane," in *The Mfecane Aftermath: Reconstructive Debates in Southern African History* (1995), 338–41. See also Eldredge, "Sources of Conflict," in Hamilton, ed., 157–160.
37. Legassick, "The Griqua, the Sotho-Tswana and the Missionaries," Ph.D. dissertation, UCLA, 1969, 141, 225–41; Parsons; "Prelude to Difiqane," in *The Mfecane Aftermath: Reconstructive Debates in Southern African History* (1995), 336–7.
38. Wikar, *The Journal* (1935), 155.
39. School of Oriental and African Studies, London, Council for World Mission Archive, London Missionary Society, Africa South, Incoming Letters [hereafter LMS] 15/2/D, Moffat, November 23, 1836.
40. For such examples, see C. Murray and W. Lye, *Transformations on the Highveld: the Tswana and Southern Sotho* (Cape Town: David Philip, 1980).
41. Margaret Kinsman, "Notes on the Southern Tswana Social Formation," in *Africa Seminar Collected Papers*, vol. 2, K. Gottschalk and C. Saunders, eds. (Cape Town: Centre for African Studies, University of Cape Town Press, 1981), 189.
42. The Comaroffs have characterized the lower classes in this period as "non-Tswana serfs." See Comaroff and Comaroff, *Of Revelation and Revolution*, 1(1991), 144. Eldredge sees class among the Tlhaping after the model of Moshoeshoe's kingdom, resulting from the incorporation of outsiders. See Eldredge, "Slave Raiding," in *Slavery in South Africa: Captive Labor on the Dutch Frontier* (1994), 104.
43. Gary Okihiro, "Precolonial Economic Change Among the BaTlhaping, c. 1795–1817," *International Journal of African Historical Studies*, 17, 1(1984): 72–8; Peter Kallaway, "Tribesman, Trader, Peasant and Proletarian: The Process of Transition from a Pre-Capitalist to a Capitalist Mode of Production in the Immediate Hinterland of the Kimberley Diamond Fields during the Nineteenth Century: A Case Study of the Tlhaping," in *Working Papers in Southern African Studies*, vol. 2, Philip Bonner, ed. (Johannesburg: Raven, 1981), 12–13; and Edwin Wilmsen, *A Land Filled With Flies: A Political Economy of the Kalahari* (Chicago: University of Chicago Press, 1989), passim, but see especially pp. 52–3.
44. On the food production of a similar Tswana lower class group, the "Kgalagadi," see Okihiro, "Hunters, Herders, Cultivators, and Traders," Ph.D. dissertation, UCLA, 1976, 144–55.
45. Iliffe, *The African Poor* (Cambridge: Cambridge University Press, 1987), 78.
46. Richard Elphick, *Kraal and Castle: Khoikhoi and the Founding of White South Africa* (New Haven: Yale University Press, 1977), 23–42.
47. Elphick, *Kraal and Castle* (1977), 38–9.
48. For evidence refuting these misconceptions by showing an unequal distribution of food, see Eldredge, "Drought, Famine and Disease in Lesotho," *African Economic History* 16(1987): 61–93; Diana Wylie, "The Changing Face of Hunger in Southern African History," *Past and Present* 122(1989): 159–99.

49. On wild foods, see Burchell, *Travels*, 2(1953), 415; Campbell, *Second Journey*, 2(1967), 217; and Gustav Fritsch, *Drei Jahre Süd-Afrika: Reiseskizzen nach Notizen des Tagebuchs Zusammengestellt* (Breslau: Ferdinand Hirt, 1868), 254.

50. Tania Anderson, "Edible Veld Plants: A Food Source for the Future?" *MacGregor Miscellany* 3(1991). For a comprehensive account of wild foods throughout southern Africa, see F. W. Fox and M. E. Norwood Young, *Food from the Veld: Edible Wild Plants of Southern Africa* (Johannesburg: Delta, 1982).

51. Burchell, *Travels* 2(1953), 298; Borcherds, *Memoir* (1963), 125; Barrow, *Voyage* (1975), 386; R. Gordon Cumming, *A Hunter's Life in South Africa*, vol. 1, (London: 1857; reprint ed., Bulawayo: Books of Zimbabwe, 1980), 295. See also Okihiro, "Hunters, Herders, Cultivators, and Traders," Ph.D. dissertation, UCLA, 1976, 66–7, 149–52.

52. E. Solomon, *Two Lectures on the Native Tribes of the Interior* (Cape Town: Saul Solomon, 1855), 51; Comaroff and Comaroff, *Of Revelation and Revolution*, 1(1991), 153. These people were also called "poor Bechuana," see Campbell, *Travels* (1974), 218.

53. On the use of the term "lala" in Nguni languages and its ethnic meaning, see Hamilton and John Wright, "The Making of the amaLala: Ethnicity, Ideology and Relations of Subordination in a Precolonial Context," *South African Historical Journal* 22(1990): 3–23.

54. Moffat, *Missionary Labours* (1842), 9. On the "practically vegetarian" diet of the poor, see also Lichtenstein, *About the Bechuanas* (1973), 66.

55. Campbell, *Second Journey*, 2(1967), 186. For evidence on smallpox epidemics, see Gordon, *Cape Travels*, 2(1988), 338, 350, 354; Smith, *Diary of Dr. Andrew Smith*, 1(1939), 390–1.

56. Campbell, *Second Journey*, 2(1967), 189.

57. Campbell, *Travels* (1974), 194.

58. Burchell, *Travels*, 2(1953), 249.

59. Burchell, *Travels*, 2(1953), 216.

60. Moffat, *Missionary Labours* (1842), 8.

61. For an example see Campbell, *Second Journey*, 1(1967), 288–9.

62. Lichtenstein was first to use a form of the term *batlhanka*, but he did not mention *balala*. *About the Bechuanas* (1973), 76, and *Travels*, 2(1930), 416; Burchell, *Travels*, 2(1953), 267, 248.

63. Lichtenstein, *Travels*, 2(1930), 396–397, and *About the Bechuanas* (1973), 75; Burchell, *Travels*, 2(1953), 334, 377–8.

64. John Philip, *Researches in South Africa*, vol. 2 (London: James Duncan, 1828), 141.

65. Lichtenstein, *Travels*, 2(1930), 365; David Livingstone, *Family Letters, 1841–1856*, vol. 1, I. Schapera, ed. (London: Chatto and Windus, 1959), 39; Fritsch, *Drei Jahre* (1868), 262–3; Campbell, *Second Journey*, 1(1967), 101, 194–5, and 2(1967), 136; Zimbabwe National Archives [hereafter ZNA], Frederick Courtenay Selous Journal [Hereafter SE], November 2, 1871.

66. Burchell, *Travels*, 2(1953), 383.

67. Borcherds, *Memoir* (1963), 125, 130; Somerville, *Narrative* (1979), 127; Barrow, *A Voyage* (1975), 393; Lichtenstein, *Travels*, 2(1930), 410; Burchell, *Travels*, 2(1953), 413; and Campbell, *Second Journey*, 2(1967), 218. On nineteenth-century herding

techniques, see Okihiro, "Hunters, Herders, Cultivators, and Traders," Ph.D. dissertation, UCLA, 1976, 169–71.

68. On sheep, see Burchell, *Travels* 2(1953), 368; Lichtenstein, *About the Bechuanas* (1973), 81.
69. Borcherds, *Memoir* (1963), 126–7. See also Somerville, *Narrative* (1979), 125, 134.
70. Somerville, *Narrative* (1979), 112.
71. Comaroff and Comaroff, *Of Revelation and Revolution*, 1(1991), 145–6; Jean Comaroff, *Body of Power, Spirit of Resistance: The Culture and History of a South African People* (Chicago: University of Chicago Press, 1985), 67–74.
72. Somerville, *Narrative* (1979), 110; Lichtenstein, *About the Bechuanas* (1973), 66; Campbell, *Travels* (1974), 202.
73. Burchell, *Travels*, 2(1953), 358.
74. Burchell, *Travels*, 2(1953), 368; Campbell, *Second Journey*, 1(1967), 63–64; Lichtenstein, *Travels*, 2(1930), 365.
75. Burchell, *Travels*, 2(1953), 362.
76. Somerville, *Narrative* (1979), 125.
77. Somerville, *Narrative* (1979), 141.
78. Campbell, *Travels* (1974), 203.
79. Somerville, *Narrative* (1979), 149.
80. For more stock disease, see Chapter 3. I am indebted to Pieter Snyman for first alerting me to the historical importance of these diseases and sharing evidence about them with me. See Snyman, "Die Bydrae van Droogtes and Veesiektes to die Verarming van die Landboubevolking in Noord-Kaapland, 1880–1920," *Tydskrif vir Geesteswetenskappe* 29(1989): 32–49.
81. Lichtenstein, *Travels*, 2(1930), 394.
82. Somerville, *Narrative* (1979), 142.
83. For a description of early herding practices in the Bechuanaland protectorate, see Duggan, *An Economic Analysis* (1986), 74–9.
84. Borcherds, *Memoir* (1963), 130; Barrow, *A Voyage* (1975), 390.
85. Comaroff and Comaroff, *Of Revelation and Revolution*, 1(1991), 151.
86. Not all these rights are documented in records for the Tlhaping at this period. For some examples, see Burchell, *Travels*, 2(1953), 377, 384; Lichtenstein, *Travels*, 2(1930), 413–4; Moffat, *Apprenticeship* (1951), 125–6; Smith, *Diary of Dr. Andrew Smith*, 1(1939), 296. On the position of the chief in this and other southern Tswana groups, see Comaroff and Comaroff, *Of Revelation and Revolution*, 1(1991), 146–52; Kinsman, "Social Formation," in *Africa Seminar Collected Papers*, 2(1981): 181–6; Okihiro, "Hunters, Herders, Cultivators, and Traders," Ph.D. dissertation, UCLA, 1976, 91–5.
87. Campbell, *Second Journey*, 2(1967), 154.
88. William C. Willoughby, *Soul of the Bantu* (Garden City, New York: Doubleday, Doran, 1928), 179, 204, 224, 258–9; Jean Comaroff, *Body of Power* (1985), 66–7; Comaroff and Comaroff, *Of Revelation and Revolution*, 1(1991), 158, 202–3, 206–13; Paul Landau, *The Realm of the Word: Language, Gender and Christianity in a Southern African Kingdom* (Portsmouth: Heinemann, 1995), 14, 25.
89. Pauline Peters, *Dividing the Commons: Politics, Policy and Culture in Botswana* (Charlottesville: University of Virginia Press, 1994), 30.

90. Peters, *Dividing the Commons* (1994), 34–5.
91. Burchell, *Travels*, 2(1953), 362.
92. Smith, *Andrew Smith's Journal*, William Lye, ed. (Cape Town: A. A. Balkema, 1975), 173.
93. Campbell, *Second Journey*, 2(1967), 214.
94. Burchell, *Travels*, 2(1953), 383.
95. Burchell, *Travels*, 2(1953), 362; Campbell, *Travels* (1974), 187, 202; and Campbell, *Second Journey*, 2(1967), 82.
96. Lichtenstein, *Travels*, 2(1930), 409.
97. Lichtenstein, *About the Bechuanas* (1973), 78.
98. On mafisa relationships in Botswana, see Schapera, *A Handbook of Tswana Law and Custom*, 2nd ed. (London: Oxford University for the International African Institute, 1955), 246–7. See also Kinsman, "Social Formation," in *Africa Seminar Collected Papers*, 2(1981): 175–6, 179–80; Okihiro, "Hunters, Herders, Cultivators, and Traders," Ph.D. dissertation, UCLA, 1976, 89–91.
99. Burchell, *Travels*, 2(1953), 248. His emphasis.
100. Burchell, *Travels*, 2(1953), 248. His emphasis.
101. Burchell, *Travels*, 2(1953), 383.
102. Lichtenstein, *About the Bechuanas* (1973), 77; Moffat, *Apprenticeship* (1951), 125; and Campbell, *Second Journey*, 2(1967), 210–11.
103. Moffat, *Missionary Labours* (1842), 8; Campbell, *Second Journey*, 2(1967), 167. See also Okihiro, "Hunters, Herders, Cultivators, and Traders," Ph.D. dissertation, UCLA, 1976, 158–60.
104. Jean Comaroff, *Body of Power* (1985), 54–60, 65, 67–70. See also Comaroff and Comaroff, *Of Revelation and Revolution*, 1(1991), 129–30, 152–60.
105. Campbell, *Second Journey*, 2(1967), 59. See also Willoughby, *Soul* (1928), 5.
106. Boserup, *Conditions* (1965), 15–6, 28–31, 44–8.
107. Based on fieldwork among the Kwena people near Molepolole in Botswana in 1975, Gary Okihiro has produced a valuable reconstruction of nineteenth-century hoe cultivation. He also holds that people began cultivating as a supplement to herding and foraging. See Okihiro, "Hunters, Herders, Cultivators, and Traders," Ph.D. dissertation, UCLA, 1976, 68–84.
108. Somerville, *Narrative* (1979), 142. On desert cultivation with sticks rather than plows in early nineteenth-century Botswana, see Okihiro, "Hunters, Herders, Cultivators, and Traders," Ph.D. dissertation, UCLA, 1976, 144–6.
109. Burchell, *Travels*, 2(1953), 362.
110. Burchell, *Travels*, 1(1953), 242. Here he is generalizing about various "wandering African nations" encountered in his travels, including the Tlhaping. For other evidence for the low value put on land, see Barrow, *A Voyage* (1975), 400. For contradictory reports on whether the Tlhaping fenced fields, see Somerville, *Narrative* (1979), 129 and Lichtenstein *Travels*, 2(1930), 410. On female ownership of fields, see Campbell, *Second Journey*, 2(1967), 148–9.
111. Fritsch, *Drei Jahre* (1868), 262, 266; Smith, *Journal* (1975), 183–4. Not all settlements were near water. Campbell, *Travels* (1974), 203.
112. Burchell, *Travels*, 2(1953), 414. His emphasis. See also James Backhouse and Charles Tyler, *The Life and Labours of George Washington Walker of Hobart Town, Tasmania* (London: A. W. Bennet, 1862), 447.

113. Somerville, *Narrative* (1979), 135–6; Campbell, *Second Journey*, 1(1967), 248.
114. LMS 14/2/F, Moffat, February 3, 1834. A missionary to the Griqua concurred, contrasting "squandering" among the Griqua with Tswana prudence and successful adaptation to the dry environment. LMS 14/1/A, Wright at Griquatown, January 25, 1834, June 19, 1834, September 25, 1835.
115. Somerville, *Narrative* (1979), 141. See also Somerville, *Narrative* (1979), 139; Campbell, *Second Journey*, 1(1967), 64.
116. Barrow, *A Voyage* (1975), 394; Somerville, *Narrative* (1979), 129.
117. Mary Moffat, *Apprenticeship* (1951), 108; Philip, *Researches*, 2(1828), 117.
118. Moffat, *Missionary Labours* (1842), 330–1. See also Burchell, *Travels*, 2(1953), 218, 361. On Moffat's environmental thought, see Richard Grove, "Scottish Missionaries, Evangelical Discourses and the Origins of Conservation Thinking in Southern Africa 1820–1900," *Journal of Southern African Studies* 15(1989): 163–87.
119. Somerville, *Narrative* (1979), 139.
120. Shillington, *Colonisation* (1985), 14–5.
121. Campbell, *Second Journey*, 2(1967), 206–7.
122. Somerville, *Narrative* (1979), 139.
123. Barrow, *A Voyage* (1975), 392, 394; Somerville, *Narrative* (1979), 129; Burchell, *Travels*, 2(1953), 366, 413; Campbell, *Second Journey*, 2(1967), 215–16; Gustav Fritsch, *Die Eingeborenen Süd-Afrikas* (Breslau: Ferdinand Hirt, 1872), 188; Henry Methuen, *Life in the Wilderness; or Wanderings in South Africa* (London: Richard Bentler, 1846), 107; LMS 11/2/B, Moffat, September 12, 1828. For a description of early cultivation techniques in the Bechuanaland protectorate, see Duggan, *An Economic Analysis* (1986), 69–74.
124. My emphasis on the extensive agriculture among the Tlhaping contrasts with Eldredge's depiction of cultivation at Dithakong producing high enough yields to earn it a reputation as a cultivation center. See "Sources of Conflict," 159–60.
125. Moffat, *Missionary Labours* (1842), 8–9; Smith, *Diary of Dr. Andrew Smith*, 1(1939), 296.
126. See Jeff Guy, "Analysing Pre-Capitalist Societies in Southern Africa," *Journal of Southern African Studies* 14(1987): 18–37.
127. Iris Berger, " 'Beasts of Burden' Revisited: Interpretations of Women and Gender in Southern African Societies," in Harms et al., eds., *Paths toward the Past: African Historical Essays in Honor of Jan Vansina* (Atlanta: African Studies Association, 1994), 123–41. For Berger's insightful critique of Guy's argument, see pp. 124–6. For more of my critique, see Nancy Jacobs, "Environment, Production and Social Difference in the Kalahari Thornveld, c. 1750–1830," *Journal of Southern African Studies* 25(1999): 370–1.
128. Kinsman, " 'Beasts of Burden': The Subordination of Southern Tswana Women, ca. 1800–1840," *Journal of Southern African Studies* 10(1983): 42. Kinsman argues that mothers and daughters held grain communally. On their control over grain stores, see Schapera, *Native Land Tenure in the Bechuanaland Protectorate* ([Alice]: Lovedale, 1943), 199.
129. Okihiro, "Hunters, Herders, Cultivators, and Traders," Ph.D. dissertation, UCLA, 1976, 79–80.
130. Borcherds, *Memoir* (1963), 128.

131. Eldredge, "Women in Production: The Economic Role of Women in Nineteenth Century Lesotho," *Signs* 16(1991): 707–31.
132. Somerville, *Narrative* (1979), 126.
133. Campbell, *Travels* (1974), 201.
134. Anon., "Mission to the Bechuanas," *South African Christian Recorder* (March 1831): 23.
135. Borcherds, *Memoir* (1963), 130; Burchell, *Travels*, 2(1953), 366; A. A. Anderson, *Twenty Five Years in a Wagon in the Gold Regions of Africa* (London: Chapman and Hall, 1888), 81.
136. Solomon, *Two Lectures* (1855), 44.
137. Campbell, *Travels* (1974), 190.
138. Campbell, *Second Journey*, 2(1967), 63.
139. Lichtenstein, *About the Bechuanas* (1973), 77.
140. Berger, "'Beasts of Burden' Revisited," in *Paths toward the Past* (1994), 125–6.
141. Campbell, *Travels* (1974), 200.
142. Berger, "'Beasts of Burden' Revisited," in *Paths toward the Past* (1994), 136.
143. Guy, "Analysing Pre-Capitalist Societies," *Journal of Southern African Studies* 14(1987): 22.
144. Somerville, *Narrative* (1979), 122; Burchell, *Travels*, 2(1953), 398.
145. Englebrecht, *The Korana* (1936), 135–6; Schapera, *The Khoisan Peoples of South Africa: Bushmen and Hottentots* (London: George Routledge and Sons, 1930), 247–8. On continuing intermarriage between Korana and Tlhaping after 1800, see Legassick, "The Griqua, the Sotho-Tswana and the Missionaries," Ph.D. dissertation, UCLA, 1969, 68–9.
146. On different approaches to the significance of bridewealth, see John Comaroff, "Introduction," in *The Meaning of Marriage Payments*, John Comaroff, ed. (London: Academic, 1980), 1–47.
147. Elias Mandala, who describes subordination by age and not gender, makes the same point about the work assigned to young people in the Tchiri Valley in the nineteenth century. See Mandala, *Work and Control* (1990), 30.
148. Jean Comaroff, *Body of Power* (1985), 84–120.
149. Eugenia Herbert, *Iron, Gender, and Power: Rituals of Transformation in African Societies* (Bloomington: Indiana University Press, 1993), 220.
150. This is most clear in the comparison of Meru and Arusha cultivation on Mount Meru in Thomas Spear, *Mountain Farmers*.

CHAPTER 3

1. Campbell, *Second Journey*, 2(1967), 60.
2. P. J. van der Merwe includes environmental factors in his analysis of Trekboers. For an English translation, see *The Migrant Farmer in the History of the Cape Colony, 1657–1842*, trans. Roger Beck (Athens: Ohio University Press, 1995). On the environmental impact for the Khoikhoi, see Leonard Guelke and Robert Shell, "Landscape of Conquest: Frontier Water Alienation and Khoikhoi Strategies of Survival, 1652–1780," *Journal of Southern African Studies* 18(1992): 803–24. On the environment dynamics of another frontier, see Crosby, "The Past and Present of Environmental History," *American Historical Review*

100(October 1995): 1185; White, "American Environmental History: The Development of a New Field," *Pacific Historical Review* 54(1985): 297–335.

3. Campbell, *Second Journey* 1(1967), 113; Lichtenstein, *About the Bechuanas* (1973), 66.

4. Smith, *Diary of Dr. Andrew Smith*, 1(1939), 295–6.

5. Moffat, *Missionary Labours* (1842), 374; Campbell, *Travels* (1974), 203.

6. Shillington, *Colonisation* (1985), 15; Campbell, *Travels* (1974), 236.

7. Legassick, "The Griqua, the Sotho-Tswana and the Missionaries," Ph.D. dissertation, UCLA, 1969, 170.

8. Legassick, "The Griqua, the Sotho-Tswana and the Missionaries," Ph.D. dissertation, UCLA, 1969, 225–54. See also Legassick, "The Northern Frontier to c. 1840," in Richard Elphick and Herman Giliomee, eds., *The Shaping of South African Society, 1652–1840*, revised edition (Middletown: Wesleyan University, 1988), 358–420.

9. This was the Truter-Somerville expedition. Accounts of this journey are found in Borcherds, *Memoir* (1963); Barrow, *A Voyage* (1975); Somerville, *Narrative* (1979).

10. Roger Beck, "Beads and Bibles: Missionaries as Traders in Southern Africa in the Early Nineteenth Century," *Journal of African History* 39(1989): 211 4; J. T. Du Bruyn, "Die Tlhaping en die Eerste Sendelinge, 1801–1806," *South African Historical Journal* 14(1982): 8–34; and Du Bruyn, "Die Aanvangsjare van die Christelike Sending onder die Tlhaping," *South African Archives Yearbook* 52(1989).

11. Du Bruyn, "James Read en die Tlhaping, 1816–1820," *Historia* 35(May 1990): 23–38.

12. Campbell, *Second Journey*, 2(1967), 60.

13. Grove, "Scottish Missionaries in Southern Africa, 1820–1900," *Journal of Southern African Studies* 15(1989).

14. Comaroff and Comaroff, *Of Revelation and Revolution*, 2(1997), 174–5, 206–14.

15. In the light of the Moffats' food shortages, the practical incentive to irrigate must not be underestimated. See *Apprenticeship* (1951), 60; Cecil Northcott, *Robert Moffat, Pioneer in Africa* (London: Lutterworth, 1961), 114.

16. Moffat, *Apprenticeship* (1951), 22–3; Moffat, *Missionary Labours* (1842), 285–6; LMS 9/1/B, Hamilton, February 17, 1823.

17. LMS 9/2/A, Moffat, January 20, 1824; Moffat, *Apprenticeship* (1951), 113. The size was given at 550 acres.

18. Campbell, *Second Journey*, 2(1967), 85.

19. Mary Moffat, *Apprenticeship* (1951), 108; Philip, *Researches*, 2(1828), 117.

20. Campbell, *Second Journey* 1(1967), 101, and 2(1967), 215–6; Philip, *Researches*, 2(1828), 118; LMS 9/4/2, Moffat and Hamilton, December 1, 1825.

21. Philip, *Researches*, 2(1828), 118.

22. On the history of tobacco trade and production, see Burchell, *Travels*, 2(1953), 230; Barrow, *A Voyage* (1975), 395; Campbell, *Travels* (1974), 241; Mary Moffat, *Apprenticeship* (1951), 224; Robert Moffat, *Missionary Labours* (1951), 558; LMS 9/4/B, Moffat and Hamilton, December 1, 1825; W. C. Harris, *Wild Sports of Southern Africa* (London: Henry G. Bohn, 1852; reprint ed. Cape Town: C. Struik, 1963), 43.

23. On this subject, see Grove, "Scottish Missionaries in Southern Africa, 1820–1900," *Journal of Southern African Studies* 15(1989). See also A. A. Anderson, *Twenty Five*

Years (1888), 74; Fritsch, *Drei Jahre* (1868), 255; Smith, "Report of the Expedition for Exploring Central Africa," *Journal of the Royal Geographic Society* 6(1836): 402–3; James Fox Wilson, "Water Supply in the Basin of the River Orange, or 'Gariep,' South Africa," *Journal of the Royal Geographical Society* 35(1865): 106–29; E. H. L. Schwarz, *The Kalahari; or Thirstland Redemption* (Cape Town: T. Maskew Miller, [1920]).

24. Tyson, *Climatic Change and Variability* (1987), 59.
25. For example, see Campbell, *Second Journey*, 2(1967), 109, 111–2.
26. Campbell, *Second Journey*, 2(1967), 93.
27. Snyman, "Die Bydrae van Droogtes and Veesiektes," *Tydskrif vir Geestesweten-skappe* 29(1989).
28. M. W. Henning, *Animal Diseases in South Africa*, 2nd ed. (Pretoria: Central News Agency, 1949), on anthrax see pp. 3–13, on botulism see pp. 324–53; H. T. B. Hall, *Diseases and Parasites of Livestock in the Tropics* (London: Longman, 1977), on anthrax see pp. 129–31, on botulism see pp. 131–3.
29. Burchell, *Travels*, 2(1953), 335, 415–6; Campbell, *Second Journey* 1(1967), 82.
30. Somerville, *Narrative* (1979), 139; Robert Moffat, *Apprenticeship* (1951), 43, 161, 211, 212; Testimonies of Masse Mahura, and Jantjie, son of Mothibi, in *Evidence Taken at Bloemhof* [The Bloemhof Blue Book] (1871), 61–2, 91.
31. Smith, *Diary of Dr. Andrew Smith* (1939), 241, 247–8, 390. There is some question whether kwatsi was anthrax or black quarter. However, black quarter does not affect humans. See Henning, *Animal Diseases* (1949), 284–93. See also Schapera, ed., *Apprenticeship* (1951), 179–80, note 3; LMS 15/2/D, Moffat, November 23, 1836.
32. David Livingstone, *Livingstone's Missionary Correspondence, 1841–1856*, Schapera, ed. (Berkeley: University of California, 1961), 35; Mackenzie, *Ten Years North of the Orange River* (Edinburgh: Edmonston and Douglas, 1871, reprint ed., London: Frank Cass and Company, 1971), 70.
33. J. D. Omer-Cooper, *Zulu Aftermath: A Nineteenth Century Revolution in Bantu Africa* (London: Longman, 1966). On events at Dithakong, see Julian Cobbing, "Mfecane as Alibi: Thoughts on Dithakong and Mbolompo," *Journal of African History* 29(1988): 487–519; Eldredge, "Sources of Conflict." On the events at Dithakong, see Jan-Bart Gewald, "'Mountaineers' as Mantatees: A Critical Re-assessment of Events leading up to the Battle of Dithakong," MA thesis, State University Leiden, 1989; and Guy Hartley, "The Battle of Dithakong and 'Mfecane' Theory," in *Mfecane Aftermath*, Caroline Hamilton, ed., 395–416.
34. Eldredge, "Slave Raiding," in *Slavery in South Africa* (1994).
35. LMS 8/2/E, Moffat at Griquatown, n. d., 1820; Smith, *Diary of Dr. Andrew Smith* (1939), 369.
36. Moffat, *Missionary Labours* (1842), 480.
37. LMS 8/2/C, Philip at Cape Town, copying letter from Campbell at Dithakong, July 29, 1820.
38. Moffat, *Missionary Labours* (1842), 447.
39. Robert Moffat, *Apprenticeship* (1951), 281–2. See also John Smith Moffat, *The Lives of Robert and Mary Moffat* (New York: A. C. Armstrong & Son, 1886), 156.
40. LMS 13/4/E, Hamilton, Moffat and Edwards, September 30, 1833.
41. Moffat, *Missionary Labours* (1842), 480. See also Mackenzie, *Ten Years* (1971), 71–2.

42. Mary Moffat, *Apprenticeship* (1951), 292. On tobacco production and trade among the Kwena people, see Okihiro, "Hunters, Herders, Cultivators, and Traders," Ph.D. dissertation, UCLA, 1976, 83–5.
43. LMS 11/3/D, Moffat and Hamilton, August 12, 1829.
44. LMS 9/2A, Moffat in Cape Town, January 20, 1824.
45. LMS 11/3/D, Moffat and Hamilton, August 12, 1829.
46. LMS 14/2F, 1834 Annual Schedule of Returns, 1834.
47. James Backhouse, *A Narrative of a Visit to the Mauritius and South Africa* (London: Hamilton, Adams and Co., 1844), 456; Gordon Cumming, *A Hunter's Life* (1980), 134.
48. LMS 13/4/E, Moffat, September 30, 1833; LMS 20/1/B, Hamilton, Moffat and Ashton, October 12, 1844. For a detailed description of irrigation works, see LMS 45/3/D, Roger Price, October 23, 1888.
49. Andrew Geddes Bain, *Journal of Andrew Geddes Bain*, Margaret Hermina Lister, ed. (Cape Town: The Van Riebeeck Society, 1949), 154.
50. Moffat, Missionary Labours (1842), 558.
51. LMS 24/1/B, Ashton, September 24, 1849.
52. LMS 28/1/C, Moffat, November 12, 1853. For the history of irrigated cultivation in a western Transvaal village, see J. H. Drummond, "Rural Land Use and Agricultural Production in Dinokana Village, Bophuthatswana," *GeoJournal* 22(1990): 335–43.
53. Robert Unwin Moffat, *John Smith Moffat* (London: John Murray, 1921; reprint ed., New York: Negro Universities Press, 1969), 71.
54. LMS 25/1/D, William Ross at Mamusa, October 18, 1850; LMS 26/1/A, Holloway Helmore, April 9, 1851; and LMS 27/1/B, Moffat, November 22, 1851.
55. LMS 26/1/A, Helmore, January 1, 1851 and April 2, 1851. For a history of this and other irrigation on the Harts River, see Shillington, "Irrigation, Agriculture and the State: The Harts Valley in Historical Perspective," in *Putting a Plough to the Ground*, Beinart, Delius, and Trapido, eds., 311–35.
56. Henning, *Animal Diseases* (1949), 170–1.
57. J. B. Peires, *The Dead Will Arise: Nonqawuse and the Great Xhosa Cattle-Killing Movement of 1856–57* (Johannesburg: Raven Press, 1989). An interesting note in the history of lungsickness in southern Africa was recorded by Robert Moffat, Jr., who encountered a quarantine in Griqualand against foreign cattle in August 1856. Robert Moffat, Jr., "Journey from Little Namaqualand Eastward along the Orange River in August 1856," *Journal of the Royal Geographical Society* 28(1858): 174–87.
58. LMS 29/3/A, Moffat, November 14, 1855.
59. John Smith Moffat, *The Matabele Mission: A Selection from the Correspondence of John and Emily Moffat, David Livingstone and Others, 1858–1878*, J. P. R. Wallis, ed. (London: Chatto and Windus, 1945), 53.
60. LMS 31/1/B, Ross at Dikgatlhong, November 1, 1858.
61. LMS 30/1/A, Robert Moffat, October 28, 1856. Another missionary admitted that at Seodin "great distress frequently prevails." See Mackenzie, *Ten Years* (1971), 70.
62. LMS 25/1/D, Ross at Mamusa, October 18, 1850; J. Agar-Hamilton, *The Road to the North: South Africa, 1852–1886* (London: Longmans, 1937), 17–27; Anthony Sillery, *The Bechuanaland Protectorate* (Cape Town: Oxford, 1952), 16–19; Shillington, *Colonisation* (1985), 19–21.

63. Harms, *Games Against Nature* (1987).
64. Mackenzie, *Austral Africa* 1(1887), 76–7.
65. Metswetsaneng: Cape Town Archives Repository (hereafter CTAR) British Bechuanaland Land Commission series (hereafter BBLC) 34, part 1, letters from Mokwene Baepi, n. d. and Yan Makgetle, n. d., and CTAR BBLC 22, claim number 161 of John Markram to Metswetsaneng. Bothetheletsa: CTAR BBLC 34, part 1, letter from Tsheboen Sabatlan, n. d. Ga-Tlhose: LMS 32/5/B, Robert Moffat, December 1, 1862; LMS 34/3/A, Robert Moffat, June 16, 1867; CTAR BBLC 34, part 1, letter from Holele Molete, n. d. Batlharos: CTAR BBLC 9, part 2, testimony of John Nelson, March 31, 1886. Konong: CTAR BBLC 20, claim number 43 of J. G. Donovan. Manyeding: LMS 37/1/A, Ashton, March 13, 1872. Mapoteng: CTAR BBLC 9, part 2, testimony of J. S. Moffat, March 31, 1886; CTAR BBLC 23 claim number 100 of Benjamin George Willmore. Kathu: CTAR BBLC 20, claim number 42 of J. G. Donovan. Kuruman River Valley above Mamoratwe: CTAR BBLC 21, claim number 60 of Herbert Jarvis. Matlhwareng River: CTAR BBLC 34, part 1, letter from Diphokwe Yakwe, n. d. Vlakfontein: University of the Witwatersrand Collection A75, John Mackenzie Papers, No. 428, S. Lowe to F. Villiers. Gasegonyane: CTAR BBLC 22, claim number 67 of LMS.
66. Sutton, "Irrigation and Soil-Conservation in African Agricultural History," *Journal of African History* 25(1984): 30.
67. William Adams and David Anderson, "Irrigation Before Development: Indigenous and Induced Change in Agricultural Water Management in East Africa," *African Affairs* 87(1988): 519–35; David Anderson, "Cultivating Pastoralists: Ecology and Economy among the Il Chamus of Baringo, 1840–1980," in *The Ecology of Survival: Case Studies from Northeast African History*, Douglas H. Johnson and David Anderson, eds. (London: Lester Crook Academic, 1988; Boulder: Westview, 1988), 241–60.
68. Mackenzie, *Ten Years* (1971), 92. For other criticism of African irrigation techniques, see Philip, *Researches*, 2(1828), 113; Livingstone, *Missionary Travels and Researches in South Africa* (London: Murray, 1857; reprint ed., Freeport, NY: Books for Libraries, 1972), 111.
69. Mackenzie, *Ten Years* (1971), 70.
70. Comaroff and Comaroff, *Of Revelation and Revolution*, 2(1997), 127–8.
71. John Brown, "The Bechuana Tribes," *Cape Monthly Magazine*, July 1875, 1–2.
72. LMS 8/2/B, Philip at Cape Town, July 29, 1820; Philip, *Researches*, 2(1828) 131; Harris, *Wild Sports* (1963), 43.
73. Moffat, *Missionary Labours* (1842), 562; LMS 27/1/A, Robert Moffat, January 15, 1852. On the use of cash, see also Smith, *Diary of Dr. Andrew Smith*, 1(1939), 250.
74. Barrow, *A Voyage* (1975), 403; Borcherds, *Memoir* (1963), 85. As late as 1853 the Tlhaping tried to block outsiders' trips to the interior. James Chapman, *Travels into the Interior of South Africa*, vol.1 (London: Bell and Daldy, 1868), 95.
75. Shillington, *Colonisation* (1985), 21–5; Mackenzie, *Ten Years* (1971), 71–2.
76. LMS 21/1/B, Ross at Taung, October 20, 1845; Thomas Leask, *The South African Diaries of Thomas Leask*, J. P. R. Wallis, ed. (London: Chatto and Windus, 1954), 52, 108.
77. John M. MacKenzie, *Empire of Nature: Hunting, Conservation, and British Imperialism* (Manchester: Manchester University Press, 1988), 86–119.

78. Frederick Selous encountered the trading store in the Langeberg Mountains. See ZNA SE 1/4, February 5, 1872. On the history of trading in Kuruman in the mid-nineteenth century, see Snyman, *Kuruman* (1992), 34–40.

79. MacKenzie, *Empire of Nature* (1988), 124, gives documented average tusk weights per elephant shot on hunting expeditions ranging from forty-four to fifty-three pounds per animal. Using the mean figure of approximately forty-eight pounds per animal, the 1844 shipment would have represented the tusks of forty-one animals; 188 animals in 1849; 468 in 1851. Barry Morton, "Materials relating to David Hume in the Grahamstown Journal" (unpublished manuscript.)

80. LMS 33/3/A, Robert Moffat, January 11, 1864; Grove, "Early Themes in African Conservation," *Conservation in Africa* (Cambridge: Cambridge University Press, 1987), 27.

81. On game depletion in southern Africa, see MacKenzie, *Empire of Nature* (1988), 89–116.

82. William Cotton Oswell, "South Africa Fifty Years Ago," in *Big Game Shooting*, vol. 1, Clive Phillips-Wolley, ed. (London: Longmans Green, 1894), 36 7.

83. ZNA SE 1/4, February 5, 1872. See also Mackenzie, *Ten Years* (1971), 70.

84. A. A. Anderson, *Twenty-Five Years* (1888), 87.

85. Alfred James Gould, "Kuruman to Morokweng in 1883," *Botswana Notes and Records*, A. Sandilands, ed., 9(1977): 49–54; British Parliamentary Papers (hereafter BPP) C 4956 (1887) *Affairs of Bechuanaland and Adjacent Territories*, Trooper A. Querk, "Report on Patrol to Honing Vley, October 5–30, 1886," 124.

86. LMS 42/3/C, Alfred Wookey, "Review of South Bechuanaland, Part 2," June 11, 1884.

87. Shillington, *Colonisation* (1985), 35–60; Ake Holmberg, *African Tribes and European Agencies* (Goteborg: Scandinavian University Press, 1966), 37–41; Agar-Hamilton, *Road to the North* (1937), 37–131.

88. LMS 42/3/C, Wookey, "Review of South Bechuanaland, part 2," June 11, 1884; Mackenzie, *Austral Africa*, 1(1887), 30.

89. John Brown, "The Bechuana Tribes," 2–3; ZNA A. C. Baillie Papers (hereafter BA) 10/1-2, July 30, 1876.

90. Shillington, "The Impact of the Diamond Discoveries on the Kimberley Hinterland: Class Formation, Colonialism and Resistance among the Tlhaping of Griqualand West in the 1870s," in *Industrialisation and Social Change in South Africa: African Class Formation, Culture and Consciousness 1870–1930*, Shula Marks and Richard Rathbone, eds. (London: Longman, 1982), 99–118.

91. Mackenzie, *Ten Years* (1971), 89–90.

92. Backhouse and Tyler, *George Washington Walker* (1862), 448; LMS 33/5/A, Ashton at Dikgatlong, December 20, 1865; ZNA SE 1/4, November 3, 1871.

93. ZNA, SE 1/4, February 1–5, 1872. For another report of prices travelers considered exorbitant, see Public Records Office, London (hereafter PRO) Colonial Office series (hereafter CO) 879/16 no. 104 Lanyon to Bartle Frere with enclosures on Griqualand West and Bechuanaland, November 19, 1878.

94. LMS 42/3/C, Wookey, "Review of South Bechuanaland, Part 2," June 11, 1884. For an overview of wood sales in the northern Cape, see Shillington, *Colonisation* (1985), 102–6, 137–43.

95. LMS 42/1A, Wookey, January 12, 1883.

96. Burchell, *Travels*, 2(1953), 369; Parker Gillmore, "The Territories Adjacent to the Kalahari Desert," *Proceedings of the Royal Colonial Institute* 14(1883): 126–7.

97. University of the Witwatersrand Collection A75, Mackenzie to Colonel Lanyon, August 1, 1878. LMS 40/1/C, Ashton at Barkly, July 23, 1879; LMS 92/1/C, John Mackenzie, April 5, 1880.

98. Comaroff and Comaroff, *Of Revelation and Revolution*, 2(1997), 139–65.

99. LMS 40/1/C, Ashton at Barkly, July 23, 1879.

100. Mackenzie, *Austral Africa*, 1(1887), 80–1.

101. CTAR BCC [Bechuanaland Crown Colony] 119, Price to British Bechuanaland Administrator Shippard, September 28, 1887.

102. Edward Solomon, *Two Lectures* (1855), mentions *balala* on p. 51; John Brown, "The Bechuana Tribes," (1875) mentions batlhanka on p. 2.

103. A. A. Anderson, *Twenty-Five Years* (1888), 82–3. One description uses a word from northern Tswana areas, "Bakalahari." CTAR BCC 119, Price to British Bechuanaland Administrator Shippard, September 28, 1887.

104. ZNA BA 10/1-2, July 30, 1876. The number may be exaggerated, but the point that they worked as *balala*, as they always had, is important.

105. CTAR Kuruman Resident Magistrate Series (hereafter 1/KMN) 8/2, Resident Magistrate Bam, October 3, 1894; CTAR 1/KMN 8/2, Inspector of Native Reserves St. Quintin to colonial secretary, October 9, 1894. The government of British Bechuanaland did not take action against captive labor among the Tswana or the Boers. On client labor in the southern Kalahari, see BPP C 3635 (1883) *Reports by Colonel Warren, R. E., C.M.G. and Captain Harell (Late 89th Regiment) on the Affairs of Bechuanaland, Dated April 3rd 1879 and April 27th 1880*, 13.

106. CTAR BCC 119, Price to British Bechuanaland Administrator Shippard, September 28, 1887. John Smith Moffat to Shippard, 6 April 1887. At this time Moffat was working as a resident magistrate in Taung.

107. Cape Colony Parliamentary Papers (hereafter CPP) G 19 - '97, *Blue Book for Native Affairs*, 68.

108. LMS 39/3/D, Ashton at Barkly (formerly Dikgatlhong), October 24, 1878.

109. Moffat, *Missionary Labours* (1842), 13; LMS 42/3/C, Wookey, "Review of South Bechuanaland, Part 2," June 11, 1884.

110. LMS 39/1/D, Ashton, November 27, 1877.

111. BPP C 4956 *Affairs of Bechuanaland and Adjacent Territories*, 124; CTAR Land Office series (hereafter LND) 1/441, Water Boring Foreman McCaig, July 10, 1895; A. A. Anderson, *Twenty-Five Years* (1888), 82; Gillmore, "Territories Adjacent to the Kalahari," 137; E. Wilkinson, "Notes on a Portion of the Kalahari," *Geographical Journal*, 1(1893): 327, 330, 333; R. Pöch, "Ethnographische und Geographische Ergebinisse meiner Kalaharireisen," *Petermanns Mitteilungen* 58(1912): 16; H. Anderson Bryden, *Gun and Camera in Southern Africa* (London: Edward Stanford, 1893; reprint ed., Prescott, Arizona: Wolfe Publishing, 1988) 62, 123; Molema, *The Bantu, Past and Present* (1920), 36; Breutz, *Tribes of Kuruman* (1963), 25–30; Breutz, "Ancient People in the Kalahari Desert," *Afrika and Übersee* 42(1959): 51–4; CC G 51 - '95, *Annual Report of the Forest Ranger, Bechuanaland for the Year Ending 31st of December, 1894*, 143; CTAR 1/KMN 10/3, Resident Magistrate Hilliard "Report on Local Labour Market," November 15, 1898.

112. LMS 26/1/A, Helmore at Dikgatlhong, January 1851; Anderson, *Twenty-Five Years* (1888), 81. Anderson traveled through Kuruman in 1864.
113. Mackenzie, *Ten Years* (1971), 70; LMS 38/3/A, Ashton at Likhatlong, February 9, 1876. (Copy of Letter to Lt. Col. Crossman.)
114. John Brown, "The Bechuana Tribes," (1875) 2.
115. A. J. Wookey, 24 September 1873, London Missionary Society South Africa Reports, quoted in Comaroff and Comaroff, *Of Revelation and Revolution*, 2(1997), 130.
116. Comaroff and Comaroff, *Of Revelation and Revolution*, 2(1997), 137–8.
117. Eldredge, "Women in Production," *Signs* 16(1991): 734–5. Okihiro depicts Kwena women as retaining control over some cultivated produce after men began to plow. Okihiro, "Hunters, Herders, Cultivators, and Traders," Ph.D. dissertation, UCLA, 1976, 76 7, 83.
118. CTAR BBLC 1, testimony of Herbert Jarvis and John Chapman, March 31, 1886; CTAR BBLC 1, testimony of Marienyane, April 4, 1886; LMS 46/1/A, Roger Price, January 11, 1889.
119. Merchant, *Ecological Revolutions* (1989). For a discussion of the explanatory value of the theory of the Ecological Revolution in Kuruman, see Jacobs, "The Colonial Ecological Revolution in South Africa: The Case of Kuruman," in *South Africa's Environmental History: Cases and Comparisons*, Steven Dovers et al., eds. (Cape Town: David Philip, 2003), 19–33.
120. See epigraph opening this chapter from Campbell, *Second Journey*, 2(1967), 60.
121. Quoted in Comaroff and Comaroff, *Of Revelation and Revolution*, 1(1991), 196. LMS 7, September 5, 1817.

CHAPTER 4

1. Mackenzie, *Austral Africa*, 1(1887), 77–8.
2. Crosby, *Ecological Imperialism* (1986); Carolyn Merchant, *Ecological Revolutions* (1989).
3. The environmental history of settler societies has yielded fruitful comparative work. For recent examples, see Tom Griffiths and Lilly Robin, eds., *Ecology and Empire*; William Beinart and Peter Coates, *Environment and History: The Taming of Nature in the USA and South Africa* (London and New York: Routledge, 1995).
4. Tanzania has the best-developed body of environmental history in Africa. See, for example, Giblin, *The Politics of Environmental Control* (1992); Kjekshus, *Ecology Control and Economic Development* (1996); and essays in Maddox, Giblin, and Kimambo, eds., *Custodians of the Land* (1996).
5. Ivan Evans, *Bureaucracy and Race: Native Administration in South Africa* (Berkeley: University of California, 1997), 1.
6. For descriptions of Direct Rule in the nineteenth-century Cape Colony and Indirect Rule in Natal, see Saul Dubow, *Racial Segregation and the Origins of Apartheid in South Africa 1919–36* (New York and London: St. Martin's, 1989), 99–107; Paul Rich, *State Power and Black Politics in South Africa, 1912–51* (New York: St Martin's, 1996), 31–5, 77–9; Mamdani, *Citizen and Subject* (1996), 16–18, 62–72; Evans, *Bureaucracy and Race* (1997), 15, 166–8.

7. Peires, *The Dead Will Arise* (1989), 60–9, 290–2. Here, I disagree with Mamdani, who believes Cape governance after Governor Grey underwent the transition from Direct to Indirect Rule. See Mamdani, *Citizen and Subject* (1996), 66–7. As evidence, he cites government willingness to rule through headmen, although it was reluctant to use chiefs. In contrast, Ivan Evans shows the structural difference between chiefs and headmen in the Cape system and charts the growing role of chiefs in later colonial governance, especially under Separate Development. Evans, *Bureaucracy and Race* (1997), 207–13.

8. The nineteenth-century French policy of assimilation was a form of Direct Rule. It endured in the twentieth century in the Four Communes of Senegal. Whether association, the dominant French policy in the twentieth century, qualifies as Indirect or Direct Rule depends on definitions. Mamdani considers it one more form of the system of Indirect Rule because it relied on African middlemen. See Mamdani, *Citizen and Subject* (1996), 83–6. Yet, it did not valorize rule through chiefs and tribal structures as British Indirect Rule did. See Michael Crowder, "Indirect Rule – French and British Style," *Africa* 24(1964): 197–205.

9. BPP C 4889 (1886), *Report of the Commissioners Appointed to Determine Land Claims and to Effect a Land Settlement in British Bechuanaland*, 38.

10. On trees as tenure, see CTAR BBLC 21, claim number 194 of Jarvis to the white house in Batlharos; CTAR BBLC 20, claim number 43 of Donovan to Konong; CTAR BBLC 21, claim number 8 of Katje Klein to Mazeppa; CTAR BBLC 22, claim number 161 of John Markram to Metswetsaneng.

11. Mackenzie, *Austral Africa* 1(1887), 76.

12. See Una Long, "Plan by Robert Moffat, Jnr," *Africana Notes and News* 11(1953): 28–9; Isaac Schapera, *Africana Notes and News* 11(1953): 60.

13. LMS 31/1/B, Ashton, July 25, 1858.

14. LMS 14/1/B, Moffat, April 7, 1828.

15. LMS 38/3/A, John Smith Moffat, March 23, 1876.

16. Moffat relinquished the claim, but Mackenzie objected. Mackenzie, *Austral Africa*, 1(1887), 111–14; LMS 38/3/D, Mackenzie, December 8, 1876; LMS 39/3/D, Mackenzie, November 21, 1878; LMS 40/3/A, John Smith Moffat at Griquatown, July 23, 1880; and LMS 43/1/A, Ashton at Barkly, January 24, 1885.

17. LMS 37/3/A, Mackenzie, May 1, 1874. See also *Austral Africa*, 1(1887), 75. For a history supporting Mackenzie, see Richard Lovett, *The History of the London Missionary Society, 1795–1895*, 2 vols. (London: Henry Frowde, 1899), 1: 606–7.

18. For an account of the controversy sympathetic to John Smith Moffat, see Robert Unwin Moffat, *John Smith Moffat* (1969), 126–35.

19. See Shillington, *Colonisation* (1985), 76–82.

20. LMS 39/3/B, John Brown, July 29, 1878.

21. University of the Witwatersrand Collection A75, No. 470 November 1, 1881. John Mackenzie, *Austral Africa*, 1(1887), 107; LMS 40/1/C, Mackenzie, June 3, 1879, and January 5, 1880.

22. Holmberg, *African Tribes and European Agencies* (1966), 57–63; Sillery, *Bechuanaland Protectorate* (1952), 43–6; Agar-Hamilton, *Road to the North* (1937), 132–82; Shillington, *Colonisation* (1985), 61–89.

23. LMS 40/4/A, Mackenzie, October 7, 1880.

24. LMS 42/3/B, R. W. Thompson at Cape Town, April 1, 1884.

25. Shillington, *Colonisation* (1985); C. W. De Kiewiet, *The Imperial Factor in South Africa* (Cambridge: Cambridge University, 1937), 183–277; Sillery, *Bechuanaland Protectorate* (1952), 47–9; Holmberg, *African Tribes and European Agencies* (1966), 62–70; Anthony J. Dachs, "Missionary Imperialism – The Case of Bechuanaland," *Journal of African History* 13(1972): 647–58; and Paul Maylam, *Rhodes, The Tswana, and the British: Colonialism, Collaboration, and Conflict in the Bechuanaland Protectorate* (Westport, Connecticut: Greenwood, 1980).

26. Mackenzie, "Bechuanaland, with Some Remarks on Mashonaland and Matabeleland," *Scottish Geographical Magazine* 3(1887): 298.

27. Mackenzie, *Austral Africa*, 1(1887), 77–8. See the epigraph opening this chapter.

28. John Mackenzie, *Ten Years* (1971), 81–3; Comaroff and Comaroff, *Of Revelation and Revolution*, 1(1991), 206–13.

29. Mackenzie, *Austral Africa*, 1(1887), 30.

30. For analysis of Mackenzie's role in the history of British Bechuanaland and the Bechuanaland Protectorate, see Agar-Hamilton, *Road to the North* (1937), 278–332; Sillery, *Bechuanaland Protectorate* (1952), 51–2; Holmberg, *African Tribes and European Agencies* (1966), 45–70; Kenneth Hall, "Humanitarianism and Racial Subordination: John Mackenzie and the Transformation of Tswana Society," *International Journal of African Historical Studies* 8(1975): 97–110; Mackenzie, *The Papers of John Mackenzie*, Anthony Dachs, ed. (Johannesburg: Witwatersrand University Press, 1975). For a biography, see Sillery, *John Mackenzie of Bechuanaland, 1835–1899: A Study in Humanitarian Imperialism* (Cape Town: Balkema, 1971).

31. For a summary of Rhodes's activities as deputy commissioner of Bechuanaland, see Sillery, *Bechuanaland Protectorate* (1952), 52–3; Holmberg, *African Tribes and European Agencies* (1966), 71–88; Agar-Hamilton, *Road to the North* (1937), 333–85.

32. BPP C 4889 (1886), *Land Settlement in British Bechuanaland*, 4. My emphasis.

33. On the Land Commission, see Shillington, *Colonisation* (1985), 174–7.

34. The official measurements of the reserves varied slightly over time. Table 4-1 uses the last available statistics for each reserve; measurements are from the following sources: 1, 1a, 3, 4, 7, 8 and 9, Breutz, *Tribes of Kuruman* (1963), 56–7; 5 and 6, Surplus People Project, *Forced Removals in South Africa: The Surplus People Project Report*, 5 vols. (Pietermaritzburg: Surplus People Project, 1983), 3:100; 10, 11 12 and 13, Public Records Office, London [hereafter PRO] Colonial Office Series [hereafter CO] 879/51, "Return of Native Reserves in Bechuanaland," 47; 14, Snyman, *Kuruman* (1992), 54. Original measurements in morgen, a Cape Dutch unit of area equaling 0.8565 hectares, have been converted to hectares.

35. CTAR BBLC 20, claim number 43 of J. G. Donovan to Konong.

36. BPP C 4889, *Land Settlement in British Bechuanaland*, 30. My emphasis.

37. De Kiewiet, *Imperial Factor* (1937), 187–8.

38. John Locke promoted this argument and Immanuel Kant refuted it. Wilcomb Washburn, *Red Man's Land – White Man's Law* (New York: Charles Scribner's Sons, 1971), 38, 143, 253, note 25.

39. Giliomee, "Processes in the Development of the Southern African Frontier," in *The Frontier in History*, Lamar and Thompson, eds., 76–119. Specifically regarding hunting, see MacKenzie, *Empire of Nature* (1988).

40. Sidney Shippard, "Bechuanaland," in *British Africa*, J. Scott Keltie, II, ed. (New York: Funk and Wagnalls and Company, 1899), 59.

41. BPP C 4889, *Land Settlement in British Bechuanaland*, 30. For commentary, see Agar-Hamilton, *Road to the North* (1937), 435.

42. Shippard, "Bechuanaland," in *British Africa* (1899), 51–2. For an analysis of Shippard's record as an administrator of British Bechuanaland, see Hall, "British Bechuanaland: The Price of Protection," *The International Journal of African Historical Studies* 6(1973): 183–97.

43. Hall, "British Bechuanaland: The Price of Protection," *The International Journal of African Historical Studies* 6(1973): 188, quoting Shippard from PRO CO 417/20/9613, 335.

44. Such rulings include those by the Bloemhof Commission in 1871, Judge Stockenstrom in 1876, and Lieutenant-Colonel Moysey in 1880. See BPP C 4889, *Land Settlement in British Bechuanaland*, 36–9 for a summary of British rulings on Tswana land customs before 1886.

45. BPP C 4889, *Land Settlement in British Bechuanaland*, 12.

46. Martin Chanock, "Paradigms, Policies and Prosperity: A Review of the Customary Law of Tenure," in *Law in Colonial Africa*, K. Mann and R. Roberts, eds. (Portsmouth: Heinemann, 1991), 61–84.

47. Mamdani, *Citizen and Subject* (1996), 138–41.

48. Schapera, *Native Land Tenure in the Bechuanaland Protectorate* ([Alice]: Lovedale, 1943), 40–1. See also Isaac Schapera, *The Tswana*, 4th ed., with a supplementary chapter by John Comaroff and a supplementary bibliography by Adam Kuper (London: KPI, 1984), 53.

49. BPP C 4889, *Land Settlement in British Bechuanaland*, 38.

50. On the Glen Grey Act, see Bundy, *The Rise and Fall of the South African Peasantry* (1979), 135–6.

51. Chanock, "Paradigms, Policies and Prosperity," *Law in Colonial Africa* (1991), 66.

52. Shillington, *Colonisation* (1985), 175.

53. BPP C 4889, *Land Settlement in British Bechuanaland*, 12.

54. Shillington, *Colonisation* (1985), 177–80.

55. Chanock, "Paradigms, Policies and Prosperity," *Law in Colonial Africa* (1991), 77.

56. CTAR BCC 93, Taung Resident Magistrate J. S. Moffat, September 18, 1886.

57. BPP C 4889, *Land Settlement in British Bechuanaland*, 44. See also Shippard, "*British Africa Bechuanaland*," (1899), 59.

58. BPP C 4956, *Affairs of Bechuanaland and Adjacent Territories*, Luka Jantjie to Shippard, September 1885, 126.

59. See CTAR 1/KMN 4/1, Lerchwe v. William James Markram, September 30, 1887; David Tawane, Jr. v. V. Petros, January 19, 1888. See also the following correspondence in CTAR BCC 81, May 26, 1890; May 28, 1890; August 7, 1890; Mokwene Baepi's statement, May 26, 1890; Wookey to Shippard, May 28, 1890; Frederick Newton, Acting Administrator of British Bechuanaland, to Herbert Jarvis, August 7, 1890.

60. On overcrowding in Setlagoli reserve, see Bryden, *Gun and Camera* (1988), 125. On Taung, see CTAR BCC 104, Taung Resident Magistrate Lowe, October 18, 1890.

61. CTAR BCC 106, Newton, June 19, 1891.

62. CPP [Cape Parliamentary Papers] G 42 - 1898 *Blue Book on Native Affairs*, 66.
63. CTAR 1/KMN 10/18, Annual Report, Resident Magistrate Scholtz, September 29, 1890; CTAR BCC 102, Surveyor General Duncan, November 22, 1890.
64. CTAR BCC 82, Petition from fifty-three signatories at Bothetheletsa, August 11, 1890.
65. CTAR BCC 82, Wookey to Shippard, enclosing petition from communities on Matlhwareng River, May 28, 1890; CTAR BCC 82, Petition from Metswetsaneng, August 8, 1890; CTAR BCC 82, Petition from Mapoteng, August 20, 1890.
66. CTAR BCC 116, Field Cornet Lanham, to Resident Magistrate Bam, November 26, 1894, including petition from Chief Khibi and seventy-nine councilors, November 16, 1894.
67. BCC 116, Acting Administrator to C. Matthews, C. MacGregor and C. Monroe, January 3, 1895.
68. CTAR BCC 116, Resident Magistrate Bam, October 29, 1894; CTAR BCC 116, Matthews Commission Report on Crown Reserve, March 8, 1895.
69. Snyman, *Kuruman* (1992), 53.
70. Shillington, *Colonisation* (1985), 179–80.
71. Peters, *Dividing the Commons* (1994), 30 3.
72. Evans, *Bureaucracy and Race* (1997), 9–13, 164–76, 282–3.
73. CTAR BCC 102, Mereki to Inspector of Native Reserves St. Quintin, translated by Wookey, November 26, 1889; Resident Magistrate Scholtz, December 6, 1889.
74. PRO CO 879/29 no. 368, Resident Magistrate Streatfeild, September 1888, 73.
75. CTAR 1/KMN 10/17, Resident Magistrate Scholtz, September 30, 1899.
76. CPP G 19 – 1897, *Blue Book on Native Affairs*, 68.
77. See PRO CO 879/29 no. 368, Resident Magistrate Streatfeild, 73; CTAR 1/KMN 10/17, Resident Magistrate Scholtz, September 30, 1899. Other historians have also noted these land disputes, see Shillington, *Colonisation* (1985), 209; Comaroff and Comaroff, *Of Revelation and Revolution*, 2(1997), 143–7.
78. Bryden, *Gun and Camera* (1988), 15–16.
79. PRO CO 879/29 no. 368, Resident Magistrate Streatfeild, September 30, 1888, 68.
80. John Mackenzie, *Austral Africa*, 2(1887), 168. There is ample evidence on rain-fed cultivation, see LMS 43/1/B, John Brown at Taung, February 7, 1889; Bryden, *Gun and Camera* (1988), 117; and CPP G 13 - 1891, *Report of Commission to Select Land in British Bechuanaland*, 6.
81. LMS 27/1/B, Holloway Helmore at Dikgatlhong, September 4, 1852; Bryden, *Gun and Camera* (1988), 117.
82. Robert Wallace, *Farming Industries of the Cape Colony* (London: P. S. King and Son; Cape Town: J. C. Juta, 1896), 439. I would like to thank Geoff Palmer for providing me with this reference.
83. UG 17 – 1911, *Department of Native Affairs Report*, 135. One informant, born in 1920, remembered it from his childhood. Interview with Prince Setungwane in Appendix C1. On the use of the "American plough" in the Bechuanaland Protectorate, see Landau, *The Realm of the Word* (1995), 74.
84. BPP C 4956 *Affairs of Bechuanaland and Adjacent Territories*, 126. This letter continues the correspondence previously cited in Ref. 58.
85. CTAR BCC 72, Surveyor General Watermeyer, February 9, 1895.
86. Bryden, *Gun and Camera* (1988), 126–7.

87. CTAR BBLC 20, claim number 43 of J. G. Donovan to Konong.
88. CTAR BCC 102, Resident Magistrate Scholtz to Shippard, December 6, 1889.
89. CPP G 19 – 1897, *Blue Book on Native Affairs*, 68.
90. CTAR Cape Colony Native Affairs Series (hereafter NA) 239, Taung Resident Magistrate J. S. Moffat, December 30, 1895.
91. CTAR BCC 96, Taung Resident Magistrate Lowe, October 7, 1887.
92. CTAR Cape Colony Native Affairs Series (hereafter NA) 251, Cape Colony Chief Inspector of Native Reserves Roberts, Report on trip to Bechuanaland, April 20, 1898.
93. CTAR BCC 113, Resident Magistrate Scholtz, January 6, 1893.
94. CTAR BCC 96, Inspector of Native Reserves St. Quintin, Annual Report, August 9, 1888.
95. CTAR BCC 96, Taung Resident Magistrate Lowe, October 7, 1887.
96. CTAR BCC 114, Inspector of Native Reserves St. Quintin, Annual Report, April 15, 1893.

CHAPTER 5

1. BPP C 8797 (1898), *Correspondence Relating to Native Disturbances in Bechuanaland*, 20–1.
2. Burchell, *Travels*, 2(1953), 186, 243.
3. Campbell, *Travels* (1974), 176. See also Campbell, *Second Journey*, 2(1967), 60.
4. The first quotation describes the veld just east of the Kuruman mission station in 1836. Harris, *Wild Sports* (1963), 41. The second quotation is by John Smith Moffat, describing a homecoming in 1859. John Smith Moffat, *The Matabele Mission* (1945), 52–3. See also Gordon Cumming, *A Hunter's Life* (1980), 277, 324.
5. English and scientific names were cross-checked in Christo Albertyn Smith, *Common Names of South African Plants*, Republic of South Africa, Department of Agricultural Technical Services, Botanical Research Institute, Botanical Survey Memoir, No. 35 (Pretoria: Government Printer, 1966). Tswana names were determined during fieldwork in October 1997 and in F. H. Ferreira, "Bantu Customs and Legends Protect Trees," *African Wildlife*, 3(1949): 59–65; Ferreira, "Setlhapin Nomenclature and Uses of the Indigenous Trees of Griqualand West," *Bantu Studies* 3(1929): 349–56; and Desmond Cole, *Setswana-Animals and Plants* (Gaborone: Botswana Society, 1995).
6. Barrow, *A Voyage* (1975), 388; Burchell, *Travels*, 2(1953), 209.
7. Burchell, *Travels*, 2(1953), 219, 361, 372; Moffat, *Missionary Labours* (1842), 330; and Livingstone, *Missionary Travels* (1972), 112. These similar observations date from the 1810s, 1820s, and 1840.
8. Burchell, *Travels*, 2(1953), 193. He was slightly south of Ga-Tlhose when he made this observation.
9. Barrow, *A Voyage* (1975), 388. These were probably *A. erioloba* rather than *A. mellifera*, since giraffes favored them.
10. Burchell, *Travels*, 2(1953), 218; Moffat, *Missionary Labours* (1842), 330.
11. Smith, *Diary of Dr. Andrew Smith*, 1(1939), 297.
12. Livingstone, *Missionary Travels* (1972), 112.

13. Burchell, *Travels*, 1(1953), 217.
14. Burchell, *Travels*, 2(1953), 370.
15. Pratt, "Scratches on the Face of the Country," *Critical Inquiry* 12(1985).
16. T. D. Hall demonstrated that people in the Cape Colony recognized the process of bush encroachment by the mid-eighteenth century. "South African Pastures: Retrospective and Prospective," *South African Journal of Science* 31(1934): 59–97.
17. Campbell, *Travels* (1974), 176–7.
18. Grove, "Scottish Missionaries in Southern Africa, 1820–1900," *Journal of Southern African Studies* 15(1989): 165–72.
19. W. S. W. Trollope, "Fire in Savanna," in *Ecological Effects of Fire in South African Ecosystems*, P. de V. Booysen and N. M. Tainton, eds. (Berlin: Springer, 1984), 156. Other writers witnessed fire, which may have been set by people or lightning. Burchell describes seeing an area recently burned; see Burchell *Travels*, 2(1953), 193. One traveler recorded the wild animals fleeing before a grass fire. William Cotton Oswell, *Big Game Shooting*, 1(1894), 40.
20. Fritsch, *Drei Jahre* (1868), 260–1.
21. For descriptions of bushes by Fritsch, see *Drei Jahre* (1868), 262, 264–6, 284.
22. Gillmore, "Territories Adjacent to the Kalahari," *Proceedings of the Royal Colonial Institute* 14(1883): 134–5.
23. D. Grossman and M. V. Gandar, "Land Transformation in South African Savanna Regions," *South African Geographical Journal* 71(1989): 43–4.
24. R. L. Liversidge and M. Berry, "Game Ranching in the Arid Regions," in *Game Ranch Management*, J. du P. Bothma, ed. (Pretoria: van Schaik, 1989), 620–5.
25. CTAR BCC 94, Surveyor General Duncan, July 23, 1887.
26. CPP G 13 - 1891, *Report of Commission to Select Land in British Bechuanaland*, 8.
27. It is difficult to say which species is meant by the term "khaki bush," which is the term for several species whose seeds are held to have been introduced in fodder during the South Africa War. On its presence, see CTAR 1/KMN 10/9, Acting Civil Commissioner Armstrong, October 15, 1908. On *Argemone mexicana* (Mexican poppy, *spanise*), see CTAR 1/KMN 10/9, Acting Civil Commissioner Armstrong, July 9, 1908. On *Xanthium spinosum* (burrweed; *setlhabakolobe*), see correspondence in CTAR NA 586.
28. CPP G 67 - 1899, *Reports of Inquiry into Agricultural Distress in Herbert, Hay, Barkly West, Vryburg and Kimberley*, 8.
29. Bryden, *Gun and Camera* (1988), 119. Anthrax, which was endemic to Kuruman, was often misidentified as "horsesickness." See M. W. Henning, *Animal Diseases in South Africa*, 2(1949), 3. On lungsickness, see CTAR 1/KMN 10/18, Resident Magistrate Scholtz to Colonial Secretary, September 29, 1890. On foot and mouth disease, see LMS 50/1/A, Price, January 10, 1893; CTAR BCC 114, Inspector of Native Reserves St. Quintin, Annual Report, April 15, 1893. Without identifying the diseases, Shillington reports an increase in cattle mortality in Griqualand West in the early 1890s. See Shillington, *Colonisation* (1985), 112.
30. CTAR LND 1/555, Water Boring Foreman McCaig, June 23, 1896.
31. CTAR BCC 82, Luka Jantjie to High Commissioner, translated by J. Tom Brown, September 23, 1890.

32. Interview with Julius Mogodi in Appendix C1. On Kikahela, see B. F. van Vreeden, "Plekname in Setswana," *Tydskrif vir Volkskunde en Volkstaal* 7(1950): 41–3.
33. CTAR BCC 114, Taung Resident Magistrate, Lowe, May 27, 1892.
34. CTAR LND 1/441, Surveyor General Templer-Horne, February 19, 1895. Shillington, *Colonisation* (1985), 227.
35. CTAR BCC 72, Resident Magistrate Scholtz, February 15, 1892; CTAR BCC 72, Inspector of Native Reserves St. Quintin, February 15, 1895. Later that year the treatment of "squatters" softened. See correspondence in CTAR LND 1/441.
36. CTAR BCC 82, Luka Jantjie to High Commissioner, translated by J. Tom Brown, September 23, 1890. On the Tlharo emigration to Namibia, see Breutz, *Tribes of Kuruman* (1963), 96.
37. LMS 51/1/C, Price, May 27, 1894. In my article "The Flowing Eye: Water Management in the Upper Kuruman Valley, South Africa, c.1800–1962," *Journal of African History* 37(1996): 237, I quoted a missionary who believed that the Kuruman was flowing into the Molopo River and then the Orange River. However, all floods in historic times have ended at Abiquas Puts, south of the Mier district, where a dune dams the channel. Personal communication, Kees Bootsman, June 12, 1998.
38. LMS 53/1/A, J. Tom Brown, January 6, 1895. See also CTAR BCC 117, Resident Magistrate Bam, April 10, 1895; LMS 52/2/B, Ashton at Barkly West, October 12, 1895.
39. For general information on rinderpest, see the following monographs: Henning, *Animal Diseases* (1949), 621–35; John Ford, *The Role of Trypanosomiasis in African Ecology; A Study of the Tsetse Fly Problem* (Oxford: Clarendon, 1971), 138–40. On its history in South Africa, see Charles Ballard, "The Repercussions of Rinderpest: Cattle Plague and Peasant Decline in Colonial Natal," *The International Journal of African Historical Studies* 19(1986): 421–50; van Onselen, "Reactions to Rinderpest in Southern Africa, 1896–97," *Journal of African History* 3(1972): 473–88; and Pule Phoofolo, "Epidemics and Revolutions: The Rinderpest Epidemic in Late Nineteenth Century Southern Africa," *Past and Present* 138(1993): 112–43.
40. Van Onselen, "Rinderpest," *Journal of African History* 3(1972): 473.
41. LMS 53/1/A, Price, April 1, 1896.
42. LMS 53/1/D, Price, April 12, 1896; LMS 53/1/D, Ashton at Barkly West, April 20, 1896; LMS 53/2/A, Gould, May 9, 1896.
43. CTAR 1/KMN 10/1, Resident Magistrate Bam, August 6, 1896.
44. CTAR 1/KMN 10/1, Resident Magistrate Bam, August 19, 1896; CTAR 1/KMN 10/1, Resident Magistrate Bam, November 18, 1896.
45. On Cape Colony game laws, see MacKenzie, *Empire of Nature* (1988), 202–4.
46. LMS 54/1/B, J. Tom Brown, September 6, 1897, quoting September 27, 1896 letter to Cape Colony Prime Minister Gordon Sprigg.
47. CTAR 1/KMN 10/1, various correspondence. On the LMS guarantee, see CTAR 1/KMN 10/1, Resident Magistrate Bam, November 18, 1896.
48. CTAR 1/KMN 10/1, Resident Magistrate Bam, December 16, 1896.
49. LMS 53/3/A, John Brown at Taung, August 20, 1896 and J. Thomas Brown, August 26, 1896; LMS 53/3/B, John Brown at Taung, October 25, 1896; Shillington, *Colonisation* (1985), 231–3; Henning, *Animal Diseases* (1949), 622.

50. CPP G 33 - 1897, *Special Report on Rinderpest by the Colonial Veterinary Surgeon, March 1896–February 1897*, 28; CTAR 1/KMN 10/1, Resident Magistrate Bam, November 18, 1896.
51. CTAR 1/KMN 10/1, Resident Magistrate Bam, December 2, 1896.
52. CPP G 19 - 1897, *Blue Book on Native Affairs*, 69–70.
53. CTAR 1/KMN 10/1, Resident Magistrate Bam, December 23, 1896.
54. Interview at Heunig Vley in Appendix C3.
55. CPP G 42 - 1898, *Blue Book on Native Affairs*, 66. See Chapter 4.
56. For accounts of the Langeberg war, see Shillington, *Colonisation* (1985), 215–40; Harry Saker and J. Aldridge, "The Origins of the Langeberg Rebellion," *Journal of African History* 12(1971): 299–317; and Snyman, *Kuruman* (1992), 67–73.
57. CPP G 42 - 1898, *Blue Book on Native Affairs*, 66. Isaac Seamecho, born in 1909 and a descendent of Chief Khibi, also affirmed that rinderpest came through the war. See Appendix C1, Interview A with Isaac Seamecho.
58. CPP G 72 - 1898, *Rinderpest Statistics for the Colony of the Cape of Good Hope.*
59. Shillington, *Colonisation* (1985), 240. See Chapter 4.
60. Mamdani, *Citizen and Subject* (1996), 139.
61. PRO CO 879/51 no. 547, Cape Colony Prime Minister Gordon Sprigg, February 7, 1897.
62. Shillington, *Colonisation* (1985), 186, 240–1.
63. CTAR LND 1/587, Proclamation by Alfred Milner, No. 419 of 1897.
64. PRO CO 879/51 no. 547, Shippard, June 23, 1897.
65. CTAR 1/KMN 10/2, Resident Magistrate Hilliard, January 4, 1898. Hilliard does not explain how he came to these figures.
66. CPP G 42 - 1898, *Blue Book on Native Affairs*, 66.
67. CTAR NA 247, Inspector of Native Reserves McCarthy, September 2, 1898.
68. LMS 59/1, J. Thomas Brown, July 1901; Archives at Moffat Mission Trust, Kuruman, [hereafter MMT] "Register of Lands Belonging to the London Missionary Society, Kuruman." For a description of the archival holdings at the Kuruman Moffat Mission, see Kristin Russell and Megan Waples, "The Kuruman Moffat Mission Trust Archives Unearthed," *South African Historical Journal* 40(1999): 239–46.
69. CPP G 42 - 1898, *Blue Book on Native Affairs*, 67; National Archives Repository [hereafter NAR] Native Affairs Series [hereafter NTS] 4368 268/313, Surveyor General, September 9, 1896. See also sundry correspondence on land claims in the Kuruman Crown Reserve in CTAR LND 1/659 and LND 564
70. CTAR LND 1/730, Secretary for Public Works, February 2, 1900; CPP G 25 - 1902, *Blue Book on Native Affairs*, 30.
71. CTAR 1/KMN 10/2, Resident Magistrate Hilliard, January 4, 1898.
72. The first indication that some cultivators manured their fields is in CPP G - 19 1897, *Blue Book on Native Affairs*, 68. Evidence that the loss of manure interfered with cultivation is found in CPP G 25 - 1902, *Blue Book on Native Affairs*, 30.
73. CTAR 1/KMN 10/3, Resident Magistrate Hilliard, February 15, 1899.
74. CTAR NA 242, Inspector of Native Reserves McCarthy, December 1, 1897.
75. CTAR 1/KMN 10/2, Batlharos headman Mmusi Lebwani, March 14, 1898. Interview A with Isaac Seamecho in Appendix C1.
76. CTAR NA 247, Inspector of Native Reserves McCarthy, July 1898.

77. BPP C 8797 (1898), *Correspondence Relating to Native Disturbances in Bechuanaland*, 20–1.
78. CTAR 1/KMN 10/3, Resident Magistrate Hilliard, February 15, 1899.
79. Cases against "vagrants" are found in CTAR 1/KMN 1/4, July 5, 1898, and November 30, 1898; CTAR 1/KMN 1/6, June 17, 1899.
80. CTAR 1/KMN 10/2, Resident Magistrate Hilliard, January 4, 1898.
81. CPP G 67 - 1899, *Reports by the Special Commissioner Appointed to Inquire into the Agriculture Distress and Land Matters in the Divisions of Herbert, Hay, Barkly West, Vryburg and Kimberley*, 8. (Kuruman was included in the Vryburg financial division.)
82. CTAR 1/KMN 10/3, Ga-Tlhose store owner Mattison, September 28, 1898.
83. CTAR 1/KMN 10/3, Resident Magistrate Hilliard, February 15, 1899; LMS 56/1/C, J. Thomas Brown, May 2, 1899.
84. The studies of imperialism in Kuruman exclude the events of the Boer War. Snyman's history of Kuruman contains the only detailed account of the war. See Snyman, *Kuruman* (1992), 79–86.
85. LMS 56/4/C, J. Thomas Brown, December 5, 1899.
86. CPP G 52 - 1901, *Blue Book on Native Affairs*, 30.
87. CPP G 25 - 1902, *Blue Book on Native Affairs*, 30.
88. CCP G 52 - 1901, *Blue Book on Native Affairs*, 20, 30.
89. CTAR 1/KMN 10/4, Resident Magistrate Lyne, date illegible, 1902.
90. LMS 59/1, J. Tom Brown, February 14, 1901.
91. NAR NTS 4368 268/313, Resident Magistrate Middlewick, December 6, 1901; CPP G 25 - 1902, 30.
92. LMS 60/1, J. Tom Brown, October 14, 1901 (out of sequence in series).
93. LMS 60/1, J. Tom Brown, October 14, 1901 (out of sequence in series); LMS 59/4, Brown, November 6, 1901.
94. LMS 59/4, J. Tom Brown, November 6, 1901, postscript dated November 14, 1901.
95. Snyman, *Kuruman* (1992), 85.
96. LMS 59/4, J. Tom Brown, November 6, 1901; LMS 60/1, Mary Wookey, February 2, 1902.
97. CPP G 29 - 1903, *Blue Book on Native Affairs*, 41.
98. CTAR NA 605, Resident Magistrate Lyne, May 2, 1903.
99. CTAR 1/KMN 10/4, Resident Magistrate Lyne, date illegible, 1902.
100. CTAR 1/KMN 10/6, Resident Magistrate Lyne, September 18, 1903; NAR NA 223 1/1910/F527, Inspector of Native Reserves Purchase, Monthly Reports, 1907–08. Unlike most Cape Colony Native Affairs papers, these are housed at the National Archives Repository in Pretoria. UG 17 - 1911, *Department of Native Affairs Report*, 197.
101. CTAR NA 605, Resident Magistrate Lyne, August 3, 1903.
102. CTAR 1/KMN 10/4, Resident Magistrate Lyne, May 4, 1903.
103. CTAR NA 605, correspondence from May 1903.
104. CPP G 67 - 1899, *Reports by the Special Commissioner Appointed to Inquire into the Agricultural Distress and Land Matters in the Division of Herbert, Hay, Barkly West, Vryburg and Kimberley*, 8.
105. CTAR BCC 104, Vryburg Resident Magistrate R. Tillard, October 17, 1890; Bryden, *Gun and Camera* (1988), 34.

106. CTAR BCC 110, Resident Magistrate Scholtz, April 4, 1892.
107. CTAR Native Affairs series [hereafter NA] 239, Resident Magistrate Moffat, December 30, 1895. This was Moffat's second stint as resident magistrate. His first was in 1886.
108. CTAR NA 605, correspondence between the Colonial Under Secretary and the Native Affairs Department, June and July 1903.
109. CTAR NA 605, Native Affairs Department, August 2, 1903.
110. CTAR NA 605, Resident Magistrate Lyne, August 3, 1903.
111. CTAR NA 605, see correspondence between Lyne, the Native Affairs Department, and the Public Works Department, August 1903.
112. CTAR NA 605, Chief Inspector Robert, September 5, 1903.
113. CTAR NA 605, Resident Magistrate Lyne, October 7, 1903.
114. CTAR 1/KMN 10/6, Resident Magistrate Lyne, September 18, 1903.
115. William Crossgrove, et al., "Colonialism, International Trade, and the Nation-state," in *Hunger in History: Food Shortage, Poverty and Deprivation*, Lucile Newman, et al., eds. (Cambridge, Massachusetts: Basil Blackwell, 1990), 215–40.
116. Merchant, *Ecological Revolutions* (1989); White, *Roots of Dependency* (1983).
117. Ballard, "Rinderpest," *The International Journal of African Historical Studies* 19(1986).
118. Amartya Sen, *Poverty and Famines: An Essay on Entitlement and Deprivation* (Oxford: Clarendon, 1981).
119. Iliffe, *Famine in Zimbabwe* (Gweru: Mambo, 1990). Iliffe argues that wage labor became more common during a 1916 famine.

CHAPTER 6

1. Interview D at Ncweng in Appendix C3.
2. Bundy, *Rise and Fall of the Peasantry* (1999), 1.
3. For excellent histories of rural reserves, see Beinart, *Political Economy of Pondoland* (1982); Colin Murray, *Black Mountain: Land, Class, and Power in the Eastern Orange Free State, 1880s–1980s* (Washington, DC: Smithsonian, 1992).
4. Beinart, *Twentieth-Century South Africa* (Oxford: Oxford University Press, 1994), 262–3.
5. Population statistics for 1896 are from CCP G 42 1898, *Blue Book on Native Affairs*, 66. Statistics for 1904 are from a Cape Colony census published in CCP G 19 - 1905, *Census of 1904*. Thereafter, they are drawn from Union Government official census reports: Official Publications of the Union Government [hereafter UG] 32 f - 1912 *Census of 1911*; UG 15 - 1923 *Census of 1921*; and UG 50 - 1938 *Census of 1936*. Statistics for 1946 and 1951 are found in Breutz, *Tribes of Kuruman* (1963), 47. Reserve populations for 1936 are given in NAR NTS 1948 256/278(3), Agricultural Officer Hattingh, October 13, 1938. Reserve populations for 1950 are given in CTAR 2/KMN 54 II 8/21/4, Annual agricultural report, 1950.
6. Charles Simkins, "Agricultural Production in the African Reserves of South Africa, 1918–1969," *Journal of Southern African Studies* 8(1981): 267–8. The statistics for cultivated production are so low and erratic that I have not cited them in this study. For statistics on stock population, which are more consistent, see Appendix B.

Before 1937, the agricultural census only estimated production on reserves. Thereafter, it was enumerated. UG 18 - 1939.

7. CTAR NA 657, Inspector of Native Reserves McCarthy, August 31, 1904; NAR NA 223 1/1910/F527, Inspector of Native Reserves reports for 1908; CPP G 46 - 1906, *Blue Book on Native Affairs*, 27; CPP G 36 - 1907, *Blue Book on Native Affairs*, 27; CPP G 24 - 1908, *Blue Book on Native Affairs*, 190; and UG 17 - 1911, *Report of Native Affairs Department*, 114.

8. De Kiewiet, *A History of South Africa* (1941), 178–207. For a moving and poetic restatement of this thesis, see the opening of Alan Paton, *Cry, The Beloved Country: A Story of Comfort in Desolation* (New York: Charles Scribner's Sons, 1948), 3–4.

9. Snyman, *Kuruman* (1992), 8–10; Grossman and Gandar, "Land Transformation in South African Savanna Regions," *South African Geographical Journal* 71(1989): 38–45.

10. On "received wisdom" regarding degradation, see Leach and Mearns, "Environmental Change and Policy: Challenging the Received Wisdom," in *Lie of the Land*, Leach and Mearns, eds., (1996), 1–33.

11. C. H. Donaldson, *Bush Encroachment with Special Reference to the Blackthorn Problem of the Molopo Area* (Pretoria: Government Printer, 1969); quoted by W. S. W. Trollope, "Application of Grassland Management Practices: Savanna," in *Veld and Pasture Management in South Africa*, N. M. Tainton, ed. (Pietermaritzburg: Shuter and Shooter, 1981), 404.

12. N. M. Tainton, "Introduction to the Concepts of Development, Production and Stability of Plant Communities," in *Veld and Pasture Management* (1998), 7, 33.

13. For example, see essays in D. C. Glenn-Lewin, R. K. Peet, and T. T. Veblen, eds., *Plant Succession Theory and Prediction* (London: Chapman and Hall, 1992). For such a study in the Karoo, see M. T. Hoffman and R. M. Cowling, "Vegetation Change in the Semi-Arid Eastern Karoo over the Last 200 Years: An Expanding Karoo – Fact or Fiction?" *South African Journal of Science* 86(1990): 286–94.

14. R. H. Behnke and Ian Scoones, "Rethinking Range Ecology: Implications for Rangeland Management in Africa," in *Range Ecology at Disequilibrium: New Models of Natural Variability and Pastoral Adaptation in African Savannas*, R. H. Behnke, I. Scoones, and C. Kerven, eds. (London: Overseas Development Institute, 1993), 11.

15. Regarding the predominance of C_4 species in the thornveld, see J. C. Vogel, A. Fuls, and R. P. Ellis, "The Geographical Distribution of Kranz Grasses in South Africa," *South African Journal of Science* 74(1978): 209–15. I thank Stephanie Wand for bringing this subject to my attention and Peter Heywood for explaining the processes.

16. The estimate of atmospheric CO_2 levels at 275 ppm before the Industrial Revolution is commonly accepted. Levels for 2000 are from C. D. Keeling and T. P. Whorf, "Atmospheric CO_2 Records from Sites in the SIO Air Sampling Network," in *Trends: A Compendium of Data on Global Change*, Carbon Dioxide Information Analysis Center, Oak Ridge National Laboratory, U.S. Department of Energy, Oak Ridge, TN, 2001.

17. See H. Wayne Polley, Herman S. Mayeux, Hyrum B. Johnson, and Charles R. Tishler, "Viewpoint: Atmospheric CO_2, Soil Water and Shrub/Grass Ratios

on Rangelands," *Journal of Range Management* 50(1997): 278; Stephanie Wand, "Physiological Growth Responses of Two African Species, *Acacia karoo* and *Themeda trianda*, To Combined Increases in CO_2 and UV-B Radiation," *Physiologia Plantarum* 98(1996): 882–90.

18. CTAR 2/KMN 22 N 1/15/6, Additional Native Commissioner, July 20, 1948.
19. NAR NTS 10251 40/423 1959, Report on planning for removal of Konong.
20. CTAR 2/KMN 22 N 1/15/6, Additional Native Commissioner, July 20, 1948; Breutz, *Tribes of Kuruman* (1963), 66, 78.
21. See Appendix C3, Interview B at Maiphiniki. On the pressure on poor people to sell cattle, see Duggan, *An Economic Analysis* (1986), 115–8.
22. In 1903, inhabitants of Manyeding and Konong, reserves on the Ghaap Plateau, requested permission to form cattle posts at Ga-Tlhose, on the far side of the Kuruman Hills and out of the low phosphate zone. CTAR 1/KMN 10/6, Resident Magistrate Lyne, September 18, 1903.
23. Snyman, *Kuruman* (1992), 114, 146; Thelma Gutsche, *There Was a Man: The Life and Times of Sir Arnold Theiler K.C.M.G. of Onderstepoort* (Cape Town: Howard Timmins, 1979), 328–32.
24. There were anthrax outbreaks in the Lower Kuruman Reserve in 1964 and 1970. See Interviews with Edward Motlhabane and with Vera Albutt in Appendix C2. On stock disease, see Interview A at Ga-Lotlhare, Interview C at Ga-Lotlhare, and Interview B at Maiphiniki in Appendix C3.
25. Donkeys hardly ever rate consideration in histories of rural South Africa. Van Onselen has given rare evidence about their usefulness. See van Onselen, *Seed is Mine* (1996), 137, 141, 323.
26. Mora Dickson, *Beloved Partner, Mary Moffat of Kuruman: A Biography Based on Her Letters* ([Gaborone and Kuruman]: Botswana Book Centre and Kuruman Moffat Mission Trust, 1974), 189. For a synthesis of the history of donkeys in Kuruman, from their introduction to the donkey massacre, see Nancy Jacobs, "The Great Bophuthatswana Donkey Massacre: Discourse on the Ass and Politics of Class and Grass," *American Historical Review* 108(2001): 485–507.
27. CPP G 36 1907, *Blue Book on Native Affairs*, 29; Union Government Publication UG 17 - 1912, *Blue Book on Native Affairs*, 160; UG 32 - 1912, *Census of the Union of South Africa*. On donkeys in mining, see Anthony Hocking, *Kaias and Cocopans: The Story of Mining in South Africa's Northern Cape* (Johannesburg: Hollards, 1983), especially 52–4, 81.
28. UG 12 - 1932, *Agricultural Census*, 1930. Early census data are unreliable, particularly for African reserves. For some years there is a discrepancy of twenty to thirty percent between the published census reports and data in archival records. Therefore, I am using these numbers advisedly and only to illustrate broad long-term trends.
29. Snyman, *Kuruman* (1992), 114, 120, 146. On mechanization of cultivation on white farms at this time, see van Onselen, *Seed is Mine* (1996), 276–8.
30. For a sort of "user's manual" for donkeys, see Peta Jones, *Donkeys for Development* (Pretoria: Animal Traction Network of Eastern and Southern Africa and Agricultural Research Council of South Africa Institute for Agricultural Engineering, 1997). See also Paul Starkey, ed., *Animal Traction in South Africa: Empowering*

Rural Communities (Halfway House, South Africa: The Development Bank of South Africa, 1995), 21–2, 139–51.

31. Snyman, *Kuruman* (1992), 113.
32. Homer Shantz Collection, Special Collections in the Main Library, University of Arizona, Tucson. I am grateful to Barry Morton for photocopying documents in this collection. For photographs of donkey wagons, see pp. 248, 259.
33. NAR NTS 6577 918/327, October 23, 1953; Interview with Olebile Mabahanyane in Appendix C2; Interview F at Ncweng in Appendix C3.
34. UG 77 - 1948, *Agricultural Census 1945–46*; Special Report Series No. 1–No. 24, *Agricultural Census 1949–50*, Republic of South Africa publications [hereafter RP] 10 - 1964 *Agricultural Census 1959–60* (livestock).
35. Interview with Peace Mabilo in Appendix C2.
36. Suzanne Vetter, "Investigating the Impact of Donkeys on a Communal Range in Namaqualand: How Much Does a Donkey 'Cost' in Goat Units?" (Honors thesis, University of Cape Town, 1996); Montague Demment and Peter Van Soest, "A Nutritional Explanation for Body-Size Patterns of Ruminant and Nonruminant Herbivores," *The American Naturalist* 125(1985): 641–72.
37. Humphrey C. Thompson, *Distant Horizons: An Autobiography on One Man's Forty Years of Missionary Service in and Around Kuruman, South Africa* (Kimberley: published by the author, 1976), 65. Thompson describes animals dying of thirst during the drought of 1932.
38. Similarly, in the American South mules had certain advantages over horses. See Martin A. Garrett, "The Mule in Southern Agriculture: A Requiem," *The Journal of Economic History* 4(1990): 925–30.
39. Starkey, *Animal Traction* (1995), 19, 21. See also Eldredge, "Women in Production," *Signs* 16(1991): 716.
40. CTAR GH (Government House) 35/250, "The Bechuanaland Native Reserve Disposal Act" (Number 8 of 1908).
41. NAR NA 223 1/1910/F527, Inspector of Native Reserves Purchase, July 1909, September 1909.
42. UG 22 - 1916, *Report of the Natives Land Commission*,Volume 2, 104.
43. NAR NTS 7752 22/335,Telesho Mongonarin, October 24, 1921.
44. NAR NTS 7752 22/335, Surveyor Roos, April 16, 1924.
45. The Khuis reserve was similarly enlarged through Government Notice 1885, October 25, 1929.
46. Testimonies are recorded in NAR NTS 3007 368/305 I.
47. NAR NTS 7351 176/327 (1), Agriculture Extension Officer Hensley November 20, 1933; NAR NTS 1947 256/278, Agricultural Officer Hattingh, March 31, 1940.
48. On regulations for wood use in the region, see a file on Setlagoli Reserve in Vryburg, NAR NTS 57/321. In 1998, this file was held in the Department of Land Affairs.
49. CTAR NTS 2/KMN 20 N 1/15/4 II, minutes of quarterly meeting of Chiefs, Headmen and People, March 28, 1951.
50. NAR NTS 6022 213/312, Chief Native Commissioner, November 12, 1949.
51. NAR NTS 1947 256/278 (3), Agricultural Officer Hattingh, October 13, 1938.
52. Michael Begen, John Harper, and Colin Townsend, *Ecology: Individuals, Populations and Communities*, 2nd ed. (Boston: Blackwell, 1990), 709.

53. Cronon, "A Place for Stories," *The Journal of American History* 78(1992): 1369–70.
54. Interview D at Batlharos in Appendix C3.
55. Interview E at Ga-Mopedi in Appendix C3 and Interview E at Ncweng in Appendix C3. Only one group discussed the disadvantages of many bushes (Interview I at Ga-Mopedi in Appendix C3). They reported having discussed with agricultural extension officers the possibility of removing *mongana* from camps intended for cattle.
56. Interview B at Sedibeng in Appendix C3.
57. CTAR 2/KMN 46 7/9/2, Agricultural Supervisor Prichard, October 26, 1964.
58. CTAR NA 657, Inspector of Native Reserve Purchase, July 1904; NAR NA 223 1/1910/F527, Inspector of Native Reserves Purchase, June 1909; Interview with M. Seipotlane in Appendix C1.
59. Reports of bird scaring from the first decade of the century suggest that people still grew mostly sorghum. CTAR NA 657, Inspector of Native Reserves Purchase, March 1905; NAR NA 223 1/1910/F527, Inspector of Native Reserves Purchase, February 1907; CPP G 24 - 1908, *Blue Book on Native Affairs*, 19; CPP G 36 - 1907, *Blue Book on Native Affairs* 26. By the early 1960s, according to the government ethnographer, no sorghum was grown. Breutz, *Tribes of Kuruman* (1963), 64. Furthermore, in 1997, middle-aged women ranked sorghum as a food they seldom ate in their childhood (see Interview D at Ga-Mopedi in Appendix C3). No interviews indicated that sorghum was the major crop at any time in living memory. On the decline of sorghum elsewhere, see Beinart, *Political Economy of Pondoland* (1982), 99.
60. CTAR NA 657, Inspector of Native Reserves Purchase, November 1904; NAR NA 223 1/1910/F527, Inspector of Native Reserves Purchase, April 1910, March 1907, April 1910; LMS 74/5, J. Tom Brown, November 4, 1912; Interview with Prince Setungwane in Appendix C1.
61. UG 17 - 1911, *Blue Book on Native Affairs*, 8.
62. NAR NTS 4368 268/313, M. C. Vos, August 26, 1911.
63. NAR NA 223 1/1910/F527, Inspector of Native Reserves Purchase, August 1909.
64. CTAR 2/KMN 33 N 2/11/4 II, Agricultural Officer, July 26, 1954.
65. Interview C at Ncweng in Appendix C3.
66. Interview B at Batlharos in Appendix C3. On tobacco, see Interview A with Isaac Seamecho in Appendix C1.
67. Interview A at Batlharos in Appendix C3.
68. Interview C at Ncweng in Appendix C3; Interview with Gladys Motshabe in Appendix C2; and Interview A at Maphiniki in Appendix C3.
69. CTAR NA 605, Resident Magistrate Lyne, September 18, 1903.
70. NAR NTS 7351 176/327, Extension Officer Hensley, June 1935.
71. CTAR NA 605, Resident Magistrate Lyne, September 18, 1903.
72. Interview B with Mosiane Kgokong in Appendix C1. See also Interview with N. Gaetsewe in Appendix C1.
73. Snyman, *Kuruman* (1992), 5. For a description of the flood in Prieska on the Orange River, see Hocking, *Kaias and Cocopans* (1983), 166.
74. Interview with Murial Tsebedi in Appendix C2. Interview with the Barnette siblings in Appendix C2.

75. In Appendix C3, see Interview G at Ncweng, Interview A at Batlharos, Interview E at Batlharos, and Interview H at Ga-Mopedi.
76. Similarly, the Il Chamus of Baringo experienced a catastrophic flood that ended irrigation. See Anderson, "Ecology and Economy among the Il Chamus of Baringo," *The Ecology of Survival* (1988), 254.
77. Interview D at Ncweng in Appendix C3.
78. Belinda Bozzoli, "Marxism, Feminism and Southern African Studies," *Journal of Southern African Studies* 9(1983):139–71. See also Cherryl Walker, "Gender and the Development of the Migrant Labor System c. 1850–1930: An Overview," in Cherryl Walker, ed., *Women and Gender in Southern Africa to 1945* (Cape Town: David Philip, 1990), 168–96.
79. Berger, "'Beasts of Burden' Revisited," *Paths toward the Past* (1994), 127.
80. CTAR 1/KMN 10/3, November 15, 1898.
81. NAR NA 223 1/1910/F527, Inspector of Native Reserves Purchase, April 1911.
82. Shillington, *Colonisation* (1985), 248–9.
83. CPP G 36 1907, *Blue Book on Native Affairs*, 27.
84. UG 32 - 1912, Census of 1911.
85. CPP G 19 1909, *Blue Book on Native Affairs*, 33; UG 10 - 1913, *Report of Native Affairs Department*, 80–1.
86. Beinart, *Twentieth-Century South Africa* (1994), 64–6.
87. CTAR NA 657, Inspector of Native Reserves Purchase, March 1904.
88. *Bechuanaland News*, Letter by "Old Resident," March 3, 1908. UG 17 - 1911, *Report of Native Affairs Department*, 224.
89. Interview B with Isaac Seamecho in Appendix C1.
90. NAR NA 223 1/1910/F527, Inspector of Native Reserves Purchase, January and February 1908; G-19 1909, *Report of Native Affairs Department*, 34.
91. UG 33 - 1913, *Report of Native Affairs Department* 110–1. The southern Tswana have a reputation for avoiding underground mining. See Comaroff and Comaroff, *Of Revelation and Revolution*, 2(1997), 206.
92. UG 17 - 1911, *Report of Native Affairs Department*, 224.
93. CTAR Kuruman Native (and Bantu) Affairs Comissioner Series [hereafter 2/KMN] 54 II, 8/21/4 Agricultural Report, June 20, 1951.
94. NAR NTS 7351 176/327, A. E. Hensley, Agricultural Extension Officer, June 1935. On seasonal harvesting work, see van Onselen, *Seed is Mine* (1996), 140, 215, 252.
95. CTAR 2/KMN 22 N 1/15/6 II, Bantu Commissioner, July 13, 1954.
96. Breutz, *Tribes of Kuruman* (1963), 63–4.
97. NAR NTS 7387 305/327(5), Deputy Director of Native Agriculture Trip Report no. 44, Western Areas, Winter 1950. In 1953, it was estimated that Kuruman workers shipped 15,000 20-pound bags of maize and transported 5,000 in their own wagons. CTAR 2/KMN 22 N 1/15/6 Part II, Native Commissioner, July 15, 1953.
98. Cosmos Desmond, *The Discarded People* (Harmondsworth: Penguin, 1971), 207. Returning harvesters also sought treatment for venereal disease.
99. Interview F at Ga-Mopedi in Appendix C3.
100. P. H. R. Snyman, "Safety and Health in the Northern Cape Blue Asbestos Belt," *Historia* 33(1988): 33; Hocking, *Kaias and Cocopans*, 39–43.
101. UG 23 - 1915, *Department of Mines Report*, 22.

102. A. L. Hall, *Asbestos in the Union of South Africa*, Union of South Africa Department of Mines and Industries, Geological Survey, Memoir No. 12, 1930, 92.

103. Snyman, "Blue Asbestos," 34.

104. NAR MNW [Department of Mines Series] 461 1420/19 Dec. 1921 or January 1922; March 9, 1922; October 25, 1921.

105. Hall, *Asbestos in the Union of South Africa*, 92. Isaac Seamecho, who grew up in Ga-Mopedi, which had many mines, corroborated this (see Appendix C1, Interviews B and C). For similar recollections by Faan Riekert, a mine manager near Maiping on the Lower Kuruman Reserve, see Hocking, *Kaias and Cocopans* (1983), 67–9.

106. Union of South Africa, Department of Mines, *The Mineral Resources of the Union of South Africa* (Pretoria: Government Printer, 1930), 285.

107. Hall, *Asbestos in South Africa* (1930), 92.

108. Union of South Africa Department of Mines, *The Mineral Resources of the Union of South Africa* (1930), 285.

109. Hocking, *Kaias and Cocopans* (1983), 68; Snyman, *Kuruman* (1992), 91–2.

110. Assistant Mine Inspector in 1916, quoted in Snyman, *Kuruman* (1992), 93.

111. See Interview C with Isaac Seamecho in Appendix C1.

112. Beinart gives generational interests as one reason households accepted lower, non-cash, advance payments for gold mining. A similar force may have been at work here. Beinart, *Political Economy of Pondoland* (1982), 63–9.

113. Snyman, *Kuruman* (1992), 93–4; UG 38 - 1919, *Department of Mines Report*, 4; UG 30 - 1927, *Department of Mines Report*, 187.

114. See Interview B with Isaac Seamecho in Appendix C1.

115. Snyman, *Kuruman* (1992), 116–7; Hocking, *Kaias and Cocopans* (1983), 54–66; Snyman, "The Northern Cape Manganese Fields: Development and Effect on the Surrounding Agrarian Community," *South African Journal of Economic History* 3, 1 (March 1988): 71–88.

116. NAR NTS 7846 36/336, Superintendent of Natives, November 18, 1931.

117. NAR NTS 7846 36/336, Native Commissioner Fritz, May 1, 1933; Native Commissioner Fritz, May 18, 1933.

118. NAR NTS 6318 23/128, Superintendent of Natives Brent, April 10, 1928; Superintendent of Natives Gladwin, September 7, 1929.

119. NAR NTS 7846 36/336, David L. Makgolokwe, January 21, 1932.

120. NAR NTS 7846 36/336, Native Commissioner Fritz, January 28, 1932.

121. NAR NTS 7846 36/336, Native Commissioner Fritz, May 26, 1933.

122. NAR NTS 7846 36/336, Acting Magistrate Lombard, February 12, 1932.

123. Iliffe, *Famine in Zimbabwe* (1990), 80–8.

124. NAR NTS 7846 36/336, Director of Native Agriculture Thornton, May 20, 1932.

125. Snyman, *Kuruman* (1992), 141; Hocking, *Kaias and Cocopans* (1983), 70–89.

126. NAR NTS 3007 368/305, Assistant Director of Native Agriculture, Northern Areas, n. d., probably October 1937.

127. The writer is reporting the memories of E. H. Chapman. NAR NTS 7846 36/336, Native Commissioner Coertzee, March 2, 1942.

128. MMT Kuruman Mission Annual Report for 1945. NAR NTS 1948 256/387(3), Agricultural Officer, March 31, 1940; NAR NTS 7846 36/336, Native Commissioner Coertzee, April 4, 1942.

129. Hocking, *Kaias and Cocopans* (1983), 90–100.

130. Statistics for 1961 are that the total of 7,538 black workers in Kuruman mines included 1,224 workers from local reserves. Snyman, *Kuruman* (1992), 176. Interview C at Ncweng in Appendix C3. On the local preference to avoid underground mining, see Interview C with Isaac Seamecho in Appendix C3; NAR Commissioner General Mafikeng (KGM) 87 (7) N11/2/3(6), Statement by Chief Toto in Regional Authority Minutes, November 8, 1973.

131. Breutz, *Tribes of Kuruman* (1963), 79.

132. This theme is dominant in the history of women's migration to urban areas. Elizabeth Schmidt, *Peasant Traders and Wives: Shona Women in the History of Zimbabwe, 1870–1939*, (Portsmouth: Heinemann, 1992).

133. Interview B at Ga-Mopedi in Appendix C3.

134. See Appendix C3, Interview A at Ga-Mopedi and Interview A at Ncweng. Statistics for asbestos workers show very small numbers of employed females, suggesting that piece workers were not included in the totals.

135. Interview C at Ga-Diboe in Appendix C3.

136. See Appendix C3, Interview A at Batlharos and Interview B at Ga-Sebolao. However, men probably controlled any grain produced for sale.

137. Ahmed Randeree, "Asbestos Pollution: What Needs to Be Done," unpublished paper dated April 5, 1998.

138. J. M. Talent, et al., "A Survey of Black Mineworkers of the Cape Crocidolite Mines," *Biological Effects of Mineral Fibre* 2(1980): 723–30.

139. Interview B with Isaac Seamecho in Appendix C1.

140. On rehabilitation, compensation, and health care for asbestos-related disease in Kuruman, see Lundy Braun, et al., "Asbestos-Related Disease in South Africa: Opportunities and Challenges Remaining Since the 1998 Asbestos Summit." http://www.brown.edu/Departments/African_American_Studies/Asbestos/titlepage.html.

141. Snyman, *Kuruman* (1992), 120; Interview A at Kagung in Appendix C3.

142. On the later history of this migration to the maize triangle, see Michael De Klerk, "Seasons that Will Never Return: The Impact of Farm Mechanization on Employment, Incomes and Population Distribution in the Western Transvaal," *Journal of Southern African Studies* 11(1984): 84–105.

143. Interview with Vivian Ditlholelo in Appendix C2; Interview A at Ga-Sebolao and Interview A at Maiphiniki in Appendix C3.

144. Interview B at Ga-Mopedi in Appendix C3.

145. Interview D at Ncweng in Appendix C3.

146. Desmond, *The Discarded People* (1971), 206–7.

147. Snyman, *Kuruman* (1992), 142–3, 173–81; Hocking, *Kaias and Cocopans* (1983), 104–8.

148. CTAR NA 605, Resident Magistrate Lyne, September 18, 1903.

149. For an argument that these land disputes resulted from capitalization among the rich as successful farmers dispossessed poorer ones of their land, see Comaroff and Comaroff, *Of Revelation and Revolution*, 2(1997), 143–7. Beinart, in contrast, argues that political concerns caused chiefs and headmen in Pondoland to accumulate land and restrict access to it. Beinart, *Political Economy of Pondoland* (1982), 126–30.

150. On the role of the *kgotla* in a land dispute in Batlharos, see CTAR 1/KMN 17/18, Record of Inquiry, September 24, 1908.
151. There are reports of communities divided over land allocation. For an example from Ga-Tlhose, see CTAR 1/KMN 10/13, Magistrate, October 16, 1911. For an example from Ga-Mopedi on the Lower Kuruman Reserve, see CTAR 1/KMN 17/18, Record of Inquiry, April 23, 1908. See other correspondence in that file regarding land disputes between individuals.
152. Interview B at Ga-Mopedi in Appendix C3.
153. NAR NA 223 1/1910/F527, Inspector of Native Reserves Purchase, December 16, 1908.
154. NAR NTS 1948 256/278(3), Agricultural Officer Hattingh, October 13, 1938.
155. CTAR 1/KMN 10/6, Resident Magistrate Lyne, November 11, 1903. A 1912 article asserted that "Real Bushmen are still to be seen in Griqualand West, but they are rapidly becoming extinct." See Lilian Orpen, "The Natives of Griqualand West," *The State*, February 1912, 154.
156. NAR NTS 7752 22/335, Surveyor General Bowden, January 24, 1908.
157. NAR NA 223 1/1910/F527, Inspector of Native Reserves Purchase, February 1911. Many interviews revealed that people still eat wild foods today.
158. Interview at Manyeding and Interview G at Ncweng in Appendix C3. Interview with Muriel Tshebedi in Appendix C2. Interview with M. Ditshetela and Interview B with John Molema in Appendix C1.
159. Breutz, *Tribes of Kuruman* (1963), 67.
160. Here my argument about the endurance of older forms of stratification and reciprocal relations differs from that of Comaroff and Comaroff who argue that a missionary-generated agrarian transformation occurred after the mid-nineteenth century, when Tswana society became increasingly dominated by capitalist relations. See Comaroff and Comaroff, *Of Revelation and Revolution*, 2(1997), 151–65. On the endurance of the precolonial agrarian dynamic after the beginning of capitalist production, see also Jack Lewis, "The Rise and Fall of the South African Peasantry: A Critique and Reassessment," *Journal of Southern African Studies* 11(1984): 1–24.
161. Interview A at Seodin in Appendix C3.
162. Interview with Johannes Itumeleng in Appendix C1.
163. For an argument that these relations were based on cash, see Comaroff and Comaroff, *Of Revelation and Revolution*, 2(1997), 453–4, note 122. However, in his history of food production in Botswana, William Duggan offers evidence that people shared labor on the basis of reciprocity more often than cash. See Duggan, *An Economic Analysis* (1986), 103–28.
164. Interview with Johannes Itumeleng in Appendix C1.
165. Interview with M. Ditshetela in Appendix C1.
166. See also Duggan, *An Economic Analysis* (1986), 111–2.
167. Interview with Johannes Itumeleng in Appendix C1.
168. Interview B with Isaac Seamecho in Appendix C1.
169. In Appendix C1, see Interviews A and B with Mosiane Kgokong, Interview with M. Lekalake, Interview with Simon Moeti, Interview with Evangelist Moholeng, and Interview with Marry Seamecho.

170. Interview C at Ga-Diboe in Appendix C3.
171. In *Cutting Down Trees* (1994), Vaughan and Moore have used rich evidence in colonial anthropological studies to analyze gender, food production, and migrant labor in Zambia. Their case differs from this in that there were practically no market opportunities for farmers in Kuruman and men were less motivated to take control of land and labor.
172. Belinda Bozzoli has made the same point in *Women of Phokeng: Consciousness, Life Strategy, and Migrancy in South Africa, 1900–1983* (Portsmouth: Heinemann, 1991), 45–7.
173. Interview B at Batlharos in Appendix C3.
174. Interview B with Isaac Seamecho in Appendix C1; Interview B at Batlharos and Interview C at Ga-Diboe in Appendix C3.
175. This statement was by Father Johannes Itumeleng, an Anglican priest. Women at the interview assented. See Interview C at Ga-Diboye in Appendix C3.
176. Interview B at Ga-Mopedi in Appendix C3. See also Duggan, *An Economic Analysis* (1986), 203–4.
177. Interview with M. Ditshetela in Appendix C1.
178. Interview with Rose Ilanka Peme in Appendix C2.
179. Interview B at Batlharos in Appendix C3.
180. Interview with Johannes Itumeleng in Appendix C1.
181. Interview C at Ga-Mopedi in Appendix C3. Eldredge also makes the point that work parties were less beneficial to women than to men. "Women in Production," *Signs* 16(1991): 722.
182. Interview with Violet Orapeleng and Interview with Gladys Mokosi in Appendix C2.
183. Interview B with Mosiane Kgokong in Appendix C1. "NJ" is Nancy Jacobs.
184. Interview B at Batlharos in Appendix C3.
185. Interview B with Isaac Seamecho in Appendix C1.
186. Interview B with John Molema in Appendix C1. The "Damaras" were refugees from violence in South-West Africa before 1910. Hocking, *Kaias and Cocopans* (1983), claims they were misnamed and were actually Herero, 40. On these refugees, see NAR NTS 7770 122/335, J. P. Frylinck, March 14, 1930. They were often laborers in asbestos mines off Tswana reserves.
187. Interview with Irene Molema in Appendix C1.
188. Interview with Vivian Ditlholelo in Appendix C2; Interview D at Ncweng in Appendix C3.
189. Comaroff and Comaroff, *Of Revelation and Revolution*, 1(1991), 140–4.
190. NAR NTS 1948 256/278(3), Agricultural Officer Hattingh, October 13, 1938.
191. Hoyt Alverson, *Mind in the Heart of Darkness: Value and Self-Identity among the Tswana of Southern Africa* (New Haven: Yale, 1978), 77.
192. Interview B with John Molema in Appendix C1.
193. Interview F at Batlharos in Appendix C3.
194. See Interview B at Ncweng, Interview F at Batlharos, and Interview F at Ncweng in Appendix C3.
195. De Klerk, "Seasons that Will Never Return," *Journal of Southern African Studies* 11(1984).

196. Interview B at Batlharos in Appendix C3.
197. Interview with White Koikanyang in Appendix C2; Interview with Simon Moeti in Appendix C1; Interview F at Ncweng in Appendix C3.
198. Interview B at Ga-Diboye in Appendix C3.
199. Chris De Wet, *Moving Together, Drifting Apart: Betterment Planning and Villagisation in a South African Homeland* (Johannesburg: University of Witwatersrand Press, 1995), 75–6, 106–7, 198.
200. Interview C at Ncweng in Appendix C3.
201. Interview D at Ncweng in Appendix C3.

CHAPTER 7

1. Desmond, *The Discarded People* (1971), 209.
2. Mamdani, *Citizen and Subject* (1996), 21.
3. Dubow, *Racial Segregation* (1989); Marion Lacey, *Working for Boroko: The Origins of a Coercive Labour System* (Johannesburg: Raven Press, 1981); Deborah Posel, *The Making of Apartheid, 1948–1961* (Oxford: Oxford University Press, 1991).
4. UG 22 - 16, *Report of the Natives Land Commission*, Vol. II, 104–5, 107. On the Natives Land Act, see Sol T. Plaatje, *Native Life in South Africa: Before and Since the European War and the Boer Rebellion* (Johannesburg: Raven Press, 1982); Lacey, *Working for Boroko* (1981); Keegan, *Rural Transformations* (1986), 182–95.
5. Dubow, *Racial Segregation* (1989), 132.
6. C. M. Tatz, *Shadow and Substance in South Africa: A Study in Land and Franchise Policies Affecting Africans, 1910–1960* (Pietermaritzburg: University of Natal Press, 1962), 27–37; Lacey, *Working for Boroko* (1981), 19–35; Laurine Platzky and Cherryl Walker, *The Surplus People: Forced Removals in South Africa* (Johannesburg: Raven Press, 1985), 82–93; Murray, *Black Mountain* (1992), 122–8.
7. Lacey, *Working for Boroko* (1981), 97–101; Dubow, *Racial Segregation* (1989), 115–6; Rich, *State Power and Black Politics* (1996), 31–6; Evans, *Bureaucracy and Race* (1997), 168–9, 178.
8. Tatz, *Shadow and Substance* (1962), 99 and 204, note 6.
9. BPP C 4889, *Land Settlement in British Bechuanaland*, 95–6; CTAR BCC 116, Surveyor General Watermeyer, December 17, 1895.
10. LMS 55/1/A, J. Tom Brown, June 20, 1898; CTAR LND 1/1730, Secretary for Public Works, February 2, 1900.
11. CTAR 1/KMN 10/4, Resident Magistrate Lyne, June 29, 1903; CTAR LND 1/730, Native Affairs Assistant Secretary, January 21, 1902.
12. LMS 64/2, J. Tom Brown, April 4, 1904 and August 10, 1904; CTAR Public Works Department 1/5/28, B44 Annexure J, n. d. 1905; NAR Land Department (hereafter LND) 1/710, Surveyor General, December 7, 1908; NAR NTS 4368 268/313, M. C. Vos, Report on the Kuruman Crown Reserve, August 26, 1911; NAR Irrigation Department Series [hereafter IRR] 801/08, map "Kuruman River Irrigation," February 2, 1917; NAR LND 1/710, Surveyor General, December 7, 1908; and Snyman, *Kuruman* (1992), 87–8.
13. NAR NTS 4368 268/313, M. C. Vos, August 26, 1911.

14. For a fuller discussion on the segregation of the Kuruman Crown Reserve and water from the Kuruman Eye, see Jacobs, "The Flowing Eye: Water Management in the Upper Kuruman Valley, South Africa, c.1800–1962," *Journal of African History* 37(1996): 237–60.

15. The act was Number 32 of 1909. On Cape Location Laws, see Bundy, *Rise and Fall of the Peasantry* (1979), 134–7. Bundy sees the 1909 law as a precursor to the 1913 Natives Land Act. See also Lacey, *Working for Boroko* (1981), 123–4. On events at the mission, see LMS 72/5, J. Tom Brown, March 14, 1910; LMS 72/7, J. Tom Brown, September 1, 1910; and LMS 72/8, J. Tom Brown, October 10, 1910.

16. Snyman, *Kuruman* (1992), 100–1, 106.

17. Snyman, *Kuruman* (1992), 107; MMT, Memorandum of Agreement between the London Missionary Society and the Municipal Council of Kuruman, February 7, 1917.

18. NAR NTS 4638 268/313, Director of Irrigation, June 19, 1924; *Northern News* (Vryburg), "Kuruman Kuttings," February 6, 1918 and August 3, 1920; Snyman, *Kuruman* (1992), 149.

19. Snyman, *Kuruman* (1992), 107.

20. Dubow, *Racial Segregation* (1989), 79; Rich, *State Power and Black Politics* (1996), 26, 29.

21. NAR NTS 4368 268/313, M. C. Vos, July 15, 1921.

22. See correspondence in NAR NTS 4638 268/313. For a map of the Kuruman Crown Reserve, see 2/KMN 13/43 N 9/15/3/2, July 9, 1948.

23. NAR NTS 7933 165/337, A. E. Jennings, December 3, 1923.

24. D. G. Beare, District Surgeon of Kuruman, claimed in 1897 that water from the Kuruman Eye flowed for forty miles downstream. CAB KMN 10/1, February 16, 1897. In contrast, the missionary Brown reported in 1900 that water was so scarce that he had to irrigate by night. LMS 58/3, J. Tom Brown, September 18, 1900.

25. NAR IRR 801/08, map, February 2, 1917.

26. NAR NTS 6882 165/337, Galeboe's testimony to the Native Affairs Commission, May 16, 1941.

27. MMT, Memorandum of Agreement between the London Missionary Society and the Municipal Council of Kuruman, February 7, 1917.

28. NAR NTS 4638 268/3/3, Director of Irrigation, June 19, 1924.

29. NAR NTS 6882 165/337, A. E. Jennings, September 1, 1924.

30. NAR NTS 6882 165/337, Native Affairs Acting Under Secretary, May 27, 1931; CTAR Provincial Administration [hereafter PAS] 2/747 L52 C4, Cape Provincial Secretary, June 23, 1924.

31. NAR NTS 6882 165/337, Native Affairs Secretary, October 18, 1939.

32. MMT, H. C. Thompson 1939 report for Kuruman; NAR NTS 6882 165/337, H. C. Thompson, January 25, 1940.

33. NAR NTS 6882 165/337, Galeboe's testimony to the Native Affairs Commission (NAC) May 16, 1941.

34. NAR NTS 6882 165/337, Testimony of J. Robinson of Landbou-Unie to the NAC, December 9, 1948.

35. Interview A at Seodin and Interview F at Ncweng in Appendix C3; Interview with Edward Motlhabane in Appendix C2.

36. Interview with Eddie van Wyk in Appendix C1.
37. NAR NTS 6882 165/337, correspondence on Seodin boreholes, 1941–8.
38. NAR NTS 7846 36/336, Native Commissioner Coertzee, April 4, 1942; CTAR 2/KMN 54 8/20/2, Additional Native Commissioner, May 20, 1948; and CTAR 2 KMN 54 8/20/3, Tussentydse Komitee Besproeiingskema, Kuruman Distrik, October 21, 1951.
39. Breutz, *Tribes of Kuruman* (1963), 64.
40. Snyman, *Kuruman* (1992), 110, 230.
41. For an environmentally aware treatment of the hydraulic society thesis, see Worster, *Rivers of Empire* (1985).
42. The establishment of the Kuruman municipal irrigation scheme was a precursor to the much larger Vaal-Harts project constructed near Taung as a relief project for whites during the Great Depression. Shillington, "Irrigation, Agriculture and the State." *Putting a Plough to the Ground* (1986), 311–35.
43. NAR NTS 7752 22/335, Magistrate Viljoen, October 2, 1924. For observations of similar connections between extensive land use and land alienation, see Bundy, *Rise and Fall* (1979), 188; Ballard, "Rinderpest," *The International Journal of African Historical Studies* 19(1986): 449.
44. NAR NTS 7752 22/335, Native Affairs Commission, November 5, 1924.
45. South African Native Affairs Commission, Volume 4, *Minutes of Evidence* (Cape Town: Cape Times, Government Printers, 1904), 265–6. Regarding Kuruman, see also *Northern News*, "Natives and Dryland Cultivation," December 3, 1913; NAR NTS 6318 23/218, Superintendent of Natives Brent, April 10, 1928.
46. Dubow, *Racial Segregation* (1989), 95.
47. Quoted in Dubow, *Racial Segregation* (1989), 69. See also Beinart, *Twentieth-Century South Africa* (1994), 117–8.
48. NAR NTS 7846 36/336, Director of Native Agriculture Thornton, May 20, 1932. This file contains much correspondence on the establishment of irrigation projects.
49. See correspondence in NAR NTS 7930 159/337.
50. NAR NTS 3007 368/305, Assistant Director of Native Agriculture, Northern Areas, n. d., probably October 1937.
51. NAR NTS 7930 159/337, Deputy Director of Native Agriculture, April 12, 1939.
52. NAR NTS 1947 256/278 III, March 31, 1940. People did grow vegetables when the government provided seed and fencing in the food shortage during World War II. NAR NTS 7351, 3, 176/327, see agriculture extension reports from 1941 and 1942.
53. NAR NTS 7351 I, 176/327, Extension Officer Hensley, November 1933.
54. NAR NTS 3007 368/305, Assistant Director of Native Agriculture, Northern Areas, n. d., probably October 1937.
55. Interview B with Isaac Seamecho in Appendix C1.
56. Interview A at Batlharos in Appendix C3.
57. NTS 7931 159/337, Assistant Native Commissioner, Kuruman, November 22, 1944.
58. NAR NTS 7933 165/337, Tussentydse Komitee Besproeiingskema, Kuruman Distrik, October 3, 1951.
59. NAR NTS 6882 165/337, unsigned memo in Afrikaans, May 1952.

60. For trust released areas by province, see Tatz, *Shadow and Substance* (1962), 99. Statistics for land purchase for Kuruman are from NAR 3007 368/305, Native Affairs Commission, October 6, 1937. The official census of the black population in Kuruman in 1936 counted 24,477 people (see Figure 6-1). The countrywide total was 6,595,597. See Beinart, *Twentieth-Century South Africa* (1994), 262.

61. NAR NTS 3773 2328/308, "Purchase of Land by the Trust in the Kuruman District," March 14, 1938; NAR 3007 368/305, Native Affairs Commission, October 6, 1937.

62. CTAR 2/KMN 22 N 1/15/6, Assistant Native Commissioner, September 30, 1945.

63. Breutz, *Tribes of Kuruman* (1963), 57–9.

64. Muriel Horrell, *A Survey of Race Relations in South Africa, 1964* (Johannesburg: South African Institute for Race Relations, 1965), 161.

65. CTAR 2/KMN 22 N 1/15/6, Assistant Native Commissioner, September 30, 1945.

66. See correspondence in NAR NTS 3079 1003/305 I.

67. NAR NTS 1947 256/278 III, Agricultural Officer Hattingh, October 13, 1938. He was referring to the horseshoe block farms, which had been acquired before the major trust purchases.

68. See Appendix B.

69. On renting land to white farmers, see correspondence in 8134 377/340 Parts I–IV. White farmers also leased trust land in Thaba Nchu. Murray, *Black Mountain* (1992), 163.

70. For records of such concerns, see NAR NTS 7933 165/337, Meeting at Dikgweng with Native Affairs Commission, December 10, 1948.

71. The Surplus People Project, *Forced Removals in South Africa* (1983), 3, 89. The reported population removed from villages in Postmasburg, Kimberley, and Vryburg Districts is 2,000 from Groenwater, 3,101 from Di Takwanen, and 3,000–6,000 from Schmidtsdrift and Skeyfontein. Populations for 1936 given in Table 7-1 are from NAR NTS 1947 256/278 III, Agricultural Officer Hattingh, October 13, 1938. Populations from 1960 are from Breutz, *Tribes of Kuruman* (1963), 47.

72. That these were desirable parcels is evident in that in the 1880s they were the third, fourth, and fifth farms in the district to be settled by whites. Snyman, *Kuruman* (1992), 57.

73. AnCRA, Peter Mokomele, n. d., "Community Profile of Smouswane – Preliminary Information Gathering Meeting at Ellendale."

74. NAR NTS 4368 268/313, M. C. Vos, August 26, 1911.

75. NAR NTS 6082 268/313, Native Commissioner, October 17, 1941.

76. NAR NTS 6082 218/313, Kuruman Town Clerk, July 11, 1941; NAR NTS 6082 218/313, Native Commissioner, August 11, 1941.

77. CTAR 1/KMN 13/43 N 9/15/3(2), correspondence from 1944.

78. CTAR 1/KMN 13/43 N 9/15/3(2), June 20, 1948. CTAR 1/KMN 13/43 N 9/15/3(2), minutes of meeting, December 10, 1948. AnCRA, Dikgweng correspondence, Peter Mokomele, "Dikgweng Profile," n. d.

79. AnCRA, Dikgweng correspondence, Moonawadibe Mmolaeng, "Land Claim Form" puts the amount of compensation at R40. This was, of course, before the rand became the currency, so the amount was probably about £20. On Dikgweng, see also Snyman, *Kuruman* (1992), 100, 150–1, 154–6, 162, 198.

80. Snyman, *Kuruman* (1992), 196.

81. MMT, LMS Annual Reports for the Kuruman District, B. J. Haai, March, 1950, 4; December 1951, 7.
82. For commentary on the thin line between voluntary exodus and evictions from farms, see Murray, *Black Mountain* (1992), 214.
83. Interview A at Ga-Sebolao in Appendix C3. See also Interview with Joseph Kopman in Appendix C2.
84. For the official population of Konong, see NAR NTS 7791 228/335, Chief Native Commissioner, April 20, 1956.
85. See requests from white farmers and responses to them from 1935, 1946, and 1948 in NAR NTS 7791 228/335.
86. NAR NTS 7791 228/335, minutes of meeting of the Native Affairs Commission, October 7, 1949.
87. NAR NTS 7791 228/335, Attorney Barnard, March 8, 1955.
88. Interview A and Interview B at Churchill in Appendix C3.
89. Interview B at Churchill in Appendix C3.
90. Quoted in AnCRA, "Kono correspondence," Konong Community Committee, Land Claim. In my interviews, people corroborated each of these statements.
91. Interview B at Churchill in Appendix C3.
92. AnCRA "Kono correspondence," undated, unsigned document.
93. AnCRA "Kono correspondence," quoted in brief by Kate Owen, Deneys Reitz Attorneys [n. d.], 3.
94. See correspondence in NAR Bantu Administration and Development Series (hereafter BAO) 7761 44/335.
95. NAR BAO 7761 44/335, minutes of meeting, January 12, 1954.
96. NAR BAO 7761 44/335, notes from undersecretary, October 7, 1959. For the 1959 census, see NAR BAO 7761 44/335, June 23, 1959.
97. A comparison of farms purchased before 1949 (found in 2/KMN 30 2/7/2 II) and farms purchased by 1963 (found in Breutz, *Tribes of Kuruman* [1963], 59–62) shows only five additional properties. However, some of the pre-1949 farms may have been only portions of the named properties.
98. The secretary of native affairs ruled Maremane was not a black spot in 1941. NAR NTS 7806 316/335 I, Secretary of Native Affairs, October 31, 1941. See also NAR NTS 7791 228/335, Secretary of Native Affairs, March 26, 1955; NAR NTS 3126 1746/305, Secretary of Native Affairs, November 9, 1953.
99. On Bophuthatswana, see Jeffrey Butler, Robert I. Rotberg, and John Adams, *The Black Homelands of South Africa: The Political and Economic Development of Bophuthatswana and KwaZulu* (Berkeley: University of California Press, 1977).
100. Thompson, *A History of South Africa* (1990), 191.
101. NAR BAO 4437 D4/1363/01, Prime Minister Verwoerd, February 7, 1962.
102. CTAR 2/KMN 31 II N 2/7/2 5, Secretary BAO, October 31, 1963; Desmond, *The Discarded People* (1971), 207–18.
103. Snyman, *Kuruman* (1992), 144, 183.
104. NAR NTS 3126 1746/305, Reivilo Town Management Board, March 10, 1954. For the decision to remove the reserve, see NAR NTS 3126 1746/305, minutes of meeting, September 23, 1963. In the 1960s, government records sometimes referred to this reserve as Metsi-Matsi, which was a village on the reserve.
105. Interview B at Kagung in Appendix C3.

106. AnCRA, Kagung Correspondence, March 23, 1996; Interview B at Kagung in Appendix C3.
107. See correspondence in NAR BAO 3319 c43/1363.
108. CTAR 2/KMN 233 N 2/10/3/(5), minutes of a meeting, July 17, 1967.
109. AnCRA 84/1995 "Khuis correspondence."
110. The Surplus People Project, *Forced Removals in South Africa* (1983), 3, 89. For the official population, see Department of Cooperation and Development 8/7/2/2/K69/43, September 16, 1969. In 1998, investigators in the Department of Land Affairs shared files of the Department of Cooperation and Development and the Department of Regional and Land Affairs with me.
111. For a report during the interim, see Desmond, *The Discarded People* (1971), 114–5.
112. For records about planning the removal process, see Department of Cooperation and Development 188/1363/46, volumes 18 and 24.
113. Department of Cooperation and Development 188/1363/43, report of visit by Tlharo Chief J. B. Toto, October 1, 1976. Complaints about a shortage of water for stock continued. See minutes of meeting at Bendell, November 8, 1976.
114. Department of Regional and Land Affairs 6/7/2/K19/43, Case no. 958/93. 5, 1992. Affidavit by Bokhutlo Denis Holele in the Supreme Court of South Africa (Northern Cape Division) in the matter of the Minister of Defense and Joseph Free and 44 others.
115. Platzky and Walker, *The Surplus People* (1985), 55, 285; The Surplus People Project, *Forced Removals in South Africa* (1983), 3, 89.

CHAPTER 8

1. CTAR 2/KMN 20 N 1/15/4 I, statement by Headman Smous Holele of Ga-Tlhose at meeting of Headmen and Councilors, April 13, 1943.
2. For an overview the history of Betterment, see De Wet, *Moving Together, Drifting Apart* (1995), 39–57, 196–203.
3. On policy motivations, see De Wet, *Moving Together, Drifting Apart* (1995), 57–67. On cheap labor and Betterment, see Fred Hendricks, *The Pillars of Apartheid: Land Tenure, Rural Planning and the Chieftaincy* (Uppsala: Uppsala University Press, 1990). On political control, see Joanne Yawitch, *Betterment: The Myth of Homeland Agriculture* (Johannesburg: South African Institute of Race Relations, 1981). On fears of environmental degradation, see Beinart, "Soil Erosion, Conservationism and Ideas about Development: A Southern African Exploration, 1900–1960," *Journal of Southern African Studies* 11(1984): 52–83.
4. Isabel Hofmeyr, *"We Spend Our Years as a Tale That Is Told": Oral Historical Narrative in a South African Chiefdom* (Portsmouth, NH: Heinemann, 1993), 80–3; De Wet, *Moving Together, Drifting Apart* (1995).
5. Mamdani, *Citizen and Subject* (1996), 124, 138–79.
6. Breutz, *Tribes of Kuruman* (1963), 8, 160; CTAR 2/KMN 57 11/1/2 I, Native Commissioner, November 13, 1952.
7. Proclamation by governor general No. 206 1948; by minister of native affairs No. 1644, August 6, 1948.

8. On the Transkei council system, see Evans, *Bureaucracy and Race* (1997), 183–5.
9. UG 51 - 1950, *Report of the Department of Native Affairs for the Years 1948–49*, 6; UG 61 - 1951, *Report of the Department of Native Affairs for the Years 1949–50*, 8.
10. Delius, *A Lion Amongst the Cattle: Reconstruction and Resistance in the Northern Transvaal* (Portsmouth: Heinemann, 1996), 55–62, 69–71; Tom Lodge, *Black Politics in South Africa since 1945* (New York: Longman, 1983), 269–73, 281–3; Rich, *State Power* (1996), 153–6; Murray, *Black Mountain* (1992), 172–84.
11. On the Apartheid policy of segregated administration, see Posel, *The Making of Apartheid 1948–1961: Conflict and Compromise* (1991).
12. Butler, Rotberg, and Adams, *The Black Homelands of South Africa* (1977), 28.
13. NAR NTS 8963 185/362(2)(a), Secretary of Native Affairs, June 17, 1957; Breutz, *Tribes of Kuruman* (1963), 102, 170.
14. Breutz, *Tribes of Kuruman* (1963), 10.
15. Butler, Rotberg, and Adams, *Black Homelands of South Africa* (1977), 33–4.
16. Observations of the relative weakness of Tlhaping chiefs appeared already in the 1880s, see Mackenzie *Austral Africa*, 1(1887), 76. They continued in the twentieth century: Breutz, *Tribes of Kuruman* (1963), 39; John Comaroff, "Tswana Transformation, 1952–1975," in Schapera, *The Tswana*, [4th ed] with a supplementary chapter by John Comaroff and a supplementary bibliography by Adam Kuper (London: KPI, 1984), 73–4.
17. See Leach and Mearns, "Introduction," in *Lie of the Land* (1996), 8–9.
18. The drought commission mentioned the northern Cape only as a contrast to the midlands. It considered that damage to the veld and the impact of drought was less severe in the northern Cape because the limited number of water sources protected the veld from overuse. UG 49 - 1923, *Drought Investigation Commission Final Report*, 274.
19. Beinart, "Soil Erosion," *Journal of Southern African Studies* 11(1984). For an east African comparison, see David Anderson, "Depression, Dust Bowl, Demography and Drought: The Colonial State and Soil Conservation in East Africa during the 1930s," *African Affairs* 83(1984): 321–43.
20. For observations of the more coercive character of development and agricultural programs after the mid-1930s, see Beinart, "Soil Erosion," *Journal of Southern African Studies* 11(1984), 69; Rich, *Black Politics* (1996), 131; Evans, *Bureaucracy and Race* (1997), 175, 201.
21. CTAR 2/KMN 48 N 8/5/2 I, Additional Native Commissioner, June 30, 1947.
22. NAR NTS 9352 19/380, Native Commissioner Vryburg, August 24, 1932.
23. NAR NTS 7387 305/327(5), Deputy Director of Native Agriculture Trip Report no. 44, Western Areas, Winter 1950. See also NAR NTS 3007 368/305, Assistant director of Native Agriculture, Northern Areas, n. d., (probably October 1937).
24. Peta Jones, *Donkeys for Development* (1997), 12.
25. CTAR 1/KMN 13/43 N 9/15/3(2). See correspondence in this file from late 1944 and early 1945.
26. NAR NTS 3079 1003/305 II, Additional Native Commissioner Hattingh, September 9, 1947.
27. NAR NTS 3079 1003/305 II, Senior Agricultural Officer, September 15, 1948.

28. UG 61 - 1951, *Report of the Department of Native Affairs for the Years 1949–50*, 3.
29. Michael Stocking, "Soil Erosion: Breaking New Ground," in *Lie of the Land* (1996), Leach and Mearns, eds., 140–54.
30. The reports are found in CTAR 2/KMN 22 N 1/15/6 II and CTAR 2/KMN 54 II, N 8/21/4.
31. Breutz, *Tribes of Kuruman* (1963), 63, 81. One white farmer denied that dust storms were ever a problem in Kuruman, compared with those in wetter areas with more plowing. Interview with J. J. van der Merwe in Appendix C1.
32. CTAR 2/KMN 47 N 8/4/2, Chief Bantu Affairs Commissioner, Western Areas, February 6, 1962, quoting proclamation by the Secretary of Native Affairs dated July 17, 1941.
33. Hendrick, *Pillars of Apartheid* (1990), 126–32; De Wet, *Moving Together, Drifting Apart* (1995), 47, 54–5; Murray, *Black Mountain* (1992), 179–80.
34. Quoted in Evans, *Bureaucracy and Race* (1997), 243. On the later development of Betterment policy and the Tomlinson Commission, see De Wet, *Moving Together, Drifting Apart* (1995), 45–8; Evans, *Bureaucracy and Race* (1997), 203–4, 239–45.
35. On the absence of conservationist concerns in Southern Rhodesian interventions into black agriculture, see Ian Phimister, "Discourse and the Discipline of Historical Context: Conservationism and Ideas about Development in Southern Rhodesia 1930–1950," *Journal of Southern African Studies* 12(1986): 263–75. On the waning of conservation as a motive behind Betterment in South Africa, see Hendricks, *Pillars of Apartheid* (1990), 122–40.
36. On "loose" and "detailed" planning, see Hendricks, *Pillars of Apartheid* (1990), 107–19; personal communication, Derick Fay, January 30, 2001.
37. CTAR 2/KMN 33 N 2/11/4 II, ad hoc planning committee, June 1, 1956.
38. Department of Cooperation and Development 8/7/2/2K69/43, report on removal of Ga-Tlhose and Maremane, September 16, 1969. This file was held in the Department of Land Affairs. For other development reports and proposals, see NAR NTS 10251 40/423(1), Correspondence from 1952–8 on Vlakfontein; NAR NTS 10251 40/423(3), Correspondence from 1952–8 on Konong; and CTAR 2/KMN 33 N 2/11/4 II, correspondence on SANT farms.
39. Interview I at Batlharos and Interview A at Seodin in Appendix C3.
40. Snyman, *Kuruman* (1992), 198–9.
41. Interview F at Ncweng and Interview A at Seodin in Appendix C3.
42. On water development in Kuruman, see correspondence in NAR NTS 7931 159/337. CTAR 2/KMN 40 N 5/1/2 IX contains a list of all boreholes and wells and describing their reliability before 1961.
43. A 1965 list in CTAR 2/KMN 33 N 2/11/4 III stated that all the reserves except Ga-Tlhose and Maremane as well as many of the inhabited SANT farms were "95%" or "100%" planned.
44. Interview I at Ga-Mopedi in Appendix C3; Breutz, *Tribes of Kuruman*, 75.
45. Snyman, *Kuruman* (1992), 196.
46. CTAR 2/KMN 33 N 2/11/4 I, Humphrey Thompson, November 1, 1958; Interview with Don Riekert in Appendix C1; Interview B at Seodin in Appendix C3.
47. Breutz, *Tribes of Kuruman* (1963), 77.
48. CTAR 2/KMN 19 1/12/10 I, Humphrey Thompson, April 25, 1951.
49. CTAR 2/KMN 57 N 11/1/2 I, minutes of meeting, May 15, 1954.

50. NAR NTS 10251 40/423(1) Correspondence from 1952–8.
51. Breutz, *Tribes of Kuruman* (1963), 58.
52. CTAR 2/KMN 30 N 2/7/2 IV, 1959 correspondence regarding the case of E. Mantanga.
53. For requests to buy land, see CTAR 2/KMN 31 II, N 2/7/2 V, correspondence with Adam Molema from 1961–3; CTAR 2/KMN 30 N 2/7/2 IV, correspondence with L. Gaetsewe in 1961.
54. Interview with Peace Mabilo in Appendix C2.
55. Interview with people from Ga-Tlhose and Interview B at Ga-Diboe in Appendix C3.
56. Interview A at Logobate in Appendix C3.
57. Interview with White Koikanyang in Appendix C2.
58. Interview I at Ga-Mopedi and Interview A at Batlharos in Appendix C3; Interview with Gladys Motshabe, Interview with Private Koikanyang, and Interview with White Koikanyang in Appendix C3.
59. On overgrazing on SANT lands rented to white herders, see NAR NTS 8134 377/340, ad hoc committee, September 3, 1958.
60. See discussions of grazing-caused erosion and rotational grazing as the antidote. UG 44 - 1946, *Report of the Department of Native Affairs for the year 1944–45*; UG 48 - 1955, *Report of the Department of Native Affairs for the Year 1952–53,* 61.
61. Behnke and Scoones, "Rethinking Range Ecology," in *Range Ecology* (1993), 6. For a discussion on the concept of carrying capacity, see pp. 2–8 in that article. The carrying capacity for Kuruman reserves was mandated in Government Notice 625 of March 25 1948. CTAR 2/KMN 48 N 8/5/2 I.
62. See Appendix C3, Interview with people removed from Ga-Tlhose, Interview I at Ga-Mopedi, Interview B at Maphiniki, and Interview B at Churchill.
63. On fencing, see correspondence in CTAR 2/KMN 23 II, N 2/1/2 and CTAR 2/KMN 24 N 2/1/2. See Appendix C3, Interview B at Maphiniki, Interview I at Ga-Mopedi, Interview C at Ga-Sebolao, and Interview with people from Ga-Tlhose. The acceptance of camp fencing in Kuruman contrasts with resistance to it elsewhere. Writing on Valtyn in the Northern Province, Isabel Hofmeyr has argued that fencing represented "a type of demarcation or 'writing' that fixes white authority in the countryside" and describes struggles over fencing — camp and boundary fencing alike – as a challenge to white domination. Hofmeyr, *We Spend Our Years as A Tale that is Told* (1993), 68–77. However, my interviews in Kuruman suggest that herders responded to the effect of fencing on animal keeping more than to its symbolic content. They differentiated between types of fences and did not believe that camp fencing restricted land or harmed herding.
64. Interview B at Maphiniki in Appendix C3.
65. CTAR 2/KMN 55 N 10/1/3 I, Ga-Mopedi headman P. Gaesitsiwe, August 22, 1949. That plowing was legal on reserves and SANT farms in Vryburg was a sore point with blacks in Kuruman. CTAR 2/KMN 20 N 1/15/4 II, minutes of meeting, March 30, 1955.
66. CTAR 2/KMN 47 N 8/1/5 (1), minutes of meeting, February 15, 1951.
67. CTAR 2 KMN 33 N 2/11/4 II, ad hoc committee report, June 1, 1956, 5. On whether plowing in river valleys should be allowed to continue, see also CTAR 2/KMN 23 II, N 2/1/2, Native Commissioner, April 24, 1953. This letter reported that people

in the Lower Kuruman Reserve were greatly concerned about losing plowing rights on irrigable reserves.

68. CTAR 2/KMN 20 N 1/15/4 II, minutes of the quarterly meeting of chiefs and head-men, June 24, 1952. CTAR 2/KMN 55 N 10/1/3 I, E. Mantanga wrote five letters in 1949 and 1950 asking for permission to plow. NAR NTS 8962 185/362 II, minutes of meeting, August 13, 1954. During preparations for their removal, Smouswane people negotiated plowing rights at their new settlement. NAR NTS 7806 316/335 part I, Native Comissioner, October 14, 1941. Dikgweng people also attempted, un-successfully, to secure plowing rights. CTAR 1/KMN 13/43 N9 15/3/(2), minutes of meeing, September 10, 1952.

69. De Wet, *Moving Together, Drifting Apart* (1995), 51.

70. CTAR 2/KMN 49 N 8/5/3 (3) IV, minutes of meeting of the Baga Motlhware Tribal Authority, May 10, 1960; March 27, 1961; April 21, 1961.

71. CTAR 2/KMN 49 N 8/5/3 (3) IV, Bantu Affairs Commissioner, August 18, 1961.

72. CTAR 2/KMN 49 N 8/5/3 (3) IV, *Government Gazette*, November 16, 1962, Procla-mation 1886. The proclamation inaugurating Betterment on Tlhaping reserves was CTAR 2/KMN 49 N 8/5/3 IV, *Government Gazette*, April 19, 1963, Proclamation 532.

73. Interview A at Batlharos in Appendix C3.

74. See correspondence in NAR NTS 7546 789/327 Part I.

75. See correspondence from 1949–56 in CTAR 2/KMN 47 N 8/4/2.

76. CTAR 2/KMN 47 N 8/1/5(2), minutes of meeting, April 21, 1951.

77. Snyman, *Kuruman* (1992), 190; Breutz, *Tribes of Kuruman* (1963), 65–6, 77. Breutz appears to give proceeds only for cattle sales. When South Africa became a republic it replaced the South African pound with a new currency, the rand, valued at two per pound.

78. For example, see the difficulties in Vlakfontein NAR NTS 10251 40/423(1), Cor-respondence from 1952–8.

79. NAR NTS 2299 798/280, memorandum of conversation, August 7, 1955.

80. NAR NTS 10251 40/423(5) B, Margin notes on 1959 report on Konong.

81. De Wet, *Moving Together, Drifting Apart* (1995), 67. See, for example, NAR NTS 5405 H 62/15/1/1363, October 2, 1961; and October 31, 1961.

82. NAR NTS 6577 918/327, Agricultural Officer, March 13, 1956.

83. CTAR 2/KMN 48 8/5/2 (1). The donkey limitation proclamation was 256 of February 6, 1953. For the numbers of culled animals, see CTAR 2/KMN 48 8/5/2(1), Agricultural Officer, October 23, 1953; Breutz, *Tribes of Kuruman* (1963), 66.

84. CTAR 2/KMN 20 N 1/15/4 IV, minutes of meetings, July 1, 1959; March 29, 1966; March 23, 1967; March 28, 1968; June 27, 1968; September 26, 1968.

85. CTAR 2/KMN 20 N 1/15/4 IV, minutes of meeting, June 29, 1967. Starkey claims that voluntary selling was also unsuccessful in Kwa-Zulu. See Starkey, *Animal Traction in South Africa* (1995), 22.

86. UG 77 1948, *Agricultural Census*, 1945 6.

87. CTAR 2/KMN 20 N 1/15/4 II, minutes of meeting, September 25, 1953.

88. CTAR 2/KMN 20 N 1/15/4 II, minutes of meetings, May 28, 1951 and September 19, 1952. See also CTAR 2/KMN 20 N 1/15/4 I, minutes of meeting, April 13, 1943.

89. Vetter, "Investigating the Impact of Donkeys," Honors thesis, University of Cape Town, 1996; Starkey, *Animal Traction in South Africa* (1995), 142–51.

90. The photographs for the southern sample set were 1958 – strip 10/job number 414/photos 7,714–7,706 and 1,899–1,890; 1965 – strip 5/job number 537/photos 220–210; 1972 – strip 6/job number 700/photos 9,599–9,611; 1981 – strip 2/job number 854/photos 446–435. The photographs for the northern sample set were 1958 – strip 4/job number 414/photos 2,824–2,802; 1965 – strip 2/job number 537/photos 73–62; 1972 – strip 6/job number 700/photos 9,400–9,385; 1981 – strip 2/job number 854/photos 521–532. All photos were 25-centimeter-square contact prints. The 1958 photos were 1:30,000; 1965 photos were 1:60,000; 1972 photos were 1:50,000; and 1981 photos were 1:150,000. I am grateful to the American Historical Association for awarding me a Bernadotte E. Schmitt Grant to purchase these photographs.

91. The 1973 1:50,000 maps for the southern strip were 2723 AD, 2723 BC, 2724 AC, for the northern strip, they were 2723 AA, 2723 AB, and 2723 BA.

92. Purchase dates are given in CTAR 2/KMN 33 N 2/11/4.

93. Tribal authorities in this area were created by Government Notice 806 of 1955 and Government Notice 1932 of 1956. Regional authorities were created by Government Notice 358 of March 7, 1958. On their responsibilities, see Butler, Rotberg, and Adams, *Black Homelands* (1977), 28, 33, 157–78. On the structure of the Bophuthatswana bureaucracy, see D. A. Kotze *Bibliography of Official Publications of the Black South African Homelands*, 2nd ed. (Pretoria: University of South Africa, 1983), xvi–xvii.

94. On homeland constitutions and elections in Bophuthatswana, see Butler, Rotberg, and Adams, *Black Homelands* (1977), 36–7, 50–5; see also John Seiler, "Bophuthatswana: A State of Politics," in *Transforming Mangope's Bophuthatswana*, John Seiler, ed., Electronic publication by *Daily Mail and Guardian*, 1999. http://www.mg.co.za/mg/projects/bop/ch_one.html.

95. *Mail and Guardian*, July 24, 1998. http://web.sn.apc.org/wmail/issues/980724/NEWS19.html. Seiler, "The North West Province from 1996 to 1999," in *Transforming Mangope's Bophuthatswana* (1999). http://www.mg.co.za/mg/projects/bop/update.html. The rand suffered serious devaluation between the foundation of Bophuthatswana and 1998, but it averaged around three or four per dollar. See also Michael Lawrence and Andrew Manson, "'The Dog of the Boers': The Rise and Fall of Mangope in Bophuthatswana," *Journal of Southern African Studies* 20(1994): 447–61; Peris Sean Jones, "'To Come Together for Progress': Modernization and Nation-Building in South Africa's Bantustan Periphery – the Case of Bophuthatswana," *Journal of Southern African Studies* 25(1999): 578–605.

96. M. Mosiamane, "What Lies Behind the Glittering Bophuthatswana Facade?" *Pace*, October 1983, 19–23. People in Batlharos, Toto's village, made clear that their chief did not support the Mangope government. Interview I at Batlharos in Appendix C3.

97. On auctions, see NAR KGM 35 4/2/4/8, minutes of regional authority meetings in 1974 and 1975. On land, see Seiler, "Bophuthatswana: A State of Politics," 1999; Interview with W. J. Seremane in Appendix C2. In 1998, Mr. Seremane was chief land claims commissioner for the Commission of Restitution of Land Rights. On the BIC, see Butler, Rotberg, and Adams, *Black Homelands* (1977), 179–218;

Bophuthatswana Department of Agriculture and Forestry, *Annual Report, 1973*, 12; Bophuthatswana Department of Agriculture and Forestry, *Annual Report, 1976*, 41.

98. Loraine Gordon, et al., *Survey of Race Relations in South Africa, 1978* (Johannesburg: South African Institute of Race Relations, 1979), 307; Loraine Gordon, et al., *Survey of Race Relations in South Africa, 1980* (Johannesburg: South African Institute of Race Relations, 1981), 433; Peter Randall, et al., *Survey of Race Relations in South Africa, 1982* (Johannesburg: South African Institute of Race Relations, 1983), 416; and Carole Cooper, et al., *Survey of Race Relations, 1983* (Johannesburg: South African Institute of Race Relations, 1984), 376.

99. Statistics on cattle and donkeys in the Tlhaping-Tlharo District are from the Bophuthatswana Department of Agriculture and Forestry, *Annual Reports*, 1972–88.

100. NAR KGM 39 5/4/6, Minutes of Regional Council Meeting September 8, 1977. Donkeys were debated in the National Assembly in 1981, but not in 1982. See Republic of Bophuthatswana, *Debates of the Fourth Session of the First National Assembly, May 6, 1981–June 17, 1981*, 1: 368–412; *Debates of the Fifth Session of the First Bophuthatswana National Assembly, April 27, 1982–June 9, 1982*. On control efforts before 1983, see Republic of Bophuthatswana, *Debates of the First Session of the Second Bophuthatswana National Assembly, June 16–July 28, 1983*, 2:773, 783.

101. Agricor *Annual Report, 1985–86*, 4. On planning land use for "middle-class farmers," see Loraine Gordon, et al., *Survey of Race Relations, 1978* (1979), 432–3.

102. Mamdani, *Citizen and Subject* (1996), 144.

103. Republic of Bophuthatswana, *Debates of the First Session of the Second Bophuthatswana National Assembly (1983)*, 2:743–9.

104. In the course of my research, I learned of a white South African Defense Force soldier who participated in the donkey killing, but I was not able to interview him.

105. Interview with W. J. Seremane in Appendix C2. On donkeys as a traffic hazard, see Republic of Bophuthatswana, *Debates of the Fourth Session of the First National Assembly (1981)*, 1:379, 386, 398.

106. The interviews on the donkey killings were Interview F at Kagung, Interview G at Kagung, Interview J at Ga-Mopedi, Interview K at Ga-Mopedi, Interview K at Ncweng, Interview C at Seodin, and Interview D at Seodin in Appendix C3.

107. Interview C at Seodin in Appendix C3; Interview with Gert Olivier in Appendix C1; Personal communication from Alan Butler, May 19, 1998.

108. Interview with A. D. Setlhodi in Appendix C2. On abuses by the Bophuthatswana police in Thaba Nchu, see Murray, *Black Mountain* (1992), 221–7.

109. Interview K at Ncweng in Appendix C3.

110. Interview C at Seodin in Appendix C3.

111. Interview K at Ncweng and Interview J at Ga-Mopedi in Appendix C3.

112. Interview C at Seodin in Appendix C3.

113. Interview K at Ncweng in Appendix C3

114. Cooper, et al., *Survey of Race Relations, 1983* (1984), 376.

115. Interview J at Ga-Mopedi in Appendix C3.

116. Interview with W. J. Seremane in Appendix C2.

117. Bophuthatswana Department of Agriculture and Forestry, *Annual Report, 1982*; Bophuthatswana Department of Agriculture and Forestry, *Annual Report, 1983*.

118. De Wet, *Moving Together, Drifting Apart* (1995), 197.
119. Interview K at Ncweng in Appendix C3.
120. De Wet, *Moving Together, Drifting Apart* (1995), 67.
121. Lodge, *Black Politics* (1983), 279–89.

CHAPTER 9

1. Interview B with Isaac Seamecho in Appendix C1. "NJ" is Nancy Jacobs.
2. Interview A at Batlharos in Appendix C3.
3. Interview A at Maiphiniki in Appendix C3.
4. Interviews C and D at Churchill in Appendix C3.
5. Interview F at Batlharos in Appendix C3. Interview with Vera Albutt in Appendix C2.
6. Interview B at Batlharos in Appendix C3.
7. Interview F at Batlharos in Appendix C3.
8. Interview D at Ncweng in Appendix C3.
9. Interview C at Ncweng in Appendix C3.
10. Boserup, *The Conditions of Agricultural Growth* (1965).
11. NAR NTS 7933 165/337, minutes of meeting, December 10, 1948.
12. Interview C at Seodin in Appendix C3.
13. Interview B at Churchill in Appendix C3.
14. Interview C at Ncweng in Appendix C3. See also Interview A at Ga-Sebolao, Interview B at Sedibeng, and Interview I at Ga-Mopedi in Appendix C3; Interview with Gladys Motshabe and Interview with Joseph Kopman in Appendix C2.
15. CPSAA Mackenzie Papers no. 1575, Mackenzie, October 20, 1887.
16. Interview A at Maiphiniki.
17. Feierman, *Peasant Intellectuals* (1990). Regarding the Tswana, see Schapera, *Rainmaking Rites of Tswana Tribes* (Leiden: Afrika-Studiecentrum, 1971), 17–42, 133–8; Paul Landau, *Realm of the Word* (1995), 25.
18. Interview C at Batlharos in Appendix C3.
19. CTAR 2/KMN 233 N.2/10/3/(5), minutes of a meeting, July 17, 1967.
20. Interview K at Ncweng and Interview C at Seodin in Appendix C3.
21. Interview C at Seodin in Appendix C3.
22. *Debates of the Fourth Session of the First National Assembly* (1981), 1:391, 401. *Debates of the First Session of the Second Bophuthatswana National Assembly* (1983), 2:750–99.
23. Interview C at Seodin in Appendix C3.
24. Interview C at Seodin in Appendix C3.
25. *Debates of the Fourth Session of the First National Assembly* (1981), 1:401.
26. *Debates of the First Session of the Second Bophuthatswana National Assembly* (1983), 2:770–1.
27. Interview D at Seodin in Appendix C3.
28. Interview K at Ncweng in Appendix C3.
29. Interview C at Seodin in Appendix C3.
30. Interview C at Seodin in Appendix C3.
31. Interview C at Seodin in Appendix C3.

32. On the material and cultural value of donkeys for white South Africans, see Brian du Toit, *People of the Valley: Life in an Isolated Afrikaner Community in South Africa* (Cape Town: Balkema, 1974), 36, 45–6, 75–7. On the donkey monuments, see photographs in James Walton, *A Tribute to the Donkey* (published by the author, 1999), 24–5; Starkey, *Animal Traction in South Africa* (1995), color photograph insert, 4. There is also a donkey statue in Brazil. See Frank Brookshier, *The Burro* (Norman: University of Oklahoma Press, 1974), 223.

33. Mosiamane, "The Bophuthatswana Façade," 19–23.

34. Telephone interview with Blondie Makhene. The song was written and sung publicly shortly after the donkey massacre, but not recorded until 1991 or 1992. It was sung at opposition rallies in Bophuthatswana during the transition to majority rule, and people sang it to me in interviews. I thank Angela Impey for locating Mr. Makhene.

35. Personal communication from Alan Butler, quoting Sophie Rieters. See also Lawrence and Manson, "The Dog of the Boers"; http://www.amnesty.org/ailib/aipub/1994/AFR/532094.AFR.txt.

36. Interview C at Seodin in Appendix C3.

37. Interview K at Ncweng in Appendix C3.

38. On the 1999 election in the North–West Province, see Andrew Reynolds, ed., *Election '99 South Africa: From Mandela to Mbeki* (New York: St. Martin's, 1999), 134–6, 189, 194. I thank John Seiler for providing me with the Kuruman voting results. Information was also available on the Independent Electoral Commission web site: http://www.elections.org.za.

39. One work with some populist sympathies is Jonathan S. Adams and Thomas O. McShane, *The Myth of Wild Africa: Conservation without Illusion* (Berkeley: University of California Press, 1996).

40. Cronon, "A Place for Stories," *The Journal of American History* 78(1992): 1375.

41. http://www.explore-southafrica.co.za/explore/gameparks/tswalu/front.htm.

42. Lewis, *The Abolition of Man* (1946), 40.

43. For environmental explanations for colonialism and disparities of development, see Alfred Crosby, *Ecological Imperialism* (1986); Jared Diamond, *Guns, Germs and Steel* (New York: Norton, 1997).

44. Wylie, "The Changing Face of Hunger," *Past and Present* 122(1989). On malnutrition in South Africa in the 1980s, see Francis Wilson and Mamphela Ramphele, *Uprooting Poverty: The South African Challenge* (Cape Town: David Philip, 1989), 100–120.

45. Mamdani, *Citizen and Subject* (1996), 24–5, 288–9.

Index

Maps are indexed in italics.

A

Acacia species
  A. erioloba, 97, 123
  A. mellifera subsp. *detinins*, 97–99, 120, 127–8
  See also bushes; woodcutting
Acocks classification, 15, 239n9
Aerial surveys, 189–94, 196–8
African Nationalist Congress, 184, 216
Agriculture
  agricultural extension, 158–61
  crops. *See specific types*
  decline of, 132, 146–7, 207, 211
  erosion and, 120, 178–9
  extensive. *See* Extensive production
  fertilizer and, 49, 60–1, 94, 107, 131–2, 160, 210
  hoeing, 51, 65, 129, 250n107
  irrigation and. *See* Irrigation
  labor, 22, 30, 33, 42, 49–55, 57–61, 64–5, 69, 92–95, 107, 114, 129–33, 144–6, 160
  men and. *See* Men
  plowing. *See* Plowing
  shifting cultivation, 49–52
  tenure. *See* Land tenure; Communal tenure
  women and. *See* Women
  See also specific locations, groups
AIDS, 221
Alfalfa, 157
ANC. *See* African National Congress
AnCRA. *See* Association for Community and Rural Advancement
Annexation, 76–96

Anthrax, 44, 62, 100, 110, 123, 249n80, 254n31, 265n29
Apartheid, 66, 161, 164–7, 175, 177, 188, 214–5
Archeological studies, 32–5, 244n8
Archival sources, 235–7
Arends, Joseph, 80
Asbestos mining, 13, 135–41, 239n8, 276n134
Association for Community and Rural Advancement (AnCRA), 26, 166
Auction, stock, 123, 186, 188, 189

B

BAD. *See* Bantu Administration and Development Department
Balala class, 39, 41–3, 48–9, 63–4, 66, 70, 72–4, 118, 142, 147, 172, 208, 219–20, 248n62, 258n104
Bantu Administration and Development (BAD), 173
Bantu Authorities Act of 1951, 175–6
Bantu Investment Corporation (BIC), 184
Bantu-speaking peoples, 32, 33, 33n, 169n
Barter, 70
Batlhanka class, 42, 48, 54, 63, 73, 142, 248n80
Batlharos, *10*, 12, 14, 68, 73, 92, 130, 131, 139, 142, 159, 172, 209, 210, 216, 221
BBLC. *See* British Bechuanaland Land Commission
Bechuanaland Protectorate, 83, *84*, 88, 169
Begging, 42, 145
Beinart, William, 17, 177, 243n45, 276n149
Bergenaars, 63

293